English Fairy Tales
and
More English Fairy Tales

❧

ABC·CLIO CLASSIC FOLK AND FAIRY TALES

Jack Zipes, Series Editor

Collectors in the nineteenth and early twentieth centuries unearthed a wealth of stories from around the world and published them in English translations for the delight of general readers, young and old. Most of these anthologies have been long out of print.

The ABC-CLIO Classic Folk and Fairy Tales series brings back to life these key anthologies of traditional tales from the golden age of folklore discovery. Each volume provides a freshly typeset but otherwise virtually unaltered edition of a classic work and each is enhanced by an authoritative introduction by a top scholar. These insightful essays discuss the significance of the collection and its original collector; the original collector's methodology and translation practices; and the original period context according to region or genre.

Certain to be of interest to folklorists, these classic collections are also meant to serve as sources for storytellers and for sheer reading pleasure, reviving as they do hundreds of folk stories, both reassuringly familiar and excitingly strange.

FORTHCOMING TITLES:
Creation Myths of Primitive America, by Jeremiah Curtin;
Introduction by Karl Kroeber

Folktales from Northern India, by William Crooke and
Pandit Ram Gharib Chaube;
Introduction by Sadhana Naithani

Old Deccan Days or Hindoo Fairy Legends, by Mary Frere;
Introduction by Kirin Narayan

Popular Tales and Fictions, by William Alexander Clouston;
Introduction by Christine Goldberg

Popular Tales of Ancient Egypt, by Gaston Maspero;
Introduction by Hasan El-Shamy

ENGLISH FAIRY TALES

AND

MORE ENGLISH FAIRY TALES

JOSEPH JACOBS

EDITED AND WITH AN INTRODUCTION
BY DONALD HAASE

*Includes complete original illustrations by
John D. Batten*

A B C • C L I O

Santa Barbara, California
Denver, Colorado   Oxford, England

Cataloging-in-Publication Data is available from the Library of Congress.

1-57607-426-9 (hardcover)
1-57607-427-7 (e-book)
06 05 04 03 02 10 9 8 7 6 5 4 3 2 1 (cloth)

This edition reprints in its entirety and retains the original chapter sequence of English Fairy Tales, *collected and edited by Joseph Jacobs, published by David Nutt, London, 1890; and* More English Fairy Tales, *collected and edited by Joseph Jacobs, published by David Nutt, London, 1894. The texts of these editions have been altered only to fit an increased page dimension, to reflect contemporary typographical conventions, and to correct typographical errors and other misleading errors in the texts.*

ABC-CLIO, Inc.
130 Cremona Drive, P.O. Box 1911
Santa Barbara, California 93116–1911

This book is also available on the World Wide Web as an e-book. Visit www.abc-clio.com for details.

～

Contents

Preface to This Edition

Joseph Jacobs's *English Fairy Tales* (1890) and *More English Fairy Tales* (1894) are pioneering collections from the golden age of folktale collecting, and they have been both berated and celebrated for the way they have preserved the classic corpus of traditional English folktales. Because of their canonical status, these two books have often been reprinted. However, modern editions have shortchanged readers by underestimating the fascinating complexity and historical context of Jacobs's work. Like the influential collection of German fairy tales published by the Brothers Grimm earlier in the nineteenth century, the two books of English fairy tales produced by Joseph Jacobs are hybrid texts where folklore, children's literature, and the eclectic scholarship of the Victorian era intersect and assert their equal claims to attention. When late-twentieth-century reprints strip away Jacobs's important prefaces, notes, and references in order to target the children's book market, they remove from view the vital intellectual dynamics and sociohistorical factors that shaped his work. Similarly, the modern edition that preserves his scholarly apparatus but eliminates the original illustrations by John D. Batten betrays the integrity of a collaborative project where the art does not simply decorate, but contributes to the synergy between collector and artist in the interplay of story, image, and scholarship. In the case of Jacobs's first collection—*English Fairy Tales*—modern reprints have relied exclusively on the third revised edition of that work, as published in 1898. The dominance of the third edition, however, has obscured the fact that *English Fairy Tales* was essentially a work in progress that Jacobs revised in the course of its four editions published in 1890, 1893, 1898, and 1911. Rare as they are, these other editions of *English Fairy Tales* are significant because they document Jacobs's method of editing and adapting the tales he collected. His revisions illuminate for us his priorities and concerns as collector and adapter, and they help us to understand how the classical

English fairy tale took shape in his hands. So, in order to draw attention to the editorial history of Jacobs's fairy-tale project, this dual edition makes available the groundbreaking first edition of *English Fairy Tales* in the form that it originally appeared and had its initial impact in 1890. In coupling that pioneering edition of *English Fairy Tales* with its sequel of 1894, *More English Fairy Tales,* this two-in-one volume provides readers with a new resource for understanding, in context, the development of the classic fairy tale in late Victorian England and for reassessing the relationship of Jacobs's canonical tales to the traditional English folktale that they sought to preserve.

The texts of Jacobs's two collections are reprinted here as they first appeared in 1890 and 1894, respectively. Typographical errors present in the original editions have been corrected. In the case of *English Fairy Tales,* a few misleading errors that affect meaning and that were corrected in later editions have also been corrected here. A few minor errors in puncuation and other obvious errors affecting the sense of sentences have been corrected in both collections. However, inconsistencies in the texts (for example, in spelling and capitalization), Jacobs's mistakes in matters of fact (like misdating the publication of *English Fairy Tales* in the preface to *More English Fairy Tales*), and mistakes he made in spelling foreign words and titles have been left unaltered.

The original editions of *English Fairy Tales* and *More English Fairy Tales* used as the basis of this combined edition are housed in the Eloise Ramsey Collection of Literature for Young People in the Purdy/Kresge Library of Wayne State University. I wish to acknowledge with thanks the generous assistance of Karen Bacsanyi, Robert P. Holley, and Diane Paldan for making the volumes available and for facilitating the process of scanning and copying them. I am grateful to the Office of the Vice President for Research at Wayne State University, which provided support for this project. I am also very much indebted to Julie Arrigo and Kaushalya Krishnamoorthy for their expert research assistance. Finally, this is for Connie, whose support endures through thirty years of fairy tales and more fairy tales.

~

Introduction to This Edition

Joseph Jacobs prefaced his collection of English fairy tales with a defiant rhetorical question: "Who says that English folk have no fairy-tales of their own?" (vii). While *English Fairy Tales* (1890) and *More English Fairy Tales* (1894) intended to disprove that claim, the fact remained that a distinctly English fairy tale did not become firmly established or widely known until the Victorian era. By any measure, the English fairy-tale tradition had paled in contrast to the remarkable tales found on the continent. By the early nineteenth century, other European cultures had produced vital fairy-tale traditions that were influential even beyond their borders. Italy had given birth to the modern literary fairy tale with two groundbreaking works: Giovan Francesco Straparola's *Entertaining Nights* (1550–1553) and Giambattista Basile's *Pentamerone* (1634–1636). France could boast an entire library of literary fairy tales published in the late seventeenth and eighteenth centuries by writers such as Marie-Catherine d'Aulnoy, Marie-Jeanne Lhéritier, and Charles Perrault.[1] By the late eighteenth century, the French stock of fairy tales was so rich and so extensive that Charles-Joseph Mayer published a forty-volume collection of these tales in the *Cabinet des fées* (1785–1789). Fueled by nationalism and radically new aesthetic theories, Germany had sent forth not only the monumental collection of folktales edited by the Brothers Grimm, but also highly original literary fairy tales penned by Romantic authors such as Ludwig Tieck, Novalis, and E. T. A. Hoffmann. Moreover, the Grimms' model of collecting and editing folktales had inspired similar collections throughout Europe, so that by the time Jacobs published his *English Fairy Tales*, collectors in France and Italy had documented over one thousand tales in each of those countries, as Jacobs himself pointed out (1890, vii). Although the Grimms' stories appeared in many English translations, adaptations, and editions throughout the nineteenth century, their pervasive presence in England only underlined the absence of a comparable collection of indigenous English tales. In fact, in the first English translation of the Grimms' tales, Edgar Taylor had urged collectors "to preserve, while it can yet be done, the popular stories . . . of the British Empire" (Taylor 1826, 257).

English Fairy Tales and *More English Fairy Tales,* which Jacobs described "as the best substitute that can be offered for an English Grimm" (1894c, 215), are a belated response to this call. With the eighty-seven texts that he published in these two books, Jacobs intended to initiate a recovery of traditional English storytelling and to present his readers with "the nucleus of the English folk-tale"—however incomplete the representation may have been. As Jacobs noted, "[T]he eighty-seven tales . . . in my two volumes must represent the English folk-tale as far as my diligence has been able to preserve it at this end of the nineteenth century. There is every indication that they form but a scanty survival of the whole *corpus* of such tales which must have existed in this country" (1894c, 215–216). Current scholarship has shown that the English folktale had been suffocated by the rationalist and utilitarian strictures of Puritanism and the Enlightenment.[2] Jacobs himself believed that specific socioeconomic and cultural conditions had prevented English tales from becoming more widely known. In 1890 he surmised, "The only reason, I imagine, why such tales have not hitherto been brought to light, is the lamentable gap between the governing and recording classes and the dumb working classes of this country—dumb to others but eloquent among themselves. It would be no unpatriotic task to help to bridge over this gulf, by giving a common fund of nursery literature to all classes of the English people, and, in any case, it can do no harm to add to the innocent gaiety of the nation" (vii–viii). In 1898, in the third revised edition of *English Fairy Tales,* Jacobs offered an additional explanation. He reasoned that provincial life in England was less "conservative and tenacious" than in France, Italy, or Germany and therefore had been less hospitable to the transmission and preservation of the oral tradition. According to Jacobs, not only had the English peasant "never had so vivid a social life" as his counterparts on the continent, but in more recent times "railways and the telegraph [had] disintegrated" life in the English countryside (1898, 229). In this Jacobs echoed his contemporary Edwin Sidney Hartland, who explained that his own collection of *English Fairy and Folk Tales* could "not pretend to be more than a presentation, in a more or less literary form, of a few of the traditional stories, formerly no doubt rife in this country, but now fast disappearing under the stress of modern life" ([1890], vii).

It is significant that Jacobs frames his project to preserve the English folktale with socioeconomic, cultural, and even political perspectives. In drawing attention to the importance of social class and to the deterioration of rural society caused by urbanization and modern technology, Jacobs demonstrates that he understands the folktale as a sociohistorical product. When he refers to the "lamentable gap" between the ruling literate who *write* stories and the laboring illiterate who *tell* stories, he also reveals his awareness of the sociopolitical dynamic at work when the oral tradition of the lower classes is appropriated for print by those in power. His patriotic notion that the gap between English social classes could be bridged by the publication of a common stock of fairy tales is a utopian impulse, but one that betrays his belief that the fairy tale can promote national and cultural unity only if it has been fixed in print, the medium controlled by the literate middle and upper classes.[3] At the same time, however, Jacobs seems to disarm the sociopolitical thrust of his work when he claims that the collected stories can serve as harmless entertainment by "add[ing] to the innocent gaiety of the nation." Indeed, just a few sentences later in his preface to the 1890 edition of *English Fairy Tales,* he identifies his target audience as children when he states that "our book is intended for the little ones" (viii). So even though Jacobs initially characterizes the folktales he has collected in historical, sociopolitical, and nationalistic terms, he then summarily announces that he views his book primarily as an innocent contribution to children's literature.

The hybrid nature of *English Fairy Tales* and *More English Fairy Tales* and the controversial reception they have received stem from unresolved tensions like these—tensions between literature and folklore, between printed text and spoken word, between respect for the folk tradition and belief in the primacy of literary creation, and between sociopolitical consciousness and children's entertainment. Such competing, even contradictory, perspectives in Jacobs's work raise important questions about his intentions, his audience, his editorial methods, the role of his tales in Victorian society, and the reception and legacy of his fairy-tale collections. No wonder that Jacobs himself, a man possessed of a "brilliantly restless and inquisitive mind," has been called by one scholar the "*enfant terrible* of English folklore" (Maidment 1975, 185, 190). To understand the complex nature of these two fairy-tale collections, we must first understand something of the collector himself.

Joseph Jacobs was born in Sydney, Australia, on 29 August 1854 to John and Sarah Jacobs. He attended school in Sydney, but by 1872 he left for

England, apparently with the intention of studying law. Jacobs, however, was pulled into another orbit during his years in Cambridge, where his studies turned to literature, history, anthropology, and philosophy. Having abandoned plans to return to Australia and practice law, Jacobs moved to London upon his graduation from Cambridge in 1876 to become a writer. Book reviews by the young Jewish author garnered him increased attention as a literary critic, especially his 1877 review of George Eliot's controversial novel *Daniel Deronda* (Jacobs 1877). Hostile criticism of Eliot's book had deepened Jacobs's consciousness of British anti-Semitism, and he responded to the critical attacks with a supportive review of the novel. The review itself earned Jacobs an introduction to Eliot and to other Victorian writers and artists such as Edward Burne-Jones, Dante Gabriel Rossetti, and William Morris.

The confrontation with anti-Semitism in the *Daniel Deronda* affair not only fostered Jacobs's literary career, but it also intensified his interest in Jewish history and culture. Jacobs left London in 1877 and spent two years studying Jewish history and ethnology at the University of Berlin. In 1882 he published a series of highly influential articles in the *Times* in which he denounced the oppression of the Jews in Russia. In this Jacobs once again exhibited his commitment to addressing social and political injustice, as he did also from 1882 to 1900 as secretary of the Russo-Jewish Committee, which had been established to advance the cause of the persecuted Russian Jews. Throughout the rest of his life, Jacobs continued to pursue his interests in Jewish history and published significant, even pioneering, scholarship in that field (Marx 1948, 252). In fact, when offered the opportunity to edit *The Jewish Encyclopedia*, Jacobs left England and moved to New York in 1900, where he taught English literature at the Jewish Theological Seminary and where he lived until his death on 30 January 1916.

In addition to his influential work as a literary critic and as a Jewish historian, Jacobs played a prominent role in British folklore studies. His most important contributions came precisely during those years when folklore was establishing itself as a discipline and became institutionalized through the Folk-Lore Society, which had been founded in London in 1878. Richard M. Dorson, in his history *The British Folklorists*, has described how "the whirlpool of activity and the ferment of excitement that lasted from 1878 to the first World War drew many talented scholars and collectors into the Society" (1968, 202). Jacobs was among these talented scholars, and from 1889 to 1900 he edited *Folk-Lore,* the society's journal. Here a new breed of folklorists fervently argued and debated the ideas that shaped the emerging field of study. Jacobs himself advanced a number of influential theories about the origin, nature, and spread of folktales that sparked controversies that were as important as they were lively. Even the fairy-tale collections that Jacobs edited incorporate folkloristic debates in their prefaces and commentary, as do the critical reviews of his fairy-tale collections written by his intellectual opponents. Jacobs's work as a collector and editor of traditional texts constitutes another pillar of his activity as a folklorist. Among his most important contributions are works such as *The Earliest English Version of the Fables of Bidpai* (1888), *The Fables of Aesop as First Printed by William Caxton in 1484* (1893b), and *The Most Delectable History of Reynard the Fox* (1895). However, it is his prolific output as a collector and editor of fairy tales—including not simply *English Fairy Tales* and *More English Fairy Tales,* but also his editions of *Indian Fairy Tales* (1892b), *Celtic Fairy Tales* (1892a), *More Celtic Fairy Tales* (1894b), and *Europa's Fairy Tales* (1916)—that exemplifies his eclectic and controversial work as a folklorist.

Despite his importance and productivity in so many areas, scholars representing these fields have been reluctant to lay claim to Jacobs. Surveying the "pioneer work" that he accomplished in his Jewish scholarship, Alexander Marx asserts that Jacobs's "greatest powers" lay in English literature and folklore, and that Jewish studies was merely a "by-path" (1948, 251–252). Folklorist Richard M. Dorson, however, considers Jacobs to belong to the "second rank" of Victorian folklorists and calls him "the Judaic scholar from Australia." "Had he never written a line on folklore," Dorson claims, "he would still be known, as indeed he is principally known, as an historian of the Jews" (1968, 266). Dorson and other folklorists have also segregated Jacobs from other Victorian folklorists because he blurred the boundary between folklore studies and children's literature. For instance, Jacobs followed his scholarly edition of Aesop with a popular edition in which the fables were "told anew" for children (1894a). Critics of his fairy-tale collections were especially upset by the way he rewrote traditional tales when he adapted them for children— making him less of a genuine folklorist than a popularizer and "an enthusiastic amateur" (Maidment 1975, 186). On the other hand, some historians of children's literature have given scant attention to Jacobs because his "collections of national fairy-tales seem to be addressed more to anthropologists and folk-lorists than to children" (Muir 1954, 107).

The challenge in assessing Jacobs's work as a collector and editor of folktales lies in the way his collections straddle the border between folklore and literature. This is the direct result of his controversial theories of how folklore is created and spread. Particularly important in the editing of his fairy-tale collections—and troubling to his critics—was Jacobs's theory of folktale diffusion, which he defended in his polemical essay entitled "The Problem of Diffusion" (1894d). In contrast to most of his contemporaries in the Folk-Lore Society, Jacobs did not believe that the existence of similar folktales throughout many different societies could be explained by their having originated independently as a result of coincidence or as an expression of universal human psychology. Instead, he maintained that folktales were spread from place to place, from society to society, through contact among people and their cultures. Jacobs also questioned the claim of anthropological folklorists that the "unnatural incidents" in folktales were often survivals of primitive beliefs and customs, and that folktales could therefore tell us a good deal about prehistoric societies. Based on his theory of folktale transmission, Jacobs countered that folktales had only limited value as carriers of information about the "savage culture" in which they might have first originated. A specific tale was more valuable for the evidence it provided about the society in which that version was actually told. Therefore, Jacobs had no abiding interest in tracing tales back to their origins, "back to what the Germans call the 'Cosmic Gas,' the primeval chaos out of which the Universe has sprung. . . . I prefer to keep with my foot on the solid ground of facts which I can control. . . . The proper scientific course would be to make investigations *in loco*. . . . I am not concerned even with the universal history of the folk-tale in general. I desire to ascertain the history of certain specific folk-tales . . ." (1894d, 141–142). Jacobs, in other words, is not primarily concerned with the ultimate origin of the folktale, but with the individual folktale text and its relationship to the specific time and place of its creation. His theory of diffusion, then, is a sociohistorical theory of the folktale that is amazingly modern in stressing the fundamental importance of the individual text in its social, historical, and cultural contexts.

The theory of diffusion makes Jacobs not simply "a sociological folklorist" (Fine 1987), but also a literary folklorist. Because the spread of tales from society to society also involved printed texts as a means of transmission, Jacobs necessarily valued literary sources in collecting and studying the folktale. Moreover, because his theory emphasized the individuality of each tale and the specific sociohistorical circumstances of its creation, the boundary between folklore and literature was virtually erased. According to the theory of diffusion, tales that had more complex plots and artistic form were not only the product of "a definite folk-artist," but also more likely to survive in the "struggle for existence in the folk-mind" (1894d, 143). Consequently, Jacobs's pursuit of folklore included "the study of the evolution of man's artistic nature" (145). Folktales, as Jacobs put it, "were folk-literature, and required to be studied by literary and not by anthropological methods" (130).

The boundary between folklore and literature was further obscured in Jacobs's radical essay on "The Folk" (1893c). Applying a good bit of common sense to the conventional notion that folklore arises "among the people," Jacobs concludes that the "Folk is a fraud, a delusion, a myth" (234). "The Folk," he points out, "is simply a name for our ignorance: we do not know to whom a proverb, a tale, a custom, a myth owes its origin, so we say it originated among the Folk" (235–236). As in the theory of diffusion, Jacobs puts forth the idea of the "individual origin of folk-lore" (237); that is, the fact that specific individuals create specific texts in acts of artistic creation:

> Can we imagine the Folk [as a group] inventing *Cinderella* or *Puss-in-Boots,* or any of the innumerable novelettes of the nursery? The process is unthinkable. These little masterpieces of narrative art emanated from an artist, who had the grin of conscious creation on his face as he told *Cinderella, Puss-in-Boots,* or *Rumpelstiltskin* for the first time in the world's history. Artistry is individual: that cannot come from the Folk no more than novels can arise spontaneously and simultaneously among the subscribers of Messrs. Mudie and Smith.[4] (234–235)

Viewing folklore in this sober light—and unencumbered by romantic nostalgia for the collective voice of the peasantry—Jacobs rejects rigid distinctions between folklore and literature, and secures a place for himself and his books in the preservation and production of folktales.

> [F]rom our individualistic standpoint we shall have to break down the rather hard and fast line we draw between folk-lore and literature. While a story passes *per ora virum* we call it folk-lore, the

moment it gets written down we call it literature, and it ceases to
have interest for us *quá* folk-lorists. I cannot recognise any such hard
and fast distinction. Books are but so many telephones preserving
the lore of the folk, or more often burying it and embalming it. For,
after all, we are the Folk as well as the rustic, though their lore may
be other than ours, as ours will be different from that of those that
follow us. (237)

Driven by these controversial ideas, *English Fairy Tales* and *More
English Fairy Tales* deliberately throw into question the
conventional boundary between folklore and literary culture. Jacobs does this by inviting confusion over his
intended audience. While he states clearly in the prefaces
to both of these collections that he assembled and rewrote

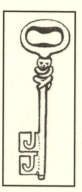

the tales for children, he makes equally dis-
tinct, if contradictory, gestures that he also
envisions an audience of folklorists. The
books' elaborate paratextual features
underline this. On the verso of the half-

title page in both *English Fairy Tales* and *More English
Fairy Tales,* Jacobs literally instructs his readers "HOW
TO GET INTO THIS BOOK." Referring to images
imprinted on each book's
binding, this playful user's
guide instructs the reader
to "Knock at the Knocker
on the Door" (depicted on
the front cover of the original editions), "Pull the
Bell at the side" (on the
spine), "Put the Key in the
Keyhole" (back and front
covers), and then "WALK
IN." By making a game of

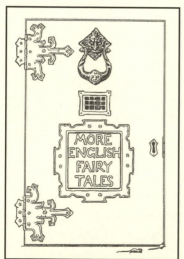

getting into the book, Jacobs not only
identifies his readers as children (even if
they are adult folklorists), but also draws attention to the physical
boards and borders of the book itself and thus to the literary nature of
the tales within. Moreover, with his name printed across the bell that is

printed on the spine and his initials in the wards of the key on the back cover, Jacobs seems to inscribe his own authority and ownership onto the collection of popular tales. These gestures in the physical construction of the book suggest that, in editing these tale collections for children, Jacobs was making a serious, if also playful statement about the role of the folklorist and the relationship between folklore and literature.

The tales in both books are also framed on one end by dedications suggesting the young audience Jacobs had in mind. *English Fairy Tales* is dedicated to his daughter, "DEAR LITTLE MAY," while the sequel is dedicated to his son Sydney "AETAT. XIII"—at age thirteen. At the other end, the tales proper are followed by a humorous illustration warning children away from the scholarly notes and references that follow. With youthful readers in mind, Jacobs also explains in the prefaces to both collections that it was necessary to alter the style and content of the stories "in order to make the tales readable for children" (1890, xi). Yet such explanations of his editorial practice and poetic license are directed obviously at folklorists and not at children. In fact, Jacobs uses the prefaces to engage in a polemical defense of his editing. In *More English Fairy Tales* he responds explicitly to his "folk-lore friends [who] look on with sadness while they view me laying profane hands on the sacred text of my originals. . . . My defence might be that I had a cause at heart as sacred as our science of folk-lore—the filling of our children's imaginations with bright trains of images" (1894c, viii).

Jacobs's scholarly polemic in the prefaces and notes to his tales, however, does not simply show that he had a bifocal vision of his audience; it also demonstrates that he believed the fairy tales he had rewritten for children retained their validity as folklore:

> [E]ven on the lofty heights of folk-lore science I am not entirely defenceless. . . . Why may I not have the same privilege as any other story-teller, especially when I know the ways of story-telling as she is told in English, at least as well as a Devonshire or Lancashire peasant? And—conclusive argument—wilt thou, oh orthodox brother folk-lorist, still continue to use Grimm and Asbjörnsen? Well, they did the same as I. (Jacobs 1894c, viii–ix)

Like the Grimms, Jacobs saw himself as just one link in the chain of storytellers who had preserved folktales by telling them. Consistent with his theory of diffusion and his concept of the folk, the authenticity he presumed his stories to have did not stem in his mind from verbatim retellings, but from his presumed ability to speak—in fact, to write—as the folk himself.

Jacobs also justified his retellings as authentic folktales by comparing the revisions he made to his sources with the editorial revisions made by the Brothers Grimm. In a review of *More English Fairy Tales,* Edwin Sidney Hartland strongly objected to Jacobs's assertion that he was following the practices of the Brothers Grimm:

> [W]e must decline to accept the editor's claim that Grimm and Asbjörnsen "did the same as" he, in re-writing at his own sweet will so many of the tales. . . . Where does Mr. Jacobs find his authority for saying that the brothers Grimm treated their tales to this wholesale doctoring? His true defence would be boldly to avow that the text he gives is not intended for students [of folklore], and there leave the matter. The student could then demand only that the genuine text of any of the tales which had not appeared elsewhere should be preserved in some accessible form—say, in the pages of FOLK-LORE. (Hartland 1894, 74)

The truth is, Jacobs was right about the Grimms. They had indeed made changes—some quite extensive—to the tales they collected.[5] In *English Fairy Tales* Jacobs had even quoted the Grimms' admission that they had altered the style and details of their stories, something Hartland had either overlooked or—like many other scholars—had not wanted to fully comprehend. Although Jacobs had expressed his hope that someday he would "reproduce [his] originals with literal accuracy" (1890, xi), the fact that he never did this proves that verbatim accuracy in recording folktales did not have a high priority for him. Instead, he felt perfectly justified in rewriting his sources and presenting his own retellings as "the nucleus of the English folk-tale."

In some cases Jacobs would recast a ballad in prose or tone down a tale's "overabundant dialect" (1894c, viii). Take, for example, the first story in *English Fairy Tales,* "Tom Tit Tot," which Jacobs adapted from the version reprinted by Edward Clodd in 1889. Contrasting the following passages highlights the kinds of lexical and orthographic changes Jacobs made in order to soften the Suffolk dialect present in his source:

Clodd's Version

Well, ivery day the flax an' the vittles, they was browt, an' ivery day that there little black impet used for to come mornins an' evenins. An' all the day the mawther she set a tryin' fur to think of names to say to it when te come at night. But she niver hot on the right one. An' as that got to-warts the ind o' the month, the impet that began for to look soo maliceful, an' that twirled that's tail faster an' faster each time she gave a guess. (Clodd 1889, 141–142)

Jacobs's Version

Well, every day the flax and the food were brought, and every day that there little black impet used to come mornings and evenings. And all the day the girl sate trying to think of names to say to it when it came at night. But she never hit on the right one. And as it got towards the end of the month, the impet began to look so mal-iceful, and that twirled that's tail faster and faster each time she gave a guess. (Jacobs 1890, 6)

Despite his occasional trimming of excessive dialect, sometime Jacobs would actually retain dialect or archaic forms. However, even when he remained faithful to his sources, Jacobs was not motivated by obedience to a rigorous notion of authenticity. Rather his treatment of his sources was guided in every case by his desire to transmit an appealing story in a printed language that could be effectively spoken. "This book," he wrote in the preface to *English Fairy Tales*, "is meant to be read aloud, and not merely taken in by the eye" (1890, xi).

However, if folklorists like Hartland faulted Jacobs for "doctoring" his sources to make them more literary and readable, literary reviewers crit-icized him for preserving dialect and slang in order to make the stories more colloquial. For example, in an 1896 review, John Hepburn Millar accepts the editorial alterations Jacobs admitted to making in his tales, but he takes Jacobs to task for reproducing language that does not live up to literary standards:

Mr Jacobs disappoints us sadly, and that is in an occasional trick of slang—and not very good slang either. We do *not* believe that Jack said "Walker!" [an exclamation of disbelief] to the butcher who sold him the beans; and it grates upon us to be told that the ogre's wife "wasn't such a bad sort after all." . . . These offences, though apparently trifling, are in reality of a grave complexion. Children are extraordinarily sharp observers and critics of style, and the impressions produced by fairy tales—the first form of literature, as a rule, to which a child is introduced—are apt to be deep and permanent. Why, then, vitiate and deprave the youthful taste by expressions which, however serviceable in private life, are essentially commonplace and undistinguished in literary use? (Millar 1976, 157)

Jacobs, however, held a less didactic view of his task and a higher opinion of children as readers. In the preface to *More English Fairy Tales* he had already responded to this type of criticism by arguing that children will not have their speech corrupted by the colloquial language they encounter in fairy tales. He also argued that "vulgar" forms contained in authentic oral sources are more easily understood by children than the artificially elevated language that his critics favored (1894c, x–xi); and he asserted that children, as much as adults, "appreciate the dramatic propriety" of vulgar speech in the mouths of vulgar characters (1890, x). Here, again, we see his overriding aesthetic interest in telling a good tale and his application of literary principles.

Although Jacobs is intent upon writing "as a good old nurse will speak when she tells Fairy Tales" (1890, x), his theory of diffusion relieves him from having to rely solely on oral sources. He does claim to have "a certain number of tales actually taken down from the mouths of the people" (1894c, x), but his prefaces and notes document quite clearly that he has relied more heavily on previously published, literary sources. Moreover, he openly admits that in some cases he has had to "re-write in simpler style the stories only extant in 'Literary' English" (1890, x). When he acknowledges that he "had to reduce the flatulent phraseology of the eighteenth-century chap-books" (1890, x), or that he had to rewrite a tale like "The Lambton Worm" because "the original was rather high falutin'" (1894c, 242), Jacobs draws attention not only to the fact that many of his sources were in fact literary texts, but also that he did not reproduce these without alteration. For example, the popular English tale "Jack the Giant-Killer" is actually Jacobs's amalgamation of two different chapbook versions, with some details inspired by yet another literary variant (1890, 237). His rendition of the Dick Whittington story—

"Whittington and His Cat"—was "cobbled . . . up out of three chap-book versions," each of which had already passed through the hands of other collectors and editors (1890, 248).[6] "Tom Hickathrift," which Jacobs considered essential for any "English child's library of folk-tales," had its source in a single chapbook version, but it had come to him in an abridged form prepared by his publisher, Alfred Nutt (1894c, 224). According to Jacobs's notes, Nutt also was responsible for rewriting "The Pedlar of Swaffham" and "The Three Wishes" from their printed sources (229, 230).

The role that Jacobs envisioned for himself as a mediator between the oral and written traditions is especially clear in the case of "Rushen Coatie." Jacobs points out that he "concocted" this version of the Cin-derella story from SIX variants among the 345 versions published in Mar-ian Roalfe Cox's monumental work of folklore scholarship, *Cinderella* (1893). Having essentially created his own version of the story, he gave his "composite" the title "Rushen Coatie" in order to distinguish it from other variants. Jacobs described this as a "folk-lore experiment," for he hoped to see whether his new story would find its way back into popu-lar storytelling: "If this book becomes generally used among English-speaking peoples, it may possibly re-introduce this and other tales among the folk. We should be able to trace this re-introduction by the variation in titles. I have done the same with 'Nix Nought Nothing,' 'Molly Whuppie,' and 'Johnny Gloke'" (1894c, 233). Here Jacobs antici-pates what late-twentieth-century folklorists have observed—namely, the reverse influence of printed folktale collections on the oral tradition.[7] The experiment also demonstrates how Jacobs hoped his book of folk-tales would bridge that "lamentable gap" between social classes and serve as "a common fund of nursery literature to all classes of the English peo-ple." In this sense, his folklore experiment serves as a social experiment as well.

Jacobs exhibits refreshing candor in describing his intentions, sources, and editorial methods. Given his view of the contiguity between folklore and literature, as well as his understanding of his own creative role in the process of transmitting stories, Jacobs has no reason to waffle about the nature of his sources or to misrepresent the extent of his revisions and rewritings. However—as with the scrupulously honest Grimms—his notion of what constitutes change is somewhat less clear, so that his statements about particular tales cannot always be taken at face value. In the note to "Jack and His Golden Snuff-Box," for example, he claims that except for one change—which he explicitly identifies—he has "otherwise . . . left the tale unaltered as one of the few English folk-tales that have been taken down from the mouths of the peasantry . . ." (1890, 236). However, when Jacobs's text is compared with his source—a version of the tale collected by Francis Hindes Groome—a number of additional alterations come to light. Many of the differences are minor and consist of changes in style or word choice that make the description more precise and the language less colloquial, as in this sample:

Groome's Version

The poor lad had not gone far, till his father called him back; when the old man drawed out of his pocket a golden snuff-box. . . . (Groome 1973, 202)

Jacobs's Version

The poor lad had not gone far, when his father called him back; then the old man drew out of his pocket a golden snuff-box. . . . (Jacobs 1890, 82)

In addition to minor changes like these, however, Jacobs also made more notable revisions, including alterations that framed the story more explicitly in what we have come to expect as the conventional fairy-tale style. Besides appending "and they all lived happy ever afterwards" to the ending, he also added a more elaborate fairy-tale formula to the story's opening:

Groome's Version

Once upon a time there was an old man and an old woman, and they had one son, and they lived in a great forest. (Groome 1973, 201)

Jacobs's Version

Once upon a time, and a very good time it was, though it was neither in my time nor in your time nor in any one else's time, there was an old man and an old woman, and they had one son, and they lived in a great forest." (Jacobs 1890, 81)

Interestingly, in the note to another tale—"The Well of the World's End"—Jacobs acknowledges that he has added this new opening formula both to that story and to "Jack and His Golden Snuff-Box" because one authority "gives it as the usual one when tramps tell folktales" (1890, 252). Apparently Jacobs incorporated this formula—altering his authentic source—in order to lend the tale authenticity. His failure to mention this change in the note to "Jack and His Golden Snuff-Box" speaks not to editorial deceit, but only to the fact that he did not consider the addition of ostensibly authentic material to be an alteration to the tale.

Jacobs had identified "Cap o' Rushes" as another of the tales "taken down from the mouths of the peasantry" and reproduced without alteration. Just how faithful Jacobs's version of "Cap o' Rushes" is to its ostensible source in oral tradition, however, becomes questionable when we scrutinize its genealogy. As Jacobs notes, fellow folklorist Andrew Lang had published this variant of the Cinderella story in both *Longman's Magazine* (1889) and in *Folk-Lore* (1890) after it had been "discovered" by Edward Clodd in the *Ipswich Journal*. The story had first been recorded there in 1877 by A. W. T., a collector whom Jacobs later identified in the third revised edition of *English Fairy Tales* as Mrs. Walter-Thomas (Jacobs 1898, 237). The *Ipswich Journal* version of the story—published under the heading "The Suffolk 'King Lear'"—was ostensibly the version that had been taken down from the mouth of the peasantry. The note prefacing Walter-Thomas's transcription of the tale in the *Ipswich Journal*, however, creates doubt about its fidelity, for it states that the story was "Told by an old servant to the writer, when a child." In other words, the 1877 printing of the story can only represent a *writer's* adult recollection of a story heard in childhood, not an accurate transcription of a storyteller's oral text—not a tale literally taken down from the mouth of a peasant. Moreover, Andrew Lang's reprintings of this text in *Longman's Magazine* and in *Folk-Lore* are not exact reproductions of the text written down by Mrs. Walter-Thomas and published in the *Ipswich Journal*. In fact, there are even alterations that occur between Lang's 1889 and 1890 reprintings of the tale. Creating an even more complex relationship with the source tale, Jacobs picks and chooses among the three tales at his disposal and, more important, even incorporates his own alterations. The following examples give just a small sampling of numerous discrepancies among these texts:

Ipswich Journal

But before the dance were done, Cap o' Rushes she slipped off and away she went home. And when the other maids was back she was framin' to be asleep with her cap o' rushes on. (Walter-Thomas 1877)

Longman's Magazine

But before the dance were done Cap o' Rushes she slipped off, and away she went home. And when the other maids was back she was framin' to be asleep with her cap o' rushes on. (Lang 1889, 442)

Folk-Lore

But before the dance was done Cap o' Rushes she slipt off, and away she went home. And when the other maids was back she was framin' to be asleep with her cap o' rushes on. (Lang 1890, 296)

English Fairy Tales

But before the dance was done Cap o' Rushes slipt off, and away she went home. And when the other maids came back she was pretending to be asleep with her cap o' rushes on. (Jacobs 1890, 53)

The changes that occur from version to version are minor, involving largely punctuation and grammar, paragraphing, and word choice. But precisely these kinds of alterations demonstrate the considerations that necessarily came into play when editors fixed folktales in printed form. They not only began negotiating the genre's lexicon and literary style, but also were compelled to impose the conventions of print itself, such as punctuation, orthography, and placement of paragraphs. If we take Jacobs at his word—that is, if we believe he spoke honestly when he claimed to have left a tale like "Cap o' Rushes" unaltered—then it is clear that the revisions these collectors and editors made on the tortuous path to print were not considered by them to be revisions at all.

Jacobs's editorial revisions, however, become even more fascinating when we take into account the fact that *English Fairy Tales* was subsequently published in revised editions—the best known of which is the third revised edition of 1898. Jacobs took advantage of a revised edition to correct mistakes and typographical errors throughout the book, and to update and expand the notes and references. In addition to citing important contributions made by other collectors and scholars, he provided cross-references to fairy-tale collections of his own that had been published in the meantime. He also used the new edition to expound on the importance of his work for the preservation of the English folktale. And although he had used the publication of *More English Fairy Tales* in 1894 to defend himself against critics who had attacked his editorial methods and rewritings, he used the 1898 revised edition of *English Fairy Tales* to respond to those who had raised questions about his selection of tales and his neglect of the anthropological folklorist's interest in survivals. The revised edition even attends to John Batten's illustrations, relocating the full-page illustration of "Mr. Fox," for example, to place it more appropriately in the narrative passage it illustrates.

Like the Brothers Grimm, however, Jacobs also used the occasion of a new edition to make further changes to the fairy tales themselves—"to revise the phraseology," as he put it in the prefatory note to the third edition (1898, x). Unlike the Grimms, Jacobs did not expunge entire tales and replace them with new texts or preferred variants; nor did he undertake the kind of major rewritings that brought about dramatic changes in character or theme. He did, however, persist at honing the style of some stories by continuing to make changes to grammar, spelling, expression, and punctuation. In revising "Molly Whuppie," for example, Jacobs intervenes only a few times in the text, but he does so in order to render the language more appropriate for the printed page, or at least more grammatically consistent with the rest of the text—changing "catcht" and "jumpt" in the first edition (1890, 128, 129) to "caught" and "jumped" in the revised edition (1898, 128, 129). In the 1898 version of "Binnorie," the changes in word choice and expression serve to make the language more direct and the description more specific. The phrase "his love grew towards her" (1890, 44) becomes the more conventional "his love went out to her" (1898, 44). Similarly, the expression "her hate grew upon her" is replaced by a simpler, more colloquial phrase: "her hate grew and grew." And instead of simply watching "for the coming of the boats," in 1898 Binnorie and her sister "watch for the beaching of the boats"—not only a more concrete expression, but also a pleasantly alliterative one at that.

But Jacobs's revisions to the "phraseology" in the third edition of *English Fairy Tales* are sometimes driven by something other than his attention to language and style. Once again, "Cap o' Rushes" offers a good example.

While most of the new emendations made to "Cap o' Rushes" are predictably stylistic and sacrifice the voice of the original storyteller to a language more appropriate for print, one small but significant alteration in the 1898 version of "Cap o' Rushes" reveals that Jacobs was also attentive to the thematic and moral dimension of his tales. This telling change occurs at the very end of the story, where Jacobs makes what might seem at first blush to be a minor addition to the fairy tale's formulaic closing:

1890 Version

And so they were happy ever after. (56)

1898 Version

And so they were all happy ever after. (56)

But this change takes on added significance in the context of the story cycle to which "Cap o' Rushes" belongs. Like "Catskin," which Jacobs published in *More English Fairy Tales,* "Cap o' Rushes" is a tale of the persecuted heroine.[8] The persecution of the heroine in "Cap o' Rushes" begins when she angers her father by telling him that she loves him "as fresh meat loves salt" (1890, 52). Driven from home by her angry father, she disguises herself in a cloak of rushes and serves as a scullery maid in a great house. At a series of dances where she wears her fine clothes, the master's son falls in love with her. When she finally reveals herself to him, they make plans to marry and invite guests from far and wide to the wedding, including her unsuspecting father. At the wedding dinner, her father is tricked into recognizing the great love his daughter had for him, whereupon Cap o' Rushes makes her true identity known to him. The daughter embraces her father, and the "happy ever after" formula brings the story to its conclusion.

Using the folktale classification system established by Annti Aarne (1987) and Stith Thompson, folklorists generally classify this tale as AT 510B, The Dress of Gold, of Silver, and of Stars (Cap o' Rushes). Most tales of this type—like Jacobs's "Catskin," Grimms' "All Fur," and Perrault's "Donkeyskin"—revolve around a father's incestuous desire to marry his daughter, which causes her to flee from him in disguise. Although the title character of Jacobs's "Cap o' Rushes" must leave her paternal home because she offends her father when she claims to love him like salt (AT 923, Love Like Salt), the story's relationship to tales of father-daughter incest is unmistakable. Jacobs himself acknowledged the connection when he identified "Cap o' Rushes" as a story belonging to the same group of Catskin-type tales as Perrault's "Donkeyskin" (1890, 233). So "Cap o' Rushes" is a tale that Jacobs knew to be deeply rooted in the theme of incest.

Incest, however, was one topic that Jacobs clearly wished to minimize in his fairy-tale collections for children. Writing about the treatment of incest in Jacobs's version of "Catskin," Maria Tatar has shown how his decision to publish a variant that replaces the villainous father with "a nasty rough old man" is motivated by the "need to choose a variant of the tale that swerves as far away as possible from the theme of incest" (Tatar 1992, 130). Jacobs's version of "Cap o' Rushes" also attempts a detour around incest—not only by virtue of the "love like salt" episode, but also by virtue of the revised ending that he provided in the 1898 version of the tale. For editors like Jacobs, who are intent upon camouflaging or eliminating the incestuous overtones of this tale type, the concluding scene poses a problem because of its ambiguity. In the classical fairy tales of marriage, it is the union of the new husband and wife that motivates the tale's proclamation that "they lived happily ever after." However, in the tale type to which "Cap o' Rushes" and "Catskin" belong, the daughter's reunion with the father from whom she has had to flee constitutes the tale's climax, overshadowing the marriage to her new husband. As Tatar has noted concerning the ending of Jacobs's "Catskin": "Husband and father return to the castle, where with Catskin they form a curious trio that 'lives happily ever afterwards'" (Tatar 1992, 131). At the end of "Cap o' Rushes," the reader is left with a tableau depicting the embrace between daughter and father—with no reference at all to the husband. Accordingly, the tale's original ending—"And so they were happy ever after"—seems to refer to the endless happiness of father and daughter, finally reunited and locked in embrace. Jacobs's revised ending—"and so they were *all* happy ever after"—eliminates that implication and makes certain that the entire fairy-tale cast of characters partakes in the happy end.

Despite his efforts at revision, Jacobs's editorial interventions were not always consistent and did not always result in a perfect uniformity of the style. To be sure, Jacobs did not strive to impose a single voice rigidly throughout his collections. Legends and sagas, for example, were composed in a more elegant language than nonsense tales (Shaner 1988, 313). But even within individual stories his revisions of grammar, spelling, and recurring expressions were not always consistently applied. Nonetheless, the differences between Jacobs's sources and his published texts, and the differences between the first edition of 1890 and the third edition of 1898 reveal Jacobs's attempt to shape the language and to some extent the thematic direction of the English fairy tale. Further research in this direction could easily tell us more about the development of the classic fairy tale in Jacobs's collections.[9]

The classic English fairy tale also took shape through Jacobs's selection of tales. Mary E. Shaner has said that *English Fairy Tales* is "one of the richest and most varied single volumes in English folk literature" (Shaner 1988, 311), and it is fair to say that *More English Fairy Tales* extends that rich variety. In the annotations to *More English Fairy Tales*, Jacobs himself spoke to the generic diversity and scope of the eighty-seven tales brought together in his two volumes:

> Of these, thirty-eight are *märchen* proper, *i.e.*, tales with definite plot and evolution; ten are sagas or legends locating romantic stories in definite localities; no less than nineteen are drolls or comic anecdotes; four are cumulative stories; six beast tales; while ten are merely ingenious nonsense tales put together in such a form as to amuse children. (1894c, 216)

While most are written in prose, a number of tales appear in verse form. And, as pointed out earlier, the tales come directly or indirectly from a wide variety of sources, including personal recollections, chapbooks, published collections of tales and ballads, periodicals and other scholarly works, as well as oral informants and collectors.

It is especially noteworthy that many tales came to Jacobs through female collectors and informants. He cites contributions from Mrs. B. Abrahams, Mrs. Balfour, Miss. C. Burne, Lady Burne-Jones, Mrs. Gomme, and Mrs. Walter-Thomas (née Fison). A number of these women were well known for their own folklore research, including M. C. Balfour, Charlotte Burne, and Alice Bertha Gomme. Jacobs benefited from tales these women told from memory, recorded from their own informants and passed on to him, or published in their own works of folklore scholarship. In the preface to *More English Fairy Tales* he takes pains to stress just how large a debt he owes to these contributors:

> The tales reported by Mrs. Balfour, with a thorough knowledge of the peasants' mind and mode of speech, are a veritable acquisition. . . . She has added to my indebtedness to her by sending me several tales

which are entirely new and inedited. Mrs. Gomme comes only second in rank among my creditors for thanks which I can scarcely pay without becoming bankrupt in gratitude. (1894c, xi-xii)

In the notes to *More English Fairy Tales,* he even reiterates his admiration by underlining yet again their contribution to his collection and their importance for the future of folktale studies more generally: "After what Miss Fison . . . , Mrs. Balfour, and Mrs. Gomme have done in the way of collecting among the folk, we may still hope for substantial additions to our stock to be garnered by ladies from the less frequented portions of English soil" (1894c, 215).

In light of the role women played as contributors to Jacobs's collections of English fairy tales, and especially in light of his high regard for their work, it is worthwhile to consider how female characters fare in the tales he published. Mary E. Shaner has noted that Jacobs's "selections are unusual in their time for the inclusion of some strong female characters" (Shaner 1988, 312). Indeed, a wide variety of his tales contradicts what we have come to think of as the stereotypical fairy-tale heroine, who is passive and dependant on male heroism. In tales like "Kate Crackernuts," "The Three Heads of the Well," "The Black Bull of Norroway," and "The Old Witch," young daughters initiate their own heroic journeys out into the world in order to "seek their fortunes"—an undertaking conventionally reserved for adventurous fairy-tale sons. Tales like "Molly Whuppie," "Catskin," and "Cap o' Rushes" depict women of strength, determination, and cunning, who fend for themselves in a hostile world. "Kate Crackernuts"—which Jacobs had "largely to rewrite" (1890, 250)—depicts not only solidarity instead of jealousy among stepsisters, but also a female rescuer who is *not* the most beautiful and who saves the prince. The tale of "Tamlane" depicts another determined female rescuer in the character of Burd Janet. In place of the traditional Bluebeard tale and its cautionary portrayal of female curiosity, Jacobs publishes the story of "Mr. Fox"—a variant of The Robber Bridegroom tale type—where the brave Lady Mary escapes marriage to a murderer by using the power of storytelling to expose his terrible deeds. Intelligent and witty women also inhabit humorous tales such as "Gobborn Seer" and "A Pottle o' Brains," where stupid men rely on women who are much more intelligent than they.

Mary E. Shaner has concluded that it is impossible to know whether Jacobs's selection of stories "was influenced by a desire to provide positive images of women" (Shaner 1988, 312). However, there is strong evidence that it was. Although Victorian culture certainly abounds with stereotypes of women as sensitive domestic angels, the social and cultural discourse of the age also embraced the contrary mythology of the new woman.[10] Victorian fiction itself was increasingly populated by mythic female figures who challenge social conventions and "exude a power that withers patriarchs" (Auerbach 1982, 8). Moreover, by the time Jacobs first arrived in England and long before he published his first collection of English fairy tales, social and political movements affecting the rights of women were well underway. Since the 1840s advances for women had occurred in laws governing labor, divorce, and education; and early feminist impulses had given rise to public and political discussions of important issues like birth control, public health, and women's suffrage. Already sensitive to anti-Semitism and religious oppression, and engaged in the fight against them, Jacobs would not have been unaware of these debates and developments concerning the rights of women. Further evidence that Jacobs endorsed progressive ideas concerning women comes from his own daughter, Mary Bradshaw Hays. In a brief reminiscence entitled "Memories of My Father, Joseph Jacobs," she makes a special point of mentioning Jacobs's association with an active women's rights advocate:

> Another innovator whom my father admired greatly was Dr. F. J. Furnivall, acknowledged authority on Chaucer and Shakespeare—and firm believer in Woman's Rights. He was the man who founded the first Rowing Club for Working Girls, and who hounded the owners of the ABC tea-shops until they provided chairs for the waitresses to sit down on when they were not working. (Hays 1966, 288–289)

By linking her father's esteem for Furnivall with his close friend's firm belief in the rights of women, Hays places her father squarely among the Victorian advocates of women's rights, giving us good reason to believe that the extraordinary female-centered tales in *English Fairy Tales* and *More English Fairy Tales* were indeed chosen because they presented strong, intelligent, brave, and adventurous women.

The value and importance of Joseph Jacobs's work as a folklorist and collector of English fairy tales lies precisely in the controversial, progressive, and even modern ideas that characterize his work. Viewed by many as a "crank and *agent provocateur*" (Maidment 1975, 190), Jacobs produced intentionally polemical fairy-tale collections that challenged conventional thinking about folklore, children's literature, and Victorian culture. The man who migrated from Australia to England and then to the United

States, who moved easily among the fields of literature, Jewish studies, and folklore, was a man who challenged, pushed, and transgressed borders. As a collector and editor of folktales, Jacobs wanted to bridge over the gulf separating socioeconomic classes. He deliberately broke down the boundary between folklore and literature. His theory of diffusion and his radical concept of the folk challenged the ideas of the leading Victorian folklorists. His insight that the creation of every folktale was an individual act of aesthetic creativity and his understanding that tales were created and transmitted in social contexts not only defied contemporary scholarship, but also anticipated modern developments in folklore studies that are still relevant today. As an editor of children's literature, Jacobs eschewed didacticism and respected children. Unlike many of his contemporaries, he claimed to have "greater confidence in my young friends" (1890, 233); and—his squeamishness about the incest theme notwithstanding—he did not think children could be morally or linguistically corrupted by his tales. Instead he encouraged imaginative experience and—applying literary concepts to folklore—believed that even gruesome folktales could be as cathartic for children as classical tragedy was for adults (1890, 246). Reflecting progressive social ideas that emerged in the late Victorian age, Jacobs did not limit his collections only to fairy tales that confirmed social stereotypes. By preserving old tales for new times, he published an exceptionally generous number of stories with strong female characters, tales that continue to be a staple in twentieth-century feminist fairy-tale anthologies.[11]

Pushing beyond conventions and boundaries as he did, it is no wonder that Jacobs's pioneering collections still have so much to offer. *English Fairy Tales* and *More English Fairy Tales*—and the ideas that shaped these classic collections—are as relevant today as ever.

Notes

1. For an excellent discussion of the genesis of the literary fairy tale in Italy and France, see the essays collected in Canepa 1997.

2. See Zipes 1987, xiii–xxix; and Seago 1998, chap. 1 and chap. 6. The powerful role of religion in the suppression and eradication of the fairy tale in England, Scotland, and Wales was noted already by the Victorian folklorist Edwin Sidney Hartland, who attributed "the loss of nursery tales" to Evangelical Protestantism: "Severer in its repression of much of the gaiety of life than any other religion influential in Europe, it has frowned upon all imagination except that of a strictly theological cast; and it has substituted for the idle tales of tradition the more edifying and veracious histories of Noah, Jacob, and Samson" (Hartland [1890], xv–xvi).

3. On Jacobs's patriotic appeal, see Szumsky 1999, 17.

4. The references are to Charles Edward Mudie and George Smith. Mudie established a very popular lending library, which had paying subscribers. Because this commercial venture was so successful, Mudie was able to influence publishers, from whom he purchased large quantities of books, to publish novels in three volumes, enabling him to loan one book simultaneously to three subscribers. George Smith was head of the publishing firm Smith, Elder and Co. and founder of *The Cornhill Magazine,* which published many serialized novels.

5. For good discussions of the Grimms' editing see Neumann 1993 and Tatar 1987.

6. Jacobs titles his version "Whittington and His Cat," although the notes and references section specifies it as "Dick Whittington." Jacobs's titles are not always consistent, as is evident from the sometimes interesting variations among the titles given in the table of contents, on the first page of the story, and in the notes.

7. See Dégh 1988; and Neumann 1993, 35.

8. On the tale of the persecuted heroine, see Bacchilega and Jones 1993.

9. If it were possible to access all his sources and manuscripts, it would be interesting to assess the accuracy of the description and defense Jacobs gave of his editing in "The Problem of Diffusion": "I have gone into the matter [of how sources have been treated] with my two volumes of English tales, and find that

one-third of them are absolutely unchanged, *verbatim et literatim* with my original, and this applies in nearly every case to the few I have collected from friends or correspondents, whose MSS. have gone untouched to the printers. Half of the stories have merely been altered in language, mostly by turning the Latinisms of the collectors into the simpler Saxon of the folk. Only in the case of some sixth of the stories have there been any considerable alterations, all of which are mentioned in the notes" (Jacobs 1894d, 144).

10. See Auerbach 1982; and Basch 1974.

11. Jacobs's tales are included, for example, in Lurie 1980; Carter 1990; and Ragan 1998.

ʚ

ᴮIBLIOGRAPHY

Aarne, Antti. 1987. *The Types of the Folktale: A Classification and Bibliography.* 2nd rev. Trans. and enl. Stith Thompson. FF Communications, no. 184. Helsinki: Suomalainen Tiedeakatemia.

Auerbach, Nina. 1982. *Woman and the Demon: The Life of a Victorian Myth.* Cambridge, MA: Harvard University Press.

Bacchilega, Cristina, and Steven Swann Jones, eds. 1993. *Perspectives on the Innocent Persecuted Heroine in Fairy Tales.* Special issue of *Western Folklore* 52, no. 1.

Basch, Françoise. 1974. *Relative Creatures: Victorian Women in Society and the Novel.* Trans. Anthony Rudolf. New York: Schocken Books.

Canepa, Nancy, ed. 1997. *Out of the Woods: The Origins of the Literary Fairy Tale in Italy and France.* Detroit: Wayne State University Press.

Carter, Angela, ed. 1990. *The Old Wives' Fairy Tale Book.* New York: Pantheon Books.

Clodd, E. 1889. "The Philosophy of Rumpelstiltskin." *Folk-Lore Journal* 7:135–163.

Cox, Marian Roalfe. 1893. *Cinderella: Three Hundred and Forty-five Variants of Cinderella, Catskin, and Cap o' Rushes.* London: David Nutt.

Dégh, Linda. 1988. "What Did the Grimm Brothers Give to and Take from the Folk?" In *The Brothers Grimm and Folktale,* ed. James M. McGlathery, pp. 66–90. Urbana: University of Illinois Press.

Dorson, Richard M. 1968. *The British Folklorists: A History.* Chicago: University of Chicago Press.

Fine, Gary Alan. 1987. "Joseph Jacobs: A Sociological Folklorist." *Folklore* 98:183–193.

Groome, Francis Hindes. 1973. *In Gipsy Tents.* 1880. Reprint, Yorkshire: EP Publishing Ltd.

Hartland, Edwin Sidney, ed. [1890]. *English Fairy and Folk Tales.* London: Walter Scott.

———. 1894. Review of *More English Fairy Tales,* by Joseph Jacobs. *Folk-Lore* 5:74–76.

Hays, May Bradshaw. 1966. "Memories of My Father, Joseph Jacobs." In *Readings about Children's Literature,* ed. Evelyn Rose Robinson, pp. 286–292. New York: McKay. Originally published in *Horn Book* 28 (Dec. 1952): 385–392.

Jacobs, Joseph. 1877. "Mordecai: A Protest against the Critics." *Macmillan's Magazine* (June): 101–111. Reprinted in *Jewish Ideals and Other Essays,* by Joseph Jacobs (New York: Macmillan, 1896), 61–83.

———, ed. 1888. *The Earliest English Version of the Fables of Bidpai; or, The Morall Philosophie of Doni.* David Nutt.

———, ed. 1890. *English Fairy Tales.* London: David Nutt.

———, ed. 1892a. *Celtic Fairy Tales.* London: David Nutt.

———, ed. 1892b. *Indian Fairy Tales.* London: David Nutt.

———, ed. 1893a. *English Fairy Tales.* 2nd ed., rev. London: David Nutt.

———, ed. 1893b. *The Fables of Aesop as First Printed by William Caxton in 1484 with Those of Avian, Alfonso, and Poggio.* 2 vols. London: David Nutt.

———. 1893c. "The Folk." *Folk-Lore* 4:233–238.

———, ed. 1894a. *The Fables of Aesop, Selected, Told Anew, and Their History Traced.* London: Macmillan.

———, ed. 1894b. *More Celtic Fairy Tales.* London: David Nutt.

———, ed. 1894c. *More English Fairy Tales.* London: David Nutt.

———. 1894d. "The Problem of Diffusion: Rejoinders." *Folk-Lore* 5:129–146.

———, ed. 1895. *The Most Delectable History of Reynard the Fox.* London: Macmillan.

———, ed. 1898. *English Fairy Tales.* 3rd ed., rev. London: David Nutt.

———, ed. 1911. *English Fairy Tales.* 4th ed, rev. London: David Nutt.

———, ed. 1916. *Europa's Fairy Tales.* New York: G. P. Putnam's Sons.

———, ed. 1967. *English Fairy Tales.* 3rd. ed., rev. 1898. Reprint, New York: Dover Publications.

———. 1968. *English Fairy Tales: Being the Two Collections of* English Fairy Tales & More English Fairy Tales. Illus. Margery Gill. 1898, 1894. Reprint (2 vols. in 1), London: The Bodley Head.

———. 1970. *English Fairy Tales.* Puffin Books. 1898, 1894. Reprint (selections), Harmondsworth: Penguin.

———. 1993. *English Fairy Tales.* Everyman's Library Children's Classics. 1898, 1894. Reprint (2 vols. in 1), New York: Alfred A. Knopf.

Lang, Andrew. 1889. "At the Sign of the Ship" (includes "Cap o' Rushes"). *Longman's Magazine* 13 (Feb.): 439–448.

———. 1890. "English and Scotch Fairy Tales" (includes "Cap o' Rushes"). *Folk-Lore* 1:289–312.

Lurie, Alison, ed. 1980. *Clever Gretchen and Other Forgotten Folktales.* New York: Crowell.

Maidment, Brian E. 1975. "Joseph Jacobs and English Folklore in the 1890s." In *Studies in the Cultural Life of the Jews in England,* ed. Dov Noy and Issachar Ben-Ami, pp. 185–196. Folklore Research Center Studies, vol. 5. Jerusalem: Magnes Press, The Hebrew University.

Marx, Alexander. 1948. "The Jewish Scholarship of Joseph Jacobs." In *Essays in Jewish Biography,* pp. 251–254. Philadelphia: Jewish Publication Society of America.

Millar, John Hepburn. 1976. "On Some Books for Boys and Girls." In *A Peculiar Gift: Nineteenth Century Writings on Books for Children,* ed. Lance Salway, pp. 154–161. Harmondsworth, Middlesex: Kestrel Books. Originally published anonymously in *Blackwood's Magazine* 159 (Mar. 1896): 389–395.

Muir, Percy. 1954. *English Children's Books: 1600 to 1900.* New York: Frederick A. Praeger.

Neumann, Siegfried. 1993. "The Brothers Grimm as Collectors and Editors of German Folktales." In *The Reception of Grimms' Fairy Tales: Responses, Reactions, Revisions,* ed. Donald Haase, pp. 24–40. Detroit: Wayne State University Press.

Ragan, Kathleen, ed. 1998. *Fearless Girls, Wise Women and Beloved Sisters: Heroines in Folktales from around the World.* New York: W. W. Norton.

Seago, Karen. 1998. "Transculturations: Making 'Sleeping Beauty.' The Translation of a Grimm Märchen into an English Fairy Tale in the Nineteenth Century." Ph.D. diss., London University.

Shaner, Mary E. 1987. "Joseph Jacobs." In *Writers for Children: Critical Studies of Major Authors since the Seventeenth Century,* ed. Jane Bingham, pp. 309–316. New York: Charles Scribner's Sons.

Szumsky, Brian E. 1999. "The House That Jack Built: Empire and Ideology in Nineteenth-Century British Versions of 'Jack and the Beanstalk.'" *Marvels & Tales: Journal of Fairy-Tale Studies* 13:11–30.

Tatar, Maria. 1987. *The Hard Facts of the Grimms' Fairy Tales.* Princeton: Princeton University Press.

———. 1992. *Off with Their Heads! Fairy Tales and the Culture of Childhood.* Princeton: Princeton University Press.

Taylor, Edgar, trans. 1826. *German Popular Stories, Translated from the Kinder und Haus-Märchen Collected by M.M. Grimm from Oral Tradition.* Vol. 2. London: James Robins; Dublin: Joseph Robins Jun.

Walter-Thomas, A. 1877. "The Suffolk 'King Lear': Cap o' Rushes." *Ipswich Journal* (7 Aug. 1877): Suffolk Notes and Queries 23, no. 62.

Zipes, Jack, ed. 1987. *Victorian Fairy Tales: The Revolt of the Fairies and Elves.* New York: Methuen.

English Fairy Tales

HOW
TO GET INTO THIS BOOK.

Knock at the Knocker on the Door,
Pull the Bell at the side,
Then, if you are very *quiet, you will hear a*
teeny tiny voice say through the grating
"Take down the Key." This you will find at the
back: you cannot mistake it, for it has J. J.
in the wards. Put the Key in the Keyhole,
which it fits exactly, unlock the door and
WALK IN.

Childe Rowland

English

Fairy Tales

COLLECTED BY

JOSEPH JACOBS

EDITOR OF "FOLK-LORE"

ILLUSTRATED BY

JOHN D. BATTEN

LONDON
DAVID NUTT, 270 STRAND
1890

To
MY DEAR LITTLE
MAY

Contents

Contents

ॐ

P REFACE

WHO says that English folk have no fairy-tales of their own ? The present volume contains only a selection out of some 140, of which I have found traces in this country. It is probable that many more exist.

A quarter of the tales in this volume, have been collected during the last ten years or so, and some of them have not been hitherto published. Up to 1870 it was equally said of France and of Italy, that they possessed no folktales. Yet, within fifteen years from that date, over 1000 tales had been collected in each country. I am hoping that the present volume may lead to equal activity in this country, and would earnestly beg any reader of this book who knows of similar tales, to communicate them, written down as they are told, to me, care of Mr. Nutt. The only reason, I imagine, why such tales have not hitherto been brought to light, is the lamentable gap between the governing and recording classes and the dumb working classes of this country—dumb to others but eloquent among themselves. It would be no unpatriotic task to help to bridge over this gulf, by giving a common fund of nursery literature to all classes of the English people, and, in any case, it can do no harm to add to the innocent gaiety of the nation.

A word or two as to our title seems necessary. We have called our stories Fairy Tales though few of them speak of fairies.* The same remark applies to the collection of the Brothers Grimm and to all the other European collections, which contain exactly the same classes of tales as ours. Yet our stories are what the little ones mean when they clamour for "Fairy Tales," and this is the only name which they give to them. One cannot imagine a child saying, "Tell us a folk-tale, nurse," or "Another nursery tale, please, grandma." As our book is intended for the little ones, we have indicated its contents by the name they use. The words "Fairy Tales" must accordingly be taken to include tales in which occurs something "fairy," something extraordinary—fairies, giants, dwarfs, speaking animals. It must be taken also to cover tales in which what is extraordinary is the

*For some recent views on fairies and tales *about* fairies, see Notes, pp. 169–172.

stupidity of some of the actors. Many of the tales in this volume, as in similar collections for other European countries, are what the folk-lorists call Drolls. They serve to justify the title of Merrie England, which used to be given to this country of ours, and indicate unsuspected capacity for fun and humour among the unlettered classes. The story of Tom Tit Tot, which opens our collection, is unequalled among all other folk-tales I am acquainted with, for its combined sense of humour and dramatic power.

The first adjective of our title also needs a similar extension of its meaning. I have acted on Molière's principle, and have taken what was good wherever I could find it. Thus, a couple of these stories have been found among descendants of English immigrants in America; a couple of others I tell as I heard them myself in my youth in Australia. One of the best was taken down from the mouth of an English Gipsy. I have also included some stories that have only been found in Lowland Scotch. I have felt justified in doing this, as of the twenty-one folk-tales contained in Chambers' "Popular Rhymes of Scotland," no less than sixteen are also to be found in an English form. With the Folk-tale as with the Ballad, Lowland Scotch may be regarded as simply a dialect of English, and it is a mere chance whether a tale is extant in one or other, or both.

I have also rescued and re-told a few Fairy Tales that only exist now-a-days in the form of ballads. There are certain indications that the "common form" of the English Fairy Tale was the *cante-fable,* a mixture of narrative and verse of which the most illustrious example in literature is "Aucassin et Nicolette." In one case I have endeavoured to retain this form, as the tale in which it occurs, "Childe Rowland," is mentioned by Shakespeare in *King Lear* and is probably, as I have shown, the source of Milton's *Comus.* Late as they have been collected, some dozen of the tales can be traced back to the sixteenth century, two of them being quoted by Shakespeare himself.

In the majority of instances I have had largely to re-write* these Fairy Tales, especially those in dialect, including the Lowland Scotch. Children, and sometimes those of larger growth, will not read dialect. I have also had to reduce the flatulent phraseology of the eighteenth-century chap-books, and to re-write in simpler style the stories only extant in

---

* It is perhaps worth remarking that the Brothers Grimm did the same with their stories. "Dass der Ausdruck," say they in their Preface, "und die Ausführung des Einzelnen grossentheils von uns herrührt versteht sich von selbst." I may add that many of their stories were taken from printed sources. In the first volume of Mrs. Hunt's translation, Nos. 12, 18, 19, 23, 32, 35, 42, 43, 44, 69, 77, 78, 83, 89, are thus derived.

"Literary" English. I have, however, left a few vulgarisms in the mouths of vulgar people. Children appreciate the dramatic propriety of this as much as their elders. Generally speaking, it has been my ambition to write as a good old nurse will speak when she tells Fairy Tales. I am doubtful as to my success in catching the colloquial-romantic tone appropriate for such narratives, but the thing had to be done or else my main object, to give a book of English Fairy Tales which English children will listen to, would have been unachieved. This book is meant to be read aloud, and not merely taken in by the eye.

In a few instances I have introduced or changed an incident. I have never done so, however, without mentioning the fact in the Notes. These have been relegated to the obscurity of small print and a back place, while the little ones have been, perhaps unnecessarily, warned off them. They indicate my sources and give a few references to parallels and variants which may be of interest to fellow-students of Folk-lore. It is, perhaps, not necessary to inform readers who are not fellow-students that the study of Folk-tales has pretensions to be a science. It has its special terminology, and its own methods of investigation, by which it is hoped, one of these days, to gain fuller knowledge of the workings of the popular mind as well as traces of archaic modes of thought and custom. I hope on some future occasion to treat the subject of the English Folk-tale on a larger scale and with all the necessary paraphernalia of prolegomena and excursus. I shall then, of course, reproduce my originals with literal accuracy, and have therefore felt the more at liberty on the present occasion to make the necessary deviations from this in order to make the tales readable for children.

Finally, I have to thank those by whose kindness in waiving their rights to some of these stories, I have been enabled to compile this book. My friends Mr. E. Clodd, Mr. F. Hindes Groome, and Mr. Andrew Lang, have thus yielded up to me some of the most attractive stories in the following pages. The Councils of the English and of the American Folk-lore Societies, and Messrs. Longmans, have also been equally generous. Nor can I close these remarks without a word of thanks and praise to the artistic skill with which my friend, Mr. J. D. Batten, has made the romance and humour of these stories live again in the brilliant designs with which he has adorned these pages. It should be added that the dainty headpieces to "Henny Penny" and "Mr. Fox" are due to my old friend, Mr. Henry Ryland.

JOSEPH JACOBS.

Full Page Illustrations

["The Castle on Twelve Golden Pillars," is from a wood engraving executed by Messrs. W. and J. Cheshire; the remainder of the full page illustrations together with all the cuts inserted in the text are from "process" blocks supplied by Messrs. J. C. Drummond & Co.]

ENGLISH FAIRY TALES

❧ Tom Tit Tot ❧

ONCE UPON A TIME there was a woman, and she baked five pies. And when they came out of the oven, they were that overbaked the crusts were too hard to eat. So she says to her daughter:

"Darter," says she, "put you them there pies on the shelf, and leave 'em there a little, and they'll come again."—She meant, you know, the crust would get soft.

But the girl, she says to herself: "Well, if they'll come again, I'll eat 'em now." And she set to work and ate 'em all, first and last.

Well, come supper-time the woman said: "Go you, and get one o' them there pies. I dare say they've come again now."

The girl went and she looked, and there was nothing but the dishes. So back she came and says she: "Noo, they ain't come again."

"Not one of 'em?" says the mother.

"Not one of 'em," says she.

"Well, come again, or not come again," said the woman, "I'll have one for supper."

"But you can't, if they ain't come," said the girl.

"But I can," says she. "Go you, and bring the best of 'em."

"Best or worst," says the girl, "I've ate 'em all, and you can't have one till that's come again."

Well, the woman she was done, and she took her spinning to the door to spin, and as she span she sang:

> "My darter ha' ate five, five pies to-day.
> My darter ha' ate five, five pies to-day."

The king was coming down the street, and he heard her sing, but what she sang he couldn't hear, so he stopped and said:

"What was that you were singing, my good woman?"

The woman was ashamed to let him hear what her daughter had been doing, so she sang, instead of that:

"My darter ha' spun five, five skeins to-day.
My darter ha' spun five, five skeins to-day."

"Stars o' mine!" said the king, "I never heard tell of any one that could do that."

Then he said: "Look you here, I want a wife, and I'll marry your daughter. But look you here," says he, "eleven months out of the year she shall have all she likes to eat, and all the gowns she likes to get, and all the company she likes to keep; but the last month of the year she'll have to spin five skeins every day, and if she don't I shall kill her."

"All right," says the woman; for she thought what a grand marriage that was. And as for the five skeins, when the time came, there'd be plenty of ways of getting out of it, and likeliest, he'd have forgotten all about it.

Well, so they were married. And for eleven months the girl had all she liked to eat, and all the gowns she liked to get, and all the company she liked to keep.

But when the time was getting over, she began to think about the skeins and to wonder if he had 'em in mind. But not one word did he say about 'em, and she thought he'd wholly forgotten 'em.

However, the last day of the last month he takes her to a room she'd never set eyes on before. There was nothing in it but a spinning-wheel and a stool. And says he: "Now, my dear, here you'll be shut in to-morrow with some victuals and some flax, and if you haven't spun five skeins by the night, your head 'll go off."

And away he went about his business.

Well, she was that frightened, she'd always been such a gatless girl, that she didn't so much as know how to spin, and what was she to do to-morrow with no one to come nigh her to help her? She sat down on a stool in the kitchen, and law! how she did cry!

However, all of a sudden she heard a sort of a knocking low down on the door. She upped and oped it, and what should she see but a small little black thing with a long tail. That looked up at her right curious, and that said:

"What are you a-crying for?"

"What's that to you?" says she.

"Never you mind," that said, "but tell me what you're a-crying for."

"This is what I'll do."

"That won't do me no good if I do," says she.

"You don't know that," that said, and twirled that's tail round.

"Well," says she, "that won't do no harm, if that don't do no good," and she upped and told about the pies, and the skeins, and everything.

"This is what I'll do," says the little black thing, "I'll come to your window every morning and take the flax and bring it spun at night."

"What's your pay?" says she.

That looked out of the corner of that's eyes, and that said: "I'll give you three guesses every night to guess my name, and if you haven't guessed it before the month's up, you shall be mine."

Well, she thought she'd be sure to guess that's name before the month was up. "All right," says she, "I agree."

"All right," that says, and law! how that twirled that's tail.

Well, the next day, her husband took her into the room, and there was the flax and the day's food.

"Now there's the flax," says he, "and if that ain't spun up this night, off goes your head." And then he went out and locked the door.

He'd hardly gone, when there was a knocking against the window.

She upped and she oped it, and there sure enough was the little old thing sitting on the ledge.

"Where's the flax?" says he.

"Here it be," says she. And she gave it to him.

Well, come the evening a knocking came again to the window. She upped and she oped it, and there was the little old thing with five skeins of flax on his arm.

"Here it be," says he, and he gave it to her.

"Now, what's my name?" says he.

"What, is that Bill?" says she.

"Noo, that ain't," says he, and he twirled his tail.

"Is that Ned?" says she.

"Noo, that ain't," says he, and he twirled his tail.

"Well, is that Mark?" says she.

"Noo, that ain't," says he, and he twirled his tail harder, and away he flew.

Well, when her husband came in, there were the five skeins ready for him. "I see I shan't have to kill you to-night, my dear," says he; "you'll have your food and your flax in the morning," says he, and away he goes.

Well, every day the flax and the food were brought, and every day that there little black impet used to come mornings and evenings. And all the day the girl sate trying to think of names to say to it when it came at night. But she never hit on the right one. And as it got towards the end of the month, the impet began to look so maliceful, and that twirled that's tail faster and faster each time she gave a guess.

At last it came to the last day but one. The impet came at night along with the five skeins, and that said:

"What, ain't you got my name yet?"

"Is that Nicodemus?" says she.

"Noo, t'ain't," that says.

"Is that Sammle?" says she.

"Noo, t'ain't," that says.

"A-well, is that Methusalem?" says she.

"Noo, t'ain't that neither," that says.

Then that looks at her with that's eyes like a coal o' fire, and that says: "Woman, there's only to-morrow night, and then you'll be mine!" And away it flew.

Well, she felt that horrid. However, she heard the king coming along the passage. In he came, and when he sees the five skeins, he says, says he:

"Well, my dear," says he. "I don't see but what you'll have your skeins ready to-morrow night as well, and as I reckon I shan't have to kill you, I'll have supper in here to-night." So they brought supper, and another stool for him, and down the two sate.

Well, he hadn't eaten but a mouthful or so, when he stops and begins to laugh.

"What is it?" says she.

"A-why," says he, "I was out a-hunting to-day, and I got away to a place in the wood I'd never seen before. And there was an old chalk-pit. And I heard a kind of a sort of a humming. So I got off my hobby, and I went right quiet to the pit, and I looked down. Well, what should there be but the funniest little black thing you ever set eyes on. And what was that doing, but that had a little spinning-wheel, and that was spinning wonderful fast, and twirling that's tail. And as that span that sang:

"Nimmy nimmy not
My name's Tom Tit Tot."

Well, when the girl heard this, she felt as if she could have jumped out of her skin for joy, but she didn't say a word.

Next day that there little thing looked so maliceful when he came for the flax. And when night came, she heard that knocking against the window panes. She oped the window, and that come right in on the ledge. That was grinning from ear to ear, and Oo! that's tail was twirling round so fast.

"What's my name?" that says, as that gave her the skeins.

"Is that Solomon?" she says, pretending to be afeard.

"Noo, t'ain't," that says, and that come further into the room.

"Well, is that Zebedee?" says she again.

"Noo, 'tain't," says the impet. And then that laughed and twirled that's tail till you couldn't hardly see it.

"Take time, woman," that says; "next guess, and you're mine." And that stretched out that's black hands at her.

Well, she backed a step or two, and she looked at it, and then she laughed out, and says she, pointing her finger at it:

NIMMY NIMMY NOT
YOUR NAME'S TOM
TIT
TOT

Well, when that heard her, that gave an awful shriek and away that flew into the dark, and she never saw it any more.

ᔆᖇ The Three Sillies ᔆᖇ

ONCE upon a time there was a farmer and his wife who had one daughter, and she was courted by a gentleman. Every evening he used to come and see her, and stop to supper at the farmhouse, and the daughter used to be sent down into the cellar to draw the beer for supper. So one evening she had gone down to draw the beer, and she happened to look up at the ceiling while she was drawing, and she saw a mallet stuck in one of the beams. It must have been there a long, long time, but somehow or other she had never noticed it before, and she began a-thinking. And she thought it was very dangerous to have that mallet there, for she said to herself: "Suppose him and me was to be married, and we was to have a son, and he was to grow up to be a man, and come down into the cellar to draw the beer, like as I'm doing now, and the mallet was to fall on his head and kill him, what a dreadful thing it would be!" And she put down the candle and the jug, and sat herself down and began a-crying.

Well, they began to wonder upstairs how it was that she was so long drawing the beer, and her mother went down to see after her, and she found her sitting on the settle crying, and the beer running over the floor. "Why, whatever is the matter?" said her mother. "Oh, mother!" says she, "look at that horrid mallet! Suppose we was to be married, and was to have a son, and he was to grow up, and was to come down to the cellar to draw the beer, and the mallet was to fall on his head and kill him, what a dreadful thing it would be!" "Dear, dear! what a dreadful thing it would be!" said the mother, and she sat her down aside of the daughter and started a-crying too. Then after a bit the father began to wonder that they didn't come back, and he went down into the cellar to look after them himself, and there they two sat a-crying, and the beer running all over the floor. "Whatever is the matter?" says he. "Why," says the mother, "look at that horrid mallet. Just suppose, if our daughter and her sweetheart was to be married, and was to have a son, and he was to grow up, and was to come down into the cellar to draw the beer, and the mallet was to fall on his head and kill him, what a dreadful thing it would be!" "Dear, dear, dear! so it would!" said the father, and he sat himself down aside of the other two, and started a-crying.

Now the gentleman got tired of stopping up in the kitchen by himself, and at last he went down into the cellar too, to see what they were after; and there they three sat a-crying side by side, and the beer running all over the floor. And he ran straight and turned the tap. Then he said: "Whatever are you three doing, sitting there crying, and letting the beer run all over the floor?" "Oh!" says the father, "look at that horrid mallet! Suppose you and our daughter was to be married, and was to have a son, and he was to grow up, and was to come down into the cellar to draw the beer, and the mallet was to fall on his head and kill him!" And then they all started a-crying worse than before. But the gentleman burst out a-laughing, and reached up and pulled out the mallet, and then he said: "I've travelled many miles, and I never met three such big sillies as you three before; and now I shall start out on my travels again, and when I can find three bigger sillies than you three, then I'll come back and marry your daughter." So he wished them good-bye, and started off on his travels, and left them all crying because the girl had lost her sweetheart.

Well, he set out, and he travelled a long way, and at last he came to a woman's cottage that had some grass growing on the roof. And the woman was trying to get her cow to go up a ladder to the grass, and the poor thing durst not go. So the gentleman asked the woman what she was doing. "Why, lookye," she said, "look at all that beautiful grass. I'm going to get the cow on to the roof to eat it. She'll be quite safe, for I shall tie a string round her neck, and pass it down the chimney, and tie it to my wrist as I go about the house, so she can't fall off without my knowing it." "Oh, you poor silly!" said the gentleman, "you should cut the grass and throw it down to the cow!" But the woman thought it was easier to get the cow up the ladder than to get the grass down, so she pushed her and coaxed her and got her up, and tied a string round her neck, and passed it down the

chimney, and fastened it to her own wrist. And the gentleman went on his way, but he hadn't gone far when the cow tumbled off the roof, and hung by the string tied round her neck, and it strangled her. And the weight of the cow tied to her wrist pulled the woman up the chimney, and she stuck fast half-way and was smothered in the soot.

Well, that was one big silly.

And the gentleman went on and on, and he went to an inn to stop the night, and they were so full at the inn that they had to put him in a double-bedded room, and another traveller was to sleep in the other bed. The other man was a very pleasant fellow, and they got very friendly together; but in the morning, when they were both getting up, the gentleman was surprised to see the other hang his trousers on the knobs of the chest of drawers and run across the room and try to jump into them, and he tried over and over again, and couldn't manage it; and the gentleman wondered whatever he was doing it for. At last he stopped and wiped his face with his handkerchief. "Oh dear," he says, "I do think trousers are the most awkwardest kind of clothes that ever were. I can't think who could have invented such things. It takes me the best part of an hour to get into mine every morning, and I get so hot! How do you manage yours?" So the gentleman burst out a-laughing, and showed him how to put them on; and he was very much obliged to him, and said he never should have thought of doing it that way.

So that was another big silly.

Then the gentleman went on his travels again; and he came to a village, and outside the village there was a pond, and round the pond was a crowd of people. And they had got rakes, and brooms, and pitchforks, reaching into the pond; and the gentleman asked what was the matter. "Why," they say, "matter enough! Moon's tumbled into the pond, and we can't rake her out anyhow!" So the gentleman burst out a-laughing, and told them to look up into the sky, and that it was only the shadow in the water. But they wouldn't listen to him, and abused him shamefully, and he got away as quick as he could.

So there was a whole lot of sillies bigger than them three sillies at home. So the gentleman turned back home again and married the farmer's daughter, and if they didn't live happy for ever after, that's nothing to do with you or me.

ᔇ The Rose-Tree ᔇ

THERE was once upon a time a good man who had two children: a girl by a first wife, and a boy by the second. The girl was as white as milk, and her lips were like cherries. Her hair was like golden silk, and it hung to the ground. Her brother loved her dearly, but

MY LIT- TLE BRO- THER WHOM I LOVE SITS BE- LOW AND SING A- BOVE

her wicked stepmother hated her. "Child," said the stepmother one day, "go to the grocer's shop and buy me a pound of candles." She gave her the money; and the little girl went, bought the candles, and started on her return. There was a stile to cross. She put down the candles whilst she got over the stile. Up came a dog and ran off with the candles.

She went back to the grocer's, and she got a second bunch. She came to the stile, set down the candles, and proceeded to climb over. Up came the dog and ran off with the candles.

She went again to the grocer's, and she got a third bunch; and just the same happened. Then she came to her stepmother crying, for she had spent all the money and had lost three bunches of candles.

The stepmother was angry, but she pretended not to mind the loss. She said to the child: "Come, lay your head on my lap that I may comb your hair." So the little one laid her head in the woman's lap, who proceeded to comb the yellow silken hair. And when she combed the hair fell over her knees, and rolled right down to the ground.

Then the stepmother hated her more for the beauty of her hair; so she said to her, "I cannot part your hair on my knee, fetch a billet of wood." So she fetched it. Then said the stepmother, "I cannot part your hair with a comb, fetch me an axe." So she fetched it.

"Now," said the wicked woman, "lay your head down on the billet whilst I part your hair."

Well! she laid down her little golden head without fear; and whist! down came the axe, and it was off. So the mother wiped the axe and laughed.

Then she took the heart and liver of the little girl, and she stewed them and brought them into the house for supper. The husband tasted them and shook his head. He said they tasted very strangely. She gave some to the little boy, but he would not eat. She tried to force him, but he refused, and ran out into the garden, and took up his little sister, and put her in a box, and buried the box under a rose-tree; and every day he went to the tree and wept, till his tears ran down on the box.

One day the rose-tree flowered. It was spring, and there among the flowers was a white bird; and it sang, and sang, and sang like an angel out of heaven. Away it flew, and it went to a cobbler's shop, and perched itself on a tree hard by; and thus it sang:

> "My wicked mother slew me,
> My dear father ate me,
> My little brother whom I love
> Sits below, and I sing above
>   Stick, stock, stone dead."

"Sing again that beautiful song," asked the shoemaker. "If you will first give me those little red shoes you are making." The cobbler gave the shoes, and the bird sang the song; then flew to a tree in front of a watch-maker's, and sang:

> "My wicked mother slew me,
> My dear father ate me,
> My little brother whom I love
> Sits below, and I sing above
> Stick, stock, stone dead."

"Oh, the beautiful song! sing it again, sweet bird," asked the watch-maker. "If you will give me first that gold watch and chain in your hand." The jeweller gave the watch and chain. The bird took it in one foot, the shoes in the other, and, after having repeated the song, flew away to where three millers were picking a millstone. The bird perched on a tree and sang:

> "My wicked mother slew me,
> My dear father ate me,
> My little brother whom I love
> Sits below, and I sing above
> Stick!

Then one of the men put down his tool and looked up from his work,
"Stock!
Then the second miller's man laid aside his tool and looked up,
"Stone!
Then the third miller's man laid down his tool and looked up,
"Dead!"

Then all three cried out with one voice: "Oh, what a beautiful song! Sing it, sweet bird, again." "If you will put the millstone round my neck," said the bird. The men did what the bird wanted and away to the tree it flew with the millstone round its neck, the red shoes in one foot, and the gold watch and chain in the other. It sang the song and then flew home. It rattled the millstone against the eaves of the house, and the stepmother said: "It thunders." Then the little boy ran out to see the thunder, and down dropped the red shoes at his feet. It rattled the millstone against the eaves of the house once more, and the stepmother said again: "It thunders." Then the father ran out and down fell the chain about his neck.

In ran father and son, laughing and saying, "See, what fine things the thunder has brought us!" Then the bird rattled the millstone against the eaves of the house a third time; and the stepmother said: "It thunders again, perhaps the thunder has brought something for me," and she ran out; but the moment she stepped outside the door, down fell the millstone on her head; and so she died.

⁓ The Old Woman and her Pig ⁓

AN old woman was sweeping her house, and she found a little crooked sixpence. "What," said she, "shall I do with this little sixpence? I will go to market, and buy a little pig."

As she was coming home, she came to a stile: but the piggy wouldn't go over the stile.

She went a little further, and she met a dog. So she said to the dog: "Dog! bite pig; piggy won't go over the stile; and I shan't get home to-night." But the dog wouldn't.

She went a little further, and she met a stick. So she said: "Stick! stick! beat dog! dog won't bite pig; piggy won't get over the stile; and I shan't get home to-night." But the stick wouldn't.

She went a little further, and she met a fire. So she said: "Fire! fire! burn stick; stick

But the dog wouldn't.

won't beat dog; dog won't bite pig; piggy won't get over the stile; and I shan't get home to-night." But the fire wouldn't.

She went a little further, and she met some water. So she said: "Water, water! quench fire; fire won't burn stick; stick won't beat dog; dog won't bite pig; piggy won't get over the stile; and I shan't get home to-night." But the water wouldn't.

She went a little further, and she met an ox. So she said: "Ox! ox! drink water; water won't quench fire; fire won't burn stick; stick won't beat dog; dog won't bite pig; piggy won't get over the stile; and I shan't get home to-night." But the ox wouldn't.

She went a little further, and she met a butcher. So she said: "Butcher! butcher! kill ox; ox won't drink water; water won't quench fire; fire won't burn stick; stick won't beat dog; dog won't bite pig; piggy won't get over the stile; and I shan't get home to-night." But the butcher wouldn't.

She went a little further, and she met a rope. So she said: "Rope! rope! hang butcher; butcher won't kill ox; ox won't drink water; water won't quench fire; fire won't burn stick; stick won't beat dog; dog won't bite pig; piggy won't get over the stile; and I shan't get home to-night." But the rope wouldn't.

She went a little further, and she met a rat. So she said: "Rat! rat! gnaw rope; rope won't hang butcher; butcher won't kill ox; ox won't .drink water; water won't quench fire; fire

But the butcher wouldn't.

won't burn stick; stick won't beat dog; dog won't bite pig; piggy won't get over the stile; and I shan't get home to-night." But the rat wouldn't.

She went a little further, and she met a cat. So she said: "Cat! cat! kill rat; rat won't gnaw rope; rope won't hang butcher; butcher won't kill ox; ox won't drink water; water won't quench fire; fire won't burn stick; stick won't beat dog; dog won't bite pig; piggy won't get over the stile; and I shan't get home to-night." But the cat said to her, "If you will go to yonder cow, and fetch me a saucer of milk, I will kill the rat." So away went the old woman to the cow.

But the cow said to her: "If you will go to yonder hay-stack, and fetch me a handful of hay, I'll give you the milk." So away went the old woman to the hay-stack; and she brought the hay to the cow.

As soon as the cow had eaten the hay, she gave the old woman the milk; and away she went with it in a saucer to the cat.

As soon as the cat had lapped up the milk, the cat began to kill the rat; the rat began to gnaw the rope; the rope began to hang the butcher; the butcher began to kill the ox; the ox began to drink the water; the water began to quench the fire; the fire began to burn the stick; the stick began to beat the dog; the dog began to bite the pig; the little pig in a fright jumped over the stile; and so the old woman got home that night.

How Jack went to Seek his Fortune

ꙮ How Jack went to Seek his Fortune ꙮ

ONCE on a time there was a boy named Jack, and one morning he started to go and seek his fortune.

He hadn't gone very far before he met a cat.

"Where are you going, Jack?" said the cat.

"I am going to seek my fortune."

"May I go with you?"

"Yes," said Jack, "the more the merrier."

So on they went, jiggelty-jolt, jiggelty-jolt.

They went a little further and they met a dog.

"Where are you going, Jack?" said the dog.

"I am going to seek my fortune."

"May I go with you?"

"Yes," said Jack, "the more the merrier."

So on they went, jiggelty-jolt, jiggelty-jolt.

They went a little further and they met a goat.

"Where are you going, Jack?" said the goat.

"I am going to seek my fortune."

"May I go with you?"

"Yes," said Jack, "the more the merrier."

So on they went, jiggelty-jolt, jiggelty-jolt.

They went a little further and they met a bull.

"Where are you going, Jack?" said the bull.

"I am going to seek my fortune."

"May I go with you?"

"Yes," said Jack, "the more the merrier."

So on they went, jiggelty-jolt, jiggelty-jolt.

They went a little further and they met a rooster.

"Where are you going, Jack?" said the rooster.

"I am going to seek my fortune."

"May I go with you?"

"Yes," said Jack, "the more the merrier."

So on they went, jiggelty-jolt, jiggelty-jolt.

Well, they went on till it was about dark, and they began to think of some place where they could spend the night. About this time they came in sight of a house, and Jack told them to keep still while he went up and looked in through the window. And there were some robbers counting over their money. Then Jack went back and told them to wait till he gave the word, and then to make all the noise they could. So when they were all ready Jack gave the word, and the cat mewed, and the dog barked, and the goat bleated, and the bull bellowed, and the rooster crowed, and all together they made such a dreadful noise that it frightened the robbers all away.

And then they went in and took possession of the house. Jack was afraid the robbers would come back in the night, and so when it came time to go to bed he put the cat in the rocking-chair, and he put the dog under the table, and he put the goat upstairs, and he put the bull down cellar, and the rooster flew up on to the roof, and Jack went to bed.

By-and-by the robbers saw it was all dark and they sent one man back to the house to look after their money. Before long he came back in a great fright and told them his story.

"I went back to the house," said he, "and went in and tried to sit down in the rocking-chair, and there was an old woman knitting, and she stuck her knitting-needles into me." That was the cat, you know.

"I went to the table to look after the money and there was a shoemaker under the table, and he stuck his awl into me." That was the dog, you know.

"I started to go upstairs, and there was a man up there threshing, and he knocked me down with his flail." That was the goat, you know.

"I started to go down cellar, and there was a man down there chopping wood, and he knocked me up with his axe." That was the bull, you know.

"But I shouldn't have minded all that if it hadn't been for that little fellow on top of the house, who kept a-hollering, 'Chuck him up to me-e! Chuck him up to me-e!'" Of course that was the cock-a-doodle-do.

⁓ Mr. Vinegar ⁓

MR. and Mrs. Vinegar lived in a vinegar bottle. Now, one day, when Mr. Vinegar was from home, Mrs. Vinegar, who was a very good housewife, was busily sweeping her house, when an unlucky thump of the broom

brought the whole house clitter-clatter, clitter-clatter, about her ears. In an agony of grief she rushed forth to meet her husband. On seeing him she exclaimed, "Oh, Mr. Vinegar, Mr. Vinegar, we are ruined, we are ruined: I have knocked the house down, and it is all to pieces!" Mr. Vinegar then said: "My dear, let us see what can be done. Here is the door; I will take it on my back, and we will go forth to seek our fortune." They walked all that day, and at nightfall entered a thick forest. They were both very, very tired, and Mr. Vinegar said: "My love, I will climb up into a tree, drag up the door, and you shall follow." He accordingly did so, and they both stretched their weary limbs on the door, and fell fast asleep. In the middle of the night Mr. Vinegar was disturbed by the sound of voices underneath, and to his horror and dismay found that it was a band of thieves met to divide their booty. "Here, Jack," said one, "here's five pounds for you; here, Bill, here's ten pounds for you; here, Bob, here's three pounds for you." Mr. Vinegar could listen no longer; his terror was so great that he trembled and trembled, and shook down the door on their heads. Away scampered the thieves, but Mr. Vinegar dared not quit his retreat till broad daylight. He then scrambled out of the tree, and went to lift up the door. What did he see but a number of golden guineas. "Come down, Mrs. Vinegar," he cried; "come down, I say; our fortune's made, our fortune's made! Come down, I say." Mrs. Vinegar got down as fast as she could, and when she saw the money she jumped for joy. "Now, my dear," said she, "I'll tell you what you shall do. There is a fair at the neighbouring town; you shall take these forty guineas and buy a cow. I can make butter and cheese, which you shall sell at market, and we shall then be able to live very comfortably." Mr. Vinegar joyfully agrees, takes the money, and off he goes to the fair. When he arrived, he walked up and down, and at length saw a beautiful red cow. It was an excellent milker, and perfect in every way. "Oh," thought Mr. Vinegar, "if I had but that cow, I should be the happiest man alive." So he offers the forty guineas for the cow, and the owner said that, as he was a friend, he'd oblige him. So the bargain was made, and he got the cow and he drove it backwards and forwards to show it. By-and-by he saw a man playing the bagpipes—Tweedle-dum tweedle-dee. The children followed him about, and he appeared to be pocketing money on all sides. "Well," thought Mr. Vinegar, "if I had but that beautiful instrument I should be the happiest man alive—my fortune would be made." So he went up to the man. "Friend," says he, "what a beautiful instrument that is, and what a deal of money you must make." "Why, yes," said the man, "I make a great deal of money, to be sure, and it is a wonderful instrument." "Oh!" cried Mr. Vinegar, "how I should like to possess it!" "Well," said the man, "as you are a friend, I don't much mind parting with it; you shall have it for that red cow." "Done!" said the delighted Mr. Vinegar. So the beautiful red cow was given for the bagpipes. He walked up and down with his purchase; but it was in vain he tried to play a tune, and instead of pocketing pence, the boys followed him hooting, laughing, and pelting.

Poor Mr. Vinegar, his fingers grew very cold, and, just as he was leaving the town, he met a man with a fine thick pair of gloves. "Oh, my fingers are so very cold," said Mr. Vinegar to himself. "Now if I had but those beautiful gloves I should be the happiest man alive." He went up to the man, and said to him: "Friend, you seem to have a capital pair of gloves there." "Yes, truly," cried the man; "and my hands are as warm as possible this cold November day." "Well," said Mr. Vinegar, "I should like to have them." "What will you give?" said the man; "as you are a friend, I don't much mind letting you have them for those bagpipes." "Done!" cried Mr. Vinegar. He put on the gloves, and felt perfectly happy as he trudged homewards.

At last he grew very tired, when he saw a man coming towards him with a good stout stick in his hand.

"Oh," said Mr. Vinegar, "that I had but that stick! I should then be the happiest man alive." He said to the man: "Friend! what a rare good stick you have got." "Yes," said the man; "I have used it for many a long mile, and a good friend it has been; but if you have a fancy for it, as you are a friend, I don't mind giving it to you for that pair of gloves." Mr. Vinegar's hands were so warm, and his legs so tired, that he gladly made the exchange. As he drew near to the wood where he had left his wife, he heard a parrot on a tree calling out his name: "Mr. Vinegar, you foolish man, you blockhead, you simpleton; you went to the fair, and laid out all your money in buying a cow. Not content with that, you changed it for bagpipes, on which you could not play, and which were not worth one-tenth of the money. You fool, you—you had no sooner got the bagpipes than you changed them for the gloves, which were not worth one-quarter of the money; and when you had got the gloves, you changed them for a poor miserable stick; and now for your forty guineas, cow, bagpipes, and gloves, you have nothing to show but that poor mis-  erable stick, which you might have cut in any hedge." On this the bird laughed and laughed, and Mr. Vinegar, falling into a violent rage, threw the stick at its head. The stick lodged in the tree, and he returned to his wife without money, cow, bagpipes, gloves, or stick, and she instantly gave him such a sound cudgelling that she almost broke every bone in his skin.

✺ Nix Nought Nothing ✺

THERE once lived a king and a queen as many a one has been. They were long married and had no children; but at last a baby-boy came to the queen when the king was away in the far countries. The queen would not christen the boy till the king came back, and she said, "We will just call him *Nix Nought Nothing* until his father comes home." But it was long before he came home, and the boy had grown a nice little laddie. At length the king was on his way back; but he had a big river to cross, and there was a whirlpool, and he could not get over the water. But a giant came up to him, and said: "I'll carry you over." But the king said: "What's your pay?" "O give me Nix, Nought, Nothing, and I will carry you over the water on my back." The king had never heard that his son was called Nix Nought Nothing, and so he said: "O, I'll give you that and my thanks into the bargain." When the king got home again, he was very happy to see his wife again, and his young son. She told him that she had not given the child any name, but just Nix Nought Nothing, until he should come home again himself. The poor king was in a terrible case. He said: "What have I done? I promised to give the giant who carried me over the river on his back, Nix Nought Nothing." The king and the queen were sad and sorry, but they said: "When the giant comes we will give him the hen-wife's boy; he will never know the difference." The next day the giant came to claim the king's promise, and he sent for the hen-wife's boy; and the giant went away with the boy on his back. He travelled till he came to a big stone, and there he sat down to rest. He said:

"Hidge, Hodge, on my back, what time of day is that?"

The poor little boy said: "It is the time that my mother, the hen-wife, takes up the eggs for the queen's breakfast."

The Giant was very angry, and dashed the boy's head on the stone and killed him.

So he went back in a tower of a temper and this time they gave him the gardener's boy. He went off with him on his back till they got to the stone again when the giant sat down to rest. And he said:

"Hidge, Hodge, on my back, what time of day do you make that?"

The gardener's boy said: "Sure it's the time that my mother takes up the vegetables for the queen's dinner."

Then the giant was right wild and dashed his brains out on the stone.

Then the giant went back to the king's house in a terrible temper and said he would destroy them all if they did not give him Nix Nought

Nothing this time. They had to do it; and when he came to the big stone, the giant said: "What time of day is that?" Nix Nought Nothing said: "It is the time that my father the king will be sitting down to supper." The giant said: "I've got the right one now"; and took Nix Nought Nothing to his own house and brought him up till he was a man.

The giant had a bonny daughter, and she and the lad grew very fond of each other. The giant said one day to Nix Nought Nothing: "I've work for you to-morrow. There is a stable seven miles long and seven miles broad, and it has not been cleaned for seven years, and you must clean it to-morrow, or I will have you for my supper."

The giant's daughter went out next morning with the lad's breakfast, and found him in a terrible state, for always as he cleaned out a bit, it just fell in again. The giant's daughter said she would help him, and she cried all the beasts in the field, and all the fowls of the air, and in a minute they all came, and carried away everything that was in the stable and made it all clean before the giant came home. He said: "Shame on the wit that helped you; but I have a worse job for you to-morrow." Then he said to Nix Nought Nothing: "There's a lake seven miles long, and seven miles deep, and seven miles broad, and you must drain it to-morrow by night-fall, or else I'll have you for my supper." Nix Nought Nothing began early next morning and tried to lave the water with his pail, but the lake was never getting any less, and he didn't know what to do; but the giant's daughter called on all the fish in the sea to come and drink the water, and very soon they drank it dry. When the giant saw the work done he was in a rage, and said: "I've a worse job for you to-morrow; there is a tree, seven miles high, and no branch on it, till you get to the top, and there is a nest with seven eggs in it, and you must bring down all the eggs without break-ing one, or else I'll have you for my supper." At first the giant's daughter did not know how to help Nix Nought Nothing; but she cut off first her fingers and then her toes, and made steps of them, and he clomb the tree and got all the eggs safe till he came just to the bottom, and then one was broken. So they determined to run away together and after the giant's daughter had tidied up her hair a bit and got her magic flask they set out together as fast as they could run. And they hadn't got but three fields away when they looked back and saw the giant walking along at top speed after them. "Quick, quick," called out the giant's daughter, "take my comb from my hair and throw it down." Nix Nought Nothing took her comb from her hair and threw it down, and out of every one of its prongs there sprung up a fine thick briar in the way of the giant. You may be sure it took him a long time to work his way through the briar bush and by the time he was well through Nix Nought Nothing and his sweetheart had

run on a tidy step away from him. But he soon came along after them and was just like to catch 'em up when the giant's daughter called out to Nix Nought Nothing, "Take my hair dagger and throw it down, quick, quick." So Nix Nought Nothing threw down the hair dagger and out of it grew as quick as lightning a thick hedge of sharp razors placed criss cross. The giant had to tread very cautiously to get through all this and meanwhile the young lovers ran on, and on, and on, till they were nearly out of sight. But at last the giant was through, and it wasn't long before he was like to catch them up. But just as he was stretching out his hand to catch Nix Nought Nothing his daughter took out her magic flask and dashed it on the ground. And as it broke out of it welled a big, big wave that grew, and that grew, till it reached the giant's waist and then his neck, and when it got to his head, he was drowned dead, and dead, and dead indeed. So he goes out of the story.

But Nix Nought Nothing fled on till where do you think they came to? Why, to near the castle of Nix Nought Nothing's father and mother. But the giant's daughter was so weary that she couldn't move a step further. So Nix Nought Nothing told her to wait there while he went and found out a lodging for the night. And he went on towards the lights of the castle, and on the way he came to the cottage of the hen-wife whose boy had had his brains dashed out by the giant. Now she knew Nix Nought Nothing in a moment, and hated him because he was the cause of her son's death. So when he asked his way to the castle she put a spell upon him, and when he got to the castle, no sooner was he let in than he fell down dead asleep upon a bench in the hall. The king and queen tried all they could do to wake him up, but all in vain. So the king promised that if any lady could wake him up she should marry him. Meanwhile the giant's daughter was waiting and waiting for him to come back. And she went up into a tree to watch for him. The gardener's daughter, going to draw water in the well, saw the shadow of the lady in the water and thought it was herself, and said: "If I'm so bonny, if I'm so brave, why do you send me to draw water?" So she threw down her pail and went to see if she could wed the sleeping stranger. And she went to the hen-wife, who taught her an unspelling catch which would keep Nix Nought Nothing awake as long as the gardener's daughter liked. So she went up to the castle and sang her catch and Nix Nought Nothing was wakened for a bit and they promised to wed him to the gardener's daughter. Meanwhile the gardener went down to draw water from the well and saw the shadow of the lady in the water. So he looks up and finds her, and he brought the lady from the tree, and led her into his house. And he told her that a stranger was to marry his daughter, and took her up to the castle and showed her the man: and it was Nix Nought Nothing asleep in a chair. And she saw him, and cried to him: "Waken, waken, and speak to me!" But he would not waken, and soon she cried:

> "I cleaned the stable, I laved the lake, and I
>   clomb the tree,
> And all for the love of thee,
> And thou wilt not waken and speak to me."

The king and the queen heard this, and came to the bonny young lady, and she said:

"I cannot get Nix Nought Nothing to speak to me for all that I can do."

Then were they greatly astonished when she spoke of Nix Nought Nothing, and asked where he was, and she said: "He that sits there in the chair." Then they ran to him and kissed him and called him their own dear son; so they called for the gardener's daughter and made her sing her charm, and he wakened, and told them all that the giant's daughter had done for him, and of all her kindness. Then they took her in their arms and kissed her, and said she should now be their daughter, for their son should marry her. But they sent for the hen-wife and put her to death. And they lived happy all their days.

᳇ Jack Hannaford ᳇

THERE was an old soldier who had been long in the wars—so long, that he was quite out-at-elbows, and he did not know where to go to find a living. So he walked up moors, down glens, till at last he came to a farm, from which the good man had gone away to market. The wife of the farmer was a very foolish woman, who had been a widow when he married her; the farmer was foolish enough, too, and it is hard to say which of the two was the more foolish. When you've heard my tale you may decide.

Now before the farmer goes to market says he to his wife: "Here is ten pounds all in gold, take care of it till I come home." If the man had not been a fool he would never have given the money to his wife to keep. Well, off he went in his cart to market, and the wife said to herself: "I will keep the ten pounds quite safe from thieves"; so she tied it up in a rag, and she put the rag up the parlour chimney.

"There," said she, "no thieves will ever find it now, that is quite sure."

Jack Hannaford, the old soldier, came and rapped at the door.

"Who is there?" asked the wife.

"Jack Hannaford."

"Where do you come from?"

"Paradise."

"Lord a' mercy! and maybe you've seen my old man there," alluding to her former husband.

"Yes, I have."

"And how was he a-doing?" asked the goody.

"But middling; he cobbles old shoes, and he has nothing but cabbage for victuals."

"Deary me!" exclaimed the woman. "Didn't he send a message to me?"

"Yes, he did," replied Jack Hannaford. "He said that he was out of leather, and his pockets were empty, so you were to send him a few shillings to buy a fresh stock of leather."

"He shall have them, bless his poor soul!" And away went the wife to the parlour chimney, and she pulled the rag with the ten pounds in it from the chimney, and she gave the whole sum to the soldier, telling him that her old man was to use as much as he wanted, and to send back the rest.

It was not long that Jack waited after receiving the money; he went off as fast as he could walk.

Presently the farmer came home and asked for his money. The wife told him that she had sent it by a soldier to her former husband in Paradise, to buy him leather for cobbling the shoes of the saints and angels of Heaven. The farmer was very angry, and he swore that he had never met with such a fool as his wife. But the wife said that her husband was a greater fool for letting her have the money.

There was no time to waste words; so the farmer mounted his horse and rode off after Jack Hannaford. The old soldier heard the horse's hoofs clattering on the road behind him, so he knew it must be the farmer pursuing him. He lay down on the ground, and shading his eyes with one hand, looked up into the sky, and pointed heavenwards with the other hand.

"What are you about there?" asked the farmer, pulling up.

"Lord save you!" exclaimed Jack: "I've seen a rare sight."

"What was that?"

"A man going straight up into the sky, as if he were walking on a road."

"Can you see him still?"

"Yes, I can."

"Where?"

"Get off your horse and lie down."

"If you will hold the horse."

Jack did so readily.

"I cannot see him," said the farmer.

"Shade your eyes with your hand, and you'll soon see a man flying away from you."

Sure enough he did so, for Jack leaped on the horse, and rode away with it. The farmer walked home without his horse.

"You are a bigger fool than I am," said the wife; "for I did only one foolish thing, and you have done two."

❧ *Binnorie* ❧

ONCE upon a time there were two king's daughters lived in a bower near the bonny mill-dams of Binnorie. And Sir William came wooing the eldest and won her love and plighted troth with glove and with ring. But after a time he looked upon the youngest, with her cherry cheeks and golden hair, and his love grew towards her till he cared no longer for the eldest one. So she hated her sister for taking away Sir William's love, and day by day her hate grew upon her, and she plotted and she planned how to get rid of her.

So one fine morning, fair and clear, she said to her sister, "Let us go and see our father's boats come in at the bonny mill-stream of Binnorie." So they went there hand in hand. And when they got to the river's bank the youngest got upon a stone to watch for the coming of the boats. And her sister, coming behind her, caught her round the waist and dashed her into the rushing mill-stream of Binnorie.

"O sister, sister, reach me your hand!" she cried, as she floated away, "and you shall have half of all I've got or shall get."

"No, sister, I'll reach you no hand of mine, for I am the heir to all your land. Shame on me if I touch the hand that has come 'twixt me and my own heart's love."

"O sister, O sister, then reach me your glove!" she cried, as she floated further away, "and you shall have your William again."

"Sink on," cried the cruel princess, "no hand or glove of mine you'll touch. Sweet William will be all mine when you are sunk beneath the bonny mill-stream of Binnorie." And she turned and went home to the king's castle.

And the princess floated down the mill-stream, sometimes swimming and sometimes sinking, till she came near the mill. Now the miller's daughter was cooking that day, and needed water for her cooking. And as she went to draw it from the stream, she saw something floating towards the mill-dam, and she called out, "Father! father! draw your dam. There's something white—a merrymaid or a milk-white swan—coming down the stream." So the miller hastened to the dam and stopped the heavy cruel mill-wheels. And then they took out the princess and laid her on the bank.

Fair and beautiful she looked as she lay there. In her golden hair were pearls and precious stones; you could not see her waist for her golden girdle, and the golden fringe of her white dress came down over her lily feet. But she was drowned, drowned!

And as she lay there in her beauty a famous harper passed by the mill-dam of Binnorie, and saw her sweet pale face. And though he travelled on far away he never forgot that face, and after many days he came back to the bonny mill-stream of Binnorie. But then all he could find of her where they had put her to rest were her bones and her golden hair. So he made a harp out of her breast-bone and her hair, and travelled on up the hill from the mill-dam of Binnorie, till he came to the castle of the king her father.

That night they were all gathered in the castle hall to hear the great harper—king and queen, their daughter and son, Sir William and all their Court. And first the harper sang to his old harp, making them joy and be glad or sorrow and weep just as he liked. But while he sang he put the harp he had made that day on a stone in the hall. And presently it began to sing by itself, low and clear, and the harper stopped and all were hushed.

And this was what the harp sung:

> "O yonder sits my father, the king,
>   Binnorie, O Binnorie;
> And yonder sits my mother, the queen;
>   By the bonny mill-dams o' Binnorie,
>
> "And yonder stands my brother Hugh,
>   Binnorie, O Binnorie;
> And by him, my William, false and true;
>   By the bonny mill-dams o' Binnorie."

Then they all wondered, and the harper told them how he had seen the princess lying drowned on the bank near the bonny mill-dams o' Binnorie, and how he had afterwards made this harp out of her hair and breast-bone. Just then the harp began singing again, and this was what it sang out loud and clear:

> "And there sits my sister who drownèd me
>   By the bonny mill-dams o' Binnorie."

And the harp snapped and broke, and never sang more.

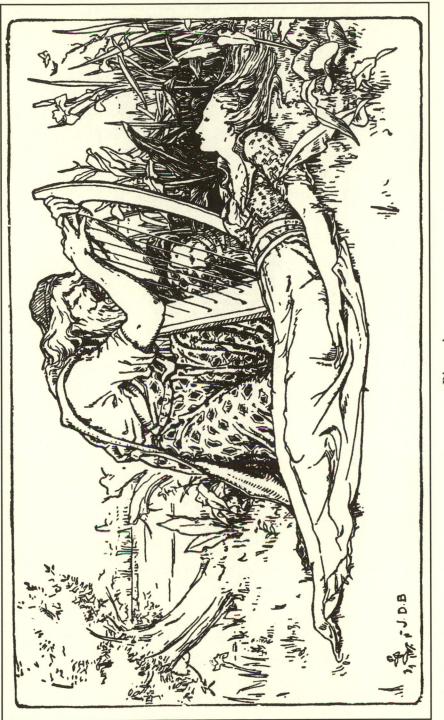

Binnorie

ᔐ *Mouse and Mouser* ᔐ

THE Mouse went to visit the Cat, and found her sitting behind the hall door, spinning.

MOUSE.
What are you doing, my lady, my lady,
What are you doing, my lady?

CAT (SHARPLY).
I'm spinning old breeches, good body, good body
I'm spinning old breeches, good body.

MOUSE.
Long may you wear them, my lady, my lady,
Long may you wear them, my lady.

CAT (GRUFFLY).
I'll wear 'em and tear 'em, good body, good body.
I'll wear 'em and tear 'em, good body.

MOUSE.
I was sweeping my room, my lady, my lady,
I was sweeping my room, my lady.

Cat.

The cleaner you'd be, good body, good body,
The cleaner you'd be, good body.

Mouse.

I found a silver sixpence, my lady, my lady,
I found a silver sixpence, my lady.

Cat.

The richer you were, good body, good body,
The richer you were, good body.

Mouse.

I went to the market, my lady, my lady,
I went to the market, my lady.

Cat.

The further you went, good body, good body,
The further you went, good body.

Mouse.

I bought me a pudding, my lady, my lady,
I bought me a pudding, my lady.

Cat (snarling).

The more meat you had, good body, good body,
The more meat you had, good body.

Mouse.

I put it in the window to cool, my lady,
I put it in the window to cool.

Cat (sharply).

The faster you'd eat it, good body, good body,
The faster you'd eat it, good body.

Mouse (timidly).

The cat came and ate it, my lady, my lady,
The cat came and ate it, my lady.

Cat (pouncingly).

And I'll eat you, good body, good body,
And I'll eat you, good body.
(Springs upon the mouse and kills it.)

⟿ Cap o' Rushes ⟿

WELL, there was once a very rich gentleman, and he'd three daughters, and he thought he'd see how fond they were of him. So he says to the first, "How much do you love me, my dear?"

"Why," says she, "as I love my life."

"That's good," says he.

So he says to the second, "How much do *you* love me my dear?"

"Why," says she, "better nor all the world."

"That's good," says he.

So he says to the third, "How much do *you* love me, my dear?"

"Why, I love you as fresh meat loves salt," says she.

Well, he was that angry. "You don't love me at all," says he, "and in my house you stay no more." So he drove her out there and then, and shut the door in her face.

Well, she went away on and on till she came to a fen, and there she gathered a lot of rushes and made them into a kind of a sort of a cloak with a hood, to cover her from head to foot, and to hide her fine clothes. And then she went on and on till she came to a great house.

"Do you want a maid?" says she.

"No, we don't," said they.

"I haven't nowhere to go," says she; "and I ask no wages, and do any sort of work," says she.

"Well," says they, "if you like to wash the pots and scrape the saucepans you may stay," said they.

So she stayed there and washed the pots and scraped the saucepans and did all the dirty work. And because she gave no name they called her "Cap o' Rushes."

Well, one day there was to be a great dance a little way off, and the servants were allowed to go and look on at the grand people. Cap o' Rushes said she was too tired to go, so she stayed at home.

But when they were gone she offed with her cap o' rushes, and cleaned herself, and went to the dance. And no one there was so finely dressed as her.

Well, who should be there but her master's son, and what should he do but fall in love with her the minute he set eyes on her. He wouldn't dance with any one else.

But before the dance was done Cap o' Rushes slipt off, and away she went home. And when the other maids came back she was pretending to be asleep with her cap o' rushes on.

Well, next morning they said to her, "You did miss a sight, Cap o' Rushes!"

"What was that?" says she.

"Why, the beautifullest lady you ever see, dressed right gay and ga'. The young master, he never took his eyes off her."

"Well, I should have liked to have seen her," says Cap o' Rushes.

"Well, there's to be another dance this evening, and perhaps she'll be there."

But, come the evening, Cap o' Rushes said she was too tired to go with them. Howsoever, when they were gone, she offed with her cap o' rushes and cleaned herself, and away she went to the dance.

The master's son had been reckoning on seeing her, and he danced with no one else, and never took his eyes off her. But, before the dance was over, she slipt off, and home she went, and when the maids came back she pretended to be asleep with her cap o' rushes on.

Next day they said to her again, "Well, Cap o' Rushes, you should ha' been there to see the lady. There she was again, gay and ga', and the young master he never took his eyes off her."

"Well, there," says she, "I should ha' liked to ha' seen her."

"Well," says they, "there's a dance again this evening, and you must go with us, for she's sure to be there."

Well, come this evening, Cap o' Rushes said she was too tired to go, and do what they would she stayed at home. But when they were gone she offed with her cap o' rushes and cleaned herself, and away she went to the dance.

The master's son was rarely glad when he saw her. He danced with none but her and never took his eyes off her. When she wouldn't tell him her name, nor where she came from, he gave her a ring and told her if he didn't see her again he should die.

Well, before the dance was over, off she slipped, and home she went, and when the maids came home she was pretending to be asleep with her cap o' rushes on.

Well, next day they says to her, "There, Cap o' Rushes, you didn't come last night, and now you won't see the lady, for there's no more dances."

"Well I should have rarely liked to have seen her," says she.

The master's son he tried every way to find out where the lady was gone, but go where he might, and ask whom he might, he never heard anything about her. And he got worse and worse for the love of her till he had to keep his bed.

"Make some gruel for the young master," they said to the cook. "He's dying for the love of the lady." The cook she set about making it when Cap o' Rushes came in.

"What are you a-doing of?" says she.

"I'm going to make some gruel for the young master," says the cook, "for he's dying for love of the lady."

"Let me make it," says Cap o' Rushes.

Well, the cook wouldn't at first, but at last she said yes, and Cap o' Rushes made the gruel. And when she had made it she slipped the ring into it on the sly before the cook took it upstairs.

The young man he drank it and then he saw the ring at the bottom.

"Send for the cook," says he.

So up she comes.

"Who made this gruel here?" says he.

"I did," says the cook, for she was frightened.

And he looked at her.

"No, you didn't," says he. "Say who did it, and you shan't be harmed."

"Well, then, 'twas Cap o' Rushes," says she.

"Send Cap o' Rushes here," says he.

So Cap o' Rushes came.

"Did you make my gruel?" says he.

"Yes, I did," says she.

"Where did you get this ring?" says he.

"From him that gave it me," says she.

"Who are you, then?" says the young man.

"I'll show you," says she. And she offed with her cap o' rushes, and there she was in her beautiful clothes.

Well, the master's son he got well very soon, and they were to be married in a little time. It was to be a very grand wedding, and every one was asked far and near. And Cap o' Rushes' father was asked. But she never told anybody who she was.

But before the wedding she went to the cook, and says she:

"I want you to dress every dish without a mite o' salt."

"That'll be rare nasty," says the cook.

"That don't signify," says she.

"Very well," says the cook.

Well, the wedding-day came, and they were married. And after they were married all the company sat down to the dinner. When they began to eat the meat, that was so tasteless they couldn't eat it. But Cap o' Rushes' father he tried first one dish and then another, and then he burst out crying.

"What is the matter?" said the master's son to him.

"Oh!" says he, "I had a daughter. And I asked her how much she loved me. And she said 'As much as fresh meat loves salt.' And I turned her from my door, for I thought she didn't love me. And now I see she loved me best of all. And she may be dead for aught I know."

"No, father, here she is!" says Cap o' Rushes. And she goes up to him and puts her arms round him.

And so they were happy ever after.

⚬ Teeny-Tiny ⚬

ONCE upon a time there was a teeny-tiny woman lived in a teeny-tiny house in a teeny-tiny village. Now, one day this teeny-tiny woman put on her teeny-tiny bonnet, and went out of her teeny-tiny house to take a teeny-tiny walk. And when this teeny-tiny woman had gone a teeny-tiny way she came to a teeny-tiny gate; so the teeny-tiny woman opened the teeny-tiny gate, and went into a teeny-tiny churchyard. And when this teeny-tiny woman had got into the teeny-tiny churchyard, she saw a teeny-tiny bone on a teeny-tiny grave, and the teeny-tiny woman said to her teeny-tiny self, "This teeny-tiny bone will make me some teeny-tiny soup for my teeny-tiny supper." So the teeny-tiny woman put the teeny-tiny bone into her teeny-tiny pocket, and went home to her teeny-tiny house.

Now when the teeny-tiny woman got home to her teeny-tiny house she was teeny-tiny tired; so she went up her teeny-tiny stairs to her teeny-tiny bed, and put the teeny-tiny bone into a teeny-tiny cupboard. And when this teeny-tiny woman had been to sleep a teeny-tiny time, she was awakened by a teeny-tiny voice from the teeny-tiny cupboard, which said:

"Give me my bone!"

And this teeny-tiny woman was a teeny-tiny frightened, so she hid her teeny-tiny head under the teeny-tiny clothes and went to sleep again. And when she had been to sleep again a teeny-tiny time, the teeny-tiny voice again cried out from the teeny-tiny cupboard a teeny-tiny louder,

"Give me my bone!"

This made the teeny-tiny woman a teeny-tiny more frightened, so she hid her teeny-tiny head a teeny-tiny further under the teeny-tiny clothes. And when the teeny-tiny woman had been to sleep again a teeny-tiny time, the teeny-tiny voice from the teeny-tiny cupboard said again a teeny-tiny louder,

"Give me my bone!"

And this teeny-tiny woman was a teeny-tiny bit more frightened, but she put her teeny-tiny head out of the teeny-tiny clothes, and said in her loudest teeny-tiny voice, "TAKE IT!"

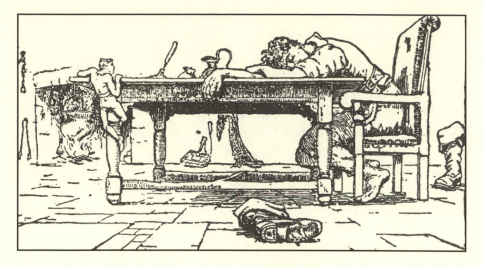

✥ Jack and the Beanstalk ✥

THERE was once upon a time a poor widow who had an only son named Jack, and a cow named Milky-white. And all they had to live on was the milk the cow gave every morning which they carried to the market and sold. But one morning Milky-white gave no milk and they didn't know what to do.

"What shall we do, what shall we do?" said the widow, wringing her hands.

"Cheer up, mother, I'll go and get work somewhere," said Jack.

"We've tried that before, and nobody would take you," said his mother; "we must sell Milky-white and with the money do something, start shop, or something."

"All right, mother," says Jack; "it's market-day to-day, and I'll soon sell Milky-white, and then we'll see what we can do."

So he took the cow's halter in his hand, and off he starts. He hadn't gone far when he met a funny-looking old man who said to him: "Good morning, Jack."

"Good morning to you," said Jack, and wondered how he knew his name.

"Well, Jack, and where are you off to?" said the man.

"I'm going to market to sell our cow here."

"Oh, you look the proper sort of chap to sell cows," said the man; "I wonder if you know how many beans make five."

"Two in each hand and one in your mouth," says Jack, as sharp as a needle.

"Right you are," said the man, "and here they are the very beans themselves," he went on pulling out of his pocket a number of strange-looking beans. "As you are so sharp," says he, "I don't mind doing a swop with you—your cow for these beans."

"Walker!" says Jack; "wouldn't you like it?"

"Ah! you don't know what these beans are," said the man; "if you plant them over-night, by morning they grow right up to the sky."

"Really?" says Jack; "you don't say so."

"Yes, that is so, and if it doesn't turn out to be true you can have your cow back."

"Right," says Jack, and hands him over Milky-white's halter and pockets the beans.

Back goes Jack home, and as he hadn't gone very far it wasn't dusk by the time he got to his door.

"What back, Jack?" said his mother; "I see you haven't got Milky-white, so you've sold her. How much did you get for her?"

"You'll never guess, mother," says Jack.

"No, you don't say so. Good boy! Five pounds, ten, fifteen, no, it can't be twenty."

"I told you you couldn't guess, what do you say to these beans; they're magical, plant them over-night and——"

"What!" says Jack's mother, "have you been such a fool, such a dolt, such an idiot, as to give away my Milky-white, the best milker in the parish, and prime beef to boot, for a set of paltry beans. Take that! Take that! Take that! And as for your precious beans here they go out of the window. And now off with you to bed. Not a sup shall you drink, and not a bit shall you swallow this very night."

So Jack went upstairs to his little room in the attic, and sad and sorry he was, to be sure, as much for his mother's sake, as for the loss of his supper.

At last he dropped off to sleep.

When he woke up, the room looked so funny. The sun was shining into part of it, and yet all the rest was quite dark and shady. So Jack jumped up and dressed himself and went to the window. And what do you think he saw? why, the beans his mother had thrown out of the window into the garden, had sprung up into a big beanstalk which went up and up and up till it reached the sky. So the man spoke truth after all.

The beanstalk grew up quite close past Jack's window, so all he had to do was to open it and give a jump on to the beanstalk which was made like a big plaited ladder. So Jack climbed and he climbed and he climbed and he climbed and he climbed and he climbed and he climbed till at last he reached the sky. And when he got there he found a long broad road going as straight as a dart. So he walked along and he walked along and he walked along till he came to a great big tall house, and on the doorstep there was a great big tall woman.

"Good morning, mum," says Jack, quite polite-like. "Could you be so kind as to give me some breakfast." For he hadn't had anything to eat, you know, the night before and was as hungry as a hunter.

"It's breakfast you want, is it?" says the great big tall woman, "it's breakfast you'll be if you don't move off from here. My man is an ogre and there's nothing he likes better than boys broiled on toast. You'd better be moving on or he'll soon be coming."

"Oh! please mum, do give me something to eat, mum. I've had nothing to eat since yesterday morning, really and truly, mum," says Jack. "I may as well be broiled, as die of hunger."

Well, the ogre's wife wasn't such a bad sort, after all. So she took Jack into the kitchen, and gave him a junk of bread and cheese and a jug of milk. But Jack hadn't half finished these when thump! thump! thump! the whole house began to tremble with the noise of some one coming.

"Goodness gracious me! It's my old man," said the ogre's wife, "what on earth shall I do? Here, come quick and jump in here." And she bundled Jack into the oven just as the ogre came in.

He was a big one, to be sure. At his belt he had three calves strung up by the heels, and he unhooked them and threw them down on the table and said: "Here, wife, broil me a couple of these for breakfast. Ah! what's this I smell?

> Fee-fi-fo-fum,
> I smell the blood of an Englishman,
> Be he alive, or be he dead
> I'll have his bones to grind my bread."

"Nonsense, dear," said his wife, "you're dreaming. Or perhaps you smell the scraps of that little boy you liked so much for yesterday's dinner. Here, go you and have a wash and tidy up, and by the time you come back your breakfast 'll be ready for you."

So the ogre went off, and Jack was just going to jump out of the oven and run off when the woman told him not. "Wait till he's asleep," says she; "he always has a snooze after breakfast."

Well, the ogre had his breakfast, and after that he goes to a big chest and takes out of it a couple of bags of gold and sits down counting them till at last his head began to nod and he began to snore till the whole house shook again.

Then Jack crept out on tiptoe from his oven, and as he was passing the ogre he took one of the bags of gold under his arm, and off he pelters till he came to the beanstalk, and then he threw down the bag of gold which of course fell in to his mother's garden, and then he climbed down and climbed down till at last he got home and told his mother and showed her the gold and said: "Well, mother wasn't I right about the beans. They are really magical, you see."

So they lived on the bag of gold for some time, but at last they came to the end of that so Jack made up his mind to try his luck once more up at the top of the beanstalk. So one fine morning he got up early, and got on to the beanstalk, and he climbed and he climbed and he climbed and he climbed and he climbed and he climbed till at last he got on the road again and came to the great big tall house he had been to before. There, sure enough, was the great big tall woman a-standing on the door-step.

"Good morning, mum," says Jack, as bold as brass, "could you be so good as to give me something to eat?"

"Go away, my boy," said the big, tall woman, "or else my man will eat you up for breakfast. But aren't you the youngster who came here once before? Do you know, that very day, my man missed one of his bags of gold."

"That's strange, mum," says Jack, "I dare say I could tell you something about that but I'm so hungry I can't speak till I've had something to eat."

Well the big tall woman was that curious that she took him in and gave him something to eat. But he had scarcely begun munching it as slowly as he could when thump! thump! thump! they heard the giant's footstep, and his wife hid Jack away in the oven.

All happened as it did before. In came the ogre as he did before, said: "Fee-fi-fo-fum," and had his breakfast off three broiled oxen. Then he said: "Wife, bring me the hen that lays the golden eggs." So she brought it, and the ogre said: "Lay," and it laid an egg all of gold. And then the ogre began to nod his head, and to snore till the house shook.

Then Jack crept out of the oven on tiptoe and caught hold of the golden hen, and was off before you could say "Jack Robinson." But this time the hen gave a cackle which woke the ogre, and just as Jack got out of the house he heard him calling: "Wife, wife, what have you done with my golden hen?"

And the wife said: "Why, my dear?"

But that was all Jack heard, for he rushed off to the beanstalk and climbed down like a house on fire. And when he got home he showed his mother the wonderful hen and said "Lay," to it; and it laid a golden egg every time he said "Lay."

Well, Jack was not content, and it wasn't very long before he determined to have another try at his luck up there at the top of the beanstalk. So one fine morning, he got up early, and went on to the beanstalk, and he climbed and he climbed and he climbed and he climbed till he got to the top. But this time he knew better than to go straight to the ogre's house. And when he got near it he waited behind a bush till he saw the ogre's wife came out with a pail to get some water, and then he crept into the house and got into the copper. He hadn't been there long when he heard thump! thump! thump! as before, and in come the ogre and his wife.

"Fee-fi-fo-fum, I smell the blood of an Englishman," cried out the ogre; "I smell him, wife, I smell him."

"Do you, my dearie?" says the ogre's wife. "Then if it's that little rogue that stole your gold and the hen that laid the golden eggs he's sure to have got into the oven." And they both rushed to the oven. But Jack wasn't there, luckily, and the ogre's wife said: "There you are again with your fee-fi-fo-fum. Why of course it's the laddie you caught last night that I've broiled for your breakfast. How forgetful I am, and how careless you are not to tell the difference between a live un and a dead un."

So the ogre sat down to the breakfast and ate it, but every now and then he would mutter: "Well, I could have sworn—" and he'd get up and search the larder and the cupboards, and everything, only luckily he did-n't think of the copper.

After breakfast was over, the ogre called out: "Wife, wife, bring me my golden harp." So she brought it and put it on the table before him. Then he said: "Sing!" and the golden harp sang most beautifully. And it went on singing till the ogre fell asleep, and commenced to snore like thunder.

Then Jack lifted up the copper-lid very quietly and got down like a mouse and crept on hands and knees till he got to the table when he got up and caught hold of the golden harp and dashed with it towards the door. But the harp called out quite loud: "Master! Master!" and the ogre woke up just in time to see Jack running off with his harp.

Jack ran as fast as he could, and the ogre came rushing after, and would soon have caught him only Jack had a start and dodged him a bit and knew where he was going. When he got to the beanstalk the ogre was not more than twenty yards away when suddenly he saw Jack disappear like, and when he got up to the end of the road he saw Jack underneath climbing down for dear life. Well, the ogre didn't like trusting himself to such a ladder, and he stood and waited, so Jack got another start. But just then the harp cried out: "Master! master!" and the ogre swung himself down on to the beanstalk which shook with his weight. Down climbs Jack, and after him climbed the ogre. By this time Jack had climbed down and climbed down and climbed down till he was very nearly home. So he called out: "Mother! mother! bring me an axe, bring me an axe." And his mother came rushing out with the axe in her hand, but when she came to the beanstalk she stood stock still with fright for there she saw the ogre just coming down below the clouds.

But Jack jumped down and got hold of the axe and gave a chop at the beanstalk which cut it half in two. The ogre felt the beanstalk shake and quiver so he stopped to see what was the matter. Then Jack gave another chop with the axe, and the beanstalk was cut in two and began to topple over. Then the ogre fell down and broke his crown, and the beanstalk came toppling after.

Then Jack showed his mother his golden harp, and what with showing that and selling the golden eggs, Jack and his mother became very rich, and he married a great princess, and they lived happy ever after.

ꙮ The Story of the Three Little Pigs ꙮ

Once upon a time when pigs spoke rhyme
And monkeys chewed tobacco,

And hens took snuff to make them tough,
And ducks went quack, quack, quack, O!

THERE was an old sow with three little pigs, and as she had not enough to keep them, she sent them out to seek their fortune. The first that went off met a man with a bundle of straw, and said to him:

"Please, man, give me that straw to build me a house."

Which the man did, and the little pig built a house with it. Presently came along a wolf, and knocked at the door, and said:

"Little pig, little pig, let me come in."

To which the pig answered:

"No, no, by the hair of my chiny chin chin."

The wolf then answered to that:

"Then I'll huff, and I'll puff, and I'll blow your house in."

So he huffed, and he puffed, and he blew his house in, and ate up the little pig.

The second little pig met a man with a bundle of furze, and said:

"Please, man, give me that furze to build a house."

Which the man did, and the pig built his house. Then along came the wolf, and said:

"Little pig, little pig, let me come in."

"No, no, by the hair of my chiny chin chin."

"Then I'll puff, and I'll huff, and I'll blow your house in."

So he huffed, and he puffed, and he puffed, and he huffed, and at last he blew the house down, and he ate up the little pig.

The third little pig met a man with a load of bricks, and said:

"Please, man, give me those bricks to build a house with."

So the man gave him the bricks, and he built his house with them. So the wolf came, as he did to the other little pigs, and said:

"Little pig, little pig, let me come in."

"No, no, by the hair of my chiny chin chin."

"Then I'll huff, and I'll puff, and I'll blow your house in."

Well, he huffed, and he puffed, and he huffed and he puffed, and he puffed and huffed; but he could *not* get the house down. When he found that he could not, with all his huffing and puffing, blow the house down, he said:

"Little pig, I know where there is a nice field of turnips."

"Where?" said the little pig.

"Oh, in Mr. Smith's Home-field, and if you will be ready to-morrow

59

morning I will call for you, and we will go together, and get some for dinner."

"Very well," said the little pig, "I will be ready. What time do you mean to go?"

"Oh, at six o'clock."

Well, the little pig got up at five, and got the turnips before the wolf came (which he did about six) and who said:

"Little Pig, are you ready?"

The little pig said: "Ready! I have been and come back again, and got a nice potful for dinner."

The wolf felt very angry at this, but thought that he would be up to the little pig somehow or other, so he said:

"Little pig, I know where there is a nice apple-tree."

"Where?" said the pig.

"Down at Merry-garden," replied the wolf, "and if you will not deceive me I will come for you, at five o'clock to-morrow and get some apples."

Well, the little pig bustled up the next morning at four o'clock, and went off for the apples, hoping to get back before the wolf came; but he had further to go, and had to climb the tree, so that just as he was coming down from it, he saw the wolf coming, which, as you may suppose, frightened him very much. When the wolf came up he said:

"Little pig, what! are you here before me? Are they nice apples?"

"Yes, very," said the little pig. "I will throw you down one."

And he threw it so far, that, while the wolf was gone to pick it up, the little pig jumped down and ran home. The next day the wolf came again, and said to the little pig:

"Little pig, there is a fair at Shanklin this afternoon, will you go?"

"Oh yes," said the pig, "I will go; what time shall you be ready?"

"At three," said the wolf. So the little pig went off before the time as usual, and got to the fair, and bought a butter-churn, which he was going home with, when he saw the wolf coming. Then he could not tell what to do. So he got into the churn to hide, and by so doing turned it round, and it rolled down the hill with the pig in it, which frightened the wolf so much, that he ran home without going to the fair. He went to the little pig's house, and told him how frightened he had been by a great round thing which came down the hill past him. Then the little pig said:

"Hah, I frightened you, then. I had been to the fair and bought a butter-churn, and when I saw you, I got into it, and rolled down the hill."

Then the wolf was very angry indeed, and declared he *would* eat up the little pig, and that he would get down the chimney after him. When the little pig saw what he was about, he hung on the pot full of water, and made up a blazing fire, and, just as the wolf was coming down, took off the cover, and in fell the wolf; so the little pig put on the cover again in an instant, boiled him up, and ate him for supper, and lived happy ever afterwards.

~ *The Master and his Pupil* ~

THERE was once a very learned man in the north-country who knew all the languages under the sun, and who was acquainted with all the mysteries of creation. He had one big book bound in black calf and clasped with iron, and with iron corners, and chained to a table which was made fast to the floor; and when he read out of this book, he unlocked it with an iron key, and none but he read from it, for it contained all the secrets of the spiritual world. It told how many angels there were in heaven, and how they marched in their ranks, and sang in their quires, and what were their several functions, and what was the name of each great angel of might. And it told of the demons, how many of them there were, and what were their several powers, and their labours, and their names, and how they might be summoned, and how tasks might be imposed on them, and how they might be chained to be as slaves to man.

Now the master had a pupil who was but a foolish lad, and he acted as servant to the great master, but never was he suffered to look into the black book, hardly to enter the private room.

One day the master was out, and then the lad, as curious as could be, hurried to the chamber where his master kept his wondrous apparatus for changing copper into gold, and lead into silver, and where was his mirror in which he could see all that was passing in the world, and where was the shell which when held to the ear whispered all the words that were being spoken by any one the master desired to know about. The lad tried in vain with the crucibles to turn copper and lead into gold and silver—he looked long and vainly into the mirror; smoke and clouds passed over it, but he saw nothing plain, and the shell to his ear produced only indistinct murmurings, like the breaking of distant seas on an unknown shore. "I can do nothing," he said; "as I don't know the right words to utter, and they are locked up in yon book." He looked round, and, see! the book was unfastened; the master had forgotten to lock it before he went out. The boy rushed to it, and unclosed the volume. It was written with red and black ink, and much of it he could not understand; but he put his finger on a line and spelled it through.

At once the room was darkened, and the house trembled; a clap of thunder rolled through the passage and the old room, and there stood before him a horrible, horrible form, breathing fire, and with eyes like burning lamps. It was the demon Beelzebub, whom he had called up to serve him.

"Set me a task!" said he, with a voice like the roaring of an iron furnace.

The boy only trembled, and his hair stood up.

"Set me a task, or I shall strangle thee!"

But the lad could not speak. Then the evil spirit stepped towards him, and putting forth his hands touched his throat. The fingers burned his flesh. "Set me a task!"

"Water yon flower," cried the boy in despair, pointing to a geranium which stood in a pot on the floor.

Instantly the spirit left the room, but in another instant he returned with a barrel on his back, and poured its contents over the flower; and again and again he went and came, and poured more and more water, till the floor of the room was ankle-deep.

"Enough, enough!" gasped the lad; but the demon heeded him not; the lad didn't know the words by which to send him away, and still he fetched water.

It rose to the boy's knees and still more water was poured. It mounted to his waist, and Beelzebub still kept on bringing barrels full. It rose to his armpits, and he scrambled to the table-top. And now the water in the room stood up to the window and washed against the glass, and swirled around his feet on the table. It still rose; it reached his breast. In vain he cried; the evil spirit would not be dismissed, and to this day he would have been pouring water, and would have drowned all Yorkshire. But the master remembered on his journey that he had not locked his book, and therefore returned, and at the moment when the water was bubbling about the pupil's chin, rushed into the room and spoke the words which cast Beelzebub back into his fiery home.

ꙮ *Titty Mouse and Tatty Mouse* ꙮ

TITTY MOUSE and Tatty Mouse both
    lived in a house,
Titty Mouse went a leasing and Tatty Mouse
    went a leasing,
So they both went a leasing.
Titty Mouse leased an ear of corn, and Tatty
    Mouse leased an ear of corn,
So they both leased an ear of corn.
Titty Mouse made a pudding, and Tatty Mouse
    made a pudding,
So they both made a pudding.
And Tatty Mouse put her pudding into the
    pot to boil,
But when Titty went to put hers in, the pot
    tumbled over, and scalded her to death.

Then Tatty sat down and wept; then a three-legged stool said: "Tatty, why do you weep?" "Titty's dead," said Tatty, and so I weep"; "then," said the stool, "I'll hop," so the stool hopped.

Then a broom in the corner of the room said, "Stool, why do you hop?" "Oh!" said the stool, "Titty's dead, and Tatty weeps, and so I hop"; "then," said the broom, "I'll sweep," so the broom began to sweep.

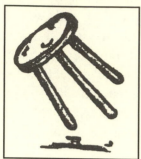

"Then," said the door, "Broom, why do you sweep?" "Oh!" said the broom, "Titty's dead, and Tatty weeps, and the stool hops, and so I sweep"; "then," said the door, "I'll jar," so the door jarred.

"Then," said the window, "Door, why do you jar?" "Oh!" said the door, "Titty's dead, and Tatty weeps, and the stool hops, and the broom sweeps, and so I jar."

So the Stool hopped.

"Then," said the window, "I'll creak," so the window creaked. Now there was an old form outside the house, and when the window creaked, the form said: "Window, why do you creak?" "Oh!" said the window, "Titty's dead, and Tatty weeps, and the stool hops, and the broom sweeps, the door jars, and so I creak."

"Then," said the old form, "I'll run round the house"; then the old form ran round the house. Now there was a fine large walnut-tree growing by the cottage, and the tree said to the form: "Form, why do you run round the house?" "Oh!" said the form, "Titty's dead, and Tatty weeps, and the stool hops, and the broom sweeps, the door jars, and the window creaks, and so I run round the house."

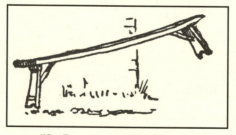

"So I run round the house."

"Then," said the walnut-tree, "I'll shed my leaves," so the walnut-tree shed all its beautiful green leaves. Now there was a little bird perched on one of the boughs of the tree, and when all the leaves fell, it said: "Walnut-tree, why do you shed your leaves?" "Oh!" said the tree, "Titty's dead, and Tatty weeps, the stool hops, and the broom sweeps, the door jars, and the window creaks, the old form runs round the house, and so I shed my leaves."

"Then," said the little bird, "I'll moult all my feathers," so he moulted all his pretty feathers. Now there was a little girl walking below, carrying a jug of milk for her brothers and sisters' supper, and when she saw the poor little bird moult all its feathers, she said: "Little bird, why do you moult all your feathers?" "Oh!" said the little bird, "Titty's dead, and Tatty weeps, the stool hops, and the broom sweeps, the door jars, and the window creaks, the old form runs round the house, the walnut-tree sheds its leaves, and so I moult all my feathers."

"So I moult all my feathers."

"Then," said the little girl, "I'll spill the milk," so she dropt the pitcher and

"So I spill the milk."

spilt the milk. Now there was an old man just by on the top of a ladder thatching a rick, and when he saw the little girl spill the milk, he said: "Little girl, what do you mean by spilling the milk, your little brothers and sisters must go without their supper." Then said the little girl: "Titty's dead, and Tatty weeps, the stool hops, and the broom sweeps, the door jars, and the window creaks, the old form runs round the house, the walnut-tree sheds all its leaves, the little bird moults all its feathers, and so I spill the milk."

"Oh!" said the old man, "then I'll tumble off the ladder and break my neck," so he tumbled off the ladder and broke his neck; and when the old man broke his neck, the great walnut-tree fell down with a crash, and upset the old form and house, and the house falling knocked the window out, and the window knocked the door down, and the door upset the broom, and the broom upset the stool, and poor little Tatty Mouse was buried beneath the ruins.

So he tumbled off the ladder.

∽ *Jack and his Golden Snuff-Box* ∽

ONCE upon a time, and a very good time it was, though it was neither in my time nor in your time nor in any one else's time, there was an old man and an old woman, and they had one son, and they lived in a great forest. And their son never saw any other people in his life, but he knew that there was some more in the world besides his own father and mother, because he had lots of books, and he used to read every day about them. And when he read about some pretty young women, he used to go mad to see some of them; till one day, when his father was out cutting wood, he told his mother that he wished to go away to look for his living in some other country, and to see some other people besides them two. And he said, "I see nothing at all here but great trees around me; and if I stay here, maybe I shall go mad before I see anything." The young man's father was out all this time, when this talk was going on between him and his poor old mother.

The old woman begins by saying to her son before leaving, "Well, well, my poor boy, if you want to go, it's better for you to go, and God be with you."—(The old woman thought for the best when she said that.)—"But stop a bit before you go. Which would you like best for me to make you, a little cake and bless you, or a big cake and curse you?" "Dear, dear!" said he, "make me a big cake. Maybe I shall be hungry on the road." The old woman made the big cake, and she went on top of the house, and she cursed him as far as she could see him.

He presently meets with his father, and the old man says to him: "Where are you going, my poor boy?" when the son told the father the same tale as he told his mother. "Well," says his father, "I'm sorry to see you going away, but if you've made your mind to go, it's better for you to go."

The poor lad had not gone far, when his father called him back; then the old man drew out of his pocket a golden snuff-box, and said to him: "Here, take this little box, and put it in your pocket, and be sure not to open it till you are near your death." And away went poor Jack upon his road, and walked till he was tired and hungry, for he had eaten all his cake upon the road; and by this time night was upon him, so he could hardly see his way before him. He could see some light a long way before him, and he made up to it, and found the back door and knocked at it, till one of the maid-servants came and asked him what he wanted. He said that night was on him, and he wanted to get some place to sleep. The maid-servant called him in to the fire, and gave him plenty to eat, good meat and bread and beer; and as he was eating his food by the fire, there came the young lady to look at him, and she loved him well and he loved her. And the young lady ran to tell her father, and said there was a pretty young man in the back kitchen; and immediately the gentleman came to him, and questioned him, and asked what work he could do. Jack said, the silly fellow, that he could do anything. (He meant that he could do any foolish bit of work, that would be wanted about the house.)

"Well," says the gentleman to him, "if you can do anything, at eight o'clock in the morning I must have a great lake and some of the largest man-of-war vessels sailing before my mansion, and one of the largest vessels must fire a royal salute, and the last round must break the leg of the bed where my young daughter is sleeping. And if you don't do that, you will have to forfeit your life."

"All right," said Jack; and away he went to his bed, and said his prayers quietly, and slept till it was near eight o'clock, and he had hardly any time to think what he was to do, till all of a sudden he remembered about the little golden box that his father gave him. And he said to himself: "Well, well, I never was so near my death as I am now"; and then he felt in his pocket, and drew the little box out. And when he opened it, out there hopped three little red men, and asked Jack: "What is your will with us?" "Well," said Jack, "I want a great lake and some of the largest man-of-war vessels in the world before this mansion, and one of the largest vessels to fire a royal salute, and the last round to break one of the legs of the bed where this young lady is sleeping." "All right," said the little men; "go to sleep."

Jack had hardly time to bring the words out of his mouth, to tell the little men what to do, but what it struck eight o'clock, when Bang, bang went one of the largest man-of-war vessels; and it made Jack jump out of bed to look through the window; and I can assure you it was a wonderful sight for him to see, after being so long with his father and mother living in a wood.

By this time Jack dressed himself, and said his prayers, and came down laughing; for he was proud, he was, because the thing was done so well. The gentleman comes to him, and says to him: "Well, my young man, I must say that you are very clever indeed. Come and have some breakfast." And the gentleman tells him, "Now there are two more things you have to do, and then you shall have my daughter in marriage." Jack gets his breakfast, and has a good squint at the young lady, and also she at him.

The other thing that the gentleman told him to do was to fell all the great trees for miles around by eight o'clock in the morning; and, to make my long story short, it was done, and it pleased the gentleman well. The gentleman said to him: "The other thing you have to do"—(and it was the last thing)—"you must get me a great castle standing on twelve golden pillars; and there must come regiments of soldiers and go through their drill. At eight o'clock the commanding officer must say, 'Shoulder up.'" "All right," said Jack; when the third and last morning came the third great feat was finished, and he had the young daughter in marriage. But, oh dear! there is worse to come yet.

The gentleman now makes a large hunting party, and invites all the gentlemen around the country to it, and to see the castle as well. And by this time Jack has a beautiful horse and a scarlet dress to go with them. On that morning his valet, when putting Jack's clothes by, after changing them to go a hunting, put his hand in one of Jack's waistcoat-pockets, and pulled out the little golden snuffbox, as poor Jack left behind in a mistake. And that man opened the little box, and there hopped the three little red men out, and asked him what he wanted with them. "Well," said the valet to them, "I want this castle to be moved from this place far and far across the sea." "All right," said the little red men to him; "do you wish to go with it?" "Yes," said he. "Well, get up," said they to him; and away they went far and far over the great sea.

Now the grand hunting party comes back, and the castle upon the twelve golden pillars had disappeared, to the great disappointment of those gentlemen as did not see it before. That poor silly Jack is threatened by taking his beautiful young wife from him, for taking them in in the way he did. But the gentleman at last made an agreement with him, and he is to have a twelvemonths and a day to look for it; and off he goes with a good horse and money in his pocket.

Now poor Jack goes in search of his missing castle, over hills, dales, valleys, and mountains, through woolly woods and sheepwalks, further than I can tell you or ever intend to tell you. Until at last he comes up to the place where lives the King of all the little mice in the world. There was one of the little mice on sentry at the front gate going up to the palace, and did try to stop Jack from going in. He asked the little mouse: "Where does the King live? I should like to see him." This one sent another with him to show him the place; and when the King saw him, he called him in. And the King questioned him, and asked him where he was going that way. Well, Jack told him all the truth, that he had lost the great castle, and was going to look for it, and he had a whole twelvemonths and a day to find it out. And Jack asked him whether he knew anything about it; and the King said: "No, but I am the King of all the little mice in the world, and I will call them all up in the morning, and maybe they have seen something of it."

Then Jack got a good meal and bed, and in the morning he and the King went on to the fields; and the King called all the mice together, and asked them whether they had seen the great beautiful castle standing on golden pillars. And all the little mice said, No, there was none of them had seen it. The old King said to him that he had two other brothers: "One is the King of all the frogs; and my other brother, who is the oldest, he is the King of all the birds in the world. And if you go there, may be they know something about the missing castle." The King said to him: "Leave your horse here with me till you come back, and take one of my best horses under you, and give this cake to my brother; he will know then who you got it from. Mind and tell him I am well, and should like dearly to see him." And then the King and Jack shook hands together.

And when Jack was going through the gates, the little mouse asked him, should he go with him; and Jack said to him: "No, I shall get myself into trouble with the King." And the little thing told him: "It will be better for you to let me go with you; maybe I shall do some good to you some time without you knowing it." "Jump up, then." And the little mouse ran up the horse's leg, and made it dance; and Jack put the mouse in his pocket.

The Castle on Twelve Golden Pillars

Now Jack, after wishing good morning to the King and pocketing the little mouse which was on sentry, trudged on his way; and such a long way he had to go and this was his first day. At last he found the place; and there was one of the frogs on sentry, and gun upon his shoulder, and did try to hinder Jack from going in; but when Jack said to him that he wanted to see the King, he allowed him to pass; and Jack made up to the door. The King came out, and asked him his business; and Jack told him all from beginning to end. "Well, well, come in." He gets good entertainment that night; and in the morning the King made such a funny sound, and collected all the frogs in the world. And he asked them, did they know or see anything of a castle that stood upon twelve golden pillars; and they all made a curious sound, *Kro-kro, kro-kro,* and said, No.

Jack had to take another horse, and a cake to this King's brother, who is the King of all the fowls of the air; and as Jack was going through the gates, the little frog that was on sentry asked John should he go with him. Jack refused him for a bit, but at last he told him to jump up, and Jack put him in his other waistcoat pocket. And away he went again on his great long journey; it was three times as long this time as it was the first day; however, he found the place, and there was a fine bird on sentry. And Jack passed him, and he never said a word to him; and he talked with the King, and told him everything, all about the castle. "Well," said the King to him, "you shall know in the morning from my birds, whether they know anything or not." Jack put up his horse in the stable, and then went to bed, after having something to eat. And when he got up in the morning the King and he went on to some field, and there the King made some funny noise, and there came all the fowls that were in all the world. And the King asked them; "Did they see the fine castle?" and all the birds answered, No. "Well," said the King, "where is the great bird?" They had to wait then for a long time for the eagle to make his appearance, when at last he came all in a perspiration, after sending two little birds high up in the sky to whistle on him to make all the haste he possibly could. The King asked the great bird, Did he see the great castle? and the bird said: "Yes, I came from there where it now is." "Well," says the King to him; "this young gentleman has lost it, and you must go with him back to it; but stop till you get a bit of something to eat first."

They killed a thief, and sent the best part of it to feed the eagle on his journey over the seas, and had to carry Jack on his back. Now when they came in sight of the castle, they did not know what to do to get the little golden box. Well, the little mouse said to them: "Leave me down, and

I will get the little box for you." So the mouse stole into the castle, and got hold of the box; and when he was coming down the stairs, it fell down, and he was very near being caught. He came running out with it, laughing his best. "Have you got it?" Jack said to him; he said: "Yes"; and off they went back again, and left the castle behind.

As they were all of them (Jack, mouse, frog, and eagle) passing over the great sea, they fell to quarrelling about which it was that got the little box, till down it slipped into the water. (It was by them looking at it and handing it from one hand to the other that they dropped the little box to the bottom of the sea.) "Well, well," said the frog, "I knew that I would have to do something, so you had better let me go down in the water." And they let him go, and he was down for three days and three nights; and up he comes, and shows his nose and little mouth out of the water; and all of them asked him, Did he get it? and he told them, No. "Well, what are you doing there, then?" "Nothing at all," he said, "only I want my full breath"; and the poor little frog went down the second time, and he was down for a day and a night, and up he brings it.

And away they did go, after being there four days and nights; and after a long tug over seas and mountains, arrive at the palace of the old King, who is the master of all the birds in the world. And the King is very proud to see them, and has a hearty welcome and a long conversation. Jack opens the little box, and told the little men to go back and to bring the castle here to them; "and all of you make as much haste back again as you possibly can."

The three little men went off; and when they came near the castle they were afraid to go to it till the gentleman and lady and all the servants were gone out to some dance. And there was no one left behind there only the cook and another maid with her; and the little red men asked them which would they rather—go, or stop behind? and they both said: "I will go with you"; and the little men told them to run upstairs quick. They were no sooner up and in one of the drawing-rooms than here comes just in sight the gentleman and lady and all the servants; but it was too late. Off the castle went at full speed, with the women laughing at them through the window, while they made motions for them to stop, but all to no purpose.

They were nine days on their journey, in which they did try to keep the Sunday holy, when one of the little men turned to be the priest, the other the clerk, and third presided at the organ, and the women were the singers, for they had a grand chapel in the castle already. Very remarkable, there was a discord made in the music, and one of the little men ran up one of the organ-pipes to see where the bad sound came from, when he found out it only happened to be that the two women were laughing at the little red man stretching his little legs full length on the bass pipes, also his two arms the same time, with his little red nightcap, which he never forgot to wear, and what they never witnessed before, could not help calling forth some good merriment while on the face of the deep. And poor thing! through them not going on with what they begun with, they very near came to danger, as the castle was once very near sinking in the middle of the sea.

At length, after a merry journey, they come again to Jack and the King. The King was quite struck with the sight of the castle; and going up the golden stairs, went to see the inside.

The King was very much pleased with the castle, but poor Jack's time of a twelvemonths and a day was drawing to a close; and he, wishing to go home to his young wife, gives orders to the three little men to get ready by the next morning at eight o'clock to be off to the next brother, and to stop there for one night; also to proceed from there to the last or the youngest brother, the master of all the mice in the world, in such place where the castle shall be left under his care until it's sent for. Jack takes a farewell of the King, and thanks him very much for his hospitality.

Away went Jack and his castle again, and stopped one night in that place; and away they went again to the third place, and there left the castle under his care. As Jack had to leave the castle behind, he had to take to his own horse, which he left there when he first started.

Now poor Jack leaves his castle behind and faces towards home; and after having so much merriment with the three brothers every night, Jack became sleepy on horseback, and would have lost the road if it was not for the little men a-guiding him. At last he arrived weary and tired, and they did not seem to receive him with any kindness whatever, because he had not found the stolen castle; and to make it worse, he was disappointed in not seeing his young and beautiful wife to come and meet him, through being hindered by her parents. But that did not stop long. Jack put full power on and despatched the little men off to bring the castle from there, and they soon got there.

Jack shook hands with the King, and returned many thanks for his kingly kindness in minding the castle for him; and then Jack instructed the little men to spur up and put speed on. And off they went, and were not long before they reached their journey's end, when out comes the young wife to meet him with a fine lump of a young SON, and they all lived happy ever afterwards.

∽ *The Story of the Three Bears* ∽

ONCE upon a time there were Three Bears, who lived together in a house of their own, in a wood. One of them was a Little, Small Wee Bear; and one was a Middle-sized Bear, and the other was a Great, Huge Bear. They had each a pot for their porridge, a little pot for the Little, Small, Wee Bear; and a middle-sized pot for the Middle Bear, and a great pot for the Great, Huge Bear. And they had each a chair to sit in; a little chair for the Little, Small, Wee Bear; and a middle-sized chair for the Middle Bear; and a great chair for the Great, Huge Bear. And they had each a bed to sleep in; a little bed for the Little, Small, Wee Bear; and a middle-sized bed for the Middle Bear; and a great bed for the Great, Huge Bear.

One day, after they had made the porridge for their breakfast, and poured it into their porridge-pots, they walked out into the wood while the porridge was cooling, that they might not burn their mouths, by beginning too soon to eat it. And while they were walking, a little old Woman came to the house. She could not have been a good, honest old Woman; for first she looked in at the window, and then she peeped in at the keyhole; and seeing nobody in the house, she lifted the latch. The door was not fastened, because the Bears were good Bears, who did nobody any harm, and never suspected that anybody would harm them. So the little old Woman opened the door, and went in; and well pleased she was when she saw the porridge on the table. If she had been a good little old Woman, she would have waited till the Bears came home, and then, per-haps, they would have asked her to breakfast; for they were good Bears— a little rough or so, as the manner of Bears is, but for all that very good-natured and hospitable. But she was an impudent, bad old Woman, and set about helping herself.

So first she tasted the porridge of the Great, Huge Bear, and that was too hot for her; and she said a bad word about that. And then she tasted the porridge of the Middle Bear, and that was too cold for her; and she said a bad word about that too. And then she went to the porridge of the Little, Small, Wee Bear, and tasted that; and that was neither too hot, nor too cold, but just right; and she liked it so well, that she ate it all up: but the naughty old Woman said a bad word about the little porridge-pot, because it did not hold enough for her.

Then the little old Woman sate down in the chair of the Great, Huge Bear, and that was too hard for her. And then she sate down in the chair of the Middle Bear, and that was too soft for her. And then she sat down in the chair of the Little, Small, Wee Bear, and that was neither too hard, nor too soft, but just right. So she seated herself in it, and there she sate till the bottom of the chair came out, and down she came, plump upon the ground. And the naughty old Woman said a wicked word about that too.

Then the little old Woman went upstairs into the bedchamber in which the three Bears slept. And first she lay down upon the bed of the Great, Huge Bear; but that was too high at the head for her. And next she lay down upon the bed of the Middle Bear; and that was too high at the foot for her. And then she lay down upon the bed of the Little, Small, Wee Bear; and that was neither too high at the head, nor at the foot, but just right. So she covered herself up comfortably, and lay there till she fell fast asleep.

By this time the Three Bears thought their porridge would be cool enough; so they came home to breakfast. Now the little old Woman had left the spoon of the Great, Huge Bear, standing in his porridge.

"Somebody has been at my porridge!"

said the Great, Huge Bear, in his great, rough, gruff voice. And when the Middle Bear looked at his, he saw that the spoon was standing in it too. They were wooden spoons; if they had been silver ones, the naughty old Woman would have put them in her pocket.

"Somebody has been at my porridge!"

said the Middle Bear in his middle voice.

Then the Little, Small, Wee Bear looked at his, and there was the spoon in the porridge-pot, but the porridge was all gone.

"Somebody has been at my porridge, and has eaten it all up!"

said the Little, Small, Wee Bear, in his little, small, wee voice.

Upon this the Three Bears, seeing that some one had entered their house, and eaten up the Little, Small, Wee Bear's breakfast, began to look about them. Now the little old Woman had not put the hard cushion straight when she rose from the chair of the Great, Huge Bear.

"Somebody has been sitting in my chair!"

said the Great, Huge Bear, in his great, rough, gruff voice.

And the little old Woman had squatted down the soft cushion of the Middle Bear.

"Somebody has been sitting in my chair!"

said the Middle Bear, in his middle voice.

And you know what the little old Woman had done to the third chair.

"Somebody has been sitting in my chair and has sate the bottom out of it!"

said the Little, Small, Wee Bear, in his little, small, wee voice.

Then the Three Bears thought it necessary that they should make farther search; so they went upstairs into their bedchamber. Now the little old Woman had pulled the pillow of the Great, Huge Bear, out of its place.

"Somebody has been lying in my bed!"

said the Great, Huge Bear, in his great, rough, gruff voice.

And the little old Woman had pulled the bolster of the Middle Bear out of its place.

"Somebody has been lying in my bed!"

said the Middle Bear, in his middle voice.

And when the Little, Small, Wee Bear came to look at his bed, there was the bolster in its place; and the pillow in its place upon the bolster; and upon the pillow was the little old Woman's ugly, dirty head,—which was not in its place, for she had no business there.

"Somebody has been lying in my bed,—and here she is!"

said the Little, Small, Wee Bear, in his little, small, wee voice.

The little old Woman had heard in her sleep the great, rough, gruff voice of the Great, Huge Bear; but she was so fast asleep that it was no more to her than the roaring of wind, or the rumbling of thunder. And she had heard the middle voice, of the Middle Bear, but it was only as if she had heard some one speaking in a dream. But when she heard the little, small, wee voice of the Little, Small, Wee Bear, it was so sharp, and so shrill, that it awakened her at once. Up she started; and when she saw the Three Bears on one side of the bed, she tumbled herself out at the other, and ran to the window. Now the window was open, because the Bears, like good, tidy Bears, as they were, always opened their bed-chamber window when they got up in the morning. Out the little old Woman jumped; and whether she broke her neck in the fall; or ran into the wood and was lost there; or found her way out of the wood, and was taken up by the constable and sent to the House of Correction for a vagrant as she was, I cannot tell. But the Three Bears never saw anything more of her.

༄ *Jack the Giant-Killer* ༄

WHEN good King Arthur reigned, there lived near the Land's End of England, in the county of Cornwall, a farmer who had one only son called Jack. He was brisk and of a ready lively wit, so that nobody or nothing could worst him.

In those days the Mount of Cornwall was kept by a huge giant named Cormoran. He was eighteen feet in height, and about three yards round the waist, of a fierce and grim countenance, the terror of all the neighbouring towns and villages. He lived in a cave in the midst of the Mount, and whenever he wanted food he would wade over to the main-land, where he would furnish himself with whatever came in his way. Everybody at his approach ran out of their houses, while he seized on their cattle, making nothing of carrying half-a-dozen oxen on his back at a time; and as for their sheep and hogs, he would tie them round his waist like a bunch of tallow-dips. He had done this for many years, so that all Cornwall was in despair.

One day Jack happened to be at the town-hall when the magistrates were sitting in council about the Giant. He asked: "What reward will be given to the man who kills Cormoran?" "The giant's treasure," they said, "will be the reward." Quoth Jack: "Then let me undertake it."

So he got a horn, shovel, and pickaxe, and went over to the Mount in the beginning of a dark winter's evening, when he fell to work, and before morning had dug a pit twenty-two feet deep, and nearly as broad, covering it over with long sticks and straw. Then he strewed a little mould over it, so that it appeared like plain ground. Jack then placed himself on the opposite side of the pit, farthest from the giant's lodging, and, just at the break of day, he put the horn to his mouth, and blew, Tantivy, Tantivy. This noise roused the giant, who rushed from his cave, crying: "You incorrigible villain, are you come here to disturb my rest? You shall pay dearly for this. Satisfaction I will have, and this it shall be, I will take you whole and broil you for breakfast." He had no sooner uttered this, than he tumbled into the pit, and made the very foundations of the Mount to shake. "Oh, Giant," quoth Jack, "where are you now? Oh, faith, you are gotten now into Lob's Pound, where I will surely plague you for your threatening words: what do you think now of broiling me for your breakfast? Will no other diet serve you but poor Jack?" Then having tantalised the giant for a while, he gave him a most weighty knock with his pickaxe on the very crown of his head, and killed him on the spot.

Jack then filled up the pit with earth, and went to search the cave, which he found contained much treasure. When the magistrates heard of this they made a declaration he should henceforth be termed

JACK THE GIANT-KILLER,

and presented him with a sword and a belt, on which were written these words embroidered in letters of gold:

"Here's the right valiant Cornish man,
Who slew the giant Cormoran."

The news of Jack's victory soon spread over all the West of England, so that another giant, named Blunderbore, hearing of it, vowed to be revenged on Jack, if ever he should light on him. This giant was the lord of an enchanted castle situated in the midst of a lonesome wood. Now Jack, about four months afterwards, walking near this wood in his journey to Wales, being weary, seated himself near a pleasant fountain and fell fast asleep. While he was sleeping, the giant, coming there for water, discovered him, and knew him to be the far-famed Jack the Giant-killer by the lines written on the belt. Without ado, he took Jack on his shoulders and carried him towards his castle. Now, as they passed through a thicket, the rustling of the boughs awakened Jack, who was strangely surprised to find himself in the clutches of the giant. His terror was only begun, for, on entering the castle, he saw the ground strewed with human bones, and the giant told him his own would ere long be among them. After this the giant locked poor Jack in an immense chamber, leaving him there while he went to fetch another giant, his brother, living in the same wood, who might share in the meal on Jack.

After waiting some time Jack, on going to the window beheld afar off the two giants coming towards the castle. "Now," quoth Jack to himself, "my death or my deliverance is at hand." Now, there were strong cords in a corner of the room in which Jack was, and two of these he took, and made a strong noose at the end; and while the giants were unlocking the iron gate of the castle he threw the ropes over each of their heads. Then he drew the other ends across a beam, and pulled with all his might, so that he throttled them. Then, when he saw they were black in the face, he slid down the rope, and drawing his sword, slew them both. Then, taking the giant's keys, and unlocking the rooms, he found three fair ladies tied by the hair of their heads, almost starved to death. "Sweet ladies," quoth Jack, "I have destroyed this monster and his brutish brother, and obtained your liberties." This said he presented them with the keys, and so proceeded on his journey to Wales.

Jack made the best of his way by travelling as fast as he could, but lost his road, and was benighted, and could find no habitation until, coming into a narrow valley, he found a large house, and in order to get shelter took courage to knock at the gate. But what was his surprise when there came forth a monstrous giant with two heads; yet he did not appear so fiery as the others were, for he was a Welsh giant, and what he did was by private and secret malice under the false show of friendship. Jack, having told his condition to the giant, was shown into a bedroom, where, in the dead of night, he heard his host in another apartment muttering these words:

> "Though here you lodge with me this night,
> You shall not see the morning light:
> My club shall dash your brains outright!"

"Say'st thou so," quoth Jack; "that is like one of your Welsh tricks, yet I hope to be cunning enough for you." Then, getting out of bed, he laid a billet in the bed in his stead, and hid himself in a corner of the room. At the dead time of the night in came the Welsh giant, who struck several heavy blows on the bed with his club, thinking he had broken every bone in Jack's skin. The next morning Jack, laughing in his sleeve, gave him hearty thanks for his night's lodging. "How have you rested?" quoth the giant; "did you not feel anything in the night?" "No," quoth Jack, "nothing but a rat, which gave me two or three slaps with her tail." With that, greatly wondering, the giant led Jack to breakfast, bringing him a bowl containing four gallons of hasty pudding. Being loth to let the giant think it too much for him, Jack put a large leather bag under his loose coat, in such a way that he could convey the pudding into it without its being perceived. Then, telling the giant he would show him a trick, taking a knife, Jack ripped open the bag, and out came all the hasty pudding. Whereupon, saying, "Odds splutters hur nails, hur can do that trick hurself," the monster took the knife, and ripping open his belly, fell down dead.

Now, it happened in these days that King Arthur's only son asked his father to give him a large sum of money, in order that he might go and seek his fortune in the principality of Wales, where lived a beautiful lady possessed with seven evil spirits. The king did his best to persuade his son from it, but in vain; so at last gave way and the prince set out with two horses, one loaded with money, the other for himself to ride upon. Now, after several days' travel, he came to a market-town in Wales, where he beheld a vast crowd of people gathered together. The prince asked the reason of it, and was told that they had arrested a corpse for several large sums of money which the deceased owed when he died. The prince replied that it was a pity creditors should be so cruel, and said: "Go bury the dead, and let his creditors come to my lodging, and there their debts shall be paid." They came, in such great numbers that before night he had only twopence left for himself.

Now Jack the Giant-Killer, coming that way, was so taken with the generosity of the prince, that he desired to be his servant. This being agreed upon, the next morning they set forward on their journey together, when, as they were riding out of the town, an old woman called after the prince, saying, "He has owed me twopence these seven years; pray pay me as well as the rest." Putting his hand to his pocket, the prince gave the woman all he had left, so that after their day's food, which cost what small spell Jack had by him, they were without a penny between them.

When the sun got low, the king's son said: "Jack, since we have no money, where can we lodge this night?"

But Jack replied: "Master, we'll do well enough, for I have an uncle lives within two miles of this place; he is a huge and monstrous giant with three heads; he'll fight five hundred men in armour, and make them to fly before him."

"Alas!" quoth the prince, "what shall we do there? He'll certainly chop us up at a mouthful. Nay, we are scarce enough to fill one of his hollow teeth!"

"It is no matter for that," quoth Jack; "I myself will go before and prepare the way for you; therefore stop here and wait till I return." Jack then rode away at full speed, and coming to the gate of the castle, he knocked so loud that he made the neighbouring hills resound. The giant roared out at this like thunder: "Who's there?"

Jack answered: "None but your poor cousin Jack."

Quoth he: "What news with my poor cousin Jack?"

He replied: "Dear uncle, heavy news, God wot!"

"Prithee," quoth the giant, "what heavy news can come to me? I am a giant with three heads, and besides thou knowest I can fight five hundred men in armour, and make them fly like chaff before the wind."

"Oh, but," quoth Jack, "here's the king's son a-coming with a thousand men in armour to kill you and destroy all that you have!"

"Oh, cousin Jack," said the giant, "this is heavy news indeed! I will immediately run and hide myself, and thou shalt lock, bolt, and bar me in, and keep the keys until the prince is gone." Having secured the giant,

Jack fetched his master, when they made themselves heartily merry whilst the poor giant lay trembling in a vault under the ground.

Early in the morning Jack furnished his master with a fresh supply of gold and silver, and then sent him three miles forward on his journey, at which time the prince was pretty well out of the smell of the giant. Jack then returned, and let the giant out of the vault, who asked what he should give him for keeping the castle from destruction. "Why," quoth Jack, "I want nothing but the old coat and cap, together with the old rusty sword and slippers which are at your bed's head." Quoth the giant: "You know not what you ask; they are the most precious things I have. The coat will keep you invisible, the cap will tell you all you want to know, the sword cuts asunder whatever you strike, and the shoes are of extraordinary swiftness. But you have been very serviceable to me, therefore take them with all my heart." Jack thanked his uncle, and then went off with them. He soon overtook his master and they quickly arrived at the house of the lady the prince sought, who, finding the prince to be a suitor, prepared a splendid banquet for him. After the repast was concluded, she told him she had a task for him. She wiped his mouth with a handkerchief, saying: "You must show me that handkerchief to-morrow morning, or else you will lose your head." With that she put it in her bosom. The prince went to bed in great sorrow, but Jack's cap of knowledge informed him how it was to be obtained. In the middle of the night she called upon her familiar spirit to carry her to Lucifer. But Jack put on his coat of darkness and his shoes of swiftness, and was there as soon as she was. When she entered the place of the Old One, she gave the handkerchief to old Lucifer, who laid it upon a shelf, whence Jack took it and brought it to his master, who showed it to the lady next day, and so saved his life. On that day, she gave the prince a kiss and told him he must show her the lips to-morrow morning that she kissed last night, or lose his head.

"Ah!" he replied, "if you kiss none but mine, I will."

"That is neither here nor there," said she; "if you do not, death's your portion!"

At midnight she went as before, and was angry with old Lucifer for letting the handkerchief go. "But now," quoth she, "I will be too hard for the king's son, for I will kiss thee, and he is to show me thy lips." Which she did, and Jack, when she was not standing by, cut off Lucifer's head and brought it under his invisible coat to his master, who the next morning pulled it out by the horns before the lady. This broke the enchantment and the evil spirit left her, and she appeared in all her beauty. They were married the next morning, and soon after went to the court of King Arthur, where Jack for his many great exploits, was made one of the Knights of the Round Table.

Jack soon went searching for giants again, but he had not ridden far, when he saw a cave, near the entrance of which he beheld a giant sitting upon a block of timber, with a knotted iron club by his side. His goggle eyes were like flames of fire, his countenance grim and ugly, and his cheeks like a couple of large flitches of bacon, while the bristles of his beard resembled rods of iron wire, and the locks that hung down upon his brawny shoulders were like curled snakes or hissing adders. Jack alighted from his horse, and, putting on the coat of darkness, went up close to the giant, and said softly: "Oh! are you there? It will not be long before I take you fast by the beard." The giant all this while could not see him, on account of his invisible coat, so that Jack, coming up close to the monster, struck a blow with his sword at his head, but, missing his aim, he cut off the nose instead. At this, the giant roared like claps of thunder, and began to lay about him with his iron club like one stark mad. But Jack, running behind, drove his sword up to the hilt in the giant's back, so that he fell down dead. This done, Jack cut off the giant's head, and sent it, with his brother's also, to King Arthur, by a waggoner he hired for that purpose.

Jack now resolved to enter the giant's cave in search of his treasure, and, passing along through a great many windings and turnings, he came at length to a large room paved with freestone, at the upper end of which was a boiling caldron, and on the right hand a large table, at which the giant used to dine. Then he came to a window, barred with iron, through which he looked and beheld a vast number of miserable captives, who, seeing him, cried out: "Alas! young man, art thou come to be one amongst us in this miserable den?"

"Ay," quoth Jack, "but pray tell me what is the meaning of your captivity?"

"We are kept here," said one, "till such time as the giants have a wish to feast, and then the fattest among us is slaughtered! And many are the times they have dined upon murdered men!"

"Say you so," quoth Jack, and straightway unlocked the gate and let them free, who all rejoiced like condemned men at sight of a pardon. Then searching the giant's coffers, he shared the gold and silver equally amongst them and took them to a neighbouring castle, where they all feasted and made merry over their deliverance.

But in the midst of all this mirth a messenger brought news that one Thunderdell, a giant with two heads, having heard of the death of his kinsmen, had come from the northern dales to be revenged on Jack, and was within a mile of the castle, the country people flying before him like chaff. But Jack was not a bit daunted, and said: "Let him come! I have a tool to pick his teeth; and you, ladies and gentlemen, walk out into the garden, and you shall witness this giant Thunderdell's death and destruction."

The castle was situated in the midst of a small island surrounded by a moat thirty feet deep and twenty feet wide, over which lay a drawbridge. So Jack employed men to cut through this bridge on both sides, nearly to the middle; and then, dressing himself in his invisible coat, he marched against the giant with his sword of sharpness. Although the giant could not see Jack, he smelt his approach, and cried out in these words:

"Fee, fi, fo, fum!
I smell the blood of an Englishman!
Be he alive or be he dead,
I'll grind his bones to make me bread!"

"Say'st thou so," said Jack; "then thou art a monstrous miller indeed."

The giant cried out again: "Art thou that villain who killed my kinsmen? Then I will tear thee with my teeth, suck thy blood, and grind thy bones to powder."

"You'll have to catch me first," quoth Jack, and throwing off his invisible coat, so that the giant might see him, and putting on his shoes of swiftness, he ran from the giant, who followed like a walking castle, so that the very foundations of the earth seemed to shake at every step. Jack led him a long dance, in order that the gentlemen and ladies might see; and at last to end the matter, ran lightly over the drawbridge, the giant, in full speed, pursuing him with his club. Then, coming to the middle of the bridge, the giant's great weight broke it down, and he tumbled headlong into the water, where he rolled and wallowed like a whale. Jack, standing by the moat, laughed at him all the while; but though the giant foamed to hear him scoff, and plunged from place to place in the moat, yet he could not get out to be revenged. Jack at length got a cart-rope and cast it over the two heads of the giant, and drew him ashore by a team of horses, and then cut off both his heads with his sword of sharpness, and sent them to King Arthur.

After some time spent in mirth and pastime, Jack, taking leave of the knights and ladies, set out for new adventures. Through many woods he passed, and came at length to the foot of a high mountain. Here, late at night, he found a lonesome house, and knocked at the door, which was opened by an aged man with a head as white as snow. "Father," said Jack, "can you lodge a benighted traveller that has lost his way?" "Yes," said the old man; "you are right welcome to my poor cottage." Whereupon Jack entered, and down they sat together, and the old man began to speak as follows: "Son, I see by your belt you are the great conqueror of giants, and behold, my son, on the top of this mountain is an enchanted castle, this is kept by a giant named Galligantua, and he by the help of an old conjurer, betrays many knights and ladies into his castle, where by magic art they are transformed into sundry shapes and forms. But above all, I grieve for a duke's daughter, whom they fetched from her father's garden, carrying her through the air in a burning chariot drawn by fiery dragons, when they secured her within the castle, and transformed her into a white hind. And though many knights have tried to break the enchantment, and work her deliverance, yet no one could accomplish it, on account of two dreadful griffins which are placed at the castle gate and which destroy every one who comes near. But you, my son, may pass by them undiscovered, where on the gates of the castle you will find engraven in large letters how the spell may be broken." Jack gave the old man his hand, and promised that in the morning he would venture his life to free the lady.

In the morning Jack arose and put on his invisible coat and magic cap and shoes, and prepared himself for the fray. Now, when he had reached the top of the mountain he soon discovered the two fiery griffins, but passed them without fear, because of his invisible coat. When he had got beyond them, he found upon the gates of the castle a golden trumpet hung by a silver chain, under which these lines were engraved:

> "Whoever shall this trumpet blow,
> Shall soon the giant overthrow,
> And break the black enchantment straight;
> So all shall be in happy state."

Jack had no sooner read this but he blew the trumpet, at which the castle trembled to its vast foundations, and the giant and conjurer were in horrid confusion, biting their thumbs and tearing their hair, knowing their wicked reign was at an end. Then the giant stooping to take up his

Jack with his Invisible Coat

club, Jack at one blow cut off his head; whereupon the conjurer, mounting up into the air, was carried away in a whirlwind. Then the enchantment was broken, and all the lords and ladies who had so long been transformed into birds and beasts returned to their proper shapes, and the castle vanished away in a cloud of smoke. This being done, the head of Galligantua was likewise, in the usual manner, conveyed to the Court of King Arthur, where, the very next day, Jack followed, with the knights and ladies who had been delivered. Whereupon, as a reward for his good services, the king prevailed upon the duke to bestow his daughter in marriage on honest Jack. So married they were, and the whole kingdom was filled with joy at the wedding. Furthermore, the king bestowed on Jack a noble castle, with a very beautiful estate thereto belonging, where he and his lady lived in great joy and happiness all the rest of their days.

ᙢ Henny-Penny ᙢ

ONE day Henny-penny was picking up corn in the cornyard when—whack!—something hit her upon the head. "Goodness gracious me!" said Henny-penny; "the sky's a-going to fall; I must go and tell the king."

So she went along and she went along and she went along till she met Cocky-locky. "Where are you going, Henny-penny?" says Cocky-locky. "Oh! I'm going to tell the king the sky's a-falling," says Henny-penny. "May I come with you?" says Cocky-locky. "Certainly," says Henny-penny. So Henny-penny and Cocky-locky went to tell the king the sky was falling.

They went along, and they went along, and they went along, till they met Ducky-daddles. "Where are you going to, Henny-penny and Cocky-locky?" says Ducky-daddles. "Oh! we're going to tell the king the sky's a-falling," said Henny-penny and Cocky-locky. "May I come with you?" says Ducky-daddles. "Certainly," said Henny-penny and Cocky-locky. So Henny-penny, Cocky-locky and Ducky-daddles went to tell the king the sky was a-falling.

So they went along, and they went along, and they went along, till they met Goosey-poosey. "Where are you going to, Henny-penny, Cocky-locky and Ducky-daddles?" said Goosey-poosey. "Oh! we're going to tell the king the sky's a-falling," said Henny-penny and Cocky-locky and Ducky-daddles. "May I come with you," said Goosey-poosey. "Certainly," said Henny-penny, Cocky-locky and Ducky-daddles. So Henny-penny, Cocky-locky, Ducky-daddles and Goosy-poosey went to tell the king the sky was a-falling.

So they went along, and they went along, and they went along, till they met Turkey-lurkey. "Where are you going, Henny-penny, Cocky-locky, Ducky-daddles, and Goosey-poosey?" says Turkey-lurkey. "Oh! we're going to tell the king the sky's a-falling," said Henny-penny, Cocky-locky, Ducky-daddles and Goosey-poosey. "May I come with you? Henny-penny, Cocky-locky, Ducky-daddles and Goosey-poosey?" said Turkey-lurkey. "Why, certainly, Turkey-lurkey," said Henny-penny, Cocky-locky, Ducky-daddles, and Goosey-poosey. So Henny-penny, Cocky-locky, Ducky-daddles, Goosey-poosey and Turkey-lurkey all went to tell the king the sky was a-falling.

So they went along, and they went along, and they went along, till they met Foxy-woxy, and Foxy-woxy said to Henny-penny, Cocky-locky, Ducky-daddles, Goosey-poosey and Turkey-lurkey: "Where are you going, Henny-penny, Cocky-locky, Ducky-daddles, Goosey-poosey, and Turkey-lurkey?" And Henny-penny, Cocky-locky, Ducky-daddles, Goosey-poosey, and Turkey-lurkey said to Foxy-woxy: "We're going to tell the king the sky's a-falling." "Oh! but this is not the way to the king, Henny-penny, Cocky-locky, Ducky-daddles, Goosey-poosey and Turkey-lurkey," says Foxy-woxy; "I know the proper way; shall I show it you?" "Why certainly, Foxy-woxy," said Henny-penny, Cocky-locky, Ducky-daddles, Goosey-poosey, and Turkey-lurkey. So Henny-penny, Cocky-locky, Ducky-daddles, Goosey-poosey, Turkey-lurkey, and Foxy-woxy all went to tell the king the sky was a-falling. So they went along, and they went along, and they went along, till they came to a narrow and dark hole.

Now this was the door of Foxy-woxy's cave. But Foxy-woxy said to Henny-penny, Cocky-locky, Ducky-daddles, Goosey-poosey, and Turkey-lurkey: "This is the short way to the king's palace: you'll soon get there if you follow me. I will go first and you come after, Henny-penny, Cocky-locky, Ducky-daddles, Goosey-poosey, and Turkey-lurkey." "Why of course, certainly, without doubt, why not?" said Henny-Penny, Cocky-locky, Ducky-daddles, Goosey-poosey, and Turkey-lurkey.

So Foxy-woxy went into his cave, and he didn't go very far but turned round to wait for Henny-penny, Cocky-locky, Ducky-daddles, Goosey-poosey and Turkey-lurkey. So at last at first Turkey-lurkey went through the dark hole into the cave. He hadn't got far when "Hrumph," Foxy-woxy snapped off Turkey-lurkey's head and threw his body over his left shoulder. Then Goosey-poosey went in, and "Hrumph," off went her head and Goosey-poosey was thrown beside Turkey-lurkey. Then Ducky-daddles waddled down, and "Hrumph," snapped Foxy-woxy, and Ducky-daddles' head was off and Ducky-daddles was thrown alongside Turkey-lurkey and Goosey-poosey. Then Cocky-locky strutted down into the cave and he hadn't gone far when "Snap, Hrumph!" went Foxy-woxy and Cocky-locky was thrown alongside of Turkey-lurkey, Goosey-poosey and Ducky-daddles.

But Foxy-woxy had made two bites at Cocky-locky, and when the first snap only hurt Cocky-locky, but didn't kill him, he called out to Henny-penny. So she turned tail and ran back home, so she never told the king the sky was a-falling.

⁓ Childe Rowland ⁓

CHILDE Rowland and his brothers twain
Were playing at the ball,

And there was their sister Burd Ellen
  In the midst, among them all.

Childe Rowland kicked it with his foot
  And caught it with his knee;
At last as he plunged among them all
  O'er the church he made it flee.

Burd Ellen round about the aisle
  To seek the ball is gone,
But long they waited, and longer still,
  And she came not back again.

They sought her east, they sought her west,
  They sought her up and down,
And woe were the hearts of those brethren,
  For she was not to be found.

So at last her eldest brother went to the Warlock Merlin and told him all the case, and asked him if he knew where Burd Ellen was. "The fair Burd Ellen," said the Warlock Merlin, "must have been carried off by the fairies, because she went round the church 'widershins'—the opposite way to the sun. She is now in the Dark Tower of the King of Elfland; it would take the boldest knight in Christendom to bring her back."

"If it is possible to bring her back," said her brother, "I'll do it, or perish in the attempt."

"Possible it is," said the Warlock Merlin, "but woe to the man or mother's son that attempts it, if he is not well taught beforehand what he is to do."

The eldest brother of Burd Ellen was not to be put off, by any fear of danger, from attempting to get her back, so he begged the Warlock Merlin to tell him what he should do, and what he should not do, in going to seek his sister. And after he had been taught, and had repeated his lesson, he set out for Elfland.

But long they waited, and longer still,
  With doubt and muckle pain,

> But woe were the hearts of his brethren,
>   For he came not back again.

Then the second brother got tired and sick of waiting, and he went to the Warlock Merlin and asked him the same as his brother. So he set out to find Burd Ellen.

> But long they waited, and longer still,
>   With muckle doubt and pain,
> And woe were his mother's and brother's heart,
>   For he came not back again.

And when they had waited and waited a good long time, Childe Rowland, the youngest of Burd Ellen's brothers, wished to go, and went to his mother, the good queen, to ask her to let him go. But she would not at first, for he was the last of her children she now had, and if he was lost, all would be lost. But he begged, and he begged, till at last the good queen let him go, and gave him his father's good brand that never struck in vain. And as she girt it round his waist, she said the spell that would give it victory.

So Childe Rowland said good-bye to the good queen, his mother, and went to the cave of the Warlock Merlin. "Once more, and but once more," he said to the Warlock, "tell how man or mother's son may rescue Burd Ellen and her brothers twain."

"Well, my son," said the Warlock Merlin, "there are but two things, simple they may seem, but hard they are to do. One thing to do, and one thing not to do. And the thing to do is this: after you have entered the land of Fairy, whoever speaks to you, till you meet the Burd Ellen, you must out with your father's brand and off with their head. And what you've not to do is this: bite no bit, and drink no drop, however hungry or thirsty you be; drink a drop, or bite a bit, while in Elfland you be, and never will you see Middle Earth again."

So Childe Rowland said the two things over and over again, till he knew them by heart, and he thanked the Warlock Merlin and went on his way. And he went along, and along, and along, and still further along, till he came to the horse-herd of the King of Elfland feeding his horses. These he knew by their fiery eyes, and knew that he was at last in the land of Fairy. "Canst thou tell me," said Childe Rowland to the horse-herd, "where the King of Elfland's Dark Tower is?" "I cannot tell thee," said the horse-herd, "but go on a little further and thou wilt come to the cow-herd, and he, maybe, can tell thee."

Then, without a word more, Childe Rowland drew the good brand that never struck in vain, and off went the horse-herd's head, and Childe Rowland went on further, till he came to the cow-herd, and asked him the same question. "I can't tell thee," said he, "but go on a little farther, and thou wilt come to the hen-wife, and she is sure to know." Then Childe Rowland out with his good brand, that never struck in vain, and off went the cow-herd's head. And he went on a little further, till he came to an old woman in a grey cloak, and he asked her if she knew where the Dark Tower of the King of Elfland was. "Go on a little further," said the hen-wife, "till you come to a round green hill, surrounded with terrace-rings, from the bottom to the top; go round it three times, widershins, and each time say:

> Open, door! open, door!
> And let me come in.

and the third time the door will open, and you may go in." And Childe Rowland was just going on, when he remembered what he had to do; so he out with the good brand, that never struck in vain, and off went the hen-wife's head.

Then he went on, and on, and on, till he came to the round green hill with the terrace-rings from top to bottom, and he went round it three times, widershins, saying each time:

> Open, door! open, door!
> And let me come in.

And the third time the door did open, and he went in, and it closed with a click, and Childe Rowland was left in the dark.

It was not exactly dark, but a kind of twilight or gloaming. There were neither windows nor candles, and he could not make out where the twilight came from, if not through the walls and roof. These were rough arches made of a transparent rock, incrusted with sheepsilver and rock spar, and other bright stones. But though it was rock, the air was quite warm, as it always is in Elfland. So he went through this passage till at last he came to two wide and high folding-doors which stood ajar. And when he opened them, there he saw a most wonderful and glorious sight. A large and spacious hall, so large that it seemed to be as long, and as broad, as the green hill itself. The roof was supported by fine pillars, so large and lofty, that the pillars of a cathedral were as nothing to them. They were all of gold and silver, with fretted work, and between them and around them, wreaths of flowers, composed of what do you think? Why, of diamonds and emeralds, and all manner of precious stones. And the very key-stones of the arches had for ornaments clusters of diamonds and rubies, and pearls, and other precious stones. And all these arches met in the middle of the roof, and just there, hung by a gold chain, an immense lamp made out of one big pearl hollowed out and quite transparent. And in the middle of this was a big, huge carbuncle, which kept spinning round and round, and this was what gave light by its rays to the whole hall, which seemed as if the setting sun was shining on it.

The hall was furnished in a manner equally grand, and at one end of it was a glorious couch of velvet, silk and gold, and there sate Burd Ellen, combing her golden hair with a silver comb. And when she saw Childe Rowland she stood up and said:

> "God pity ye, poor luckless fool,
>   What have ye here to do?
>
> "Hear ye this, my youngest brother,
>   Why didn't ye bide at home?
> Had you a hundred thousand lives
>   Ye couldn't spare any a one.
>
> "But sit ye down; but woe, O, woe,
>   That ever ye were born,
> For come the King of Elfland in,
>   Your fortune is forlorn."

Then they sate down together, and Childe Rowland told her all that he had done, and she told him how their two brothers had reached the Dark Tower, but had been enchanted by the King of Elfland, and lay there entombed as if dead. And then after they had talked a little longer Childe Rowland began to feel hungry from his long travels, and told his sister Burd Ellen how hungry he was and asked for some food, forgetting all about the Warlock Merlin's warning.

Burd Ellen looked at Childe Rowland sadly, and shook her head, but she was under a spell, and could not warn him. So she rose up, and went out, and soon brought back a golden basin full of bread and milk. Childe Rowland was just going to raise it to his lips, when he looked at his sister and remembered why he had come all that way. So he dashed the bowl to the ground, and said: "Not a sup will I swallow, nor a bit will I bite, till Burd Ellen is set free."

Just at that moment they heard the noise of some one approaching, and a loud voice was heard saying:

> "Fee, fi, fo, fum,
> I smell the blood of a Christian man,
> Be he dead, be he living, with my brand,
> I'll dash his brains from his brain-pan."

And then the folding-doors of the hall were burst open, and the King of Elfland rushed in.

"Strike then, Bogle, if thou darest," shouted out Childe Rowland, and rushed to meet him with his good brand that never yet did fail. They fought, and they fought and they fought, till Childe Rowland beat the King of Elfland down on to his knees, and caused him to yield and beg for mercy. "I grant you mercy," said Childe Rowland, "release my sister from thy spells and raise my brothers to life, and let us all go free, and thou shalt be spared." "I agree," said the Elfin King, and rising up he went to a chest from which he took a phial filled with a blood-red liquor. With this he anointed the ears, eyelids, nostrils, lips, and finger-tips, of the two brothers, and they sprang at once into life, and declared that their souls had been away, but had now returned. The Elfin king then said some words to Burd Ellen, and she was disenchanted, and they all four passed out of the hall, through the long passage, and turned their back on the Dark Tower, never to return again. And they reached home, and the good queen, their mother, and Burd Ellen never went round a church widershins again.

✌ Molly Whuppie ✌

ONCE upon a time there was a man and a wife had too many children, and they could not get meat for them, so they took the three youngest and left them in a wood. They travelled and travelled and could see never a house. It began to be dark, and they were hungry. At last they saw a light and made for it; it turned out to be a house. They knocked at the door, and a woman came to it, who said: "What do you want?" They said: "Please let us in and give us something to eat." The woman said: "I can't do that, as my man is a giant, and he would kill you if he comes home." They begged hard. "Let us stop for a little while," said they, "and we will go away before he comes." So she took them in, and set them down before the fire, and gave them milk and bread; but just as they had begun to eat a great knock came to the door, and a dreadful voice said:

"Fee, fie, fo, fum,
I smell the blood of some earthly one.

Who have you there wife?" "Eh," said the wife, "it's three poor lassies cold and hungry, and they will go away. Ye won't touch 'em, man." He said nothing, but ate up a big supper, and ordered them to stay all night. Now he had three lassies of his own, and they were to sleep in the same bed with the three strangers. The youngest of the three strange lassies was called Molly Whuppie, and she was very clever. She noticed that before they went to bed the giant put straw ropes round her neck and her sisters', and round his own lassies' necks he put gold chains. So Molly took care and did not fall asleep, but waited till she was sure every one was sleeping sound. Then she slipped out of the bed, and took the straw ropes off her own and her sisters' necks, and took the gold chains off the giant's lassies. She then put the straw ropes on the giant's lassies and the gold on herself and her sisters, and lay down. And in the middle of the night up rose the giant, armed with a great club, and felt for the necks with the straw. It was dark. He took his own lassies out of bed on to the floor, and battered them until they were dead, and then lay down again, thinking he had managed fine. Molly thought it time she and her sisters were out of that, so she wakened them and told them to be quiet, and they slipped out of the house. They all got out safe, and they ran and ran, and never stopped until morning, when they saw a grand house before them. It turned out to be a king's house: so Molly went in, and told her story to the king. He said: "Well, Molly, you are a clever girl, and you have managed well; but, if you would manage better, and go back, and steal the giant's sword that hangs on the back of his bed, I would give your eldest sister my eldest son to marry." Molly said she would try. So she went back, and managed to slip into the giant's house, and crept in below the bed. The giant came home, and ate up a great supper, and went to bed. Molly waited until he was snoring, and she crept out, and reached over the giant and got down the sword; but just as she got it out over the bed it gave a rattle, and up jumped the giant, and Molly ran out at the door and the sword with her; and she ran, and he ran, till they came to the "Bridge of one hair"; and she got over, but he couldn't, and he says, "Woe worth ye, Molly Whuppie! never ye come again." And she says: "Twice yet, carle," quoth she, "I'll come to Spain." So Molly took the sword to the king, and her sister was married to his son.

Well, the king he says: "Ye've managed well, Molly; but if ye would manage better, and steal the purse that lies below the giant's pillow, I would marry your second sister to my second son." And Molly said she would try. So she set out for the giant's house, and slipped in, and hid again below the bed, and waited till the giant had eaten his supper, and was snoring sound asleep. She slipped out, and slipped her hand below the pillow, and got out the purse; but just as she was going out the giant wakened, and ran after her; and she ran, and he ran, till they came to the "Bridge of one hair," and she got over, but he couldn't, and he said, "Woe worth ye, Molly Whuppie! never you come again." "Once yet, carle," quoth she, "I'll come to Spain." So Molly took the purse to the king, and her second sister was married to the king's second son.

After that the king says to Molly: "Molly, you are a clever girl, but if you would do better yet, and steal the giant's ring that he wears on his finger, I will give you my youngest son for yourself." Molly said she would try. So back she goes to the giant's house, and hides herself below the bed. The giant wasn't long ere he came home and, after he had eaten a great big supper, he went to his bed, and shortly was snoring loud. Molly crept out and reached over the bed, and got hold of the giant's hand, and she pulled and she pulled until she got off the ring; but just as she got it off the giant got up, and gripped her by the hand, and he says: "Now I have catcht you, Molly Whuppie, and, if I had done as much ill to you as ye have done to me, what would ye do to me?"

Molly says: "I would put you into a sack, and I'd put the cat inside wi' you, and the dog aside you, and a needle and thread and a shears, and I'd hang you up upon the wall, and I'd go to the wood, and choose the thickest stick I could get, and I would come home, and take you down, and bang you till you were dead."

"Well, Molly," says the giant, "I'll just do that to you."

So he gets a sack, and puts Molly into it, and the cat and the dog beside

her, and a needle and thread and shears, and hangs her up upon the wall, and goes to the wood to choose a stick.

Molly she sings out: "Oh, if ye saw what I see."

"Oh," says the giant's wife, "what do ye see, Molly?"

But Molly never said a word but, "Oh, if ye saw what I see!"

The giant's wife begged that Molly would take her up into the sack till she would see what Molly saw. So Molly took the shears and cut a hole in the sack, and took out the needle and thread with her, and jumpt down and helped the giant's wife up into the sack, and sewed up the hole.

The giant's wife saw nothing, and began to ask to get down again; but Molly never minded, but hid herself at the back of the door. Home came the giant, and a great big tree in his hand, and he took down the sack, and began to batter it. His wife cried, "It's me, man"; but the dog barked and the cat mewed, and he did not know his wife's voice. But Molly came out from the back of the door, and the giant saw her, and he after her; and he ran and she ran, till they came to the "Bridge of one hair," and she got over but he couldn't; and he said, "Woe worth you, Molly Whuppie! never you come again." "Never more, carle," quoth she, "will I come again to Spain."

So Molly took the ring to the king, and she was married to his youngest son, and she never saw the giant again.

ᔥ *The Red Ettin* ᔥ

THERE was once a widow that lived on a small bit of ground, which she rented from a farmer. And she had two sons; and by-and-by it was time for the wife to send them away to seek their fortune. So she told her eldest son one day to take a can and bring her water from the well, that she might bake a cake for him; and however much or however little water he might bring, the cake would be great or small accordingly, and that cake was to be all that she could give him when he went on his travels.

The lad went away with the can to the well, and filled it with water, and then came away home again; but the can being broken, the most part of the water had run out before he got back. So his cake was very small; yet small as it was, his mother asked him if he was willing to take the half of it with her blessing, telling him that, if he chose rather to take the whole, he would only get it with her curse. The young man, thinking he might have to travel a far way, and not knowing when or how he might get other provisions, said he would like to have the whole cake, come of his mother's malison what like; so she gave him the whole cake, and her malison along with it. Then he took his brother aside, and gave him a knife to keep till he should come back, desiring him to look at it every morning, and as long as it continued to be clear, then he might be sure that the owner of it was well; but if it grew dim and rusty, then for certain some ill had befallen him.

So the young man went to seek his fortune. And he went all that day, and all the next day; and on the third day, in the afternoon, he came up to where a shepherd was sitting with a flock of sheep. And he went up to the shepherd and asked him who the sheep belonged to; and he answered:

> "The Red Ettin of Ireland
>   Once lived in Ballygan,
> And stole King Malcolm's daughter,
>   The king of fair Scotland.
> He beats her, he binds her,
>   He lays her on a band;
> And every day he strikes her
>   With a bright silver wand.
> Like Julian the Roman,
> He's one that fears no man.

"It's said there's one predestinate
To be his mortal foe;
But that man is yet unborn,
And long may it be so."

This shepherd also told him to beware of the beasts he should next meet, for they were of a very different kind from any he had yet seen.

So the young man went on, and by-and-by he saw a multitude of very dreadful beasts, with two heads, and on every head four horns. And he was

sore frightened, and ran away from them as fast as he could; and glad was he when he came to a castle that stood on a hillock, with the door standing wide open to the wall. And he went into the castle for shelter, and there he saw an old wife sitting beside the kitchen fire. He asked the wife if he might stay for the night, as he was tired with a long journey; and the wife said he might, but it was not a good place for him to be in, as it belonged to the Red Ettin, who was a very terrible beast, with three heads, that spared no living man it could get hold of. The young man would have gone away, but he was afraid of the beasts on the outside of the castle; so he beseeched the old woman to hide him as best she could, and not tell the Ettin he was there. He thought, if he could put over the night, he might get away in the morning, without meeting with the beasts, and so escape. But he had not been long in his hiding-hole, before the awful Ettin came in; and no sooner was he in, than he was heard crying:

> "Snouk but and snouk ben,
> I find the smell of an earthly man,
> Be he living, or be he dead,
> His heart this night shall kitchen my bread."

The monster soon found the poor young man, and pulled him from his hole. And when he had got him out, he told him that if he could answer him three questions his life should be spared. So the first head asked: "A thing without an end, what's that?" But the young man knew not. Then the second head said: "The smaller, the more dangerous, what's that?" But the young man knew it not. And then the third head asked: "The dead carrying the living; riddle me that?" But the young man had to give it up. The lad not being able to answer one of these questions, the Red Ettin took a mallet and knocked him on the head, and turned him into a pillar of stone.

On the morning after this happened, the younger brother took out the knife to look at it, and he was grieved to find it all brown with rust. He told his mother that the time was now come for him to go away upon his travels also; so she requested him to take the can to the well for water, that she might make a cake for him. And he went, and as he was bringing home the water, a raven over his head cried to him to look, and he would see that the water was running out. And he was a young man of sense, and seeing the water running out, he took some clay and patched up the holes, so that he brought home enough water to bake a large cake. When his mother put it to him to take the half cake with her blessing, he took it in preference to having the whole with her malison; and yet the half was bigger than what the other lad had got.

So he went away on his journey; and after he had travelled a far way, he met with an old woman that asked him if he would give her a bit of his johnny-cake. And he said: "I will gladly do that," and so he gave her a piece of the johnny-cake; and for that she gave him a magical wand, that she might yet be of service to him, if he took care to use it rightly. Then the old woman, who was a fairy, told him a great deal that would happen to him, and what he ought to do in all circumstances; and after that she vanished in an instant out of his sight. He went on a great way farther, and then he came up to the old man herding the sheep; and when he asked whose sheep these were, the answer was:

> "The Red Ettin of Ireland
>   Once lived in Ballygan,
> And stole King Malcolm's daughter,
>   The king of Fair Scotland.
>
> "He beats her, he binds her,
>   He lays her on a band;
> And every day he strikes her
>   With a bright silver wand.
> Like Julian the Roman,
> He's one that fears no man.
>
> "But now I fear his end is near,
>   And destiny at hand;
> And you're to be, I plainly see,
>   The heir of all his land."

When he came to the place where the monstrous beasts were standing, he did not stop nor run away, but went boldly through amongst them. One came up roaring with open mouth to devour him, when he struck it with his wand, and laid it in an instant dead at his feet. He soon came to the Ettin's castle, where he knocked, and was admitted. The old woman who sat by the fire warned him of the terrible Ettin, and what had been the fate of his brother; but he was not to be daunted. The monster soon came in, saying:

> "Snouk but and snouk ben,
> I find the smell of an earthly man;
> Be he living, or be he dead,
> His heart shall be kitchen to my bread."

He quickly espied the young man, and bade him come forth on the floor. And then he put the three questions to him; but the young man had been told everything by the good fairy, so he was able to answer all the questions. So when the first head asked, "What's the thing without an end?" he said: "A bowl." And when the second head said: "The smaller the more dangerous; what's that?" he said at once, "A bridge." And last, the third head said: "When does the dead carry the living, riddle me that?" Then the young man answered up at once and said: "When a ship sails on the sea with men inside her." When the Ettin found this, he knew that his power was gone. The young man then took up an axe and hewed off the monster's three heads. He next asked the old woman to show him where the king's daughter lay; and the old woman took him upstairs, and opened a great many doors, and out of every door came a beautiful lady who had been imprisoned there by the Ettin; and one of the ladies was the king's daughter. She also took him down into a low room, and there stood a stone pillar, that he had only to touch with his wand, when his brother started into life. And the whole of the prisoners were overjoyed at their deliverance, for which they thanked the young man. Next day they all set out for the king's court, and a gallant company they made. And the king married his daughter to the young man that had delivered her, and gave a noble's daughter to his brother; and so they all lived happily all the rest of their days.

꙾ *The Golden Arm* ꙾

THERE was once a man who travelled the land all over in search of a wife. He saw young and old, rich and poor, pretty and plain, and could not meet with one to his mind. At last he found a woman, young, fair, and rich, who possessed a right arm of solid gold. He married her at once, and thought no man so fortunate as he was. They lived happily together, but, though he wished people to think otherwise, he was fonder of the golden arm than of all his wife's gifts besides.

At last she died. The husband put on the blackest black, and pulled the longest face at the funeral; but for all that he got up in the middle of the night, dug up the body, and cut off the golden arm. He hurried home to hide his treasure, and thought no one would know.

The following night he put the golden arm under his pillow, and was just falling asleep, when the ghost of his dead wife glided into the room. Stalking up to the bedside it drew the curtain, and looked at him reproachfully. Pretending not to be afraid, he spoke to the ghost, and said: "What hast thou done with thy cheeks so red?"

"All withered and wasted away," replied the ghost, in a hollow tone.

"What hast thou done with thy red rosy lips?"

"All withered and wasted away."

"What hast thou done with thy golden hair?"

"All withered and wasted away."

"What hast thou done with thy *Golden Arm?*"

"THOU HAST IT!"

ෆ *The History of Tom Thumb* ෆ

IN THE DAYS of the great Prince Arthur, there lived a mighty magician, called Merlin, the most learned and skilful enchanter the world has ever seen.

This famous magician, who could take any form he pleased, was travelling about as a poor beggar, and being very tired, he stopped at the cottage of a ploughman to rest himself, and asked for some food.

The countryman bade him welcome, and his wife, who was a very good-hearted woman, soon brought him some milk in a wooden bowl, and some coarse brown bread on a platter.

Merlin was much pleased with the kindness of the ploughman and his wife; but he could not help noticing that though everything was neat and comfortable in the cottage, they seemed both to be very unhappy. He therefore asked them why they were so melancholy, and learned that they were miserable because they had no children.

The poor woman said, with tears in her eyes: "I should be the happiest creature in the world if I had a son; although he was no bigger than my husband's thumb, I would be satisfied."

Merlin was so much amused with the idea of a boy no bigger than a man's thumb, that he determined to grant the poor woman's wish. Accordingly, in a short time after, the ploughman's wife had a son, who, wonderful to relate! was not a bit bigger than his father's thumb.

The queen of the fairies, wishing to see the little fellow, came in at the window while the mother was sitting up in the bed admiring him. The queen kissed the child, and, giving it the name of Tom Thumb, sent for some of the fairies, who dressed her little godson according to her orders;

> An oak-leaf hat he had for his crown;
> His shirt of web by spiders spun;
> With jacket wove of thistle's down;
> His trowsers were of feathers done.
> His stockings, of apple-rind, they tie
> With eyelash from his mother's eye:
> His shoes were made of mouse's skin,
> Tann'd with the downy hair within.

Tom never grew any larger than his father's thumb, which was only of ordinary size; but as he got older he became very cunning and full of tricks. When he was old enough to play with the boys, and had lost all his own cherry-stones, he used to creep into the bags of his playfellows, fill his pockets, and, getting out without their noticing him, would again join in the game.

One day, however, as he was coming out of a bag of cherry-stones, where he had been stealing as usual, the boy to whom it belonged chanced to see him. "Ah, ah! my little Tommy," said the boy, "so I have caught you stealing my cherry-stones at last, and you shall be rewarded for your thievish tricks." On saying this, he drew the string tight round his neck, and gave the bag such a hearty shake, that poor little Tom's legs, thighs, and body were sadly bruised. He roared out with pain, and begged to be let out, promising never to steal again.

A short time afterwards his mother was making a batter-pudding, and Tom, being very anxious to see how it was made, climbed up to the edge of the bowl; but his foot slipped, and he plumped over head and ears into the batter, without his mother noticing him, who stirred him into the pudding-bag, and put him in the pot to boil.

The batter filled Tom's mouth, and prevented him from crying; but, on feeling the hot water, he kicked and struggled so much in the pot, that his mother thought that the pudding was bewitched, and, pulling it out of the pot, she threw it outside the door. A poor tinker, who was passing by, lifted up the pudding, and, putting it into his budget, he then walked off. As Tom had now got his mouth cleared of the batter, he then began to cry aloud, which so frightened the tinker that he flung down the pudding and ran away. The pudding being broke to pieces by the fall, Tom crept out covered all over with the batter, and walked home. His mother, who was very sorry to see her darling in such a woful state, put him into a teacup, and soon washed off the batter; after which she kissed him, and laid him in bed.

Soon after the adventure of the pudding, Tom's mother went to milk her cow in the meadow, and she took him along with her. As the wind was very high, for fear of being blown away, she tied him to a thistle with a piece of fine thread. The cow soon observed Tom's oak-leaf hat, and liking the appearance of it, took poor Tom and the thistle at one mouthful. While the cow was chewing the thistle Tom was afraid of her great teeth, which threatened to crush him in pieces, and he roared out as loud as he could: "Mother, mother!"

"Where are you, Tommy, my dear Tommy?" said his mother.

"Here, mother," replied he, "in the red cow's mouth."

His mother began to cry and wring her hands; but the cow, surprised at the odd noise in her throat, opened her mouth and let Tom drop out. Fortunately his mother caught him in her apron as he was falling to the ground, or he would have been dreadfully hurt. She then put Tom in her bosom and ran home with him.

Tom's father made him a whip of a barley straw to drive the cattle with, and having one day gone into the fields, he slipped a foot and rolled into the furrow. A raven, which was flying over, picked him up, and flew with him over the sea, and there dropped him.

A large fish swallowed Tom the moment he fell into the sea, which was soon after caught, and bought for the table of King Arthur. When they opened the fish in order to cook it, every one was astonished at finding such a little boy, and Tom was quite delighted at being free again. They carried him to the king, who made Tom his dwarf, and he soon grew a great favourite at court; for by his tricks and gambols he not only amused the king and queen, but also all the Knights of the Round Table.

It is said that when the king rode out on horseback, he often took Tom along with him, and if a shower came on, he used to creep into his majesty's waistcoat-pocket, where he slept till the rain was over.

King Arthur one day asked Tom about his parents, wishing to know if they were as small as he was, and whether they were well off. Tom told the king that his father and mother were as tall as anybody about the court, but in rather poor circumstances. On hearing this, the king carried Tom to his treasury, the place where he kept all his money, and told him to take as much money as he could carry home to his parents, which made the poor little fellow caper with joy. Tom went immediately to procure a purse, which was made of a water-bubble, and then returned to the treasury, where he received a silver threepenny-piece to put into it.

Our little hero had some difficulty in lifting the burden upon his back; but he at last succeeded in getting it placed to his mind, and set forward on his journey. However, without meeting with any accident, and after resting himself more than a hundred times by the way, in two days and two nights he reached his father's house in safety.

Tom had travelled forty-eight hours with a huge silver-piece on his back, and was almost tired to death, when his mother ran out to meet him, and carried him into the house. But he soon returned to Court.

As Tom's clothes had suffered much in the batter-pudding, and the inside of the fish, his majesty ordered him a new suit of clothes, and to be mounted as a knight on a mouse.

> Of Butterfly's wings his shirt was made,
>   His boots of chicken's hide;
> And by a nimble fairy blade,
> Well learnèd in the tailoring trade,
>   His clothing was supplied.
> A needle dangled by his side;
> A dapper mouse he used to ride,
> Thus strutted Tom in stately pride!

It was certainly very diverting to see Tom in this dress and mounted on the mouse, as he rode out a-hunting with the king and nobility, who were all ready to expire with laughter at Tom and his fine prancing charger.

The king was so charmed with his address that he ordered a little chair to be made, in order that Tom might sit upon his table, and also a palace of gold, a span high, with a door an inch wide, to live in. He also gave him a coach, drawn by six small mice.

The queen was so enraged at the honours conferred on Sir Thomas that she resolved to ruin him, and told the king that the little knight had been saucy to her.

The king sent for Tom in great haste, but being fully aware of the danger of royal anger, he crept into an empty snail-shell, where he lay for a long time until he was almost starved with hunger; but at last he ventured to peep out, and seeing a fine large butterfly on the ground, near the place of his concealment, he got close to it and jumping astride on it, was carried up into the air. The butterfly flew with him from tree to tree and from field to field, and at last returned to the court, where the king and nobility all strove to catch him; but at last poor Tom fell from his seat into a watering-pot, in which he was almost drowned.

When the queen saw him she was in a rage, and said he should be beheaded; and he was again put into a mouse trap until the time of his execution.

However a cat, observing something alive in the trap, patted it about till the wires broke, and set Thomas at liberty.

The king received Tom again into favour, which he did not live to enjoy, for a large spider one day attacked him; and although he drew his sword and fought well, yet the spider's poisonous breath at last overcame him.

> He fell dead on the ground where he stood,
> And the spider suck'd every drop of his blood.

King Arthur and his whole court were so sorry at the loss of their little favourite that they went into mourning and raised a fine white marble monument over his grave with the following epitaph:

> Here lies Tom Thumb, King Arthur's knight,
> Who died by a spider's cruel bite.
> He was well known in Arthur's court,
> Where he afforded gallant sport;
> He rode at tilt and tournament,
> And on a mouse a-hunting went.
> Alive he filled the court with mirth;
> His death to sorrow soon gave birth.
> Wipe, wipe your eyes, and shake your head
> And cry,—Alas! Tom Thumb is dead!

❧ *Mr. Fox* ❧

LADY Mary was young, and Lady Mary was fair. She had two brothers, and more lovers than she could count. But of them all, the bravest and most gallant, was a Mr. Fox, whom she met when she was down at her father's country-house. No one knew who Mr. Fox was; but he was certainly brave, and surely rich, and of all her lovers, Lady Mary cared for him alone. At last it was agreed upon between them that they should be married. Lady Mary asked Mr. Fox where they should live, and he described to her his castle, and where it was; but, strange to say, did not ask her, or her brothers to come and see it.

So one day, near the wedding-day, when her brothers were out, and Mr. Fox was away for a day or two on business, as he said, Lady Mary set out for Mr. Fox's castle. And after many searchings, she came at last to it, and a fine strong house it was, with high walls and a deep moat. And when she came up to the gateway she saw written on it:

Be bold, be bold.

But as the gate was open, she went through it, and found no one there. So she went up to the doorway, and over it she found written:

Be bold, be bold, but not too bold.

Still she went on, till she came into the hall, and went up the broad stairs till she came to a door in the gallery, over which was written:

Be bold, be bold, but not too bold,
Lest that your heart's blood should run cold.

But Lady Mary was a brave one, she was, and she opened the door, and what do you think she saw? Why, bodies and skeletons of beautiful young ladies all stained with blood. So Lady Mary thought it was high time to get out of that horrid place, and she closed the door, went through the gallery, and was just going down the stairs, and out of the hall, when who should she see through the window, but Mr. Fox dragging a beautiful young lady along from the gateway to the door. Lady Mary rushed downstairs, and hid herself behind a cask, just in time, as Mr. Fox came in with the poor young lady who seemed to have fainted. Just as he got near Lady Mary, Mr. Fox saw a diamond ring glittering on the finger of the young lady he was dragging, and he tried to pull it off. But it was tightly fixed, and would not come off, so Mr. Fox cursed and swore, and drew his sword, raised it, and brought it down upon the hand of the poor lady. The sword cut off the hand, which jumped up into the air, and fell of all places in the world into Lady Mary's lap. Mr. Fox looked about a bit, but did not think of looking behind the cask, so at last he went on dragging the young lady up the stairs into the Bloody Chamber.

As soon as she heard him pass through the gallery, Lady Mary crept out of the door, down through the gateway, and ran home as fast as she could.

Now it happened that the very next day the marriage contract of Lady Mary and Mr. Fox was to be signed, and there was a splendid breakfast before that. And when Mr. Fox was seated at table opposite Lady Mary, he looked at her. "How pale you are this morning, my dear." "Yes," said she, "I had a bad night's rest last night. I had horrible dreams." "Dreams go by contraries," said Mr. Fox; "but tell us your dream, and your sweet voice will make the time pass till the happy hour comes."

"I dreamed," said Lady Mary, "that I went yestermorn to your castle, and I found it in the woods, with high walls, and a deep moat, and over the gateway was written:

Be bold, be bold.

"But it is not so, nor it was not so," said Mr. Fox.
"And when I came to the doorway over it was written:

Be bold, be bold, but not too bold.

"It is not so, nor it was not so," said Mr. Fox.
"And then I went upstairs, and came to a gallery, at the end of which was a door, on which was written:

Be bold, be bold, but not too bold,
Lest that your heart's blood should run cold.

"It is not so, nor it was not so," said Mr. Fox.
"And then—and then I opened the door, and the room was filled with bodies and skeletons of poor dead women, all stained with their blood."
"It is not so, nor it was not so. And God forbid it should be so," said Mr. Fox.
"I then dreamed that I rushed down the gallery, and just as I was going down the stairs, I saw you, Mr. Fox, coming up to the hall door, dragging after you a poor young lady, rich and beautiful."
"It is not so, nor it was not so. And God forbid it should be so," said Mr. Fox.
"I rushed downstairs, just in time to hide myself behind a cask, when you, Mr. Fox, came in dragging the young lady by the arm. And, as you passed me, Mr. Fox, I thought I saw you try and get off her diamond ring, and when you could not, Mr. Fox, it seemed to me in my dream, that you out with your sword and hacked off the poor lady's hand to get the ring."
"It is not so, nor it was not so. And God forbid it should be so," said Mr. Fox, and was going to say something else as he rose from his seat, when Lady Mary cried out:
"But it is so, and it was so. Here's hand and ring I have to show," and pulled out the lady's hand from her dress, and pointed it straight at Mr. Fox.
At once her brothers and her friends drew their swords and cut Mr. Fox into a thousand pieces.

Mister Fox

↳ *Lazy Jack* ↲

ONCE upon a time there was a boy whose name was Jack, and he lived with his mother on a common. They were very poor, and the old woman

got her living by spinning, but Jack was so lazy that he would do nothing but bask in the sun in the hot weather, and sit by the corner of the hearth in the winter-time. So they called him lazy Jack. His mother could not get him to do anything for her, and at last told him, one Monday, that if he did not begin to work for his porridge she would turn him out to get his living as he could.

This roused Jack, and he went out and hired himself for the next day to a neighbouring farmer for a penny; but as he was coming home, never having had any money before, he lost it in passing over a brook. "You stupid boy," said his mother, "you should have put it in your pocket." "I'll do so another time," replied Jack.

On Wednesday, Jack went out again and hired himself to a cowkeeper, who gave him a jar of milk for his day's work. Jack took the jar and put it into the large pocket of his jacket, spilling it all, long before he got home. "Dear me!" said the old woman; "you should have carried it on your head." "I'll do so another time," said Jack.

So on Thursday, Jack hired himself again to a farmer, who agreed to give him a cream cheese for his services. In the evening Jack took the cheese, and went home with it on his head. By the time he got home the cheese was all spoilt, part of it being lost, and part matted with his hair. "You stupid lout," said his mother, "you should have carried it very carefully in your hands." "I'll do so another time," replied Jack.

On Friday, Lazy Jack again went out, and hired himself to a baker, who would give him nothing for his work but a large tom-cat. Jack took the cat, and began carrying it very carefully in his hands, but in a short time pussy scratched him so much that he was compelled to let it go. When he got home, his mother said to him, "You silly fellow, you should have tied it with a string, and dragged it along after you." "I'll do so another time," said Jack.

So on Saturday, Jack hired himself to a butcher, who rewarded him by the handsome present of a shoulder of mutton. Jack took the mutton, tied it to a string, and trailed it along after him in the dirt, so that by the time he had got home the meat was completely spoilt. His mother was this time quite out of patience with him, for the next day was Sunday, and she was obliged to do with cabbage for her dinner. "You ninney-hammer," said she to her son; "you should have carried it on your shoulder." "I'll do so another time," replied Jack.

On the next Monday, Lazy Jack went once more, and hired himself to a cattle-keeper, who gave him a donkey for his trouble. Jack found it hard to hoist the donkey on his shoulders, but at last he did it, and began walking slowly home with his prize. Now it happened that in the course of his journey there lived a rich man with his only daughter, a beautiful girl, but deaf and dumb. Now she had never laughed in her life, and the doctors said she would never speak till somebody made her laugh. This young lady happened to be looking out of the window when Jack was passing with the donkey on his shoulders, with the legs sticking up in the air, and the sight was so comical and strange that she burst out into a great fit of laughter, and immediately recovered her speech and hearing. Her father was overjoyed, and fulfilled his promise by marrying her to Lazy Jack, who was thus made a rich gentleman. They lived in a large house, and Jack's mother lived with them in great happiness until she died.

ꙮ Johnny-Cake ꙮ

ONCE upon a time there was an old man, and an old woman, and a little boy. One morning the old woman made a Johnny-cake, and put it in the oven to bake. "You watch the Johnny-cake while your father and I go out to work in the garden." So the old man and the old woman went out and began to hoe potatoes, and left the little boy to tend the oven. But he didn't watch it all the time, and all of a sudden he heard a noise, and he looked up and the oven door popped open, and out of the oven jumped Johnny-cake, and went rolling along end over end, towards the open door of the house. The little boy ran to shut the door,

but Johnny-cake was too quick for him and rolled through the door, down the steps, and out into the road long before the little boy could catch him. The little boy ran after him as fast as he could clip it, crying out to his father and mother, who heard the uproar, and threw down their hoes and gave chase too. But Johnny-cake outran all three a long way, and was soon out of sight, while they had to sit down, all out of breath, on a bank to rest.

On went Johnny-cake, and by-and-by he came to two well-diggers who looked up from their work and called out: "Where ye going, Johnny-cake?"

He said: "I've outrun an old man, and an old woman, and a little boy, and I can outrun you too-o-o!"

"Ye can, can ye? we'll see about that?" said they; and they threw down their picks and ran after him, but couldn't catch up with him, and soon they had to sit down by the roadside to rest.

On ran Johnny-cake, and by-and-by he came to two ditch-diggers who were digging a ditch. "Where ye going, Johnny-cake?" said they. He said: "I've outrun an old man, and an old woman, and a little boy, and two well-diggers, and I can outrun you too-o-o!"

"Ye can, can ye? we'll see about that!" said they; and they threw down their spades, and ran after him too. But Johnny-cake soon outstripped them also, and seeing they could never catch him, they gave up the chase and sat down to rest.

On went Johnny-cake, and by-and-by he came to a bear. The bear said: "Where are ye going, Johnny-cake?"

He said: "I've outrun an old man, and an old woman, and a little boy, and two well-diggers, and two ditch-diggers, and I can outrun you too-o-o!"

"Ye can, can ye?" growled the bear, "we'll see about that!" and trotted as fast as his legs could carry him after Johnny-cake, who never stopped to look behind him. Before long the bear was left so far behind that he saw he might as well give up the hunt first as last, so he stretched himself out by the roadside to rest.

On went Johnny-cake, and by-and-by he came to a wolf. The wolf said: "Where ye going, Johnny-cake?" He said: I've outrun an old man, and an old woman, and a little boy, and two well-diggers, and two ditch-diggers and a bear, and I can outrun you too-o-o!"

"Ye can, can ye?" snarled the wolf, "we'll see about that!" And he set into a gallop after Johnny-cake, who went on and on so fast that the wolf too saw there was no hope of overtaking him, and he too lay down to rest.

On went Johnny-cake, and by-and-by he came to a fox that lay quietly in a corner of the fence. The fox called out in a sharp voice, but without getting up: "Where ye going Johnny-cake?"

He said: "I've outrun an old man, and an old woman, and a little boy, and two well-diggers, and two ditch-diggers, a bear, and a wolf, and I can outrun you too-o-o!"

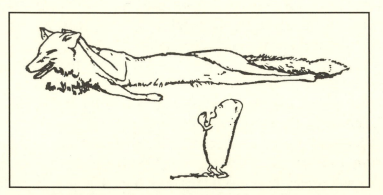

The fox said: "I can't quite hear you, Johnny-cake, won't you come a little closer?" turning his head a little to one side.

Johnny-cake stopped his race for the first time, and went a little closer, and called out in a very loud voice: "*I've outrun an old man, and an old woman, and a little boy, and two well-diggers, and two ditch-diggers, and a bear, and a wolf, and I can outrun you too-o-o.*"

"Can't quite hear you; won't you come a *little* closer?" said the fox in a feeble voice, as he stretched out his neck towards Johnny-cake, and put one paw behind his ear.

Johnny-cake came up close, and leaning towards the fox screamed out: I'VE OUTRUN AN OLD MAN, AND AN OLD WOMAN, AND A LITTLE BOY, AND TWO WELL-DIGGERS, AND TWO DITCH-DIGGERS, AND A BEAR, AND A WOLF, AND I CAN OUTRUN YOU TOO-O-O!"

"You can, can you?" yelped the fox, and he snapped up the Johnny-cake in his sharp teeth in the twinkling of an eye.

✒ Earl Mar's Daughter ✒

ONE fine summer's day Earl Mar's daughter went into the castle garden, dancing and tripping along. And as she played and sported she would stop from time to time to listen to the music of the birds. After a while as she sat under the shade of a green oak tree she looked up and spied a sprightly dove sitting high up on one of its branches.

She looked up and said: "Coo-my-dove, my dear, come down to me and I will give you a golden cage. I'll take you home and pet you well, as well as any bird of them all." Scarcely had she said these words when the dove flew down from the branch and settled on her shoulder, nestling up against her neck while she smoothed its feathers. Then she took it home to her own room.

The day was done and the night came on and Earl Mar's daughter was thinking of going to sleep when, turning round, she found at her side a handsome young man. She *was* startled, for the door had been locked for hours. But she was a brave girl and said: "What are you doing here, young man, to come and startle me so? The door was barred these hours ago; how ever did you come here?"

"Hush! hush!" the young man whispered. "I was that cooing dove that you coaxed from off the tree."

"But who are you then?" she said quite low; "and how came you to be changed into that dear little bird?"

"My name is Florentine, and my mother is a queen, and something more than a queen, for she knows magic and spells, and because I would not do as she wished she turned me into a dove by day, but at night her spells lose their power and I become a man again. To-day I crossed the sea and saw you for the first time and I was glad to be a bird that I could come near you. Unless you love me, I shall never be happy more."

"But if I love you," says she, "will you not fly away and leave me one of these fine days?"

"Never, never," said the prince; "be my wife and I'll be yours for ever. By day a bird, by night a prince, I will always be by your side as a husband, dear."

So they were married in secret and lived happily in the castle and no one knew that every night Coo-my-dove became Prince Florentine. And every year a little son came to them as bonny as bonny could be. But as each son was born Prince Florentine carried the little thing away on his back over the sea to where the queen his mother lived and left the little one with her.

Seven years passed thus and then a great trouble came to them. For the Earl Mar wished to marry his daughter to a noble of high degree who came wooing her. Her father pressed her sore but she said: "Father dear I do not wish to marry; I can be quite happy with Coo-my-dove here."

Then her father got into a mighty rage and swore a great big oath, and said: "To-morrow, so sure as I live and eat, I'll twist that birdie's neck," and out he stamped from her room.

"Oh, oh!" said Coo-my-dove; "it's time that I was away," and so he jumped upon the window-sill and in a moment was flying away. And he flew and he flew till he was over the deep, deep sea, and yet on he flew till he came to his mother's castle. Now the queen his mother was taking her walk abroad when she saw the pretty dove flying overhead and alighting on the castle walls.

"Here, dancers come and dance your jigs," she called, "and pipers, pipe you well, for here's my own Florentine, come back to me to stay for he's brought no bonny boy with him this time."

"No, mother," said Florentine, "no dancers for me and no minstrels, for my dear wife, the mother of my seven boys, is to be wed to-morrow, and sad's the day for me."

"What can I do, my son?" said the queen, "tell me and it shall be done if my magic has power to do it."

"Well then, mother dear, turn the twenty-four dancers and pipers into twenty-four grey herons, and let my seven sons become seven white swans, and let me be a goshawk and their leader."

"Alas! alas! my son," she said, "that may not be; my magic reaches not so far. But perhaps my teacher, the spaewife of Ostree, may know better." And away she hurries to the cave of Ostree, and after a while comes out as white as white can be and muttering over some burning herbs she brought out of the cave. Suddenly Coo-my-dove changed into a goshawk and around him flew twenty-four grey herons and above them flew seven cygnets.

Without a word or a good-bye off they flew over the deep blue sea which was tossing and moaning. They flew and they flew till they swooped down on Earl Mar's castle just as the wedding party were setting out for the church. First came the men-at-arms and then the bridegroom's friends, and then Earl Mar's men, and then the bridegroom, and lastly, pale and beautiful, Earl Mar's daughter herself. They moved down slowly to stately music till they came past the trees on which the birds were settling. A word from Prince Florentine, the goshawk, and they all rose into the air, herons beneath, cygnets above, and goshawk circling above all. The weddineers wondered at the sight when, swoop! the herons were down among them scattering the men-at-arms. The swanlets took charge of the bride while the goshawk dashed down and tied the bridegroom to a tree. Then the herons gathered themselves together into one feather bed and the cygnets placed their mother upon them, and suddenly they all rose in the air bearing the bride away with them in safety towards Prince Florentine's home. Surely a wedding party was never so disturbed in this world. What could the weddineers do? They saw their pretty bride carried away and away till she and the herons and the swans and the goshawk disappeared, and that very day Prince Florentine brought Earl Mar's daughter to the castle of the queen his mother, who took the spell off him and they lived happy ever afterwards.

↤ Mr. Miacca ↦

TOMMY GRIMES was sometimes a good boy, and sometimes a bad boy; and when he was a bad boy, he was a very bad boy. Now his mother used to say to him: "Tommy, Tommy, be a good boy, and don't go out of the street, or else Mr. Miacca will take you." But still when he was a bad boy he would go out of the street; and one day, sure enough, he had scarcely got round the corner, when Mr. Miacca did catch him and popped him into a bag upside down, and took him off to his house.

When Mr. Miacca got Tommy inside, he pulled him out of the bag and set him down, and felt his arms and legs. "You're rather tough," says he; "but you're all I've got for supper, and you'll not taste bad boiled. But body o' me, I've forgot the herbs, and it's bitter you'll taste without herbs. Sally! Here, I say, Sally!" and he called Mrs. Miacca.

So Mrs. Miacca came out of another room and said: "What d'ye want, my dear?"

"Oh, here's a little boy for supper," said Mr. Miacca, "and I've forgot the herbs. Mind him, will ye, while I go for them."

"All right, my love," says Mrs. Miacca, and off he goes.

Then Tommy Grimes said to Mrs. Miacca: "Does Mr. Miacca always have little boys for supper?"

"Mostly, my dear," said Mrs. Miacca, "if little boys are bad enough, and get in his way."

"And don't you have anything else but boy-meat? No pudding?" asked Tommy.

"Ah, I loves pudding," says Mrs. Miacca. "But it's not often the likes of me gets pudding."

"Why, my mother is making a pudding this very day," said Tommy Grimes, "and I am sure she'd give you some, if I ask her. Shall I run and get some?"

"Now, that's a thoughtful boy," said Mrs. Miacca, "only don't be long and be sure to be back for supper."

So off Tommy pelters, and right glad he was to get off so cheap; and for many a long day he was as good as good could be, and never went round the corner of the street. But he couldn't always be good; and one day he went round the corner, and as luck would have it, he hadn't scarcely got round it when Mr. Miacca grabbed him up, popped him in his bag, and took him home.

When he got him there, Mr. Miacca dropped him out; and when he saw him, he said: "Ah, you're the youngster what served me and my missus that shabby trick, leaving us without any supper. Well, you shan't do it again. I'll watch over you myself. Here, get under the sofa, and I'll set on it and watch the pot boil for you."

So poor Tommy Grimes had to creep under the sofa, and Mr. Miacca sate on it and waited for the pot to boil. And they waited, and they waited, but still the pot didn't boil, till at last Mr. Miacca got tired of waiting, and he said: "Here, you under there, I'm not going to wait any longer; put out your leg, and I'll stop your giving us the slip."

So Tommy put out a leg, and Mr. Miacca got a chopper, and chopped it off, and pops it in the pot.

Suddenly he calls out: "Sally, my dear, Sally!" and nobody answered. So he went into the next room to look out for Mrs. Miacca, and while he was there, Tommy crept out from under the sofa and ran out of the door. For it was a leg of the sofa that he had put out.

So Tommy Grimes ran home, and he never went round the corner again till he was old enough to go alone.

✑ Whittington and his Cat ✑

IN the reign of the famous King Edward III. there was a little boy called Dick Whittington, whose father and mother died when he was very young. As poor Dick was not old enough to work, he was very badly off; he got but little for his dinner, and sometimes nothing at all for his breakfast; for the people who lived in the village were very poor indeed, and could not spare him much more than the parings of potatoes, and now and then a hard crust of bread.

Now Dick had heard a great many very strange things about the great city called London; for the country people at that time thought that folks in London were all fine gentlemen and ladies; and that there was singing and music there all day long; and that the streets were all paved with gold.

One day a large waggon and eight horses, all with bells at their heads, drove through the village while Dick was standing by the sign-post. He thought that this waggon must be going to the fine town of London; so he took courage, and asked the waggoner to let him walk with him by the side of the waggon. As soon as the waggoner heard that poor Dick had no father or mother, and saw by his ragged clothes that he could not be worse off than he was, he told him he might go if he would, so off they set together.

So Dick got safe to London, and was in such a hurry to see the fine streets paved all over with gold, that he did not even stay to thank the kind waggoner; but ran off as fast as his legs would carry him, through many of the streets, thinking every moment to come to those that were paved with gold; for Dick had seen a guinea three times in his own little village, and remembered what a deal of money it brought in change; so he thought he had nothing to do but to take up some little bits of the pavement, and should then have as much money as he could wish for.

Poor Dick ran till he was tired, and had quite forgot his friend the waggoner; but at last, finding it grow dark, and that every way he turned he saw nothing but dirt instead of gold, he sat down in a dark corner and cried himself to sleep.

Little Dick was all night in the streets; and next morning, being very hungry, he got up and walked about, and asked everybody he met to give him a halfpenny to keep him from starving; but nobody stayed to answer him, and only two or three gave him a halfpenny; so that the poor boy was soon quite weak and faint for the want of victuals.

In this distress he asked charity of several people, and one of them said crossly: "Go to work for an idle rogue." "That I will," says Dick, "I will to go work for you, if you will let me." But the man only cursed at him and went on.

At last a good-natured looking gentleman saw how hungry he looked. "Why don't you go to work my lad?" said he to Dick. "That I would, but I do not know how to get any," answered Dick. "If you are willing, come along with me," said the gentleman, and took him to a hay-field, where Dick worked briskly, and lived merrily till the hay was made.

After this he found himself as badly off as before; and being almost starved again, he laid himself down at the door of Mr. Fitzwarren, a rich merchant. Here he was soon seen by the cook-maid, who was an ill-tempered creature, and happened just then to be very busy dressing dinner for her master and mistress; so she called out to poor Dick: "What business have you there, you lazy rogue? there is nothing else but beggars; if you do not take yourself away, we will see how you will like a sousing of some dish-water; I have some here hot enough to make you jump."

Just at that time Mr. Fitzwarren himself came home to dinner; and when he saw a dirty ragged boy lying at the door, he said to him: "Why do you lie there, my boy? You seem old enough to work; I am afraid you are inclined to be lazy."

"No, indeed, sir," said Dick to him, "that is not the case, for I would work with all my heart, but I do not know anybody, and I believe I am very sick for the want of food."

"Poor fellow, get up; let me see what ails you."

Dick now tried to rise, but was obliged to lie down again, being too weak to stand, for he had not eaten any food for three days, and was no longer able to run about and beg a halfpenny of people in the street. So the kind merchant ordered him to be taken into the house, and have a good dinner given him, and be kept to do what work he was able to do for the cook.

Little Dick would have lived very happy in this good family if it had not been for the ill-natured cook. She used to say: "You are under me, so look sharp; clean the spit and the dripping-pan, make the fires, wind up the jack, and do all the scullery work nimbly, or——" and she would shake the ladle at him. Besides, she was so fond of basting, that when she had no meat to baste, she would baste poor Dick's head and shoulders with a broom, or anything else that happened to fall in her way. At last her ill-usage of him was told to Alice, Mr. Fitzwarren's daughter, who told the cook she should be turned away if she did not treat him kinder.

The behaviour of the cook was now a little better; but besides this Dick had another hardship to get over. His bed stood in a garret, where there were so many holes in the floor and the walls that every night he was tormented with rats and mice. A gentleman having given Dick a penny for cleaning his shoes, he thought he would buy a cat with it. The next day he saw a girl with a cat, and asked her, "Will you let me have that cat for a penny?" The girl said: "Yes, that I will, master, though she is an excellent mouser."

Dick hid his cat in the garret, and always took care to carry a part of his dinner to her; and in a short time he had no more trouble with the rats and mice, but slept quite sound every night.

Soon after this, his master had a ship ready to sail; and as it was the custom that all his servants should have some chance for good fortune as well as himself, he called them all into the parlour and asked them what they would send out.

They all had something that they were willing to venture except poor Dick, who had neither money nor goods, and therefore could send nothing. For this reason he did not come into the parlour with the rest; but Miss Alice guessed what was the matter, and ordered him to be called in. She then said: "I will lay down some money for him, from my own purse;" but her father told her: "This will not do, for it must be something of his own."

When poor Dick heard this, he said: "I have nothing but a cat which I bought for a penny some time since of a little girl."

"Fetch your cat then, my lad," said Mr. Fitzwarren, "and let her go."

Dick went upstairs and brought down poor puss, with tears in his eyes, and gave her to the captain; "For," he said, "I shall now be kept awake all night by the rats and mice." All the company laughed at Dick's odd venture; and Miss Alice, who felt pity for him, gave him some money to buy another cat.

This, and many other marks of kindness shown him by Miss Alice, made the ill-tempered cook jealous of poor Dick, and she began to use him more cruelly than ever, and always made game of him for sending his cat to sea. She asked him: "Do you think your cat will sell for as much money as would buy a stick to beat you?"

At last poor Dick could not bear this usage any longer, and he thought he would run away from his place; so he packed up his few things, and started very early in the morning, on All-hallows Day, the first of November. He walked as far as Holloway; and there sat down on a stone, which to this day is called "Whittington's Stone," and began to think to himself which road he should take.

While he was thinking what he should do, the Bells of Bow Church, which at that time were only six, began to ring, and their sound seemed to say to him:

"Turn again, Whittington,
Thrice Lord Mayor of London."

"Lord Mayor of London!" said he to himself. "Why, to be sure, I would put up with almost anything now, to be Lord Mayor of London, and ride in a fine coach, when I grow to be a man! Well, I will go back, and think nothing of the cuffing and scolding of the old cook, if I am to be Lord Mayor of London at last."

Dick went back, and was lucky enough to get into the house, and set about his work, before the old cook came downstairs.

We must now follow Miss Puss to the coast of Africa. The ship with the cat on board, was a long time at sea; and was at last driven by the winds on a part of the coast of Barbary, where the only people were the Moors, unknown to the English. The people came in great numbers to see the sailors, because they were of different colour to themselves, and treated them civilly; and, when they became better acquainted, were very eager to buy the fine things that the ship was loaded with.

When the captain saw this, he sent patterns of the best things he had to the king of the country; who was so much pleased with them, that he sent for the captain to the palace. Here they were placed, as it is the custom of the country, on rich carpets flowered with gold and silver. The king and queen were seated at the upper end of the room; and a number of dishes were brought in for dinner. They had not sat long, when a vast number of rats and mice rushed in, and devoured all the meat in an instant. The captain wondered at this, and asked if these vermin were not unpleasant.

"Oh yes," said they, "very offensive; and the king would give half his treasure to be freed of them, for they not only destroy his dinner, as you see, but they assault him in his chamber, and even in bed, and so that he is obliged to be watched while he is sleeping, for fear of them."

The captain jumped for joy; he remembered poor Whittington and his cat, and told the king he had a creature on board the ship that would despatch all these vermin immediately. The king jumped so high at the joy which the news gave him, that his turban dropped off his head. "Bring this creature to me," says he; "vermin are dreadful in a court, and if she will perform what you say, I will load your ship with gold and jewels in exchange for her."

The captain, who knew his business, took this opportunity to set forth the merits of Miss Puss. He told his majesty: "It is not very convenient to part with her, as, when she is gone, the rats and mice may destroy the goods in the ship—but to oblige your majesty, I will fetch her."

"Run, run!" said the queen; "I am impatient to see the dear creature."

Away went the captain to the ship, while another dinner was got ready. He put Puss under his arm, and arrived at the place just in time to see the table full of rats. When the cat saw them, she did not wait for bidding, but jumped out of the captain's arms, and in a few minutes laid almost all the rats and mice dead at her feet. The rest of them in their fright scampered away to their holes.

The king was quite charmed to get rid so easily of such plagues, and the queen desired that the creature who had done them so great a kindness might be brought to her, that she might look at her. Upon which the captain called: "Pussy, pussy, pussy!" and she came to him. He then presented her to the queen, who started back, and was afraid to touch a creature who had made such a havoc among the rats and mice. However, when the captain stroked the cat and called: "Pussy, pussy," the queen also touched her and cried: "Putty, putty," for she had not learned English. He then put her down on the queen's lap, where she purred and played with her majesty's hand, and then purred herself to sleep.

The king, having seen the exploits of Mrs. Puss, and being informed that her kittens would stock the whole country, and keep it free from rats, bargained with the captain for the whole ship's cargo, and then gave him ten times as much for the cat as all the rest amounted to.

The captain then took leave of the royal party, and set sail with a fair wind for England, and after a happy voyage arrived safe in London.

One morning, early, Mr. Fitzwarren had just come to his counting-house and seated himself at the desk, to count over the cash, and settle the business for the day, when somebody came tap, tap, at the door. "Who's there?" said Mr. Fitzwarren. "A friend," answered the other; "I come to bring you news of your ship *Unicorn*." The merchant, bustling up in such a hurry that he forgot his gout, opened the door, and who should he see waiting but the captain and factor, with a cabinet of jewels, and a bill of lading; when he looked at this the merchant lifted up his eyes and thanked Heaven for sending him such a prosperous voyage.

They then told the story of the cat, and showed the rich present that the king and queen had sent for her to poor Dick. As soon as the merchant heard this, he called out to his servants:

"Go send him in, and tell him of his fame;
Pray call him Mr. Whittington by name."

Mr. Fitzwarren now showed himself to be a good man; for when some of his servants said so great a treasure was too much for him, he answered: "God forbid I should deprive him of the value of a single penny, it is his own, and he shall have it to a farthing."

He then sent for Dick, who at that time was scouring pots for the cook, and was quite dirty. He would have excused himself from coming into the counting-house, saying, "The room is swept, and my shoes are dirty and full of hob-nails." But the merchant ordered him to come in.

Mr. Fitzwarren ordered a chair to be set for him, and so he began to think they were making game of him, at the same time said to them: "Do not play tricks with a poor simple boy, but let me go down again, if you please, to my work."

"Indeed, Mr. Whittington," said the merchant, "we are all quite in earnest with you, and I most heartily rejoice in the news that these gentlemen have brought you; for the captain has sold your cat to the King of Barbary, and brought you in return for her more riches than I possess in the whole world; and I wish you may long enjoy them!"

Mr. Fitzwarren then told the men to open the great treasure they had brought with them; and said: "Mr. Whittington has nothing to do but to put it in some place of safety."

Poor Dick hardly knew how to behave himself for joy. He begged his master to take what part of it he pleased, since he owed it all to his kindness. "No, no," answered Mr. Fitzwarren, "this is all your own; and I have no doubt but you will use it well."

Dick next asked his mistress, and then Miss Alice, to accept a part of his good fortune; but they would not, and at the same time told him they felt great joy at his good success. But this poor fellow was too kind-hearted to keep it all to himself; so he made a present to the captain, the mate, and the rest of Mr. Fitzwarren's servants; and even to the ill-natured old cook.

After this Mr. Fitzwarren advised him to send for a proper tailor and get himself dressed like a gentleman; and told him he was welcome to live in his house till he could provide himself with a better.

When Whittington's face was washed, his hair curled, his hat cocked, and he was dressed in a nice suit of clothes he was as handsome and genteel as any young man who visited at Mr. Fitzwarren's; so that Miss Alice, who had once been so kind to him, and thought of him with pity, now looked upon him as fit to be her sweetheart; and the more so, no doubt, because Whittington was now always thinking what he could do to oblige her, and making her the prettiest presents that could be.

Mr. Fitzwarren soon saw their love for each other, and proposed to join them in marriage; and to this they both readily agreed. A day for the wedding was soon fixed; and they were attended to church by the Lord Mayor, the court of aldermen, the sheriffs, and a great number of the richest merchants in London, whom they afterwards treated with a very rich feast.

History tells us that Mr. Whittington and his lady lived in great splendour, and were very happy. They had several children. He was Sheriff of London, thrice Lord Mayor, and received the honour of knighthood by Henry V.

He entertained this king and his queen at dinner after his conquest of France so grandly, that the king said: "Never had prince such a subject"; when Sir Richard heard this, he said: "Never had subject such a prince."

The figure of Sir Richard Whittington with his cat in his arms, carved in stone, was to be seen till the year 1780 over the archway of the old prison of Newgate, which he built for criminals.

✄ *The Strange Visitor* ✄

A WOMAN was sitting at her reel one night;
   And still she sat, and still she reeled, and still she wished for
     company.

In came a pair of broad broad soles, and sat down at the fireside;
   And still she sat, and still she reeled, and still she wished for
     company.

In came a pair of small small legs, and sat down on the broad broad soles;
  And still she sat, and still she reeled, and still she wished for company.

In came a pair of thick thick knees, and sat down on the small small legs;
  And still she sat, and still she reeled, and still she wished for company.

In came a pair of thin thin thighs, and sat down on the thick thick knees;
  And still she sat, and still she reeled, and still she wished for company.

In came a pair of huge huge hips, and sat down on the thin thin thighs;
  And still she sat, and still she reeled, and still she wished for company.

In came a wee wee waist, and sat down on the huge huge hips;
  And still she sat, and still she reeled, and still she wished for company.

In came a pair of broad broad shoulders, and sat down on the wee wee waist;
  And still she sat, and still she reeled, and still she wished for company.

In came a pair of small small arms, and sat down on the broad broad shoulders;
  And still she sat, and still she reeled, and still she wished for company.

In came a pair of huge huge hands, and sat down on the small small arms;
  And still she sat, and still she reeled, and still she wished for company.

In came a small small neck, and sat down on the broad broad shoulders;
  And still she sat, and still she reeled, and still she wished for company.

In came a huge huge head, and sat down on the small small neck.

"How did you get such broad broad feet?" quoth the woman.

"Much tramping, much tramping" (*gruffly*).

"How did you get such small small legs?"

"*Aih-h-h!*—late—and *wee-e-e*—moul" (*whiningly*).

"How did you get such thick thick knees?"

"Much praying, much praying" (*piously*).

"How did you get such thin thin thighs?"

"Aih-h-h!—late—and wee-e-e—moul" (*whiningly*).

"How did you get such big big hips?"

"Much sitting, much sitting" (*gruffly*).

"How did you get such a wee wee waist?"

"Aih-h-h!—late—and wee-e-e—moul" (*whiningly*).

"How did you get such broad broad shoulders?"

"With carrying broom, with carrying broom" (*gruffly*).

"How did you get such small small arms?"

"Aih-h-h!—late—and wee-e-e—moul" (*whiningly*).

"How did you get such huge huge hands?"

"Threshing with an iron flail, threshing with an iron flail" (*gruffly*).

"How did you get such a small small neck?"

"Aih-h-h!—late—wee-e-e—moul" (*pitifully*).

"How did you get such a huge huge head?"

"Much knowledge, much knowledge" (*keenly*).

"What do you come for?"

"FOR YOU!" (*At the top of the voice, with a wave of the arm and a stamp of the feet.*)

⌁ The Laidly Worm of Spindleston Heugh ⌁

IN Bamborough Castle once lived a king who had a fair wife and two children, a son named Childe Wynd and a daughter named Margaret. Childe Wynd went forth to seek his fortune, and soon after he had gone the queen his mother died. The king mourned her long and faithfully, but one day while he was hunting he came across a lady of great beauty, and became so much in love with her that he determined to marry her. So he sent word home that he was going to bring a new queen to Bamborough Castle.

Childe·Wynd·thrice·kisses·the
Laidly·Worm·&·rescues·his·Sister
the·Princess·Margaret·

The Laidly Worm of Spindleston Heugh

Princess Margaret was not very glad to hear of her mother's place being taken, but she did not repine but did her father's bidding. And at the appointed day came down to the castle gate with the keys all ready to hand over to her stepmother. Soon the procession drew near, and the new queen came towards Princess Margaret who bowed low and handed her the keys of the castle. She stood there with blushing cheeks and eye on ground, and said: "O welcome, father dear, to your halls and bowers, and welcome to you my new mother, for all that's here is yours," and again she offered the keys. One of the king's knights who had escorted the new queen, cried out in admiration: "Surely this northern Princess is the loveliest of her kind." At that the new queen flushed up and cried out: "At least your courtesy might have excepted me," and then she muttered below her breath: "I'll soon put an end to her beauty."

That same night the queen, who was a noted witch, stole down to a lonely dungeon wherein she did her magic and with spells three times three, and with passes nine times nine she cast Princess Margaret under her spell. And this was her spell:

> I weird ye to be a Laidly Worm,
>   And borrowed shall ye never be,
> Until Childe Wynd, the King's own son
>   Come to the Heugh and thrice kiss thee;
> Until the world comes to an end,
>   Borrowed shall ye never be.

So Lady Margaret went to bed a beauteous maiden, and rose up a Laidly Worm. And when her maidens came in to dress her in the morning they found coiled up on the bed a dreadful dragon, which uncoiled itself and came towards them. But they ran away shrinking, and the Laidly Worm crawled and crept, and crept and crawled till it reached the Heugh or rock of the Spindlestone, round which it coiled itself, and lay there basking with its terrible snout in the air.

Soon the country round about had reason to know of the Laidly Worm of Spindleston Heugh. For hunger drove the monster out from its cave and it used to devour everything it could come across. So at last they went to a mighty warlock and asked him what they should do. Then he consulted his works and his familiar, and told them: "The Laidly Worm is really the Princess Margaret and it is hunger that drives her forth to do such deeds. Put aside for her seven kine, and each day as the sun goes down, carry every drop of milk they yield to the stone trough at the foot of the Heugh, and the Laidly Worm will trouble the country no longer. But if ye would that she be borrowed to her natural shape, and that she who bespelled her be rightly punished, send over the seas for her brother, Childe Wynd."

All was done as the warlock advised, the Laidly Worm lived on the milk of the seven kine, and the country was troubled no longer. But when Childe Wynd heard the news, he swore a mighty oath to rescue his sister and revenge her on her cruel stepmother. And three-and-thirty of his men took the oath with him. Then they set to work and built a long ship, and its keel they made of the rowan tree. And when all was ready, they out with their oars and pulled sheer for Bamborough Keep.

But as they got near the keep, the stepmother felt by her magic power that something was being wrought against her, so she summoned her familiar imps and said: "Childe Wynd is coming over the seas; he must never land. Raise storms, or bore the hull, but nohow must he touch shore." Then the imps went forth to meet Childe Wynd's ship, but when they got near, they found they had no power over the ship, for its keel was made of the rowan tree. So back they came to the queen witch, who knew not what to do. She ordered her men-at-arms to resist Childe Wynd if he should land near them, and by her spells she caused the Laidly Worm to wait by the entrance of the harbour.

As the ship came near, the Worm unfolded its coils, and dipping into the sea, caught hold of the ship of Childe Wynd, and banged it off the shore. Three times Childe Wynd urged his men on to row bravely and strong, but each time the Laidly Worm kept it off the shore. Then Childe Wynd ordered the ship to be put about, and the witch-queen thought he had given up the attempt. But instead of that, he only rounded the next point and landed safe and sound in Budle Creek, and then, with sword drawn and bow bent, rushed up followed by his men, to fight the terrible Worm that had kept him from landing.

But the moment Childe Wynd had landed, the witch-queen's power over the Laidly Worm had gone, and she went back to her bower all alone, not an imp, nor a man-at-arms to help her, for she knew her hour was come. So when Childe Wynd came rushing up to the Laidly Worm it made no attempt to stop him or hurt him, but just as he was going to raise his sword to slay it, the voice of his own sister Margaret came from its jaws saying:

> "O, quit your sword, unbend your bow,
> And give me kisses three;
> For though I am a poisonous worm,
> No harm I'll do to thee."

Childe Wynd stayed his hand, but he did not know what to think if some witchery were not in it. Then said the Laidly Worm again:

> "O, quit your sword, unbend your bow,
> And give me kisses three,
> If I'm not won ere set of sun,
> Won never shall I be."

Then Childe Wynd went up to the Laidly Worm and kissed it once; but no change came over it. Then Childe Wynd kissed it once more; but yet no change came over it. For a third time he kissed the loathsome thing, and with a hiss and a roar the Laidly Worm reared back and before Childe Wynd stood his sister Margaret. He wrapped his cloak about her, and then went up to the castle with her. When he reached the keep, he went off to the witch queen's bower, and when he saw her, he touched her with a twig of a rowan tree. No sooner had he touched her than she shrivelled up and shrivelled up, till she became a huge ugly toad, with bold staring eyes and a horrible hiss. She croaked and she hissed, and then hopped away down the castle steps, and Childe Wynd took his father's place as king, and they all lived happy afterwards.

But to this day, the loathsome toad is seen at times, haunting the neighbourhood of Bamborough Keep, and the wicked witch-queen is a Laidly Toad.

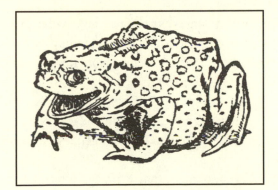

ঔ *The Cat and the Mouse* ঔ

The cat and the mouse
Play'd in the malt-house:

THE cat bit the mouse's tail off. "Pray, puss, give me my tail." "No," says the cat, "I'll not give you your tail, till you go to the cow, and fetch me some milk."

First she leapt and then she ran,
Till she came to the cow, and thus began:

"Pray, Cow, give me milk, that I may give cat milk, that cat may give me my own tail again." "No," said the cow, "I will give you no milk, till you go to the farmer and get me some hay."

First she leapt, and then she ran,
Till she came to the farmer and thus began:

"Pray, Farmer, give me hay, that I may give cow hay, that cow may give me milk, that I may give cat milk, that cat may give me my own tail again." "No," says the farmer, "I'll give you no hay, till you go to the butcher and fetch me some meat."

First she leapt, and then she ran,
Till she came to the butcher, and thus began:

"Pray, Butcher, give me meat, that I may give farmer meat, that farmer may give me hay, that I may give cow hay, that cow may give me milk, that I may give cat milk, that cat may give me my own tail again." "No," says the butcher, "I'll give you no meat, till you go to the baker and fetch me some bread."

> First she leapt and then she ran,
> Till she came to the baker, and thus began:

"Pray, Baker, give me bread, that I may give butcher bread, that butcher may give me meat, that I may give farmer meat, that farmer may give me hay, that I may give cow hay, that cow may give me milk, that I may give cat milk, that cat may give me my own tail again."

> "Yes," says the baker, "I'll give you some bread,
> But if you eat my meal, I'll cut off your head."

Then the baker gave mouse bread, and mouse gave butcher bread, and butcher gave mouse meat, and mouse gave farmer meat, and farmer gave mouse hay, and mouse gave cow hay, and cow gave mouse milk, and mouse gave cat milk, and cat gave mouse her own tail again!

ꕥ *The Fish and the Ring* ꕥ

ONCE upon a time, there was a mighty baron in the North Countrie who was a great magician that knew everything that would come to pass. So one day, when his little boy was four years old, he looked into the Book of Fate to see what would happen to him. And to his dismay, he found that his son would wed a lowly maid that had just been born in a house under the shadow of York Minster. Now the Baron knew the father of the little girl was very, very poor, and he had five children already. So he called for his horse, and rode into York, and passed by the father's house, and saw him sitting by the door, sad and doleful. So he dismounted and went up to him and said: "What is the matter, my good man?" And the man said: "Well, your honour, the fact is, I've five children already, and now a sixth's come, a little lass, and where to get the bread from to fill their mouths, that's more than I can say."

"Don't be downhearted, my man," said the Baron. "If that's your trouble, I can help you I'll take away the last little one, and you won't have to bother about her."

"Thank you kindly, sir," said the man; and he went in and brought out the lass and gave her to the Baron, who mounted his horse and rode away with her. And when he got by the bank of the river Ouse, he threw the little thing into the river, and rode off to his castle.

But the little lass didn't sink; her clothes kept her up for a time, and she floated, and she floated, till she was cast ashore just in front of a fisherman's hut. There the fisherman found her, and took pity on the poor little thing and took her into his house, and she lived there till she was fifteen years old, and a fine handsome girl.

One day it happened that the Baron went out hunting with some companions along the banks of the River Ouse, and stopped at the fisherman's hut to get a drink, and the girl came out to give it to them. They all noticed her beauty, and one of them said to the Baron: "You can read fates, Baron, whom will she marry, d'ye think?"

"Oh! that's easy to guess," said the Baron; "some yokel or other. But I'll cast her horoscope. Come here girl, and tell me on what day you were born?"

"I don't know, sir," said the girl, "I was picked up just here after having been brought down by the river about fifteen years ago."

Then the Baron knew who she was, and when they went away, he rode back and said to the girl: "Hark ye, girl, I will make your fortune. Take this letter to my brother in Scarborough, and you will be settled for life." And the girl took the letter and said she would go. Now this was what he had written in the letter:

"DEAR BROTHER,—Take the bearer and put her to death immediately.
"Yours affectionately,
"ALBERT."

So soon after the girl set out for Scarborough, and slept for the night at a little inn. Now that very night a band of robbers broke into the inn, and searched the girl, who had no money, and only the letter. So they opened this and read it, and thought it a shame. The captain of the robbers took a pen and paper and wrote this letter:

"DEAR BROTHER,—Take the bearer and marry her to my son immediately.
"Yours affectionately,
"ALBERT."

And then he gave it to the girl, bidding her begone. So she went on to the Baron's brother at Scarborough, a noble knight, with whom the Baron's son was staying. When she gave the letter to his brother, he gave orders for the wedding to be prepared at once, and they were married that very day.

Soon after, the Baron himself came to his brother's castle, and what was his surprise to find that the very thing he had plotted against had come to pass. But he was not to be put off that way; and he took out the girl for a walk, as he said, along the cliffs. And when he got her all alone, he took her by the arms, and was going to throw her over. But she begged hard for her life. "I have not done anything," she said: "if you will only spare me, I will do whatever you wish. I will never see you or your son again till you desire it." Then the Baron took off his gold ring and threw it into the sea, saying: "Never let me see your face till you can show me that ring"; and he let her go.

The poor girl wandered on and on, till at last she came to a great noble's castle, and she asked to have some work given to her; and they made her the scullion girl of the castle, for she had been used to such work in the fisherman's hut.

Now one day, who should she see coming up to the noble's house but the Baron and his brother and his son, her husband. She didn't know what to do; but thought they would not see her in the castle kitchen. So she went back to her work with a sigh, and set to cleaning a huge big fish that was to be boiled for their dinner. And, as she was cleaning it, she saw something shine inside it, and what do you think she found? Why, there was the Baron's ring, the very one he had thrown over the cliff at Scarborough. She was right glad to see it, you may be sure. Then she cooked the fish as nicely as she could, and served it up.

Well, when the fish came on the table, the guests liked it so well that they asked the noble who cooked it. He said he didn't know, but called to his servants: "Ho, there, send up the cook that cooked that fine fish." So they went down to the kitchen and told the girl she was wanted in the hall. Then she washed and tidied herself and put the Baron's gold ring on her thumb and went up into the hall.

When the banqueters saw such a young and beautiful cook they were surprised. But the Baron was in a tower of a temper, and started up as if he would do her some violence. So the girl went up to him with her hand before her with the ring on it; and she put it down before him on the table. Then at last the Baron saw that no one could fight against Fate, and he handed her to a seat and announced to all the company that this was his son's true wife; and he took her and his son home to his castle; and they all lived as happy as could be ever afterwards.

❧ The Magpie's Nest ❧

Once upon a time when pigs spoke rhyme
And monkeys chewed tobacco,
And hens took snuff to make them tough,
And ducks went quack, quack, quack, O!

ALL the birds of the air came to the magpie and asked her to teach them how to build nests. For the magpie is the cleverest bird of all at building nests. So she put all the birds round her and began to show them how to do it. First of all she took some mud and made a sort of round cake with it.

"Oh, that's how it's done," said the thrush; and away it flew, and so that's how thrushes build their nests.

Then the magpie took some twigs and arranged them round in the mud.

"Now I know all about it," says the blackbird, and off he flew; and that's how the blackbirds make their nests to this very day.

Then the magpie put another layer of mud over the twigs.

"Oh that's quite obvious," said the wise owl, and away it flew; and owls have never made better nests since.

After this the magpie took some twigs and twined them round the outside.

"The very thing!" said the sparrow, and off he went; so sparrows make rather slovenly nests to this day.

Well, then Madge Magpie took some feathers and stuff and lined the nest very comfortably with it.

"That suits me," cried the starling, and off it flew; and very comfortable nests have starlings.

So it went on, every bird taking away some knowledge of how to build nests, but none of them waiting to the end. Meanwhile Madge Magpie went on working and working without looking up till the only bird that remained was the turtle-dove, and that hadn't paid any attention all along, but only kept on saying its silly cry: "Take two, Taffy, take two-o-o-o."

At last the magpie heard this just as she was putting a twig across. So she said: "One's enough."

But the turtle-dove kept on saying: "Take two, Taffy, take two-o-o-o."

Then the magpie got angry and said: "One's enough, I tell you."

Still the turtle-dove cried: "Take two, Taffy, take two-o-o-o."

At last, and at last, the magpie looked up and saw nobody near her but the silly turtle-dove, and then she got rare angry and flew away and refused to tell the birds how to build nests again. And that is why different birds build their nests differently.

ঌ Kate Crackernuts ঌ

ONCE upon a time there was a king and a queen, as in many lands have been. The king had a daughter, Anne, and the queen had one named Kate, but Anne was far bonnier than the queen's daughter, though they loved one another like real sisters. The queen was jealous of the king's daughter being bonnier than her own, and cast about to spoil her beauty. So she took counsel of the henwife, who told her to send the lassie to her next morning fasting.

So next morning early, the queen said to Anne, "Go, my dear, to the henwife in the glen, and ask her for some eggs." So Anne set out, but as she passed through the kitchen she saw a crust, and she took and munched it as she went along.

When she came to the henwife's she asked for eggs, as she had been told to do; the henwife said to her, "Lift the lid off that pot there and see." The lassie did so, but nothing happened. "Go home to your minnie and tell her to keep her larder door better locked," said the henwife. So she went home to the queen and told her what the henwife had said. The queen knew from this that the lassie had had something to eat, so watched the next morning and sent her away fasting; but the princess saw some country-folk picking peas by the roadside, and being very kind she spoke to them and took a handful of the peas, which she eat by the way.

When she came to the henwife's, she said, "Lift the lid off the pot and you'll see." So Anne lifted the lid but nothing happened. Then the henwife was rare angry and said to Anne, "Tell your minnie the pot won't boil if the fire's away." So Anne went home and told the queen.

The third day the queen goes along with the girl herself to the henwife. Now, this time, when Anne lifted the lid off the pot, off falls her own pretty head, and on jumps a sheep's head.

So the queen was now quite satisfied, and went back home.

Her own daughter, Kate, however, took a fine linen cloth and wrapped it round her sister's head and took her by the hand and they both went out to seek their fortune. They went on, and they went on, and they went on, till they came to a castle. Kate knocked at the door and asked for a night's lodging for herself and a sick sister. They went in and found it was a king's castle, who had two sons, and one of them was sickening away to death and no one could find out what ailed him. And the curious thing was that whoever watched him at night was never seen any more. So the king had offered a peck of silver to any one who would stop up with him. Now Katie was a very brave girl, so she offered to sit up with him.

Till midnight all goes well. As twelve o'clock rings, however, the sick prince rises, dresses himself, and slips downstairs. Kate followed, but he didn't seem to notice her. The prince went to the stable, saddled his horse, called his hound, jumped into the saddle, and Kate leapt lightly up behind him. Away rode the prince and Kate through the greenwood, Kate, as they pass, plucking nuts from the trees and filling her apron with them. They rode on and on till they came to a green hill. The prince here drew bridle and spoke, "Open, open, green hill, and let the young prince in with his horse and his hound," and Kate added, "and his lady him behind."

Immediately the green hill opened and they passed in. The prince entered a magnificent hall, brightly lighted up, and many beautiful fairies surrounded the prince and led him off to the dance. Meanwhile, Kate, without being noticed, hid herself behind the door. There she sees the prince dancing, and dancing, and dancing, till he could dance no longer and fell upon a couch. Then the fairies would fan him till he could rise again and go on dancing.

At last the cock crew, and the prince made all haste to get on horseback; Kate jumped up behind, and home they rode. When the morning sun rose they came in and found Kate sitting down by the fire and cracking her nuts. Kate said the prince had a good night; but she would not sit up another night unless she was to get a peck of gold. The second night passed as the first had done. The prince got up at midnight and rode away to the green hill and the fairy ball, and Kate went with him, gathering nuts as they rode through the forest. This time she did not watch the prince, for she knew he would dance and dance, and dance. But she sees a fairy baby playing with a wand, and overhears one of the fairies say:

"Three strokes of that wand would make Kate's sick sister as bonnie as ever she was." So Kate rolled nuts to the fairy baby, and rolled nuts till the baby toddled after the nuts and let fall the wand, and Kate took it up and put it in her apron. And at cock crow they rode home as before, and the moment Kate got home to her room she rushed and touched Anne three times with the wand, and the nasty sheep's head fell off and she was her own pretty self again. The third night Kate consented to watch, only if she should marry the sick prince. All went on as on the first two nights.

This time the fairy baby was playing with a birdie; Kate heard one of the fairies say: "Three bites of that birdie would make the sick prince as well as ever he was." Kate rolled all the nuts she had to the fairy baby till the birdie was dropped, and Kate put it in her apron.

At cockcrow they set off again, but instead of cracking her nuts as she used to do, this time Kate plucked the feathers off and cooked the birdie. Soon there arose a very savoury smell. "Oh!" said the sick prince, "I wish I had a bite of that birdie," so Kate gave him a bite of the birdie, and he rose up on his elbow. By-and-by he cried out again: "Oh, if I had another bite of that birdie!" so Kate gave him another bite, and he sat up on his bed. Then he said again: "Oh! if I only had a third bite of that birdie!" So Kate gave him a third bite, and he rose quite well, dressed himself, and sat down by the fire, and when the folk came in next morning they found Kate and the young prince cracking nuts together. Meanwhile his brother had seen Annie and had fallen in love with her, as everybody did who saw her sweet pretty face. So the sick son married the well sister, and the well son married the sick sister, and they all lived happy and died happy, and never drank out of a dry cappy.

ᔓ *The Cauld Lad of Hilton* ᔓ

AT HILTON HALL, long years ago, there lived, a Brownie that was the contrariest Brownie you ever knew. At night, after the servants had gone

to bed, it would turn everything topsy-turvy, put sugar in the salt-cellars, pepper into the beer, and was up to all kinds of pranks. It would throw the chairs down, put tables on their backs, rake out fires, and do as much mischief as could be. But sometimes it would be in a good temper, and then!—"What's a Brownie?" you say. Oh, it's a kind of a sort of a Bogle, but it isn't so cruel as a Redcap! What! you don't know what's a Bogle or a Redcap! Ah, me! what's the world a-coming to? Of course a Brownie is a funny little thing, half man, half goblin, with pointed ears and hairy hide. When you bury a treasure, you scatter over it blood drops of a newly slain kid or lamb, or, better still, bury the animal with the treasure, and a Brownie will watch over it for you, and frighten everybody else away.

Where was I? Well, as I was a-saying, the Brownie at Hilton Hall would play at mischief, but if the servants laid out for it a bowl of cream, or a knuckle cake spread with honey, it would clear away things for them, and make everything tidy in the kitchen. One night, however, when the servants had stopped up late, they heard a noise in the kitchen, and, peeping in, saw the Brownie swinging to and fro on the Jack chain, and saying:

> "Woe's me! woe's me!
> The acorn's not yet
> Fallen from the tree,
> That's to grow the wood,
> That's to make the cradle,
> That's to rock the bairn,
> That's to grow to the man,
> That's to lay me.
> Woe's me! woe's me!"

So they took pity on the poor Brownie, and asked the nearest henwife what they should do to send it away. "That's easy enough," said the henwife, and told them that a Brownie that's paid for its service, in aught that's not perishable, goes away at once. So they made a cloak of Lincoln green, with a hood to it, and put it by the hearth and watched. They saw the Brownie come up, and seeing the hood and cloak, put them on and frisk about, dancing on one leg and saying:

> "I've taken your cloak, I've taken your hood;
> The Cauld Lad of Hilton will do no more good."

And with that it vanished, and was never seen or heard of afterwards.

❧ The Ass, the Table, and the Stick ❧

A LAD named Jack was once so unhappy at home through his father's ill-treatment, that he made up his mind to run away and seek his fortune in the wide world.

He ran, and he ran, till he could run no longer, and then he ran right up against a little old woman who was gathering sticks. He was too much

out of breath to beg pardon, but the woman was good-natured, and she said he seemed to be a likely lad, so she would take him to be her servant, and would pay him well. He agreed, for he was very hungry, and she brought him to her house in the wood, where he served her for a twelve-months and a day. When the year had passed, she called him to her, and said she had good wages for him. So she presented him with an ass out of the stable, and he had but to pull Neddy's ears to make him begin at once to ee—aw! And when he brayed there dropped from his mouth silver sixpences, and halfcrowns, and golden guineas.

The lad was well pleased with the wage he had received, and away he rode till he reached an inn. There he ordered the best of everything, and when the innkeeper refused to serve him without being paid before-hand, the boy went off to the stable, pulled the ass's ears and obtained his pocket full of money. The host had watched all this through a crack in the door, and when night came on he put an ass of his own for the precious Neddy of the poor youth. So Jack without knowing that any change had been made, rode away next morning to his father's house.

Now, I must tell you that near his home dwelt a poor widow with an only daughter. The lad and the maiden were fast friends and trueloves; but when Jack asked his father's leave to marry the girl, "Never till you have the money to keep her," was the reply. "I have that, father," said the lad, and going to the ass he pulled its long ears; well, he pulled, and he pulled, till one of them came off in his hands; but Neddy, though he hee-hawed and he hee-hawed let fall no halfcrowns or guineas. The father picked up a hayfork and beat his son out of the house. I promise you he ran. Ah! he ran and ran till he came bang against the door, and burst it open, and there he was in a joiner's shop. "You're a likely lad," said the joiner; "serve me for a twelvemonths and a day and I will pay you well." So he agreed, and served the carpenter for a year and a day. "Now," said the master, "I will give you your wage"; and he presented him with a table, telling him he had but to say, "Table, be covered," and at once it would be spread with lots to eat and drink.

Jack hitched the table on his back, and away he went with it till he came to the inn. "Well, host," shouted he, "my dinner to-day, and that of the best."

"Very sorry, but there is nothing in the house but ham and eggs."

"Ham and eggs for me!" exclaimed Jack. "I can do better than that.— Come, my table, be covered!"

At once the table was spread with turkey and sausages, roast mutton, potatoes, and greens. The publican opened his eyes, but he said nothing, not he.

That night he fetched down from his attic a table very like that of Jack, and exchanged the two. Jack, none the wiser, next morning hitched the worthless table on to his back and carried it home. "Now, father, may I marry my lass?" he asked.

"Not unless you can keep her," replied the father.

"Look here!" exclaimed Jack. "Father, I have a table which does all my bidding."

"Let me see it," said the old man.

The lad set it in the middle of the room, and bade it be covered; but all in vain, the table remained bare. In a rage, the father caught the warming-pan down from the wall and warmed his son's back with it so that the boy fled howling from the house, and ran and ran till he came to a river and tumbled in. A man picked him out and bade him assist him in making a bridge over the river; and how do you think he was doing it. Why, by casting a tree across; so Jack climbed up to the top of the tree and threw his weight on it, so that when the man had rooted the tree up, Jack and the tree-head dropped on the farther bank.

"Thank you," said the man; "and now for what you have done I will pay you"; so saying, he tore a branch from the tree, and fettled it up into a club with his knife. "There," exclaimed he; "take this stick, and when you say to it, 'Up stick and bang him,' it will knock any one down who angers you."

The lad was overjoyed to get this stick—so away he went with it to the inn, and as soon as the publican appeared, "Up stick and bang him!" was his cry. At the word the cudgel flew from his hand and battered the old publican on the back, rapped his head, bruised his arms, tickled his ribs, till he fell groaning on the floor; still the stick belaboured the prostrate man, nor would Jack call it off till he had got back the stolen ass and table. Then he galloped home on the ass, with the table on his shoulders, and the stick in his hand. When he arrived there he found his father was dead, so he brought his ass into the stable, and pulled its ears till he had filled the manger with money.

It was soon known through the town that Jack had returned rolling in wealth, and accordingly all the girls in the place set their caps at him. "Now," said Jack, "I shall marry the richest lass in the place; so to-morrow do you all come in front of my house with your money in your aprons."

Next morning the street was full of girls with aprons held out, and gold and silver in them; but Jack's own sweetheart was among them, and she had neither gold nor silver, nought but two copper pennies, that was all she had.

"Stand aside, lass," said Jack to her, speaking roughly. "Thou hast no silver nor gold—stand off from the rest." She obeyed, and the tears ran down her cheeks, and filled her apron with diamonds.

"Up stick and bang them!" exclaimed Jack; whereupon the cudgel leaped up, and running along the line of girls, knocked them all on the heads and left them senseless on the pavement. Jack took all their money and poured it into his truelove's lap. "Now, lass," he exclaimed, "thou art the richest, and I shall marry thee."

ॐ *Fairy Ointment* ॐ

DAME GOODY was a nurse that looked after sick people, and minded babies. One night she was woke up at midnight, and when she went downstairs, she saw a strange squinny-eyed, little ugly old fellow, who asked her to come to his wife who was too ill to mind her baby. Dame Goody didn't like the look of the old fellow, but business is business; so she popped on her things, and went down to him. And when she got down to him, he whisked her up on to a large coal-black horse with fiery eyes, that stood at the door; and soon they were going at a rare pace, Dame Goody holding on to the old fellow like grim death.

They rode, and they rode, till at last they stopped before a cottage door. So they got down and went in and found the good woman abed with the children playing about; and the babe, a fine bouncing boy, beside her.

Dame Goody took the babe, which was as fine a baby boy as you'd wish to see. The mother, when she handed the baby to Dame Goody to mind, gave her a box of ointment, and told her to stroke the baby's eyes with it as soon as it opened them. After a while it began to open its eyes. Dame Goody saw that it had squinny eyes just like its father. So she took the box of ointment and stroked its two eyelids with it. But she couldn't help wondering what it was for, as she had never seen such a thing done before. So she looked to see if the others were looking, and, when they were not noticing she stroked her own right eyelid with the ointment.

No sooner had she done so, than everything seemed changed about her. The cottage became elegantly furnished. The mother in the bed was a beautiful lady, dressed up in white silk. The little baby was still more beautiful than before, and its clothes were made of a sort of silvery gauze. Its little brothers and sisters around the bed were flat-nosed imps with pointed ears, who made faces at one another, and scratched their polls. Sometimes they would pull the sick lady's ears with their long and hairy paws. In fact, they were up to all kinds of mischief; and Dame Goody knew that she had got into a house of pixies. But she said nothing to nobody, and as soon as the lady was well enough to mind the baby, she asked the old fellow to take her back home. So he came round to the door with the coal-black horse with eyes of fire, and off they went as fast as before, or perhaps a little faster, till they came to Dame Goody's cottage, where the squinny-eyed old fellow lifted her down and left her, thanking her civilly enough, and paying her more than she had ever been paid before for such service.

Now next day happened to be market-day, and as Dame Goody had been away from home, she wanted many things in the house, and trudged off to get them at the market. As she was buying the things she wanted, who should she see but the squinny-eyed old fellow who had taken her on the coal-black horse. And what do you think he was doing? Why he went about from stall to stall taking up things from each, here some fruit, and there some eggs, and so on; and no one seemed to take any notice.

Now Dame Goody did not think it her business to interfere, but she thought she ought not to let so good a customer pass without speaking. So she ups to him and bobs a curtsey and said: "Gooden, sir, I hopes as how your good lady and the little one are as well as—"

But she couldn't finish what she was a-saying, for the funny old fellow started back in surprise, and he says to her, says he: "What! do you see me to-day?"

"See you," says she, "why, of course I do, as plain as the sun in the skies, and what's more," says she, "I see you are busy too, into the bargain."

"Ah, you see too much," said he; "now, pray, with which eye do you see all this?"

"With the right eye to be sure," said she, as proud as can be to find him out.

"The ointment! The ointment!" cried the old pixy thief. "Take that for meddling with what don't concern you: you shall see me no more." And with that he struck her on her right eye, and she couldn't see him any more; and, what was worse, she was blind on the right side from that hour till the day of her death.

The Well of the World's End

ONCE upon a time, and a very good time it was, though it wasn't in my time, nor in your time, nor any one else's time, there was a girl whose mother had died, and her father had married again. And her stepmother hated her because she was more beautiful than herself, and she was very cruel to her. She used to make her do all the servant's work, and never let her have any peace. At last, one day, the stepmother thought to get rid of her altogether; so she handed her a sieve and said to her: "Go, fill it at the Well of the World's End and bring it home to me full, or woe betide you." For she thought she would never be able to find the Well of the World's End, and, if she did, how could she bring home a sieve full of water?

Well, the girl started off, and asked every one she met to tell her where was the Well of the World's End. But nobody knew, and she didn't know what to do, when a queer little old woman, all bent double, told her where it was, and how she could get to it. So she did what the old woman told her, and at last arrived at the Well of the World's End. But when she dipped the sieve in the cold, cold water, it all ran out again. She tried and she tried again, but every time it was the same; and at last she sate down and cried as if her heart would break.

Suddenly she heard a croaking voice, and she looked up and saw a great frog with goggle eyes looking at her and speaking to her.

"What's the matter, dearie?" it said.

"Oh, dear, oh dear," she said, "my stepmother has sent me all this long way to fill this sieve with water from the Well of the World's End, and I can't fill it no how at all."

"Well," said the frog, "if you promise me to do whatever I bid you for a whole night long, I'll tell you how to fill it."

So the girl agreed, and then the frog said:

> "Stop it with moss and daub it with clay,
> And then it will carry the water away";

and then it gave a hop, skip and jump, and went flop into the Well of the World's End.

So the girl looked about for some moss, and lined the bottom of the sieve with it, and over that she put some clay, and then she dipped it once again into the Well of the World's End; and this time, the water didn't run out, and she turned to go away.

Just then the frog popped up its head out of the Well of the World's End, and said: "Remember your promise."

"All right," said the girl; for thought she, "what harm can a frog do me?"

So she went back to her stepmother, and brought the sieve full of water from the Well of the World's End. The stepmother was fine and angry, but she said nothing at all.

That very evening they heard something tap tapping at the door low down, and a voice cried out:

> "Open the door, my hinny, my heart,
>   Open the door, my own darling;
> Mind you the words that you and I spoke,
>   Down in the meadow, at the World's End Well."

The Well of the World's End

"Whatever can that be?" cried out the stepmother, and the girl had to tell her all about it, and what she had promised the frog.

"Girls must keep their promises," said the stepmother. "Go and open the door this instant." For she was glad the girl would have to obey a nasty frog.

So the girl went and opened the door, and there was the frog from the Well of the World's End. And it hopped, and it skipped, and it jumped, till it reached the girl, and then it said:

> "Lift me to your knee, my hinny, my heart;
> Lift me to your knee, my own darling;
> Remember the words you and I spoke,
> Down in the meadow by the World's End Well."

But the girl didn't like to, till her stepmother said: "Lift it up this instant, you hussy! Girls must keep their promises!"

So at last she lifted the frog up on to her lap, and it lay there for a time, till at last it said:

> "Give me some supper, my hinny, my heart,
> Give me some supper, my darling;
> Remember the words you and I spake,
> In the meadow, by the Well of the World's End."

Well, she didn't mind doing that, so she got it a bowl of milk and bread, and fed it well. And when the frog had finished, it said:

> "Go with me to bed, my hinny, my heart,
> Go with me to bed, my own darling;
> Mind you the words you spake to me,
> Down by the cold well, so weary."

But that the girl wouldn't do, till her stepmother said: "Do what you promised, girl; girls must keep their promises. Do what you're bid, or out you go, you and your froggie."

So the girl took the frog with her to bed, and kept it as far away from her as she could. Well, just as the day was beginning to break what should the frog say but:

> "Chop off my head, my hinny, my heart,
> Chop off my head, my own darling;
> Remember the promise you made to me,
> Down by the cold well so weary."

At first the girl wouldn't, for she thought of what the frog had done for her at the Well of the World's End. But when the frog said the words over again, she went and took an axe and chopped off its head, and lo! and behold, there stood before her a handsome young prince, who told her that he had been enchanted by a wicked magician, and he could never be unspelled till some girl would do his bidding for a whole night, and chop off his head at the end of it.

The stepmother was that surprised when she found the young prince instead of the nasty frog, and she wasn't best pleased, you may be sure, when the prince told her that he was going to marry her stepdaughter because she had unspelled him. So they were married and went away to live in the castle of the king, his father, and all the stepmother had to console her was, that it was all through her that her stepdaughter was married to a prince.

ᔕ *Master of all Masters* ᔕ

A GIRL once went to the fair to hire herself for servant. At last a funny-looking old gentleman engaged her, and took her home to his house.

When she got there, he told her that he had something to teach her, for that in his house he had his own names for things.

He said to her: "What will you call me?"

"Master or mister, or whatever you please sir," says she.

He said: "You must call me 'master of all masters.' And what would you call this?" pointing to his bed.

"Bed or couch, or whatever you please, sir."

"No, that's my 'barnacle.' And what do you call these?" said he pointing to his pantaloons.

"Breeches or trousers, or whatever you please, sir."

"You must call them 'squibs and crackers.' And what would you call her?" pointing to the cat.

"Cat or kit, or whatever you please, sir."

"You must call her 'white-faced simminy.' And this now," showing the fire, "what would you call this?"

"Fire or flame, or whatever you please, sir."

"You must call it 'hot cockalorum,' and what this?" he went on, pointing to the water.

"Water or wet, or whatever you please, sir."

"No, 'pondalorum' is its name. And what do you call all this?" asked he, as he pointed to the house.

"House or cottage, or whatever you please, sir."

"You must call it 'high topper mountain.'"

That very night the servant woke her master up in a fright and said: "Master of all masters, get out of your barnacle and put on your squibs and crackers. For white-faced simminy has got a spark of hot cockalorum on its tail, and unless you get some pondalorum high topper mountain will be all on hot cockalorum." ... That's all.

❧ *The Three Heads of the Well* ❧

LONG before Arthur and the Knights of the Round Table, there reigned in the eastern part of England a king who kept his Court at Colchester.

In the midst of all his glory, his queen died, leaving behind her an only daughter, about fifteen years of age who for her beauty and kindness was the wonder of all that knew her. But the king hearing of a lady who had likewise an only daughter, had a mind to marry her for the sake of her riches, though she was old, ugly, hook-nosed, and hump-backed. Her daughter was a yellow dowdy, full of envy and ill-nature; and, in short, was much of the same mould as her mother. But in a few weeks the king, attended by the nobility and gentry, brought his deformed bride to the palace, where the marriage rites were performed. They had not been long in the Court before they set the king against his own beautiful daughter by false reports. The young princess having lost her father's love, grew weary of the Court, and one day, meeting with her father in the garden, she begged him, with tears in her eyes, to let her go and seek her fortune; to which the king consented, and ordered her mother-in-law to give her what she pleased. She went to the queen, who gave her a canvas bag of brown bread and hard cheese, with a bottle of beer; though this was but a pitiful dowry for a king's daughter. She took it, with thanks, and proceeded on her journey, passing through groves, woods, and valleys, till at length she saw an old man sitting on a stone at the mouth of a cave, who said: "Good morrow, fair maiden, whither away so fast?"

"Aged father," says she, "I am going to seek my fortune."

"What have you got in your bag and bottle?"

"In my bag I have got bread and cheese, and in my bottle good small beer. Would you like to have some?"

"Yes," said he, "with all my heart."

With that the lady pulled out her provisions, and bade him eat and welcome. He did so, and gave her many thanks, and said: "There is a thick thorny hedge before you, which you cannot get through, but take this wand in your hand, strike it three times, and say, 'Pray, hedge, let me come through,' and it will open immediately; then, a little further, you will find a well; sit down on the brink of it, and there will come up three golden heads, which will speak; and whatever they require, that do." Promising she would, she took her leave of him. Coming to the hedge and using the old man's wand, it divided, and let her through; then, coming to the well, she had no sooner sat down than a golden head came up singing:

> "Wash me, and comb me,
> And lay me down softly.
> And lay me on a bank to dry,
> That I may look pretty,
> When somebody passes by."

"Yes," said she, and taking it in her lap combed it with a silver comb, and then placed it upon a primrose bank. Then up came a second and a third head, saying the same as the former. So she did the same for them, and then, pulling out her provisions, sat down to eat her dinner.

Then said the heads one to another: "What shall we weird for this damsel who has used us so kindly?"

The first said: "I weird her to be so beautiful that she shall charm the most powerful prince in the world."

The second said: "I weird her such a sweet voice as shall far exceed the nightingale."

The third said: "My gift shall be none of the least, as she is a king's daughter, I'll weird her so fortunate that she shall become queen to the greatest prince that reigns."

She then let them down into the well again, and so went on her journey. She had not travelled long before she saw a king hunting in the park with his nobles. She would have avoided him, but the king, having caught a sight of her, approached, and what with her beauty and sweet voice, fell desperately in love with her, and soon induced her to marry him.

This king finding that she was the King of Colchester's daughter, ordered some chariots to be got ready, that he might pay the king, his father-in-law, a visit. The chariot in which the king and queen rode was adorned with rich gems of gold. The king, her father, was at first astonished that his daughter had been so fortunate, till the young king let him know of all that had happened. Great was the joy at Court amongst all, with the exception of the queen and her club-footed daughter, who were ready to burst with envy. The rejoicings, with feasting and dancing, continued many days. Then at length they returned home with the dowry her father gave her.

The hump-backed princess, perceiving that her sister had been so lucky in seeking her fortune, wanted to do the same; so she told her mother, and all preparations were made, and she was furnished not only with rich dresses, and sugar, almonds, and sweetmeats, in great quantities, and a large bottle of Malaga sack. With these she went the same road as her sister; and coming near the cave, the old man said: "Young woman, whither so fast?"

"What's that to you?" said she.

"Then," said he, "what have you in your bag and bottle?"

She answered: "Good things, which you shall not be troubled with."

"Won't you give me some?" said he.

"No, not a bit, nor a drop, unless it would choke you."

The old man frowned, saying: "Evil fortune attend ye!"

Going on, she came to the hedge, through which she espied a gap, and thought to pass through it; but the hedge closed, and the thorns ran into her flesh, so that it was with great difficulty that she got through. Being now all over blood, she searched for water to wash herself, and, looking round, she saw the well. She sat down on the brink of it, and one of the heads came up, saying: "Wash me, comb me, and lay me down softly," as before, but she banged it with her bottle, saying, "Take that for your washing." So the second and third heads came up, and met with no better treatment than the first. Whereupon the heads consulted among themselves what evils to plague her with for such usage.

The first said: "Let her be struck with leprosy in her face."

The second: "Let her voice be as harsh as a corncrake's."

The third said: "Let her have for husband but a poor country cobbler."

Well, she goes on till she came to a town, and it being market-day, the people looked at her, and, seeing such a mangy face, and hearing such a squeaky voice, all fled but a poor country cobbler. Now he not long before had mended the shoes of an old hermit, who, having no money, gave him a box of ointment for the cure of the leprosy, and a bottle of spirits for a harsh voice. So the cobbler having a mind to do an act of charity, was induced to go up to her and ask her who she was.

"I am," said she, "the King of Colchester's daughter-in-law."

"Well," said the cobbler, "if I restore you to your natural complexion, and make a sound cure both in face and voice, will you in reward take me for a husband?"

"Yes, friend," replied she, "with all my heart!"

With this the cobbler applied the remedies, and they made her well in a few weeks; after which they were married, and so set forward for the Court at Colchester. When the queen found that her daughter had married nothing but a poor cobbler, she hanged herself in wrath. The death of the queen so pleased the king, who was glad to get rid of her so soon, that he gave the cobbler a hundred pounds to quit the Court with his lady, and take to a remote part of the kingdom, where he lived many years mending shoes, his wife spinning the thread for him.

Notice to Little Children

Notes and References

In the following notes I give first the *source* whence I obtained the various tales. Then come *parallels* in some fulness for the United Kingdom, but only a single example for foreign countries, with a bibliographical reference where further variants can be found. Finally, a few *remarks* are sometimes added where the tale seems to need it. In two cases (Nos. xvi. and xxi.) I have been more full.

I. Tom Tit Tot

Source.—Unearthed by Mr. E. Clodd from the Suffolk Notes and Queries of the *Ipswich Journal,* and reprinted by him in a paper on "The Philosophy of Rumpelstiltskin" in *Folk-Lore Journal,* vii. 138-43. I have reduced the Suffolk dialect.

Parallels.—In Yorkshire this occurs as "Habetrot and Scantlie Mab," in Henderson's *Folk-Lore of Northern Counties,* 221–6; in Devonshire as "Duffy and the Devil" in Hunt's *Romances and Drolls of the West of England,* 239-47; in Scotland two variants are given by *Chambers, Popular Rhymes of Scotland,* under the title "Whuppity Stourie." The "name-guessing wager" is also found in "Peerifool," printed by Mr. Andrew Lang in *Longman's Magazine,* July 1889, also *Folk-Lore,* September, 1890. It is clearly the same as Grimm's "Rumpelstiltskin" (No. 14); for other Continental parallels see Mr. Clodd's article, and Cosquin, *Contes pop. de Lorraine,* i. 269 *seq.*

Remarks.—One of the best folk-tales that have ever been collected, far superior to any of the continental variants of this tale with which I am acquainted. Mr. Clodd sees in the class of name-guessing stories, a "survival" of the superstition that to know a man's name gives you power over him, for which reason savages object to tell their names. It may be necessary, I find, to explain to the little ones that Tom Tit can only be referred to as "that," because his name is not known till the end.

II. The Three Sillies

Source.—From *Folk-Lore Journal,* ii. 40-3; to which it was communicated by Miss C. Burne.

Parallels.—Prof. Stephens gave a variant from his own memory in *Folk-Lore Record,* iii. 155, as told in Essex at the beginning of the century. Mr. Toulmin Smith gave another version in *The Constitutional,* July 1, 1853, which was translated by his daughter, and contributed to *Mélusine,* t. ii. An Oxfordshire version was given in *Notes and Queries,* April 17, 1852. It occurs also in Ireland, Kennedy, *Fireside Stories,* p. 9. It is Grimm's *Kluge Else,* No. 34, and is spread through the world. Mr. Clouston devotes the seventh chapter of his *Book of Noodles* to the Quest of the Three Noodles.

III. THE ROSE TREE

Source.—From the first edition of Henderson's *Folk-Lore of Northern Counties*, p. 314, to which it was communicated by the Rev. S. Baring-Gould.

Parallels.—This is better known under the title, "Orange and Lemon," and with the refrain:

> "My mother killed me,
> My father picked my bones,
> My little sister buried me,
> Under the marble stones."

I heard this in Australia. Mr. Jones gives part of it in *Folk Tales of the Magyars,* 418–20, and another version occurs in 4 *Notes and Queries,* vi. 496. Mr. I. Gollancz informs me he remembers a version entitled "Pepper, Salt, and Mustard," with the refrain just given. Abroad it is Grimm's "Juniper Tree" (No. 47), where see further parallels. The German rhyme is sung by Margaret in the mad scene of Goethe's "Faust."

IV. OLD WOMAN AND PIG

Source.—Halliwell's *Nursery Rhymes and Tales,* 114.

Parallels.—*Cf.* Miss Burne, *Shropshire Folk-Lore,* 529; also No. xxxiv. *infra* ("Cat and Mouse"). It occurs also in Scotch, with the title "The Wife and her Bush of Berries," Chambers's *Pop. Rhymes,* p. 57. Newell, *Games and Songs of American Children,* gives a game named "Club-fist" (No. 75), founded on this, and in his notes refers to German, Danish, and Spanish variants. (*Cf.* Cosquin, ii. 36 *seq.*)

Remarks.—One of the class of Accumulative stories, which are well represented in England. (*Cf. infra,* Nos. xvi., xx., xxxiv.)

V. HOW JACK SOUGHT HIS FORTUNE

Source.—*American Folk-Lore Journal,* l., 227-8. I have eliminated a malodorous and un-English skunk.

Parallels.—Two other versions are given in the *Journal l.c.* One of these, however, was probably derived from Grimm's "Town Musicians of Bremen" (No. 27). That the others came from across the Atlantic is shown by the fact that it occurs in Ireland (Kennedy, *Fictions,* pp. 5-10) and Scotland (Campbell, No. 11). For other variants, see R. Köhler in Gonzenbach, *Sicil. Märchen,* ii. 245.

VI. MR. VINEGAR

Source.—Halliwell, p. 149.

Parallels.—This is the *Hans im Glück* of Grimm (No. 83). *Cf.* too, "Lazy Jack," *infra,* No. xxvii. Other variants are given by M. Cosquin, *Contes pop. de Lorraine,* i. 241. On surprising robbers, see preceding tale.

Remarks.—In some of the variants the door is carried, because Mr. Vinegar, or his equivalent, has been told to "mind the door," or he acts on the principle "he that is master of the door is master of the house." In other stories he makes the foolish exchanges to the entire satisfaction of his wife. (*Cf.* Cosquin, i. 156-7.)

VII. NIX NOUGHT NOTHING

Source.—From a Scotch tale, "Nicht Nought Nothing," collected by Mr. Andrew Lang in Morayshire, published by him first in *Revue Celtique,* t. iii.; then in his *Custom and Myth,* p. 89; and again in *Folk-Lore,* Sept. 1890. I have changed the name so as to retain the *équivoque* of the giant's reply to the King. I have also inserted the incidents of the flight, the usual ones in tales of this type, and expanded the conclusion, which is very curtailed and confused in the original. The usual ending of tales of this class contains the "sale of bed" incident, for which see Child, i. 391.

Parallels.—Mr. Lang, in the essay "A Far-travelled Tale" in which he gives the story, mentions several variants of it, including the classical myth of Jason and Medea. A fuller study in Cosquin, *l.c.,* ii. 12-28. For the finger ladder, see Köhler, in *Orient und Occident,* ii. 111.

VIII. JACK HANNAFORD

Source.—Henderson's *Folk-Lore of Northern Counties* (first edition), p. 319. Communicated by the Rev. S. Baring-Gould.

Parallels.—"Pilgrims from Paradise" are enumerated in Clouston's *Book of Noodles,* pp. 205, 214-8. See also Cosquin, *l.c.,* i. 239.

IX. BINNORIE

Source.—From the ballad of the "Twa Sisters o' Binnorie." I have used the longer version in Roberts's *Legendary Ballads,* with one or two touches from Mr. Allingham's shorter and more powerful variant in *The Ballad Book.* A tale is the better for length, a ballad for its curtness.

Parallels.—The story is clearly that of Grimm's "Singing Bone"(No. 28), where one brother slays the other and buries him under a bush. Years after a shepherd passing by finds a bone under the bush, and, blowing through this, hears the bone denounce the murderer. For numerous variants in Ballads and Folk Tales, see Prof. Child's *English and Scotch Ballads* (ed. 1886), i. 125, 493; iii. 499.

X. MOUSE AND MOUSER

Source.—From memory by Mrs. E. Burne-Jones.

Parallels.—A fragment is given in Halliwell, 43; Chambers's *Popular Rhymes* has a Scotch version, "The Cattie sits in the Kiln-ring spinning"(p. 53). The surprise at the end, similar to that in Perrault's "Red Riding Hood," is a frequent device in English folk-tales. (*Cf. infra,* Nos. xii., xxiv., xxix., xxxiii., xli.)

XI. CAP O' RUSHES

Source.—Discovered by Mr. E. Clodd, in "Suffolk Notes and Queries" of the *Ipswich Journal,* published by Mr. Lang in *Longman's Magazine,* vol. xiii., also in *Folk-Lore,* Sept. 1890.

Parallels.—The beginning recalls "King Lear." For "loving like salt," see the parallels collected by Cosquin, i. 288. The whole story is a version of the numerous class of Cinderella stories, the particular variety being the Catskin sub-species analogous to Perrault's *Peau d'Ane.* "Catskin" was told by Mr. Burchell to the young Primroses in "The Vicar of Wakefield," and has been elaborately studied by the late H. C. Coote, in *Folk-Lore Record,* iii. 1-25. It is only now extant in ballad form, of which "Cap o' Rushes" may be regarded as a prose version.

XII. Teeny-Tiny

Source.—Halliwell, 148.

XIII. Jack and the Beanstalk

Source.—I tell this as it was told me in Australia, somewhere about the year 1860.

Parallels.—There is a chap-book version which is very poor; it is given by Mr. E. S. Hartland, *English Folk and Fairy Tales* (Camelot Series), p. 35, *seq.* In this, when Jack arrives at the top of the Beanstalk, he is met by a fairy, who gravely informs him that the ogre had stolen all his possessions from Jack's father. The object of this was to prevent the tale becoming an encouragement to theft! I have had greater confidence in my young friends, and have deleted the fairy who did not exist in the tale as told to me. For the Beanstalk elsewhere, see Ralston, *Russian Folk Tales,* 293-8. Cosquin has some remarks on magical ascents (i. 14).

XIV. Three Little Pigs

Source.—Halliwell, p. 16.

Parallels.—The only known parallels are one from Venice, Bernoni, *Trad. Pop.,* punt. iii. p. 65, given in Crane, *Italian Popular Tales,* p. 267, "The Three Goslings"; and a negro tale in *Lippincott's Magazine,* December, 1877, p. 753 ("Tiny Pig").

Remarks.—As little pigs do not have hair on their chinny chin-chins, I suspect that they were originally kids, who have. This would bring the tale close to the Grimms' "Wolf and Seven Little Kids," (No. 5). In Steel and Temple's "Lambikin" (*Wide-awake Stories,* p. 71), the Lambikin gets inside a Drumikin, and so nearly escapes the jackal.

XV. Master and Pupil

Source.—Henderson, *Folk-Lore of Northern Counties,* first edition, p. 343, communicated by the Rev. S. Baring-Gould. The rhymes on the open book have been supplied by Mr. Batten, in whose family, if I understand him rightly, they have been long used for raising the ——; something similar occurs in Halliwell, p. 243, as a riddle rhyme. The mystic signs in Greek are a familiar "counting-out rhyme": these have been studied in a monograph by Mr. H. C. Bolton; he thinks they are "survivals" of incantations. Under the circumstances, it would be perhaps as well if the reader did not read the lines out when alone. One never knows what may happen.

Parallels.—Sorcerers' pupils seem to be generally selected for their stupidity—in folk-tales. Friar Bacon was defrauded of his labour in producing the Brazen Head in a similar way. In one of the legends about Virgil he summoned a number of demons, who would have torn him to pieces if he had not set them at work (J. S. Tunison, *Master Virgil,* Cincinatti, 1888, p. 30).

XVI. Titty Mouse and Tatty Mouse

Source.—Halliwell, p. 115.

Parallels.—This curious droll is extremely widespread; references are given in

Cosquin, i. 204 *seq.*, and Crane, *Italian Popular Tales,* 375-6. As a specimen I may indicate what is implied throughout these notes by such bibliographical references by drawing up a list of the variants of this tale noticed by these two authorities, adding one or two lately printed. Various versions have been discovered in

ENGLAND: Halliwell, *Nursery Rhymes,* p. 115.

SCOTLAND: K. Blind, in *Arch. Rev.* iii. ("Fleakin and Lousikin," in the Shetlands).

FRANCE: *Mélusine,* 1877, col. 424; Sebillot, *Contes pop. de la Haute Bretagne,* No. 55, *Litterature orale,* p. 232; *Magasin picturesque,* 1869, p. 82; Cosquin, *Contes pop. de Lorraine,* Nos. 18 and 74.

ITALY: Pitrè, *Novelline popolari siciliane,* No. 134 (translated in Crane, *Ital. Pop. Tales,* p. 257); Imbriani, *La novellaja Fiorentina,* p. 244; Bernoni, *Tradizione popolari veneziane,* punt. iii. p. 81; Gianandrea, *Biblioteca delle tradizioni popolari marchigiane,* p. 11; Papanti, *Novelline popolari livornesi,* p. 19 ("Vezzino e Madonna Salciccia"); Finamore, *Trad. pop. abruzzesi,* p. 244; Morosi, *Studi sui Dialetti Greci della Terra d'Otranto,* p. 75; *Giamb. Basile,* 1884, p. 37.

GERMANY: Grimm, *Kinder und-Haus-Märchen,* No. 30; Kuhn und Schwarz, *Nord-deutsche Sagen,* No. 16.

NORWAY: Asbjornsen, No. 103 (translated in Sir G. Dasent's *Tales from the Fjeld,* p. 30, "Death of Chanticleer").

SPAIN: Maspons, *Cuentos populars catalans,* p. 12; Fernan Caballero, *Cuentos y refranes populares,* p. 3 ("La Hormiguita").

PORTUGAL: Coelho, *Contos popolares portuguezes,* No. 1.

ROUMANIA: Kremnitz, *Rumänische Mährchen,* No. 15.

ASIA MINOR: Von Hahn, *Griechische und Albanesische Mährchen,* No. 56.

INDIA: Steel and Temple, *Wide-awake Stories,* p. 157 ("The Death and Burial of Poor Hen-Sparrow").

Remarks.—These 25 variants of the same jingle scattered over the world from India to Spain, present the problem of the diffusion of folk-tales in its simplest form. No one is likely to contend with Prof. Müller and Sir George Cox, that we have here the detritus of archaic Aryan mythology, a parody of a sun-myth. There is little that is savage and archaic to attract the school of Dr. Tylor, beyond the speaking powers of animals and inanimates. Yet even Mr. Lang is not likely to hold that these variants arose by coincidence and independently in the various parts of the world where they have been found. The only solution is that the curious succession of incidents was invented once for all at some definite place and time by some definite entertainer for children, and spread thence through all the Old World. In a few instances we can actually trace the passage—*e.g.,* the Shetland version was certainly brought over from Hamburg. Whether the centre of dispersion was India or not, it is impossible to say, as it might have spread east from Smyrna (Hahn, No. 56). Benfey *(Einleitung zu Pantschatantra,* i. 190-91) suggests that this class of accumulative story may be a sort of parody on the Indian stories, illustrating the moral, "what great events from small occasions rise." Thus, a drop of honey falls on the ground; a fly goes after it, a bird snaps at the fly, a dog goes for the bird, another dog goes for the first, the masters of the two dogs—who happen to be kings—quarrel and go to war, whole provinces are devastated, and all for a drop of honey! "Titty Mouse and Tatty Mouse" also ends in a universal calamity which seems to arise from a cause of no great importance. Benfey's suggestion is certainly ingenious, but perhaps too ingenious to be true.

XVII. JACK AND HIS SNUFF-BOX

Source.—Mr. F. Hindes Groome, *In Gipsy Tents*, p. 201 *seq.* I have eliminated a superfluous Gipsy who makes her appearance towards the end of the tale *à propos des bottes*, but otherwise have left the tale unaltered as one of the few English folk-tales that have been taken down from the mouths of the peasantry: this applies also to i., ii., xi.

Parallels.—There is a magic snuff-box with a friendly power in it in Kennedy's *Fictions of the Irish Celts*, p. 49. The choice between a small cake with a blessing, &c., is frequent (*cf.* No. xxiii.), but the closest parallel to the whole story, including the mice, is afforded by a tale in Carnoy and Nicolaides' *Traditions populaires de l'Asie Mineure*, which is translated as the first tale in Mr. Lang's *Blue Fairy Book*. There is much in both that is similar to Aladdin, I beg his pardon, Allah-ed-din.

XVIII. THE THREE BEARS

Source.—*Verbatim et literatim* from Southey, *The Doctor, &c.*, quarto edition, p. 327.

Parallels.—None, as the story was invented by Southey. There is an Italian translation, *I tre Orsi*, Turin, 1868, and it would be curious to see if the tale ever acclimatises itself in Italy.

Remarks.—"The Three Bears" is the only example I know of where a tale that can be definitely traced to a specific author has become a folk-tale. Not alone is this so, but the folk has developed the tale in a curious and instructive way, by substituting a pretty little girl with golden locks for the naughty old woman. In Southey's version there is nothing of Little Silverhair as the heroine: she seems to have been introduced in a metrical version by G. N., much be-praised by Southey. Silverhair seems to have become a favourite, and in Mrs. Valentine's version of "The Three Bears," in "The Old, Old Fairy Tales," the visit to the bear-house is only the preliminary to a long succession of adventures of the pretty little girl, of which there is no trace in the original (and this in "The Old, Old Fairy Tales." Oh! Mrs. Valentine!). I have, though somewhat reluctantly, cast back to the original form. After all, as Prof. Dowden remarks, Southey's memory is kept alive more by "The Three Bears" than anything else, and the text of such a nursery classic should be retained in all its purity.

XIX. JACK THE GIANT-KILLER

Source.—From two chap-books at the British Museum (London, 1805, Paisley, 1814?). I have taken some hints from "Felix Summerly's" (Sir Henry Cole's) version, 1845. From the latter part, I have removed the incident of the Giant dragging the lady along by her hair.

Parallels.—The chap-book of "Jack the Giant-Killer" is a curious jumble. The second part, as in most chap-books, is a weak and late invention of the enemy, and is not *volkstümlich* at all. The first part is compounded of a comic and a serious theme. The first is that of the Valiant Tailor (Grimm, No. 20); to this belong the incidents of the fleabite blows (for variants of which see Köhler in *Jahrb. rom. eng. Phil.*, viii. 252), and that of the slit paunch (*cf.* Cosquin, *l.c.*, ii. 51). The Thankful Dead episode, where the hero is assisted by the soul of a person whom he has caused to be buried, is found as early as the *Cento novelle antichi* and Straparola, xi. 2. It has been best studied by Köhler in *Germania*, iii. 199-209 (*cf.* Cosquin, i.

214-5; ii. 14 and note; and Crane, *Ital. Pop. Tales,* 350, note 12). It occurs also in the curious play of Peele's *The Old Wives' Tale,* in which one of the characters is the Ghost of Jack. Practically the same story as this part of Jack the Giant-Killer occurs in Kennedy, *Fictions of the Irish Celts,* p. 32, "Jack the Master and Jack the Servant"; and Kennedy adds (p. 38), "In some versions Jack the Servant is the spirit of the buried man."

The "Fee-fi-fo-fum" formula is common to all English stories of giants and ogres; it also occurs in Peele's play and in *King Lear* (see note on "Childe Rowland"). Messrs. Jones and Kropf have some remarks on it in their "Magyar Tales," pp. 340-1; so has Mr. Lang in his "Perrault," p. lxiii., where he traces it to the Furies in Æschylus' *Eumenides*.

XX. Henny-Penny

Source.—I give this as it was told me in Australia in 1860. The fun consists in the avoidance of all pronouns, which results in jaw-breaking sentences almost equal to the celebrated "She stood at the door of the fish-sauce shop, welcoming him in."

Parallels.—Halliwell, p. 151, has the same with the title "Chicken-Licken." It occurs also in Chambers's *Popular Rhymes,* p. 59, with the same names of the *dramatis personæ* as my version. For European parallels, see Crane, *Ital. Pop. Tales,* 377, and authorities there quoted.

XXI. Childe Rowland

Source.—Jamieson's *Illustrations of Northern Antiquities* 1814, p. 397 *seq.*, who gives it as told by a tailor in his youth, *c.* 1770. I have Anglicised the Scotticisms, eliminated an unneccessary ox-herd and swine-herd, who lose their heads for directing the Childe, and I have called the Erlkönig's lair the Dark Tower on the strength of the description and of Shakespeare's reference. I have likewise suggested a reason why Burd Ellen fell into his power, chiefly in order to introduce a definition of "widershins." "All the rest is the original horse," even including the erroneous description of the youngest son as the Childe or heir (*cf.* "Childe Harold" and Child Wynde, *infra,* No. xxxiii.), unless this is some "survival" of Junior Right or "Borough English," the archaic custom of letting the heirship pass to the youngest son. I should add that, on the strength of the reference to Merlin, Jamieson calls Childe Rowland's mother, Queen Guinevere, and introduces references to King Arthur and his Court. But as he confesses that these are his own improvements on the tailor's narrative I have eliminated them.

Parallels.—The search for the Dark Tower is similar to that of the Red Ettin, (*cf.* Köhler on Gonzenbach, ii. 222). The formula "Youngest best," in which the youngest of three brothers succeeds after the others have failed, is one of the most familiar in folk-tales amusingly parodied by Mr. Lang in his *Prince Prigio*. The taboo against taking food in the underworld occurs in the myth of Proserpine, and is also frequent in folk-tales (Child, i. 322). But the folk-tale parallels to our tale fade into insignificance before its brilliant literary relationships. There can be little doubt that Edgar, in his mad scene in *King Lear,* is alluding to our tale when he breaks into the lines:

"Childe Rowland to the Dark Tower came. . . .
His word was still: 'Fie, foh and fum,

I smell the blood of a British* man.'"
King Lear, act iii. sc. 4, *ad fin.*

The latter reference is to the cry of the King of Elfland. That some such story was current in England in Shakespeare's time, is proved by that curious *mélange* of nursery tales, Peele's *The Old Wives' Tale*. The main plot of this is the search of two brothers, Calypha and Thelea, for a lost sister, Delia, who has been bespelled by a sorcerer, Sacrapant (the names are taken from the "Orlando Furioso"). They are instructed by an old man (like Merlin in "Childe Rowland") how to rescue their sister, and ultimately succeed. The play has besides this the themes of the Thankful Dead, the Three Heads of the Well (which see), the Life Index, and a transformation, so that it is not to be wondered at if some of the traits of "Childe Rowland" are observed in it.

But a still closer parallel is afforded by Milton's *Comus*. Here again we have two brothers in search of a sister, who has got into the power of an enchanter. But besides this, there is the refusal of the heroine to touch the enchanted food, just as Childe Rowland finally refuses. And ultimately the bespelled heroine is liberated by a liquid, which is applied to her *lips and finger-tips*, just as Childe Rowland's brothers are unspelled. Such a minute resemblance as this cannot be accidental, and it is therefore probable that Milton used the original form of "Childe Rowland," or some variant of it, as heard in his youth, and adapted it to the purposes of the masque at Ludlow Castle, and of his allegory. Certainly no other folk-tale in the world can claim so distinguished an offspring.

Remarks.—Distinguished as "Childe Rowland" will be henceforth as the origin of *Comus,* if my affiliation be accepted, it has even more remarkable points of interest, both in form and matter, for the folk-lorist, unless I am much mistaken. I will therefore touch upon these points, reserving a more detailed examination for another occasion.

First, as to the form of the narrative. This begins with verse, then turns to prose, and throughout drops again at intervals into poetry in a friendly way like Mr. Wegg. Now this is a form of writing not unknown in other branches of literature, the *cante-fable,* of which "Aucassin et Nicolette" is the most distinguished example. Nor is the *cante-fable* confined to France. Many of the heroic verses of the Arabs contained in the *Hamâsa* would be unintelligible without accompanying narrative, which is nowadays preserved in the commentary. The verses imbedded in the *Arabian Nights* give them something of the character of a *cante-fable,* and the same may be said of the Indian and Persian story-books, though the verse is usually of a sententious and moral kind, as in the *gâthas* of the Buddhist Jatakas. Even as remote as Zanzibar, Mr. Lang notes, the folk-tales are told as *cante-fables.* There are even traces in the Old Testament of such screeds of verse amid the prose narrative, as in the story of Lamech or that of Balaam. All this suggests that this is a very early and common form of narrative.

* "British" for "English." This is one of the points that settles the date of the play; James I. was declared King of Great *Britain*, October 1604. I may add that Motherwell in his *Minstrelsy,* p. xiv. note, testifies that the story was still extant in the nursery at the time he wrote (1828).

Among folk-tales there are still many traces of the *cante-fable*. Thus, in Grimm's collection, verses occur in Nos. 1, 5, 11, 12, 13, 15, 19, 21, 24, 28, 30, 36, 38*a*, *b*, 39*a*, 40, 45, 46, 47, out of the first fifty tales, 36 per cent. Of Chambers' twenty-one folk-tales, in the *Popular Rhymes of Scotland* only five are without interspersed verses. Of the forty-three tales contained in this volume, three (ix., xxix., xxxiii.) are derived from ballads and do not therefore count in the present connection. Of the remaining forty, i., iii., vii., xvi., xix., xxi., xxiii., xxv., xxxi., xxxv., xxxviii., xli. (made up from verses), xliii., contain rhymed lines, while xiv., xxii., xxvi., and xxxvii., contain "survivals" of rhymes ("let me come in—chinny chin-chin"; "once again ... come to Spain"; "it is not so—should be so"; "and his lady, him behind"); and x. and xxxii. are rhythmical if not rhyming. As most of the remainder are drolls, which have probably a different origin, there seems to be great probability that originally all folk-tales of a serious character were interspersed with rhyme, and took therefore the form of the *cante-fable*. It is indeed unlikely that the ballad itself began as continuous verse, and the *cante-fable* is probably the protoplasm out of which both ballad and folk-tale have been differentiated, the ballad by omitting the narrative prose, the folk-tale by expanding it. In "Childe Rowland" we have the nearest example to such protoplasm, and it is not difficult to see how it could have been shortened into a ballad or reduced to a prose folk-tale pure and simple.

The subject-matter of "Childe Rowland" has also claims on our attention especially with regard to recent views on the true nature and origin of elves, trolls, and fairies. I refer to the recently published work of Mr. D. MacRitchie, "The Testimony of Tradition" (Kegan Paul, Trench, Trübner & Co.)—*i.e.*, of tradition about the fairies and the rest. Briefly put, Mr. MacRitchie's view is that the elves, trolls, and fairies represented in popular tradition are really the mound-dwellers, whose remains have been discovered in some abundance in the form of green hillocks, which have been artificially raised over a long and low passage leading to a central chamber open to the sky. Mr. MacRitchie shows that in several instances traditions about trolls or "good people" have attached themselves to mounds, which have afterwards on investigation turned out to be evidently the former residence of men of smaller build than the mortals of to-day. He goes on further to identify these with the Picts—fairies are called "Pechs" in Scotland—and other early races, but with these ethnological equations we need not much concern ourselves. It is otherwise with the mound-traditions and their relation, if not to fairy tales in general, to tales *about* fairies, trolls, elves, &c. These are very few in number, and generally bear the character of anecdotes. The fairies, &c., steal a child, they help a wanderer to a drink and then disappear into a green hill, they help cottagers with their work at night but disappear if their presence is noticed; human midwives are asked to help fairy mothers, fairy maidens marry ordinary men or girls marry and live with fairy husbands. All such things may have happened and bear no such *à priori* marks of impossibility as speaking animals, flying through the air, and similar incidents of the folk-tale pure and simple. If, as archæologists tell us, there was once a race of men in Northern Europe, very short and hairy, that dwelt in underground chambers artificially concealed by green hillocks, it does not seem unlikely that odd survivors of the race should have lived on after they had been conquered and nearly exterminated by Aryan invaders and should occasionally have performed something like the pranks told of fairies and trolls.

Certainly the description of the Dark Tower of the King of Elfland in "Childe Rowland," has a remarkable resemblance to the dwellings of the "good folk," which recent excavations have revealed. By the kindness of Mr. MacRitchie, I am enabled to give the reader illustrations of one of the most interesting of these, the Maes-How of Orkney. This is a green mound some 100 feet in length and 35 in breadth at its broadest part. Tradition had long located a goblin in its centre, but it was not till 1861 that it was discovered to be pierced by a long passage 53 feet in length, and only two feet four inches high, for half of its length. This led into a central chamber 15 feet square and open to the sky. The diagrams on the opposite page will give all further details.

Now it is remarkable how accurately all this corresponds to the Dark Tower of "Childe Rowland," allowing for a little idealisation on the part of the narrator. We have the long dark passage leading into the well-lit central chamber, and all enclosed in a green hill or mound. It is of course curious to contrast Mr. Batten's frontispiece with the central chamber of the How, but the essential features are the same.

Central chamber, Maes-How

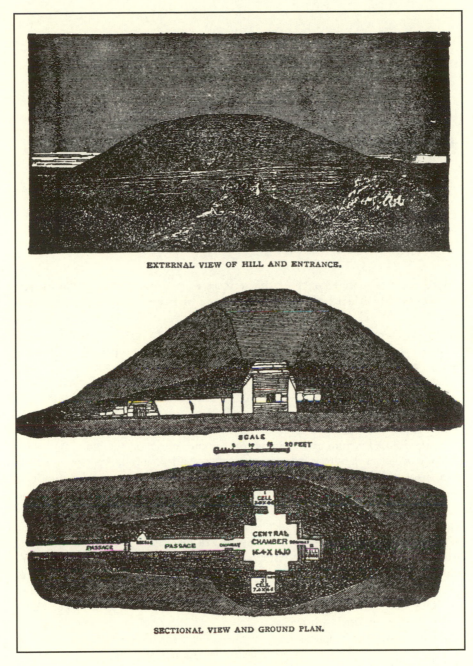

EXTERNAL VIEW OF HILL AND ENTRANCE.

SCALE

SECTIONAL VIEW AND GROUND PLAN.

The Maes-How, Orkney

Terraces at Newlands Kirk, Peebleshire

Even such a minute touch as the terraces on the hill have their bearing, I believe, on Mr. MacRitchie's "realistic" views of Faerie. For in quite another connection Mr. G. L. Gomme, in his recent "Village Community" (W. Scott), pp. 75-98, has given reasons and examples* for believing that terrace cultivation along the sides of hills was a practice of the non-Aryan and pre-Aryan inhabitants of these isles. Here then from a quarter quite unexpected by Mr. MacRitchie, we have evidence of the association of the King of Elfland with a non-Aryan mode of cultivation of the soil. By Mr. Gomme's kindness I am enabled to give an illustration of this.

Altogether it seems not improbable that in such a tale as "Childe Rowland" we have an idealised picture of a "marriage by capture" of one of the diminutive non-Aryan dwellers of the green hills with an Aryan maiden, and her re-capture by her brothers. It is otherwise difficult to account for such a circumstantial description of the interior of these mounds, and especially of such a detail as the terrace cultivation on them. At the same time it must not be thought that Mr. MacRitchie's views explain all fairy tales, or that his identifications of Finns = Fenians = Fairies = Sidhe = "Pechs" = Picts, will necessarily be accepted. His interesting book, so far as it goes, seems to throw light on tales about mermaids (Finnish women in their "kayaks,") and trolls, but not necessarily, on fairy tales in general. Thus, in the present volume, besides "Childe Rowland," there is only "Tom Tit Tot" in his hollow, the green hill in "Kate Crackernuts," the "Cauld Lad of Hilton," and perhaps the "Fairy Ointment," that are affected by his views.

Finally, there are a couple of words in the narrative that deserve a couple of words of explanation: "Widershins" is probably, as Mr. Batten suggests, analogous to the German "wider Schein," against the appearance of the sun, "counterclockwise" as the mathematicians say—*i.e.,* W., S., E., N., instead of with the sun and the hands of a clock; why it should have an unspelling influence is hard to say. "Bogle" is a provincial word for "spectre," and is analogous to the Welsh *bwg,* "goblin," and to the English

* To these may be added Iona (*cf.* Duke of Argyll, *Iona,* p. 109).

insect of similar name, and still more curiously to the Russian "Bog," God, after which so many Russian rivers are named. I may add that "Burd" is etymologically the same as "bride" and is frequently used in the early romances for "Lady."

XXII. Molly Whuppie

Source.—*Folk-Lore Journal,* ii. p. 68, forwarded by Rev. Walter Gregor. I have modified the dialect and changed "Mally" into "Molly."

Parallels.—The first part is clearly the theme of "Hop o' my Thumb," which Mr. Lang has studied in his "Perrault," pp. civ.–cxi. (*cf.* Köhler, *Occident,* ii. 301.) The change of night-dresses occurs in Greek myths. The latter part wanders off into "rob giant of three things," a familiar incident in folk-tales (Cosquin, i. 46-7), and finally winds up with the "out of sack" trick, for which see Cosquin, i. 113; ii. 209; and Köhler on Campbell, in *Occident und Orient,* ii. 489-506.

XXIII. Red Ettin

Source.—"The Red Etin" in Chambers's *Pop. Rhymes of Scotland,* p. 89. I have reduced the adventurers from three to two, and cut down the herds and their answers. I have substituted riddles from the first English collection of riddles, *The Demandes Joyous* of Wynkyn de Worde, for the poor ones of the original, which are besides not solved. "Ettin" is the Engish spelling of the word, as it is thus spelt in a passage of Beaumont and Fletcher *(Knight of Burning Pestle,* i. 1), which may refer to this very story, which, as we shall see, is quite as old as their time.

Parallels.—"The Red Etin" is referred to in *The Complaynt of Scotland,* about 1548. It has some resemblance to "Childe Rowland," which see. The "death index," as we may call tokens that tell the state of health of a parted partner, is a usual incident in the theme of the Two Brothers, and has been studied by the Grimms, i. 421, 453; ii. 403; by Köhler on Campbell, *Occ. u. Or.,* ii. 119-20; on Gonzenbach, ii. 230; on Bladé, 248; by Cosquin, *l.c.,* i. 70-2, 193; by Crane, *Ital. Pop. Tales,* 326; and by Jones and Kropf, *Magyar Tales,* 329. Riddles generally come in the form of the "riddle-bride-wager" (*cf.* Child, *Ballads,* i. 415-9; ii. 519), when the hero or heroine wins a spouse by guessing a riddle or riddles. Here it is the simpler Sphinx form of the "riddle task," on which see Köhler in *Jahrb. rom. Phil.,* vii. 273, and on Gonzenbach, 215.

XXIV. Golden Arm

Source.—Henderson, *l.c.,* p. 338, collected by the Rev. S. Baring-Gould, in Devonshire. Mr. Burne-Jones remembers hearing it in his youth in Warwickshire.

Parallels.—The first fragment at the end of Grimm (ii. 467, of Mrs. Hunt's translation), tells of an innkeeper's wife who had used the liver of a man hanging on the gallows, whose ghost comes to her and tells her what has become of his hair, and his eyes, and the dialogue concludes

> "She: Where is thy liver?
> It: Thou hast devoured it!"

For similar "surprise packets" see Cosquin, ii. 77.

Remarks.—It is doubtful how far such gruesome topics should be introduced into a book for children, but as a matter of fact the καθοσισ of pity and terror among the little ones is as effective as among the spectators of a drama, and they take the same kind of pleasant thrill from such stories. They know it is all make-believe just as much as the spectators of a tragedy. Every one who has enjoyed the blessing of a romantic imagination has been trained up on such tales of wonder.

XXV. Tom Thumb

Source.—From the chap-book contained in Halliwell, p. 199, and Mr. Hartland's *English Folk and Fairy Tales.* I have omitted much of the second part.

Parallels.—Halliwell has also a version entirely in verse. "Tom Thumb" is "Le petit Poucet" of the French, "Daumling" of the Germans, and similar diminutive heroes elsewhere (*cf.* Deulin, *Contes de ma Mère l'Oye,* 326), but of his adventures only that in the cow's stomach (*cf.* Cosquin, ii. 190) is common with his French and German cousins. M. Gaston Paris has a monograph on "Tom Thumb."

XXVI. Mr. Fox

Source.—Contributed by Blakeway to Malone's Variorum Shakespeare, to illustrate Benedick's remark in *Much Ado about Nothing* (I. i. 146): "Like the old tale, my Lord, 'It is not so, nor 'twas not so, but, indeed, God forbid it should be so'"; which clearly refers to the tale of Mr. Fox. "The Forbidden Chamber" has been studied by Mr. Hartland, *Folk-Lore Journal,* iii. 193, *seq.*

Parallels.—Halliwell, p. 166, gives a similar tale of "An Oxford Student," whose sweetheart saw him digging her grave. "Mr. Fox" is clearly a variant of the theme of "The Robber Bridegroom" (Grimm, No. 40, Mrs. Hunt's translation, i. 389, 395; and Cosquin, i. 180-1).

XXVII. Lazy Jack

Source.—Halliwell, 157.

Parallels.—The same story occurs in Lowland Scotch as "Jock and his Mother," Chambers, *l.c.,* 101; in Ireland, as "I'll be wiser next time," Kennedy, *l.c.,* 39-42. Abroad it is Grimm's *Hans im Gluck* (No. 83). The "cure by laughing" incident is "common form" in folk-tales (*cf.* Köhler on Gonzenbach, *Sizil. Märchen,* ii. 210, 224; Jones and Kropf, *Magyar Tales,* 312).

XXVIII. Johnny-Cake

Source.—*American Journal of Folk-Lore,* ii, 60.

Parallels.—Another variant is given in the same *Journal,* p. 277, where reference is also made to a version "The Gingerbread Boy," in *St. Nicholas,* May 1875. Chambers gives two versions of the same story, under the title "The Wee Bunnock," the first of which is one of the most dramatic and humorous of folk-tales. Unfortunately, the Scotticisms are so frequent as to render the Droll practically untranslatable. "The Fate of Mr. Jack Sparrow" in *Uncle Remus* is similar to that of Johnny-Cake.

XXIX. Earl Mar's Daughter

Source.—From the ballad of the same name as given in Mr. Allingham's *Ballad Book:* it is clearly a fairy tale and not a ballad proper.

Parallels.—The lover visiting his spouse in guise of a bird, is a frequent *motif* in folk-tales.

XXX. Mr. Miacca

Source.—From memory of Mrs. B. Abrahams, who heard it from her mother some x years ago ($x>40$). I have transposed the two incidents, as in her version Tommy Grimes was a clever carver and carried about with him a carven leg. This seemed to me to exceed the limits of *vraisemblance* even for a folk-tale.

Parallels.—Getting out of an ogre's clutches by playing on the simplicity of his wife, occurs in "Molly Whuppie" (No. xxii.), and its similars. In the Grimms' "Hansel and Grethel," Hansel pokes out a stick instead of his finger that the witch may not think him fat enough for the table.

Remarks.—Mr. Miacca seems to have played the double *rôle* of a domestic Providence. He not alone punished bad boys, as here, but also rewarded the good, by leaving them gifts on appropriate occasions like Santa Claus or Father Christmas, who, as is well known, only leave things for good children. Mrs. Abrahams remembers one occasion well when she nearly caught sight of Mr. Miacca, just after he had left her a gift; she saw his shadow in the shape of a bright light passing down the garden.

XXXI. Dick Whittington

Source.—I have cobbled this up out of three chap-book versions; (1) that contained in Mr. Hartland's *English Folk-tales;* (2) that edited by Mr. H. B. Wheatley for the Villon Society; (3) that appended to Messrs. Besant and Rice's monograph.

Parallels.—Whittington's cat has made the fortune of his master in all parts of the Old World, as Mr. W. A. Clouston, among others, has shown, *Popular Tales and Fictions*, ii. 65-78 (*cf.* Köhler on Gonzenbach, ii. 251).

Remarks.—If Bow Bells had pealed in the exact and accurate nineteenth century, they doubtless would have chimed

Turn again, Whittington,
Thrice and a half Lord Mayor of London.

For besides his three mayoralties of 1397, 1406, and 1419, he served as Lord Mayor in place of Adam Bamme, deceased, in the latter half of the mayoralty of 1396. It will be noticed that the chap-book puts the introduction of potatoes rather far back.

XXXII. The Strange Visitor

Source.—From Chambers, *l.c.*, 64, much Anglicised. I have retained "Aih-late-wee-moul," though I candidly confess I have not the slightest idea what it means; judging other children by myself, I do not think that makes the response less effective. The prosaic-minded may substitute "Up-late-and-little-food."

Parallels.—The man made by instalments, occurs in the Grimms' No. 4, and something like it in an English folk-tale, *The Golden Ball, ap.* Henderson, *l.c.*, p. 333.

XXXIII. The Laidly Worm

Source.—From an eighteenth-century ballad of the Rev. Mr. Lamb of Norham, as given in Prof. Child's *Ballads;* with a few touches and verses from the more ancient version "Kempion." A florid prose version appeared in *Monthly Chronicle of North Country Lore* for May 1890. I have made the obvious emendation of

> O quit your sword, unbend your bow

for

> O quit your sword, and bend your bow.

Parallels.—The ballad of "Kempe Owein" is a more general version which "The Laidly Worm" has localised near Bamborough. We learn from this that the original herd was Kempe or Champion Owain, the Welsh hero who flourished in the ninth century. Childe Wynd therefore = Childe Owein. The "Deliverance Kiss" has been studied by Prof. Child, *l.c.,* i. 207. A noteworthy example occurs in Boiardo's *Orlando Inamorato,* cc. xxv., xxvi.

Remarks.—It is perhaps unnecessary to give the equations "Laidly Worm = Loathly Worm = Loathsome Dragon," and "borrowed = changed."

XXXIV. Cat and Mouse

Source.—Halliwell, p. 154.

Parallels.—Scarcely more than a variant of the "Old Woman and her Pig" (No. iv.), which see. It is curious that a very similar "run" is added by Bengali women at the end of every folk-tale they tell (Lal Behari Day, *Folk Tales of Bengal,* Pref. *ad fin.*)

XXXV. The Fish and The Ring

Source.—Henderson, *l.c.,* p. 326, from a communication by the Rev. S. Baring-Gould.

Parallels.— "Jonah rings" have been put together by Mr. Clouston in his *Popular Tales,* i. 398, &c.: the most famous are those of Polycrates, of Solomon, and the Sanskrit drama of "Sakuntala," the plot of which turns upon such a ring. "Letters to kill bearer" have been traced from Homer downwards by Prof. Köhler on Gonzenbach, ii. 220, and "the substituted letter" by the same authority in *Occ. u. Or.,* ii. 289. Mr. Baring-Gould, who was one of the pioneers of the study of folk-tales in this country, has given a large number of instances of "the pre-ordained marriage" in folk-tales in Henderson, *l.c.*

XXXVI. The Magpie's Nest

Source.—I have built up the "Magpie's Nest" from two nidification myths, as a German professor would call them, in the Rev. Mr. Swainson's *Folk-Lore of British Birds,* pp. 80 and 166. I have received instruction about the relative values of nests from a little friend of mine named Katie, who knows all about it. If there is any mistake in the order of neatness in the various birds' nests, I must have learnt my lesson badly.

Remarks.—English popular tradition is curiously at variance about the magpie's nidificatory powers, for another legend given by Mr. Swainson represents her as refusing to be instructed by the birds and that is why she does *not* make a good nest.

XXXVII. Kate Crackernuts

Source.—Given by Mr. Lang in *Longman's Magazine*, vol. xiv. and reprinted *Folk-Lore*, Sept. 1890. It is very corrupt, both girls being called Kate, and I have had largely to rewrite.

Parallels.—There is a tale which is clearly a cousin if not a parent of this in Kennedy's *Fictions*, 54 *seq.,* containing the visit to the green hill (for which see "Childe Rowland"), a reference to nuts, and even the sesame rhyme. The prince is here a corpse who becomes revivified; the same story is in Campbell No. 13. The jealous stepmother is "universally human."(*Cf.* Köhler on Gonzenbach, ii. 206.)

XXXVIII. The Cauld Lad of Hilton

Source.—Henderson's *Folk-Lore of Northern Counties*, 2nd edition, published by the Folk-Lore Society, pp. 266-7. I have written the introductory paragraph so as to convey some information about Brownies, Bogles, and Redcaps, for which Henderson, *l.c.,* 246-53, is my authority. Mr. Batten's portrait renders this somewhat superfluous.

Parallels.—The Grimms' "Elves" (No. 39) behave in like manner on being rewarded for their services. Milton's "lubbar-fiend" in *L'Allegro* has all the characteristics of a Brownie.

XXXIX. Ass, Table and Stick

Source.—Henderson, *l.c.,* first edition, pp. 327-9, by the Rev. S. Baring-Gould.

Parallels.—Mr. Baring-Gould gives another version from the East Riding, *l.c.,* 329, in which there are three brothers who go through the adventures. He also refers to European Variants, p. 311, which could now be largely supplemented from Cosquin, i. 53-4, ii. 66, 171.

Remarks.—As an example of the sun-myth explanation of folk-tales I will quote the same authority (p. 314): "The Master, who gives the three precious gifts, is the All Father, the Supreme Spirit. The gold and jewel-dropping ass, is the spring cloud, hanging in the sky and shedding the bright productive vernal flowers. The table which covers itself is the earth becoming covered with flowers and fruit at the bidding of the New Year. But there is a check; rain is withheld, the process of vegetation is stayed by some evil influence. Then comes the thunder-cloud, out of which leaps the bolt; the rains pour down, the earth receives them, and is covered with abundance—all that was lost is recovered."

Mr. Baring-Gould, it is well-known, has since become a distinguished writer of fiction.

XL. Fairy Ointment

Source.—Mrs. Bray, *The Tamar and the Tavy*, i. 174 (letters to Southey), as quoted by Mr. Hartland in *Folk-Lore*, i. 207-8. I have christened the anonymous midwife and euphemised her profession.

Parallels.—Mr. Hartland has studied Human Midwives in the *Archæol. Review,* iv., and parallels to our story in *Folk-Lore,* i. 209, *seq.;* the most interesting of these is from Gervase of Tilbury (xiii. cent,), *Otia Imper.,* iii. 85, and three Breton tales given by M. Sebillot (*Contes*, ii. 42; *Litt. orale*, 23; *Trad. et Superst.*, i. 109). *Cf.* Prof. Child, i. 339; ii. 505.

XLI. THE WELL OF THE WORLD'S END

Source.—Leyden's edition of *The Complaynt of Scotland*, p. 234 *seq.*, with additional touches from Halliwell, 162-3, who makes up a slightly different version from the rhymes. The opening formula I have taken from Mayhew, *London Labour*, iii. 390, who gives it as the usual one when tramps tell folk-tales. I also added it to No. xvii.

Parallels.—Sir W. Scott remembered a similar story; see Taylor's *Gammer Grethel*, *ad fin.* In Scotland it is Chambers's tale of *The Paddo*, p. 87; Leyden supposes it is referred to in the *Complaynt*, (c. 1548), as "The Wolf of the Warldis End." The well of this name occurs also in the Scotch version of the "Three Heads of the Well," (No. xliii.). Abroad it is the Grimms' first tale, while frogs who would a-wooing go are discussed by Prof. Köhler, *Occ. u. Orient*, 330; by Prof. Child, i. 298; and by Messrs. Jones and Kropf, *l.c.*, p. 404. The sieve-bucket task is widespread from the Danaids of the Greeks to the leverets of *Uncle Remus*, who, curiously enough, use the same rhyme: "Fill it wid moss en dob it wid clay." *Cf.*, too, No. xxiii.

XLII. MASTER OF ALL MASTERS

Source.—I have taken what suited me from a number of sources, which shows how wide-spread this quaint droll is in England: (i) In Mayhew, *London Poor*, iii. 391, told by a lad in a workhouse; (ii) several versions in 7 *Notes and Queries*, iii. 35, 87, 159, 398.

Parallels.—Rev. W. Gregor gives a Scotch version under the title "The Clever Apprentice," in *Folk-Lore Journal*, vii. 166. Mr. Hartland, in *Notes and Queries, l.c.*, 87, refers to Pitré's *Fiabi sicil.*, iii. 120, for a variant.

Remarks.—According to Mr. Hartland, the story is designed as a satire on pedantry, and is as old in Italy as Straparola (sixteenth century). In passionate Sicily a wife disgusted with her husband's pedantry sets the house on fire, and informs her husband of the fact: is this unintelligible gibberish? he, not understanding his own lingo, falls a victim to the flames, and she marries the servant who had taken the message.

XLIII. THE THREE HEADS OF THE WELL

Source.—Halliwell, p. 158. The second wish has been somewhat euphemised.

Parallels.—The story forms part of Peele's *Old Wives' Tale*, where the rhyme was

> *A Head rises in the well,*
> Fair maiden, white and red,
> Stroke me smooth and comb my head,
> And thou shalt have some cockell-bread.

It is also in Chambers, *l.c.*, 105, where the well is at the World's End (*cf.* No. xli.). The contrasted fates of two step-sisters, is the Frau Holle (Grimm, No. 24) type of Folk-tale studied by Cosquin, i. 250, *seq.* "Kate Crackernuts" (No. xxxvii.) is a pleasant contrast to this.

FINIS

More English
Fairy Tales

YOU KNOW HOW
TO GET INTO THIS BOOK.

Knock at the Knocker on the Door,
Pull the Bell at the side,
Then, if you are very *quiet, you will hear a*
teeny tiny voice say through the grating
"Take down the Key." This you will find at the
back: you cannot mistake it, for it has J. J.
in the wards. Put the Key in the Keyhole,
which it fits exactly, unlock the door and
WALK IN

Janet casts the Flaming Sword into the Well

Tamlane

MORE ENGLISH
FAIRY TALES

COLLECTED AND EDITED BY

JOSEPH JACOBS

EDITOR OF "FOLK-LORE"

ILLUSTRATED BY

JOHN D. BATTEN

LONDON
DAVID NUTT, 270 STRAND
1894

To
MY SON SYDNEY
ÆTAT. XIII

Contents

CONTENTS

PREFACE

THIS volume will come, I fancy, as a surprise both to my brother folk-lorists and to the public in general. It might naturally have been thought that my former volume (*English Fairy Tales,* Nutt, 1889) had almost exhaust-ed the scanty remains of the traditional folk-tales of England. Yet I shall be much disappointed if the present collection is not found to surpass the for-mer in interest and vivacity, while for the most part it goes over hitherto untrodden ground. The majority of the tales in this book have either never appeared before, or have never been brought between the same boards.

In putting these tales together, I have acted on the same principles as in the preceding volume, which has already, I am happy to say, established itself as a kind of English Grimm. I have taken English tales wherever I could find them, one from the United States, some from the Lowland Scotch, and a few have been adapted from ballads, while I have left a cou-ple in their original metrical form. I have re-written most of them, and in doing so have adopted the traditional English style of folk-telling, with its "Wells" and "Lawkamercy" and archaic touches, which are known nowadays as vulgarisms. From former experience, I find that each of these principles has met with some dissent from critics who have writ-ten from the high and lofty standpoint of folk-lore, or from the lowlier vantage of "mere literature." I take this occasion to soften their ire, or per-haps give them further cause for reviling.

My folk-lore friends look on with sadness while they view me laying profane hands on the sacred text of my originals. I have actually at times introduced or deleted whole incidents, have given another turn to a tale, or finished off one that was incomplete, while I have had no scruple in pros-ing a ballad or softening down overabundant dialect. This is rank sacrilege in the eyes of the rigid orthodox in matters folk-lorical. My defence might be that I had a cause at heart as sacred as our science of folk-lore—the fill-ing of our children's imaginations with bright trains of images. But even on the lofty heights of folk-lore science I am not entirely defenceless. Do my friendly critics believe that even Campbell's materials had not been modi-fied by the various narrators before they reached the great J. F.? Why may I not have the same privilege as any other story-teller, especially when I know the ways of story-telling as she is told in English, at least as well as a Devonshire or Lancashire peasant? And—conclusive argument—wilt thou, oh orthodox brother folk-lorist, still continue to use Grimm and Asbjörnsen? Well, they did the same as I.

Then as to using tales in Lowland Scotch, whereat a Saturday Reviewer, whose identity and fatherland were not difficult to guess, was so shocked. Scots a dialect of English! Scots tales the same as English! Horror and Philistinism! was the Reviewer's outcry. Matter of fact, is my reply, which will only confirm him, I fear, in his convictions. Yet I appeal to him, why make a difference between tales told on different sides of the Border? A tale told in Durham or Cumberland in a dialect which only Dr. Murray could distinguish from Lowland Scotch, would on all hands be allowed to be "English." The same tale told a few miles farther North, why should we refuse it the same qualification? A tale in Hen-derson is English: why not a tale in Chambers, the majority of whose tales are to be found also south of the Tweed?

The truth is, my folk-lore friends and my Saturday Reviewer differ with me on the important problem of the origin of folk-tales. They think that a tale probably originated where it is found. They therefore attribute more importance than I to the exact form in which it is found and restrict it to the locality of birth. I consider the probability to lie in an origin else-where: I think it more likely than not that any tale found in a place was rather brought there than born there. I have discussed this matter else-where* with all the solemnity its importance deserves, and cannot attempt further to defend my position here. But even the reader innocent of folk-lore can see that, holding these views, I do not attribute much anthropological value to tales whose origin is probably foreign, and am certainly not likely to make a hard-and-fast division between tales of the North Countrie and those told across the Border.

As to how English folk-tales should be told authorities also differ. I am inclined to follow the tradition of my old nurse, who was not bred at Gir-ton and who scorned at times the rules of Lindley Murray and the diction

* See "The Science of Folk Tales and the Problem of Diffusion" in *Transactions of the International Folk-Lore Congress*, 1892. Mr. Lang has honoured me with a rejoinder, which I regard as a palinode, in his Preface to Miss Roalfe Cox's volume of variants of *Cinderella* (Folk-Lore Society, 1891).

of smart society. I have been recommended to adopt a diction not too remote from that of the Authorised Version. Well, quite apart from memories of my old nurse, we have a certain number of tales actually taken down from the mouths of the people, and these are by no means in Authorised form; they even trench on the "vulgar"—*i.e.,* the archaic. Now there is just a touch of snobbery in objecting to these archaisms and calling them "vulgar." These tales have been told, if not from time immemorial, at least for several generations, in a special form which includes dialect and "vulgar" words. Why desert that form for one which the children cannot so easily follow with "thous" and "werts" and all the artificialities of pseudo-Elizabethan? Children are not likely to say "darter" for "daughter," or to ejaculate "Lawkamercyme" because they come across these forms in their folk-tales. They recognise the unusual forms while enjoying the fun of them. I have accordingly retained the archaisms and the old-world formulae which go so well with the folk-tale.

In compiling the present collection I have drawn on the store of 140 tales with which I originally started; some of the best of these I reserved for this when making up the former one. That had necessarily to contain the old favourites "Jack the Giant Killer," "Dick Whittington," and the rest, which are often not so interesting or so well told as the less familiar ones buried in periodicals or folk-lore collections. But since the publication of *English Fairy Tales* I have been specially fortunate in obtaining access to tales entirely new and exceptionally well told, which have been either published during the past three years or have been kindly placed at my disposal by folk-lore friends. Among these the tales reported by Mrs. Balfour, with a thorough knowledge of the peasants' mind and mode of speech, are a veritable acquisition. I only regret that I have had to tone down so much of dialect in her versions. She has added to my indebtedness to her by sending me several tales which are entirely new and inedited. Mrs. Gomme comes only second in rank among my creditors for thanks which I can scarcely pay without becoming bankrupt in gratitude. Other friends have been equally kind, especially Mr. Alfred Nutt, who has helped by adapting some of the book versions, and by reading the proofs, while to the Councils of the American and the English Folk-Lore Societies I have again to repeat my thanks for permission to use materials which first appeared in their publications. Finally, I have had Mr. Batten with me once again— what should I or other English children do without him?

JOSEPH JACOBS.

Full Page Illustrations

[From "process" blocks supplied by Messrs. J. C. Drummond, Henrietta Street, Covent Garden.]

MORE ENGLISH
FAIRY TALES

❧ *The Pied Piper* ❧

NEWTOWN, or Franchville, as 'twas called of old, is a sleepy little town, as you all may know, upon the Solent shore. Sleepy as it is now, it was once noisy enough, and what made the noise was—rats. The place was so infested with them as to be scarce worth living in. There wasn't a barn or a corn-rick, a store-room or a cupboard, but they ate their way into it. Not a cheese but they gnawed it hollow, not a sugar puncheon but they cleared out. Why the very mead and beer in the barrels was not safe from them. They'd gnaw a hole in the top of the tun, and down would go one master rat's tail, and when he brought it up round would crowd all the friends and cousins, and each would have a suck at the tail.

Had they stopped here it might have been borne. But the squeaking and shrieking, the hurrying and scurrying, so that you could neither hear yourself speak nor get a wink of good honest sleep the livelong night! Not to mention that, Mamma must needs sit up, and keep watch and ward over baby's cradle, or there'd have been a big ugly rat running across the poor little fellow's face, and doing who knows what mischief.

Why didn't the good people of the town have cats? Well they did, and there was a fair stand-up fight, but in the end the rats were too many, and the pussies were regularly driven from the field. Poison, I hear you say? Why, they poisoned so many that it fairly bred a plague. Ratcatchers! Why there wasn't a ratcatcher from John o' Groats' House to the Land's End that hadn't tried his luck. But do what they might, cats or poison, terrier or traps, there seemed to be more rats than ever, and every day a fresh rat was cocking his tail or pricking his whiskers.

The Mayor and the town council were at their wits' end. As they were sitting one day in the town hall racking their poor brains, and bewailing their hard fate, who should run in but the town beadle. "Please your Honour," says he, "here is a very queer fellow come to town. I don't rightly know what to make of him." "Show him in," said the Mayor, and in he stept. A queer fellow, truly. For there wasn't a colour of the rainbow but you might find it in some corner of his dress, and he was tall and thin, and had keen piercing eyes.

"I'm called the Pied Piper," he began. "And pray what might you be willing to pay me, if I rid you of every single rat in Franchville?"

Well, much as they feared the rats, they feared parting with their money more, and fain would they have higgled and haggled. But the Piper was not a man to stand nonsense, and the upshot was that fifty pounds were promised him (and it meant a lot of money in those old days) as soon as not a rat was left to squeak or scurry in Franchville.

Out of the hall stept the Piper, and as he stept he laid his pipe to his lips and a shrill keen tune sounded though street and house. And as each note pierced the air you might have seen a strange sight. For out of every hole the rats came tumbling. There were none too old and none too young, none too big and none too little to crowd at the Piper's heels and

with eager feet and upturned noses to patter after him as he paced the streets. Nor was the Piper unmindful of the little toddling ones, for every fifty yards he'd stop and give an extra flourish on his pipe just to give them time to keep up with the older and stronger of the band.

Up Silver Street he went, and down Gold Street, and at the end of Gold Street is the harbour and the broad Solent beyond. And as he paced along, slowly and gravely, the townsfolk flocked to door and window, and many a blessing they called down upon his head.

As for getting near him there were too many rats. And now that he was at the water's edge he stepped into a boat, and not a rat, as he shoved off into deep water, piping shrilly all the while, but followed him, plashing, paddling, and wagging their tails with delight. On and on he played and played until the tide went down, and each master rat sank deeper and deeper in the slimy ooze of the harbour, until every mother's son of them was dead and smothered.

The tide rose again, and the Piper stepped on shore, but never a rat followed. You may fancy the townfolk had been throwing up their caps and hurrahing and stopping up rat-holes and setting the church bells a-ringing. But when the Piper stepped ashore and not so much as a single squeak was to be heard, the Mayor and the Council, and the town-folk generally, began to hum and to ha and to shake their heads.

For the town money chest had been sadly emptied of late, and where was the fifty pounds to come from? Such an easy job, too! Just getting into a boat and playing a pipe! Why the Mayor himself could have done that if only he had thought of it.

So he hummed and ha'ad and at last, "Come, my good man," said he, "you see what poor folk we are; how can we manage to pay you fifty pounds? Will you not take twenty? When all is said and done 'twill be good pay for the trouble you've taken."

"Fifty pounds was what I bargained for," said the Piper shortly; "and if I were you I'd pay it quickly. For I can pipe many kinds of tunes, as folk sometimes find to their cost."

"Would you threaten us, you strolling vagabond?" shrieked the Mayor, and at the same time he winked to the Council; "the rats are all dead and drowned," muttered he; and so "You may do your worst, my good man," and with that he turned short upon his heel.

"Very well," said the Piper, and he smiled a quiet smile. With that he laid his pipe to his lips afresh, but now there came forth no shrill notes, as it were, of scraping and gnawing, and squeaking and scurrying, but the tune was joyous and resonant, full of happy laughter and merry play. And as he paced down the streets the elders mocked, but from school-room and play-room, from nursery and workshop, not a child but ran out with eager glee and shout following gaily at the Piper's call. Dancing, laughing, joining hands and tripping feet, the bright throng moved along up Gold Street and down Silver Street, and beyond Silver Street lay the cool green forest full of old oaks and wide-spreading beeches. In and out among the oak-trees you might catch glimpses of the Piper's many-coloured coat. You might hear the laughter of the children break and fade and die away as deeper and deeper into the lone green wood the stranger went and the children followed.

All the while, the elders watched and waited. They mocked no longer now. And watch and wait as they might, never did they set their eyes again upon the Piper in his parti-coloured coat. Never were their hearts gladdened by the song and dance of the children issuing forth from amongst the ancient oaks of the forest.

✺ Hereafterthis ✺

ONCE upon a time there was a farmer called Jan, and he lived all alone by himself in a little farmhouse.

By-and-by he thought that he would like to have a wife to keep it all vitty for him.

So he went a-courting a fine maid, and said to her, "Will you marry me?"

"That I will, to be sure," said she.

So they went to church, and were wed. After the wedding was over, she got up on his horse behind him, and he brought her home. And they lived as happy as the day was long.

One day, Jan said to his wife, "Wife, can you milk-y?"

"Oh, yes, Jan, I can milk-y. Mother used to milk-y, when I lived home."

So he went to market and bought her ten red cows. All went well till one day when she had driven them to the pond to drink, she thought they did not drink fast enough. So she drove them right into the pond to make them drink faster, and they were all drowned.

When Jan came home, she up and told him what she had done, and he said, "Oh, well there, never mind, my dear; better luck next time."

So they went on for a bit, and then, one day, Jan said to his wife, "Wife can you serve pigs?"

"Oh, yes, Jan, I can serve pigs. Mother used to serve pigs when I lived home."

So Jan went to market and bought her some pigs. All went well till one day, when she had put their food into the trough she thought they did not eat fast enough, and she pushed their heads into the trough to make them eat faster, and they were all choked.

When Jan came home, she up and told him what she done, and he said, "Oh, well, there, never mind my dear, better luck next time."

So they went on for a bit, and then, one day, Jan said to his wife, "Wife can you bake-y?"

"Oh, yes, Jan, I can bake-y. Mother used to bake-y when I lived home."

So he bought everything for his wife so that she could bake bread. All went well for a bit, till one day, she thought that she would bake white bread for a treat for Jan. So she carried her meal to the top of a high hill, and let the wind blow on it, for she thought to herself that the wind would blow out all the bran. But the wind blew away meal and bran and all—so there was an end of it.

When Jan come home, she up and told him what she had done, and he said, "Oh, well, there, never mind my dear, better luck next time."

So they went on for a bit, and then, one day, Jan said to his wife, "Wife can you brew-y?"

"Oh, yes, Jan, I can brew-y. Mother used to brew-y when I lived home."

So he bought everything proper for his wife to brew ale with. All went well for a bit, till one day when she had brewed her ale and put it in the barrel, a big black dog came in and looked up in her face. She drove him out of the house, but he stayed outside the door and still looked up in her face. And she got so angry that she pulled out the plug of the barrel, threw it at the dog, and said, "What dost look in me for? I be Jan's wife." Then the dog ran down the road, and she ran after him to chase him right away. When she came back again, she found that the ale had all run out of the barrel, and so there was an end of it.

When Jan came home, she up and told him what she had done, and he said, "Oh well, there, never mind, my dear; better luck next time."

So they went on for a bit, and then one day she thought to herself, "'Tis time to clean up my house." When she was taking down her big bed she found a bag of groats on the tester. So when Jan came home, she up and said to him, "Jan, what is that bag of groats on the tester for?"

"That is for Hereafterthis, my dear."

Now, there was a robber outside the window, and he heard what Jan said. Next day, he waited till Jan had gone to market, and then he came and knocked at the door. "What do you please to want?" said Mally.

"I am Hereafterthis," said the robber, "I have come for the bag of groats."

Now the robber was dressed like a fine gentleman, so she thought to herself it was very kind of so fine a man to come for the bag of groats, so she ran upstairs and fetched the bag of groats, and gave it to the robber and he went away with it.

When Jan came home, she said to him, "Jan, Hereafterthis has been for the bag of groats."

"What do you mean, wife?" said Jan.

So she up and told him, and he said, "Then I'm a ruined man, for that money was to pay our rent with. The only thing we can do is to roam the world over till we find the bag of groats." Then Jan took the house-door off its hinges, "That's all we shall have to lie on," he said. So Jan put the door on his back, and they both set out to look for Hereafterthis. Many a long day they went, and in the night Jan used to put the door on the branches of a tree, and they would sleep on it. One night they came to a big hill, and there was a high tree at the foot. So Jan put the door up in it, and they got up in the tree and went to sleep. By-and-by Jan's wife heard a noise, and she looked to see what it was. It was an opening of a door in the side of the hill. Out came two gentlemen with a long table, and behind them, fine ladies and gentlemen, each carrying a bag, and one of them was Hereafterthis with the bag of groats. They sat round the table, and began to drink and talk and count up all the money in the bags. So then Jan's wife woke him up, and asked what they should do.

"Now's our time," said Jan, and he pushed the door off the branches, and it fell right in the very middle of the table, and frightened the robbers so that they all ran away. Then Jan and his wife got down from the tree, took as many money-bags as they could carry on the door, and went straight home. And Jan bought his wife more cows, and more pigs, and they lived happy ever after.

ᔣ *The Golden Ball* ᔣ

THERE were two lasses, daughters of one mother, and as they came from the fair, they saw a right bonny young man stand at the house-door before them. They never saw such a bonny man before. He had gold on his cap, gold on his finger, gold on his neck, a red gold watch-chain—eh! but he had brass. He had a golden ball in each hand. He gave a ball to each lass, and she was to keep it, and if she lost it, she was to be hanged. One of the lasses, 'twas the youngest, lost her ball. I'll tell thee how. She was by a park-paling, and she was tossing her ball, and it went up, and up, and up, till it went fair over the paling; and when she climbed up to look, the ball ran along the green grass, and it went right forward to the door of the house, and the ball went in and she saw it no more.

So she was taken away to be hanged by the neck till she was dead because she'd lost her ball.

But she had a sweetheart, and he said he would go and get the ball. So he went to the park-gate, but 'twas shut; so he climbed the hedge, and when he got to the top of the hedge, an old woman rose up out of the dyke before him, and said, if he wanted to get the ball, he must sleep three nights in the house. He said he would.

Then he went into the house, and looked for the ball, but could not find it. Night came on and he heard bogles move in the courtyard; so he looked out o' the window, and the yard was full of them.

Presently he heard steps coming upstairs. He hid behind the door, and was as still as a mouse. Then in came a big giant five times as tall as he, and the giant looked round but did not see the lad, so he went to the window and bowed to look out; and as he bowed on his elbows to see the bogles in the yard, the lad stepped behind him, and with one blow of his sword he cut him in twain, so that the top part of him fell in the yard, and the bottom part stood looking out of the window.

There was a great cry from the bogles when they saw half the giant come tumbling down to them, and they called out, "There comes half our master, give us the other half."

So the lad said, "It's no use of thee, thou pair of legs, standing alone at the window, as thou hast no eye to see with, so go join thy brother"; and he cast the lower part of the giant after the top part. Now when the bogles had gotten all the giant they were quiet.

Next night the lad was at the house again, and now a second giant came in at door, and as he came in the lad cut him in twain, but the legs walked on to the chimney and went up them. "Go, get thee after thy legs," said the lad to the head, and he cast the head up the chimney too.

The third night the lad got into bed, and he heard the bogles striving under the bed, and they had the ball there, and they were casting it to and fro.

Now one of them has his leg thrust out from under bed, so the lad brings his sword down and cuts it off. Then another thrusts his arm out at other side of the bed, and the lad cuts that off. So at last he had maimed them all, and they all went crying and wailing off, and forgot the ball, but he took it from under the bed, and went to seek his truelove.

Now the lass was taken to York to be hanged; she was brought out on the scaffold, and the hangman said, "Now, lass, thou must hang by the neck till thou be'st dead." But she cried out:

> "Stop, stop, I think I see my mother coming!
> Oh mother, hast brought my golden ball

And come to set me free?"

"I've neither brought thy golden ball
Nor come to set thee free,
But I have come to see thee hung
Upon this gallows-tree."

Then the hangman said, "Now, lass, say thy prayers for thou must die." But she said:

"Stop, stop, I think I see my father coming!
O father, hast brought my golden ball
And come to set me free?"

"I've neither brought thy golden ball
Nor come to set thee free,
But I have come to see thee hung
Upon this gallows-tree."

Then the hangman said, "Hast thee done thy prayers? Now, lass, put thy head into the noose."

But she answered, "Stop, stop, I think I see my brother coming!" And again she sang, and then she thought she saw her sister coming, then her uncle, then her aunt, then her cousin; but after this the hangman said, "I will stop no longer, thou'rt making game of me. Thou must be hung at once."

But now she saw her sweetheart coming through the crowd, and he held over his head in the air her own golden ball; so she said:

"Stop, stop, I see my sweetheart coming!
Sweetheart, hast brought my golden ball
And come to set me free?"

"Aye, I have brought thy golden ball
And come to set thee free,
I have not come to see thee hung
Upon this gallows-tree."

And he took her home, and they lived happy ever after.

↢ *My Own Self* ↣

IN a tiny house in the North Countrie, far away from any town or village, there lived not long ago, a poor widow all alone with her little son, a six-year-old boy.

The house-door opened straight on to the hill-side, and all round about were moorlands and huge stones, and swampy hollows; never a house nor a sign of life wherever you might look, for their nearest neighbours were the "ferlies" in the glen below, and the "will-o'-the-wisps" in the long grass along the path-side.

And many a tale she could tell of the "good folk" calling to each other in the oak-trees, and the twinkling lights hopping on to the very window sill, on dark nights; but in spite of the loneliness, she lived on from year to year in the little house, perhaps because she was never asked to pay any rent for it.

But she did not care to sit up late, when the fire burnt low, and no one knew what might be about; so, when they had had their supper she would make up a good fire and go off to bed, so that if anything terrible *did* happen, she could always hide her head under the bed-clothes.

This, however, was far too early to please her little son; so when she called him to bed, he would go on playing beside the fire, as if he did not hear her.

He had always been bad to do with since the day he was born, and his mother did not often care to cross him; indeed, the more she tried to make him obey her, the less heed he paid to anything she said, so it usually ended by his taking his own way.

But one night, just at the fore-end of winter, the widow could not make up her mind to go off to bed, and leave him playing by the fireside; for the wind was tugging at the door, and rattling the window-panes, and well she knew that on such a night, fairies and such like were bound to be out and about, and bent on mischief. So she tried to coax the boy into going at once to bed:

"The safest bed to bide in, such a night as this!" she said: but no, he wouldn't.

Then she threatened to "give him the stick," but it was no use.

The more she begged and scolded, the more he shook his head; and when at last she lost patience and cried that the fairies would surely come and fetch him away, he only laughed and said he wished they *would*, for he would like one to play with.

At that his mother burst into tears, and went off to bed in despair, certain that after such words something dreadful would happen; while her naughty little son sat on his stool by the fire, not at all put out by her crying.

But he had not long been sitting there alone, when he heard a fluttering sound near him in the chimney, and presently down by his side dropped the tiniest wee girl you could think of; she was not a span high, and had hair like spun silver, eyes as green as grass, and cheeks red as June roses.

The little boy looked at her with surprise.

"Oh!" said he; "what do they call ye?"

"My own self," she said in a shrill but sweet little voice, and she looked at him too. "And what do they call ye?"

"Just my own self too?" he answered cautiously; and with that they began to play together.

She certainly showed him some fine games. She made animals out of the ashes that looked and moved like life; and trees with green leaves waving over tiny houses, with men and women an inch high in them, who, when she breathed on them, fell to walking and talking quite properly.

But the fire was getting low, and the light dim, and presently the little boy stirred the coals with a stick, to make them blaze; when out jumped a red-hot cinder, and where should it fall, but on the fairy-child's tiny foot.

Thereupon she set up such a squeal, that the boy dropped the stick, and clapped his hands to his ears; but it grew to so shrill a screech, that it was like all the wind in the world, whistling through one tiny keyhole.

There was a sound in the chimney again, but this time the little boy did not wait to see what it was, but bolted off to bed, where he hid under the blankets and listened in fear and trembling to what went on.

A voice came from the chimney speaking sharply:

"Who's there, and what's wrong?" it said.

"It's my own self," sobbed the fairy child; "and my foot's burnt sore. O-o-h!"

"Who did it?" said the voice angrily; this time it sounded nearer, and the boy, peeping from under the clothes, could see a white face looking out from the chimney-opening.

"Just my own self too!" said the fairy-child again.

"Then if ye did it your own self," cried the elf-mother shrilly, "what's the use o' making all this fash about it?"—and with that she stretched out a long thin arm, and caught the creature by its ear, and, shaking it roughly, pulled it after her, out of sight up the chimney.

The little boy lay awake a long time, listening, in case the fairy mother

should come back after all; and next evening after supper, his mother was surprised to find that he was willing to go to bed whenever she liked.

"He's taking a turn for the better at last!" she said to herself; but he was thinking just then that, when next a fairy came to play with him, he might not get off quite so easily as he had done this time.

⤳ Black Bull of Norroway ⤳

IN Norroway, long time ago, there lived a certain lady, and she had three daughters. The oldest of them said to her mother: "Mother, bake me a bannock, and roast me a collop, for I'm going away to seek my fortune." Her mother did so; and the daughter went away to an old witch washerwife and told her purpose. The old wife bade her stay that day, and look out of her back-door, and see what she could see. She saw nought the first day. The second day she did the same, and saw nought. On the third day she looked again, and saw a coach-and-six coming along the road. She ran in and told the old wife what she saw. "Well," quoth the old woman, "yon's for you." So they took her into the coach, and galloped off.

The second daughter next says to her mother: "Mother, bake me a bannock, and roast me a collop, for I'm going away to seek my fortune." Her mother did so; and away she went to the old wife, as her sister had done. On the third day she looked out of the back-door, and saw a coach-and-four coming along the road. "Well," quoth the old woman, "yon's for you." So they took her in, and off they set.

The third daughter says to her mother: "Mother, bake me a bannock, and roast me a collop, for I'm going away to seek my fortune." Her mother did so; and away she went to the old witch. She bade her look out of her back-door, and see what she could see. She did so; and when she came back, said she saw nought. The second day she did the same, and saw nought. The third day she looked again, and on coming back said to the old wife she saw nought but a great Black Bull coming crooning along the road. "Well," quoth the old witch, "yon's for you." On hearing this she was next to distracted with grief and terror; but she was lifted up and set on his back, and away they went.

Aye they travelled, and on they travelled, till the lady grew faint with hunger. "Eat out of my right ear," says the Black Bull, "and drink out of my left ear, and set by your leaving." So she did as he said, and was wonderfully refreshed. And long they rode, and hard they rode, till they came in sight of a very big and bonny castle. "Yonder we must be this night," quoth the Bull; "for my old brother lives yonder"; and presently they were at the place. They lifted her off his back, and took her in, and sent him away to a park for the night. In the morning, when they brought the Bull home, they took the lady into a fine shining parlour, and gave her a beautiful apple, telling her not to break it till she was in the greatest strait ever mortal was in in the world, and that would bring her out of it. Again she was lifted on the Bull's back, and after she had ridden far, and farther than I can tell, they came in sight of a far bonnier castle, and far farther away than the last. Says the Bull to her: "Yonder we must be this night, for my second brother lives yonder"; and they were at the place directly. They lifted her down and took her in, and sent the Bull to the field for the night. In the morning they took the lady into a fine and rich room, and gave her the finest pear she had ever seen, bidding her not to break it till she was in the greatest strait ever mortal could be in, and that would get her out of it. Again she was lifted and set on his back, and away they went. And long they rode, and hard they rode, till they came in sight of the far biggest castle, and far farthest off, they had yet seen. "We must be yonder to night," says the Bull, "for my young brother lives yonder"; and they were there directly. They lifted her down, took her in, and sent the Bull to the field for the night. In the morning they took her into a room, the finest of all, and gave her a plum, telling her not to break it till she was in the greatest strait mortal could be in, and that would get her out of it. Presently they brought home the Bull, set the lady on his back, and away they went.

And aye they rode, and on they rode, till they came to a dark and ugsome glen, where they stopped, and the lady lighted down. Says the Bull to her: "Here ye must stay till I go and fight the Old Un. Ye must seat yourself on that stone, and move neither hand nor foot till I come back, else I'll never find ye again. And if everything round about you turns blue, I have beaten the Old Un; but should all things turn red, he'll have conquered me." She set herself down on the stone, and by-and-by all round her turned blue. Overcome with joy, she lifted one of her feet, and crossed it over the other, so glad was she that her companion was victorious. The Bull returned and sought for her, but never could find her.

Long she sat, and aye she wept, till she wearied. At last she rose and went away, she didn't know where. On she wandered, till she came to a great hill of glass, that she tried all she could to climb, but wasn't able. Round the bottom of the hill she went, sobbing and seeking a passage over, till at last she came to a smith's house; and the smith promised, if she would serve him seven years, he would make her iron shoon, wherewith she could climb over the glassy hill. At seven years' end she got her iron shoon, clomb the glassy hill, and chanced to come to the old washerwife's habitation. There she was told of a gallant young knight that had given in some clothes all over blood to wash, and whoever washed them was to be his wife. The old wife had washed till she was tired, and then she set her daughter at it, and both washed, and they washed, and they washed, in hopes of getting the young knight; but all they could do, they couldn't bring out a stain. At length they set the stranger damosel to work; and whenever she began, the stains came out pure and clean, and the old wife made the knight believe it was her daughter had washed the clothes. So the knight and the eldest daughter were to be married, and the stranger damosel was distracted at the thought of it, for she was deeply in love with him. So she bethought her of her apple, and breaking it, found it filled with gold and precious jewellery, the richest she had ever seen. "All these," she said to the eldest daughter, "I will give you, on condition that you put off your marriage for one day, and allow me to go into his room alone at night." So the lady consented; but meanwhile the old wife had prepared a sleeping drink, and given it to the knight, who drank it, and never wakened till next morning. The life-long night the damosel sobbed and sang:

> "Seven long years I served for thee,
> The glassy hill I clomb for thee,
> Thy bloody clothes I wrang for thee;
> And wilt thou not waken and turn to me?"

Next day she knew not what to do for grief. She then broke the pear, and found it filled with jewellery far richer than the contents of the apple. With these jewels she bargained for permission to be a second night in the young knight's chamber; but the old wife gave him another sleeping drink, and he again slept till morning. All night she kept sighing and singing as before:

> "Seven long years I served for thee,
> The glassy hill I clomb for thee,
> Thy bloody clothes I wrang for thee;
> And wilt thou not waken and turn to me?"

Still he slept, and she nearly lost hope altogether. But that day, when he was out hunting, somebody asked him what noise and moaning was that they heard all last night in his bedchamber. He said, "I haven't heard any

THE GLASSY HILL

THEE FOR CLOMB

The Black Bull of Norroway

noise." But they assured him there was; and he resolved to keep waking that night to try what he could hear. That being the third night, and the damosel being between hope and despair, she broke her plum, and it held far the richest jewellery of the three. She bargained as before; and the old wife, as before, took in the sleeping drink to the young knight's chamber; but he told her he couldn't drink it that night without sweetening. And when she went away for some honey to sweeten it with, he poured out the drink, and so made the old wife think he had drunk it. They all went to bed again, and the damosel began, as before, singing:

> "Seven long years I served for thee,
> The glassy hill I clomb for thee,
> Thy bloody clothes I wrang for thee;
> And wilt thou not waken and turn to me?"

He heard, and turned to her. And she told him all that had befallen her, and he told her all that had happened to him. And he caused the old washerwife and her daughter to be burnt. And they were married, and he and she are living happy to this day, for aught I know.

ᠵᡝ *Yallery Brown* ᠵᡝ

ONCE upon a time, and a very good time it was, though it wasn't in my time, nor in your time, nor any one else's time, there was a young lad of eighteen or so named Tom Tiver working on the Hall Farm. One Sunday he was walking across the west field, 'twas a beautiful July night, warm and still and the air was full of little sounds as though the trees and grass were chattering to themselves. And all at once there came a bit ahead of him the pitifullest greetings ever he heard, sob, sobbing, like a bairn spent with fear, and nigh heartbroken; breaking off into a moan and then rising again in a long whimpering wailing that made him feel sick to hark to it. He began to look everywhere for the poor creature. "It must be Sally Bratton's child," he thought to himself; "she was always a flighty thing, and never looked after it. Like as not, she's flaunting about the lanes, and has clean forgot the babby." But though he looked and looked, he could see nought. And presently the whimpering got louder and stronger in the quietness, and he thought he could make out words of some sort. He hearkened with all his ears, and the sorry thing was saying words all mixed up with sobbing—

"Ooh! the stone, the great big stone! ooh! the stones on top!"

Naturally he wondered where the stone might be, and he looked again, and there by the hedge bottom was a great flat stone, nigh buried in the mools, and hid in the cotted grass and weeds. One of the stones was called the "Strangers' Tables." However, down he fell on his knee-bones by that stone, and hearkened again. Clearer than ever, but tired and spent with greeting came the little sobbing voice—"Ooh! ooh! the stone, the stone on top." He was gey, and misliking to meddle with the thing, but he couldn't stand the whimpering babby, and he tore like mad at the stone, till he felt it lifting from the mools, and all at once it came with a sough out o' the damp earth and the tangled grass and growing things. And there in the hole lay a tiddy thing on its back, blinking up at the moon and at him. 'Twas no bigger than a year old baby, but it had long cotted hair and beard, twisted round and round its body so that you couldn't see its clothes; and the hair was all yaller and shining and silky, like a bairn's; but the face of it was old and as if 'twere hundreds of years since 'twas young and smooth. Just a heap of wrinkles, and two bright black eyne in the midst, set in a lot of shining yaller hair; and the skin was the colour of the fresh turned earth in the spring—brown as brown could be, and its bare hands and feet were brown like the face of it. The greeting had stopped, but the tears were standing on its cheek, and the tiddy thing looked mazed like in the moonshine and the night air.

The creature's eyne got used like to the moonlight, and presently he looked up in Tom's face as bold as ever was; "Tom," says he, "thou'rt a

good lad!" as cool as thou can think, says he, "Tom, thou'rt a good lad!" and his voice was soft and high and piping like a little bird twittering.

Tom touched his hat, and began to think what he ought to say. "Houts!" says the thing again, "thou needn't be feared o' me; thou'st done me a better turn than thou knowst, my lad, and I'll do as much for thee." Tom couldn't speak yet, but he thought, "Lord! for sure 'tis a bogle!"

"No!" says he as quick as quick, "I am no bogle, but ye'd best not ask me what I be; anyways I be a good friend o' thine." Tom's very knee-bones struck, for certainly an ordinary body couldn't have known what he'd been thinking to himself, but he looked so kind like, and spoke so fair, that he made bold to get out, a bit quavery like—

"Might I be axing to know your honour's name?"

"H'm," says he, pulling his beard; "as for that"—and he thought a bit— "ay so," he went on at last, "Yallery Brown thou mayst call me, Yallery Brown; 'tis my nature seest thou, and as for a name 'twill do as any other. Yallery Brown, Tom, Yallery Brown's thy friend, my lad."

"Thankee, master," says Tom, quite meek like.

"And now," he says, "I'm in a hurry to-night, but tell me quick, what'll I do for thee? Wilt have a wife? I can give thee the finest lass in the town. Wilt be rich? I'll give thee gold as much as thou can carry. Or wilt have help wi' thy work? Only say the word."

Tom scratched his head. "Well, as for a wife, I have no hankering after such; they're but bothersome bodies, and I have women folk at home as 'll mend my clouts; and for gold that's as may be, but for work, there, I can't abide work, and if thou'lt give me a helpin' hand in it I'll thank———"

"Stop," says he, quick as lightning, "I'll help thee and welcome, but if ever thou sayest that to me—if ever thou thankest me, see'st thou, thou'lt never see me more. Mind that now; I want no thanks, I'll have no thanks"; and he stampt his tiddy foot on the earth and looked as wicked as a raging bull.

"Mind that now, great lump that thou be," he went on, calming down a bit, "and if ever thou need'st help, or get'st into trouble, call on me and just say, 'Yallery Brown, come from the mools, I want thee!' and I'll be wi' thee at once; and now," says he, picking a dandelion puff, "good night to thee," and he blowed it up, and it all came into Tom's eyne and ears. Soon as Tom could see again the tiddy creature was gone, and but for the stone on end and the hole at his feet, he'd have thought he'd been dreaming.

Well, Tom went home and to bed; and by the morning he'd nigh forgot all about it. But when he went to the work, there was none to do! all was done already, the horses seen to, the stables cleaned out, everything in its proper place, and he'd nothing to do but sit with his hands in his pockets. And so it went on day after day, all the work done by Yallery Brown, and better done, too, than he could have done it himself. And if the master gave him more work, he sat down, and the work did itself, the singeing irons, or the broom, or what not, set to, and with ne'er a hand put to it would get through in no time. For he never saw Yallery Brown in daylight; only in the darklins he saw him hopping about, like a Will-o-th'-wyke without his lanthorn.

At first, 'twas mighty fine for Tom; he'd nought to do and good pay for it; but by-and-by things began to go vicey-varsy. If the work was done for Tom, 'twas undone for the other lads; if his buckets were filled, theirs were upset; if his tools were sharpened, theirs were blunted and spoiled; if his horses were clean as daisies, theirs were splashed with muck, and so on; day in and day out, 'twas the same. And the lads saw Yallery Brown flitting about o' nights, and they saw the things working without hands o' days, and they saw that Tom's work was done for him, and theirs undone for them; and naturally they begun to look shy on him, and they wouldn't speak or come nigh him, and they carried tales to the master and so things went from bad to worse.

For Tom could do nothing himself; the brooms wouldn't stay in his hand, the plough ran away from him, the hoe kept out of his grip. He thought that he'd do his own work after all, so that Yallery Brown would leave him and his neighbours alone. But he couldn't—true as death he couldn't. He could only sit by and look on, and have the cold shoulder turned on him, while the unnatural thing was meddling with the others, and working for him.

At last, things got so bad that the master gave Tom the sack, and if he hadn't, all the rest of the lads would have sacked him, for they swore they'd not stay on the same garth with Tom. Well, naturally Tom felt bad; 'twas a very good place, and good pay too; and he was fair mad with Yallery Brown, as 'd got him into such a trouble. So Tom shook his fist in the air and called out as loud as he could, "Yallery Brown, come from the mools; thou scamp, I want thee!"

You'll scarce believe it, but he'd hardly brought out the words but he felt something tweaking his leg behind, while he jumped with the smart of it; and soon as he looked down, there was the tiddy thing, with his shining hair, and wrinkled face, and wicked glinting black eyne.

Tom was in a fine rage, and he would have liked to have kicked him, but 'twas no good, there wasn't enough of it to get his boot against; but he said, "Look here, master, I'll thank thee to leave me alone after this, dost hear? I want none of thy help, and I'll have nought more to do with thee—see now."

The horrid thing broke into a screeching laugh, and pointed its brown finger at Tom. "Ho, ho, Tom!" says he. "Thou'st thanked me, my lad, and I told thee not, I told thee not!"

"I don't want thy help, I tell thee," Tom yelled at him—"I only want never to see thee again, and to have nought more to do with ee—thou can go."

The thing only laughed and screeched and mocked, as long as Tom went on swearing, but so soon as his breath gave out————

"Tom, my lad," he said with a grin, "I'll tell'ee summat, Tom. True's true I'll never help thee again, and call as thou wilt, thou'lt never see me after to-day; but I never said that I'd leave thee alone, Tom, and I never will, my lad! I was nice and safe under the stone, Tom, and could do no harm; but thou let me out thyself, and thou can't put me back again! I would have been thy friend and worked for thee if thou had been wise; but since thou bee'st no more than a born fool I'll give 'ee no more than a born fool's luck; and when all goes vice-varsy, and everything agee—thou'lt mind that it's Yallery Brown's doing though m'appen thou doesn't see him. Mark my words, will 'ee?"

And he began to sing, dancing round Tom, like a bairn with his yellow hair, but looking older than ever with his grinning wrinkled bit of a face:

> "Work as thou will
> Thou'lt never do well;
> Work as thou mayst
> Thou'lt never gain grist;
> For harm and mischance and Yallery Brown
> Thou'st let out thyself from under the stone."

Tom could never rightly mind what he said next. 'Twas all cussing and calling down misfortune on him; but he was so mazed in fright that he could only stand there shaking all over, and staring down at the horrid thing; and if he'd gone on long, Tom would have tumbled down in a fit. But by-and-by, his yaller shining hair rose up in the air, and wrapt itself round him till he looked for all the world like a great dandelion puff; and it floated away on the wind over the wall and out o' sight, with a parting skirl of wicked voice and sneering laugh.

And did it come true, sayst thou? My word! but it did, sure as death! He worked here and he worked there, and turned his hand to this and to that, but it always went agee, and 'twas all Yallery Brown's doing. And the children died, and the crops rotted—the beasts never fatted, and nothing ever did well with him; and till he was dead and buried, and m'appen even afterwards, there was no end to Yallery Brown's spite at him; day in and day out he used to hear him saying—

> "Work as thou wilt
> Thou'lt never do well;
> Work as thou mayst
> Thou'lt never gain grist;
> For harm and mischance and Yallery Brown
> Thou'st let out thyself from under the stone."

❧ Three Feathers ❧

ONCE upon a time there was a girl who was married to a husband that she never saw. And the way this was that he was only at home at night, and would never have any light in the house. So the girl thought that was funny, and all her friends told her there must be something wrong with her husband, some great deformity that made him want not to be seen.

Well, one night when he came home she suddenly lit a candle and saw him. He was handsome enough to make all the women of the world fall in love with him. But scarcely had she seen him when he began to change into a bird, and then he said: "Now you have seen me, you shall see me no more, unless you are willing to serve seven years and a day for me, so that I may become a man once more." Then he told her to take three feathers from under his side, and whatever she wished through them would come to pass. Then he left her at a great house to be laundry-maid for seven years and a day.

And the girl used to take the feathers and say: "By virtue of my three feathers may the copper be lit, and the clothes washed, and mangled, and folded, and put away to the missus's satisfaction."

And then she had no more care about it. The feathers did the rest, and the lady set great store by her for a better laundress she had never had. Well, one day the butler, who had a notion to have the pretty laundry-maid for his wife, said to her, he should have spoken before but he did not want to vex her. "Why should it when I am but a fellow-servant?" the girl said. And then he felt free to go on, and explain he had £70 laid by with the master, and how would she like him for a husband.

And the girl told him to fetch her the money, and he asked his master for it, and brought it to her. But as they were going up stairs, she cried, "O John, I must go back, sure I've left my shutters undone, and they'll be slashing and banging all night."

The butler said, "Never you trouble, I'll put them right," and he ran back, while she took her feathers, and said: "By virtue of my three feathers may the shutters slash and bang 'till morning, and John not be able to fasten them nor yet to get his fingers free from them!"

And so it was. Try as he might the butler could not leave hold, nor yet keep the shutters from blowing open as he closed them. And he *was* angry, but could not help himself, and he did not care to tell of it and get the laugh on him, so no one knew.

Then after a bit the coachman began to notice her, and she found he had some £40 with the master, and he said she might have it if she would take him with it.

So after the laundry-maid had his money in her apron as they went merrily along, she stopt, exclaiming: "My clothes are left outside, I must run back and bring them in." "Stop for me while I go; it is a cold frost night," said William, "you'd be catching your death." So the girl waited long enough to take her feathers out and say, "By virtue of my three feathers may the clothes slash and blow about 'till morning, and may William not be able to take his hand from them nor yet to gather them up." And then she was away to bed and to sleep.

The coachman did not want to be every one's jest, and he said nothing. So after a bit, the footman comes to her and said he: "I have been with my master for years and have saved up a good bit, and you have been three years here, and must have saved up as well. Let us put it together, and make us a home or else stay on at service as pleases you." Well, she got him to bring the savings to her as the others had, and then she pretended she was faint, and said to him: "James, I feel so queer, run down cellar for me, that's a dear, and fetch me up a drop of brandy." Now no sooner had he started than she said: "By virtue of my three feathers, may there be slashing and spilling, and James not be able to pour the brandy straight nor yet to take his hand from it until morning!"

And so it was. Try as he might James could not get his glass filled, and there was slashing and spilling, and right on it all, down came the master to know what it meant!

So James told him he could not make it out, but he could not get the drop of brandy the laundry-maid had asked for, and his hand would shake and spill everything, and yet come away he could not.

This got him in for a regular scrape, and the master when he got back to his wife said, "What has come over the men, they were all right until that laundry-maid of yours came. Something is up now though. They have all drawn out their pay, and yet they don't leave, and what can it be anyway?"

But his wife said she could not hear of the laundry-maid being blamed, for she was the best servant she had, and worth all the rest put together.

So it went on until one day as the girl stood in the hall door, the coachman happened to say to the footman: "Do you know how that girl served me, James?" And then William told about the clothes. The butler put in, "That was nothing to what she served me," and he told of the shutters clapping all night.

So then the master came through the hall, and the girl said: "By virtue of my three feathers may there be slashing and striving between master and men, and may all get splashed in the pond."

And so it was, the men fell to disputing which had suffered the most by her, and when the master came up all would be heard at once and none listened to him, and it came to blows all round, and the first they knew they had shoved one another into the pond.

So when the girl thought they had had enough she took the spell off, and the master asked her what had begun the row, for he had not heard in the confusion.

And the girl said, "They were ready to fall on any one; they'd have beat me if you had not come by."

So it blew over for that time, and through her feathers she made the best laundress ever known. But to make a long story short, when the seven years and a day were up, the bird-husband, who had known her doings all along, came after her, restored to his own shape again. And he told her mistress he had come to take her from being a servant, and that she should have servants under her. But he did not tell of the feathers.

And then he bade her give the men back their savings.

"That was a rare game you had with them," said he, "but now you are going where there is plenty, so leave them each their own." So she did; and they drove off to their castle, where they lived happy ever after.

⤳ *Sir Gammer Vans* ⤳

LAST Sunday morning at six o'clock in the evening as I was sailing over the tops of the mountains in my little boat, I met two men on horseback riding on one mare: so I asked them, "Could they tell me whether the little old woman was dead yet who was hanged last Saturday week for drowning herself in a shower of feathers?" They said they could not positively inform me, but if I went to Sir Gammer Vans he could tell me all about it.

"But how am I to know the house?" said I.

"Ho, 'tis easy enough," said they, "for 'tis a brick house, built entirely of flints, standing alone by itself in the middle of sixty or seventy others just like it."

"Oh, nothing in the world is easier," said I.

"Nothing *can* be easier," said they: so I went on my way.

Now this Sir G. Vans was a giant, and bottle-maker. And as all giants who *are* bottle-makers usually pop out of a little thumb-bottle from behind the door, so did Sir G. Vans.

"How d'ye do?" says he.

"Very well, I thank you," says I.

"Have some breakfast with me?"

"With all my heart," says I.

So he gave me a slice of beer, and a cup of cold veal; and there was a little dog under the table that picked up all the crumbs.

"Hang him," says I.

"No, don't hang him," says he; "for he killed a hare yesterday. And if you don't believe me, I'll show you the hare alive in a basket."

So he took me into his garden to show me the curiosities. In one corner there was a fox hatching eagle's eggs; in another there was an iron apple-tree, entirely covered with pears and lead; in the third there was the hare which the dog killed yesterday alive in the basket; and in the fourth there were twenty-four *hipper switches* threshing tobacco, and at the sight of me they threshed so hard that they drove the plug through the wall, and through a little dog that was passing by on the other side. I, hearing the dog howl, jumped over the wall; and turned it as neatly inside out as possible, when it ran away as if it had not an hour to live. Then he took me into the park to show me his deer: and I remembered that I had a warrant in my pocket to shoot venison for his majesty's dinner. So I set fire to my bow, poised my arrow, and shot amongst them. I broke seventeen ribs on one side, and twenty-one and a-half on the other; but my arrow passed clean through without ever touching it, and the worst was I lost my arrow: however, I found it again in the hollow of a tree. I felt it; it felt clammy. I smelt it; it smelt honey. "Oh, ho," said I, "here's a bee's nest," when out sprang a covey of partridges. I shot at them; some say I killed eighteen; but I am sure I killed thirty-six, besides a dead salmon which was flying over the bridge, of which I made the best apple-pie I ever tasted.

❧ *Tom Hickathrift* ❧

BEFORE the days of William the Conqueror there dwelt a man in the marsh of the Isle of Ely whose name was Thomas Hickathrift, a poor day labourer, but so stout that he could do two days' work in one. His one son he called by his own name, Thomas Hickathrift, and he put him to good learning, but the lad was none of the wisest, and indeed seemed to be somewhat soft, so he got no good at all from his teaching.

Tom's father died, and his mother being tender of him, kept him as well as she could. The slothful fellow would do nothing but sit in the chimney-corner, and eat as much at a time as would serve four or five ordinary men. And so much did he grow that when but ten years old he was already eight feet high, and his hand like a shoulder of mutton.

One day his mother went to a rich farmer's house to beg a bottle of straw for herself and Tom. "Take what you will," said the farmer, an honest, charitable man. So when she got home she told Tom to fetch the straw, but he wouldn't, and, beg as she might, he wouldn't till she borrowed him a cart rope. So off he went, and when he came to the farmer's, master and men were all a-thrashing in the barn.

"I'm come for the straw," said Tom.

"Take as much as thou canst carry," said the farmer.

So Tom laid down his rope and began to make his bottle.

"Your rope is too short," said the farmer by way of a joke; but the joke was on Tom's side, for when he had made up his load there was some twenty hundredweight of straw, and though they called him a fool for thinking he could carry the tithe of it, he flung it over his shoulder as if it had been a hundredweight, to the great admiration of master and men.

Tom's strength being thus made known there was no longer any basking by the fire for him; every one would be hiring him to work, and telling him 'twas a shame to live such a lazy life. So Tom seeing them wait on him as they did, went to work first with one, then with another. And one day a woodman desired his help to bring home a tree. Off went Tom and four men besides, and when they came to the tree they began to draw it into the cart with pulleys. At last Tom, seeing them unable to lift it, "Stand away, you fools," said he, and, taking the tree, set it on one end and laid it in the cart. "Now," said he, "see what a man can do." "Marry, 'tis true," said they, and the woodman asked what reward he'd take. "Oh, a stick for my mother's fire," said Tom; and, espying a tree bigger than was in the cart, he laid it on his shoulders and went home with it as fast as the cart and six horses could draw it.

Tom now saw that he had more strength than twenty men, and began to be very merry, taking delight in company, in going to fairs and meetings, in seeing sports and pastimes. And at cudgels, wrestling, or throwing the hammer, not a man could stand against him, so that at last none durst go into the ring to wrestle with him, and his fame was spread more and more in the country.

Far and near he would go to any meetings, as football play or the like. And one day in a part of the country where he was a stranger, and none knew him, he stopped to watch a company at football play; rare sport it was; but Tom spoiled it all, for meeting the ball he took it such a kick that away it flew none could tell whither. They were angry with Tom as you may fancy, but got nothing by that, as Tom took hold of a big spar, and laid about with a will, so that though the whole country-side was up in arms against him, he cleared his way wherever he came.

It was late in the evening ere he could turn homeward, and on the road there met him four lusty rogues that had been robbing passengers all day. They thought they had a good prize in Tom, who was all alone, and made cocksure of his money.

"Stand and deliver!" said they.

"What should I deliver?" said Tom.

"Your money, sirrah," said they.

"You shall give me better words for it first," said Tom.

"Come, come, no more prating; money we want, and money we'll have before you stir."

"Is it so?" said Tom; "nay, then come and take it."

The long and the short of it was that Tom killed two of the rogues, and grievously wounded the other two, and took all their money, which was as much as two hundred pounds. And when he came home he made his old mother laugh with the story of how he served the football players and the four thieves.

But you shall see that Tom sometimes met his match. In wandering one day in the forest he met a lusty tinker that had a good staff on his shoulder, and a great dog to carry his bag and tools.

"Whence come you and whither are you going?" said Tom, "this is no highway."

"What's that to you?" said the tinker; "fools must needs be meddling."

"I'll make you know," said Tom, "before you and I part, what it is to me."

"Well," said the tinker, "I'm ready for a bout with any man, and I hear there is one Tom Hickathrift in the country of whom great things are told. I'd fain see him to have a turn with him."

"Ay," said Tom, "methinks he might be master with you. Anyhow, I am the man; what have you to say to me?"

"Why, verily, I'm glad we are so happily met."

"Sure, you do but jest," said Tom.

"Marry, I'm in earnest," said the tinker. "A match?" "'Tis done." "Let me first get a twig," said Tom. "Ay," said the tinker, "hang him that would fight a man unarmed."

So Tom took a gate-rail for his staff, and at it they fell, the tinker at Tom, and Tom at the tinker, like two giants they laid on at each other.

The tinker had a leathern coat on, and at every blow Tom gave the tinker his coat roared again, yet the tinker did not give way one inch. At last Tom gave him a blow on the side of his head which felled him.

"Now tinker where are you?" said Tom.

But the tinker being a nimble fellow, leapt up again, gave Tom a blow that made him reel again, and followed his blow with one on the other side that made Tom's neck crack again. So Tom flung down his weapon and yielded the tinker the better on it, took him home to his house, where they nursed their bruises, and from that day forth there was no stauncher pair of friends than they two.

Tom's fame was thus spread abroad till at length a brewer at Lynn, wanting a good lusty man to carry his beer to Wisbeach went to hire Tom, and promised him a new suit of clothes from top to toe, and that he should eat and drink of the best, so Tom yielded to be his man and his master told him what way he should go, for you must understand there was a monstrous giant who kept part of the marsh-land, so that none durst go that way.

So Tom went every day to Wisbeach, a good twenty miles by the road. 'Twas a wearisome journey thought Tom and he soon found that the way kept by the giant was nearer by half. Now Tom had got more strength than ever, being well kept as he was and drinking so much strong ale as he did. One day, then, as he was going to Wisbeach, without saying anything to his master or to any of his fellow-servants, he resolved to take the nearest road or to lose his life; as they say, to win horse or lose saddle. Thus resolved, he took the near road, flinging open the gates for his cart and horses to go through. At last the giant spied him, and came up speedily, intending to take his beer for a prize.

He met Tom like a lion, as though he would have swallowed him. "Who gave you authority to come this way?" roared he. "I'll make you an example for all rogues under the sun. See how many heads hang on yonder tree. Yours shall hang higher than all the rest for a warning."

But Tom made him answer, "A fig in your teeth you shall not find me like one of them, traitorly rogue that you are."

The giant took these words in high disdain, and ran into his cave to fetch his great club, intending to dash out Tom's brains at the first blow.

Tom knew not what to do for a weapon; his whip would be but little good against a monstrous beast twelve foot in length and six foot about the waist. But whilst the giant went for his club, bethinking him of a very good weapon, he made no more ado, but took his cart, turned it upside down, and took axle-tree and wheel for shield and buckler. And very good weapons they were found!

Out came the giant and began to stare at Tom. "You are like to do great service with those weapons," roared he. "I have here a twig that will beat you and your wheel to the ground." Now this twig was as thick as some mileposts are, but Tom was not daunted for all that, though the giant made at him with such force that the wheel cracked again. But Tom gave as good as he got, taking the giant such a weighty blow on the side of the head that he reeled again. "What," said Tom, "are you drunk with my strong beer already?"

So at it they went, Tom laying such huge blows at the giant, down whose face sweat and blood ran together, so that, being fat and foggy and tired with the long fighting, he asked Tom would he let him drink a little? "Nay, nay," said Tom, "my mother did not teach me such wit; who'd be a fool then?" And seeing the giant beginning to weary and fail in his blows, Tom thought best to make hay whilst the sun shone, and, laying on as fast as though he had been mad, he brought the giant to the ground. In vain were the giant's roars and prayers and promises to yield himself and be Tom's servant. Tom laid at him till he was dead, and then, cutting off his head, he went into the cave, and found a great store of silver and gold, which made his heart to leap. So he loaded his cart, and after delivering his beer at Wisbeach, he came home and told his master what had befallen him. And on the morrow he and his master and more of the town-folk of Lynn set out for the giant's cave. Tom showed them the head, and what silver and gold there was in the cave, and not a man but leapt for joy, for the giant was a great enemy to all the country.

The news was spread all up and down the country-side how Tom Hickathrift had killed the giant. And well was he that could run to see the cave; all the folk made bonfires for joy, and if Tom was respected before, he was much more so now. With common consent he took possession of the cave and everyone said, had it been twice as much, he would have deserved it. So Tom pulled down the cave, and built himself a brave house. The ground that the giant kept by force for himself, Tom gave part to the poor for their common land, and part he turned into good wheat-land to keep himself and his old mother, Jane Hickathrift. And now he was become the chiefest man in the country-side; 'twas no longer plain Tom, but Mr. Hickathrift, and he was held in due respect I promise you. He kept men and maids and lived most bravely; made him a park to keep deer, and time passed with him happily in his great house till the end of his days.

✥ *The Hedley Kow* ✥

THERE was once an old woman, who earned a poor living by going errands and such like, for the farmers' wives round about the village where she lived. It wasn't much she earned by it; but with a plate of meat at one house, and a cup of tea at another, she made shift to get on somehow, and always looked as cheerful as if she hadn't a want in the world.

Well, one summer evening as she was trotting away homewards she came upon a big black pot lying at the side of the road.

"Now *that*," said she, stopping to look at it, "would be just the very thing for me if I had anything to put into it! But who can have left it here?" and she looked round about, as if the person it belonged to must be not far off. But she could see no one.

"Maybe it'll have a hole in it," she said thoughtfully:—

"Ay, that'll be how they've left it lying, hinny. But then it'd do fine to put a flower in for the window; I'm thinking I'll just take it home, anyways." And she bent her stiff old back, and lifted the lid to look inside.

"Mercy me!" she cried, and jumped back to the other side of the road; "*if it isn't brim full o' gold* PIECES!!"

For a while she could do nothing but walk round and round her treasure, admiring the yellow gold and wondering at her good luck, and saying to herself about every two minutes, "Well, I *do* be feeling rich and grand!" But presently she began to think how she could best take it home with her; and she couldn't see any other way than by fastening one end of her shawl to it, and so dragging it after her along the road.

"It'll certainly be soon dark," she said to herself, "and folk'll not see what I'm bringing home with me, and so I'll have all the night to myself to think what I'll do with it. I could buy a grand house and all, and live like the Queen herself, and not do a stroke of work all day, but just sit by the fire with a cup of tea; or maybe I'll give it to the priest to keep for me, and get a piece as I'm wanting; or maybe I'll just bury it in a hole at the garden-foot, and put a bit on the chimney, between the chiney teapot and the spoons—for ornament, like. Ah! I feel so grand, I don't know myself rightly!"

And by this time, being already rather tired with dragging such a heavy weight after her, she stopped to rest for a minute, turning to make sure that her treasure was safe.

But when she looked at it, it wasn't a pot of gold at all, but a great lump of shining silver!

She stared at it, and rubbed her eyes and stared at it again; but she couldn't make it look like anything but a great lump of silver. "I'd have sworn it was a pot of gold," she said at last, "but I reckon I must have been dreaming. Ay, now, that's a change for the better; it'll be far less trouble to look after, and none so easy stolen; yon gold pieces would have been a sight of bother to keep 'em safe—Ay, I'm well quit of them; and with my bonny lump I'm as rich as rich————!"

And she set off homewards again, cheerfully planning all the grand things she was going to do with her money. It wasn't very long, however, before she got tired again and stopped once more to rest for a minute or two.

Again she turned to look at her treasure, and as soon as she set eyes on it she cried out in astonishment. "Oh my!" said she; "now it's a lump o' iron! Well, that beats all; and it's just real convenient! I can sell it as *easy* as *easy*, and get a lot o' penny pieces for it. Ay, hinny, an' it's much handier than a lot o' yer gold and silver as'd have kept me from sleeping o' nights thinking the neighbours were robbing me—an' it's a real good thing to have by you in a house, ye niver can tell what ye mightn't use it for, an' it'll sell—ay, for a real lot. Rich? I'll be just *rolling!*"

And on she trotted again chuckling to herself on her good luck, till presently she glanced over her shoulder, "just to make sure it was there still," as she said to herself.

"Eh my!" she cried as soon as she saw it; "if it hasn't gone and turned itself into a great stone this time! Now, how could it have known that I was just *terrible* wanting something to hold my door open with? Ay, if that isn't a good change! Hinny, it's a fine thing to have such good luck."

And, all in a hurry to see how the stone would look in its corner by her door, she trotted off down the hill, and stopped at the foot, beside her own little gate.

When she had unlatched it, she turned to unfasten her shawl from the stone, which this time seemed to lie unchanged and peaceably on the path beside her. There was still plenty of light, and she could see the stone quite plainly as she bent her stiff back over it, to untie the shawl end; when, all of a sudden, it seemed to give a jump and a squeal, and grew in a moment as big as a great horse; then it threw down four lanky legs, and shook out two long ears, flourished a tail, and went off kicking its feet into the air, and laughing like a naughty mocking boy.

The old woman stared after it, till it was fairly out of sight.

"WELL!" she said at last, "I *do* be the luckiest body hereabouts! Fancy me seeing the Hedley Kow all to myself, and making so free with it too! I can tell you, I *do* feel that GRAND———"

And she went into her cottage and sat down by the fire to think over her good luck.

ᢌ Gobborn Seer ᢌ

ONCE there was a man Gobborn Seer, and he had a son called Jack.

One day he sent him out to sell a sheep-skin, and Gobborn said, "You must bring me back the skin and the value of it as well."

So Jack started, but he could not find any who would leave him the skin and give him its price too. So he came home discouraged.

But Gobborn Seer said, "Never mind, you must take another turn at it to-morrow."

So he tried again, and nobody wished to buy the skin on those terms.

When he came home his father said, "You must go and try your luck to-morrow," and the third day it seemed as if it would be the same thing over again. And he had half a mind not to go back at all, his father would be so vexed. As he came to a bridge, like the Creek Road one yonder, he leaned on the parapet thinking of his trouble, and that perhaps it would be foolish to run away from home, but he could not tell which to do; when he saw a girl washing her clothes on the bank below. She looked up and said, "If it may be no offence asking, what is it you feel so badly about?"

"My father has given me this skin, and I am to fetch it back and the price of it beside."

"Is that all? Give it here, and it's easy done."

So the girl washed the skin in the stream, took the wool from it, and paid him the value of it, and gave him the skin to carry back.

His father was well pleased, and said to Jack, "That was a witty woman; she would make you a good wife. Do you think you could tell her again?"

Jack thought he could, so his father told him to go by-and-by to the bridge, and see if she was there, and if so bid her come home to take tea with them.

And sure enough Jack spied her and told her how his old father had a wish to meet her, and would she be pleased to drink tea with them.

The girl thanked him kindly, and said she could come the next day; she was too busy at the moment.

"All the better," said Jack, "I'll have time to make ready."

So when she came Gobborn Seer could see she was a witty woman, and he asked her if she would marry his Jack. She said "Yes," and they were married.

Not long after, Jack's father told him he must come with him and build the finest castle that ever was seen, for a king who wished to outdo all others by his wonderful castle.

And as they went to lay the foundation-stone, Gobborn Seer said to Jack, "Can't you shorten the way for me?"

But Jack looked ahead and there was a long road before them, and he said, "I don't see, father, how I could break a bit off."

"You're no good to me, then, and had best be off home."

So poor Jack turned back, and when he came in his wife said, "Why, how's this you've come alone?" and he told her what his father had said and his answer.

"You stupid," said his witty wife, "if you had told a tale you would have shortened the road! Now listen till I tell you a story, and then catch up with Gobborn Seer and begin it at once. He will like hearing it, and by the time you are done you will have reached the foundation-stone."

So Jack sweated and overtook his father. Gobborn Seer said never a word, but Jack began his story, and the road was shortened as his wife had said.

When they came to the end of their journey, they started building of this castle which was to outshine all others. Now the wife had advised them to be intimate with the servants, and so they did as she said, and it was "Good-morning" and "Good-day to you" as they passed in and out.

Now, at the end of a twelvemonth, Gobborn, the wise man, had built such a castle thousands were gathered to admire it.

And the king said: "The castle is done. I shall return to-morrow and pay you all."

"I have just a ceiling to finish in an upper lobby," said Gobborn, "and then it wants nothing."

But after the king was gone off, the housekeeper sent for Gobborn and Jack, and told them that she had watched for a chance to warn them, for the king was so afraid they should carry their art away and build some other king as fine a castle, he meant to take their lives on the morrow. Gobborn told Jack to keep a good heart, and they would come off all right.

When the king had come back Gobborn told him he had been unable to complete the job for lack of a tool left at home, and he should like to send Jack after it.

"No, no," said the king, "cannot one of the men do the errand?"

"No, they could not make themselves understood," said the Seer, "but Jack could do the errand."

"You and your son are to stop here. But how will it do if I send my own son?"

"That will do."

So Gobborn sent by him a message to Jack's wife. "Give him *Crooked and Straight!*"

Now there was a little hole in the wall rather high up, and Jack's wife tried to reach up into a chest there after "crooked and straight," but at last she asked the king's son to help her, because his arms were longest.

But when he was leaning over the chest she caught him by the two heels, and threw him into the chest, and fastened it down. So there he was, both "crooked and straight!"

Then he begged for pen and ink, which she brought him, but he was not allowed out, and holes were bored that he might breathe.

When his letter came, telling the king, his father, he was to be let free when Gobborn and Jack were safe home, the king saw he must settle for the building, and let them come away.

As they left Gobborn told him: Now that Jack was done with this work, he should soon build a castle for his witty wife far superior to the king's, which he did, and they lived there happily ever after.

ꙅ Lawkamercyme ꙅ

THERE was an old woman, as I've heard tell,
She went to the market her eggs for to sell;
She went to the market, all on a market-day,
And she fell asleep on the king's highway.

There came by a pedlar, whose name was Stout,
He cut her petticoats round about;
He cut her petticoats up to the knees,
Which made the old woman to shiver and freeze.

When this old woman first did wake,
She began to shiver, and she began to shake;
She began to wonder, and she began to cry—
"Lawkamercyme, this is none of I!"

"But if it be I, as I do hope it be,
I've a little dog at home, and he'll know me;

If it be I, he'll wag his little tail,
And if it be not I, he'll loudly bark and wail."

Home went the little woman, all in the dark
Up got the little dog, and he began to bark;
He began to bark, so she began to cry—
"Lawkamercyme, this is none of I!"

ꙮ Tattercoats ꙮ

IN a great Palace by the sea there once dwelt a very rich old lord, who
had neither wife nor children living, only one little granddaughter, whose
face he had never seen in all her life. He hated her bitterly, because at her
birth his favourite daughter died; and when the old nurse brought him
the baby, he swore, that it might live or die as it liked, but he would never
look on its face as long as it lived.

So he turned his back, and sat by his window looking out over the sea,
and weeping great tears for his lost daughter, till his white hair and beard
grew down over his shoulders and twined round his chair and crept into
the chinks of the floor, and his tears, dropping on to the window-ledge,
wore a channel through the stone, and ran away in a little river to the
great sea. And, meanwhile, his granddaughter grew up with no one to
care for her, or clothe her; only the old nurse, when no one was by, would
sometimes give her a dish of scraps from the kitchen, or a torn petticoat
from the rag-bag; while the other servants of the Palace would drive her

from the house with blows and mocking words, calling her "Tattercoats," and pointing at her bare feet and shoulders, till she ran away crying, to hide among the bushes.

And so she grew up, with little to eat or to wear, spending her days in the fields and lanes, with only the gooseherd for a companion, who would play to her so merrily on his little pipe, when she was hungry, or cold, or tired, that she forgot all her troubles, and fell to dancing, with his flock of noisy geese for partners.

But, one day, people told each other that the King was travelling through the land, and in the town near by was to give a great ball, to all the lords and ladies of the country, when the Prince, his only son, was to choose a wife.

One of the royal invitations was brought to the Palace by the sea, and the servants carried it up to the old lord who still sat by his window, wrapped in his long white hair and weeping into the little river that was fed by his tears.

But when he heard the King's command, he dried his eyes and bade them bring shears to cut him loose, for his hair had bound him a fast prisoner and he could not move. And then he sent them for rich clothes, and jewels, which he put on; and he ordered them to saddle the white horse, with gold and silk, that he might ride to meet the King.

Meanwhile Tattercoats had heard of the great doings in the town, and she sat by the kitchen-door weeping because she could not go to see them. And when the old nurse heard her crying she went to the Lord of the Palace, and begged him to take his granddaughter with him to the King's ball.

But he only frowned and told her to be silent, while the servants laughed and said, "Tattercoats is happy in her rags, playing with the gooseherd, let her be—it is all she is fit for."

A second, and then a third time, the old nurse begged him to let the girl go with him, but she was answered only by black looks and fierce words, till she was driven from the room by the jeering servants, with blows and mocking words.

Weeping over her ill-success, the old nurse went to look for Tattercoats; but the girl had been turned from the door by the cook, and had run away to tell her friend, the gooseherd, how unhappy she was because she could not go to the King's ball.

But when the gooseherd had listened to her story, he bade her cheer up, and proposed that they should go together into the town to see the

King, and all the fine things; and when she looked sorrowfully down at her rags and bare feet, he played a note or two upon his pipe, so gay and merry, that she forgot all about her tears and her troubles, and before she well knew, the herdboy had taken her by the hand, and she, and he, and the geese before them, were dancing down the road towards the town.

Before they had gone very far, a handsome young man, splendidly dressed, rode up and stopped to ask the way to the castle where the King was staying; and when he found that they too were going thither, he got off his horse and walked beside them along the road.

The herdboy pulled out his pipe and played a low sweet tune, and the stranger looked again and again at Tattercoat's lovely face till he fell deeply in love with her, and begged her to marry him.

But she only laughed, and shook her golden head.

"You would be finely put to shame if you had a goose-girl for your wife!" said she; "go and ask one of the great ladies you will see to-night at the King's ball, and do not flout poor Tattercoats."

But the more she refused him the sweeter the pipe played, and the deeper the young man fell in love; till at last he begged her, as a proof of his sincerity, to come that night at twelve to the King's ball, just as she was, with the herdboy and his geese, and in her torn petticoat and bare feet, and he would dance with her before the King and the lords and ladies, and present her to them all, as his dear and honoured Bride.

So when night came, and the hall in the castle was full of light and music, and the lords and ladies were dancing before the King, just as the clock struck twelve, Tattercoats and the herdboy, followed by his flock of noisy geese, entered at the great doors, and walked straight up the ball-room, while on either side the ladies whispered, the lords laughed, and the King seated at the far end stared in amazement.

But as they came in front of the throne, Tattercoat's lover rose from beside the King, and came to meet her. Taking her by the hand, he kissed her thrice before them all, and turned to the King.

"Father!" he said, for it was the Prince himself, "I have made my choice, and here is my bride, the loveliest girl in all the land, and the sweetest as well!"

Before he had finished speaking, the Herdboy put his pipe to his lips and played a few low notes that sounded like a bird singing far off in the woods; and as he played, Tattercoat's rags were changed to shining robes sewn with glittering jewels, a golden crown lay upon her golden hair, and the flock of geese behind her, became a crowd of dainty pages, bearing her long train.

Tattercoats

And as the King rose to greet her as his daughter, the trumpets sounded loudly in honour of the new Princess, and the people outside in the street said to each other:

"Ah! now the Prince has chosen for his wife the loveliest girl in all the land!"

But the gooseherd was never seen again, and no one knew what became of him; while the Old Lord went home once more to his Palace by the sea, for he could not stay at Court, when he had sworn never to look on his granddaughter's face.

So there he still sits by his window, if you could only see him, as you some day may, weeping more bitterly than ever, as he looks out over the sea.

᠅ The Wee Bannock ᠅

GRANNIE, grannie, come tell us the story of the wee bannock."

"Hout, childer, ye've heard it a hundred times afore. I needn't tell it over again."

"Ah, but, grannie, it's such a fine one. You must tell it. Just once."

"Well, well, if ye'll all promise to be good, I'll tell it ye again."

There lived an old man and an old woman at the side of a burn. They had two cows, five hens and a cock, a cat and two kittens. The old man looked after the cows, and the old wife span on the distaff. The kittens oft gripped at the old wife's spindle, as it tussled over the hearthstone. "Sho, sho," she would say, "go away"; and so it tussled about.

One day, after breakfast, she thought she would have a bannock. So she baked two oatmeal bannocks, and set them on to the fire to harden. After a while, the old man came in, and sat down beside the fire, and takes one of the bannocks, and snaps it through the middle. When the other one sees this, it runs off as fast as it could, and the old wife after it, with the spindle in the one hand, and the distaff in the other. But the wee bannock ran away and out of sight, and ran till it came to a pretty large thatched house, and it ran boldly up inside to the fireside; and there were three tailors sitting on a big bench. When they saw the wee bannock come in, they jumped up, and got behind the goodwife, that was carding tow by the fire. "Hout," quoth she, "be no afeard; it's but a wee bannock. Grip it, and I'll give ye a sup of milk with it." Up she gets with the tow-cards and the tailor with the goose, and the two 'prentices, the one with the big shears, and

the other with the lawbrod; but it dodged them, and ran round about the fire; and one of the 'prentices, thinking to snap it with the shears fell into the ashes. The tailor cast the goose, and the goodwife the tow-cards; but it wouldn't do. The bannock ran away, and ran till it came to a wee house at the roadside; and in it runs, and there was a weaver sitting at the loom, and the wife winding a clue of yarn.

"Tibby," quoth he, "what's that?"

"Oh," quoth she, "it's a wee bannock."

"It's well come," quoth he, "for our porrage were but thin to-day. Grip it, my woman; grip it."

"Ay," quoth she; "what recks! That's a clever bannock. Catch it, Willie; catch it, man."

"Hout," quoth Willie, "cast the clue at it."

But the bannock dodged round about, and off it went, and over the hill, like a new-tarred sheep or a mad cow. And forward it runs to the neat-house, to the fireside; and there was the goodwife churning.

"Come away, wee bannock," quoth she; "I'll have cream and bread to-day." But the wee bannock dodged round about the churn, and the wife after it, and in the hurry she had near-hand overturned the churn. And before she got it set right again, the wee bannock was off and down the brae to the mill; and in it ran.

The miller was sifting meal in the trough; but, looking up: "Ay," quoth he, "it's a sign of plenty when ye're running about, and nobody to look after ye. But I like a bannock and cheese. Come your way hither, and I'll give ye a night's quarters." But the bannock wouldn't trust itself with the miller and his cheese. So it turned and ran its way out; but the miller didn't fash his head with it.

So it toddled away and ran till it came to the smithy; and in it runs, and up to the anvil. The smith was making horse-nails. Quoth he: "I like a glass of good ale and a well-toasted bannock. Come your way in by here." But the bannock was frightened when it heard about the ale, and turned and was off as hard as it could, and the smith after it, and cast the hammer. But it missed, and the bannock was out of sight in a crack, and ran till it came to a farmhouse with a good peat-stack at the end of it. Inside it runs to the fireside. The goodman was cloving lint, and the goodwife heckling. "O Janet," quoth he, "there's a wee bannock; I'll have the half of it."

"Well, John, I'll have the other half. Hit it over the back with the clove." But the bannock played dodgings. "Hout, tout," quoth the wife, and made the heckle flee at it. But it was too clever for her.

And off and up the burn it ran to the next house, and rolled its way to the fireside. The goodwife was stirring the soup, and the goodman plaiting sprit-binnings for the cows. "Ho, Jock," quoth the goodwife, "come here. You're always crying about a wee bannock. Here's one. Come in, haste ye, and I'll help ye to grip it."

"Ay, mother, where is it?"

"See there. Run over on that side."

But the bannock ran in behind the goodman's chair. Jock fell among the sprits. The goodman cast a binning, and the goodwife the spurtle. But it was too clever for Jock and her both. It was off and out of sight in a crack, and through among the whins, and down the road to the next house, and in and snug by the fireside. The folk were just sitting down to their soup, and the goodwife scraping the pot. "Look," quoth she, "there's a wee bannock come in to warm itself at our fireside."

"Shut the door," quoth the goodman, "and we'll try to get a grip of it."

When the bannock heard that, it ran out of the house and they after it with their spoons, and the goodman shied his hat. But it rolled away and ran, and ran, till it came to another house; and when it went in, the folk were just going to their beds. The goodman was taking off his breeches, and the goodwife raking the fire.

"What's that?" quoth he.

"Oh," quoth she, "it's a wee bannock."

Quoth he, "I could eat the half of it."

"Grip it," quoth the wife, "and I'll have a bit too."

"Cast your breeches at it!" The goodman shied his breeches, and had nearly smothered it. But it wriggled out, and ran, and the goodman after it without his breeches; and there was a clean chase over the craft park, and in among the whins; and the goodman lost it, and had to come away, trotting home half-naked. But now it was grown dark, and the wee bannock couldn't see; but it went into the side of a big whin bush, and into a fox's hole. The fox had had no meat for two days. "O welcome, welcome," quoth the fox, and snapped it in two in the middle. And that was the end of the wee bannock.

ꙮ Johnny Gloke ꙮ

JOHNNY GLOKE was a tailor by trade, but like a man of spirit he grew tired of his tailoring, and wished to follow some other path that would lead to honour and fame. But he did not know what to do at first to gain fame and fortune, so for a time he was fonder of basking idly in the sun than in plying the needle and scissors. One warm day as he was enjoying his ease, he was annoyed by the flies alighting on his bare ankles. He brought his hand down on them with force and killed a goodly number of them. On counting the victims of his valour, he was overjoyed at his success; his heart rose to the doing of great deeds, and he gave vent to his feelings in the saying:—

> "Well done! Johnny Gloke.
> Killt fifty flies at one stroke."

His resolution was now taken to cut out his path to fortune and honour. So he took down from its resting-place a rusty old sword that had belonged to some of his forebears, and set out in search of adventures. After travelling a long way, he came to a country that was much troubled by two giants, whom no one was bold enough to meet, and strong enough to overcome. He was soon told of the giants, and learned that the King of the country had offered a great reward and the hand of his daughter in marriage to the man who should rid his land of this scourge. John's heart rose to the deed, and he offered himself for the service. The great haunt of the giants was a wood, and John set out with his old sword to perform his task. When he reached the wood, he laid himself down to think what course he would follow, for he knew how weak he was compared to those he had undertaken to kill. He had not waited long, when he saw them coming with a waggon to fetch wood for fuel. My! they were big ones, with huge heads and long tusks for teeth. Johnny hid himself in the hollow of a tree, thinking only of his own safety. Feeling himself safe, he peeped out of his hiding-place, and watched the two at work. Thus watching he formed his plan of action. He picked up a pebble, threw it with force at one of them, and struck him a sharp blow on the head. The giant in his pain turned at once on his companion, and blamed him in strong words for hitting him. The other denied in anger that he had thrown the pebble. John now saw himself on the high way to gain his reward and the hand of the king's daughter. He kept still, and carefully watched for an opportunity of striking another blow. He soon found it, and right against the giant's head went another pebble. The injured giant fell on his companion in fury, and the two belaboured each other till they were utterly tired out. They sat down on a log to breathe, rest, and recover themselves.

While sitting, one of them said, "Well, all the king's army was not able to take us, but I fear an old woman with a rope's end would be too much for us now."

"If that be so," said Johnny Gloke, as he sprang, bold as a lion, from his hiding-place, "What do you say to Johnny Gloke with his old roosty sword?" So saying he fell upon them, cut off their heads, and returned in triumph. He received the king's daughter in marriage and for a time lived in peace and happiness. He never told the mode he followed in his dealing with the giants.

Some time after a rebellion broke out among the subjects of his father-in-law. John, on the strength of his former valiant deed, was chosen to quell the rebellion. His heart sank within him, but he could not refuse, and so lose his great name. He was mounted on the fiercest horse that ever saw sun or wind, and set out on his desperate task. He was not accustomed to ride on horseback, and he soon lost all control of his steed. It galloped off at full speed, in the direction of the rebel army. In its wild career it passed under the gallows that stood by the wayside. The gallows was somewhat old and frail, and down it fell on the horse's neck. Still the horse made no stop, but always forward at furious speed towards the rebels. On seeing this strange sight approaching towards them at such a speed they were seized with terror, and cried out to one another, "There comes Johnny Gloke that killed the two giants with the gallows on his horse's neck to hang us all." They broke their ranks, fled in dismay, and never stopped till they reached their homes. Thus was Johnny Gloke a second time victorious. So in due time he came to the throne and lived a long, happy, and good life as king.

❧ Coat o' Clay ❧

ONCE on a time, in the parts of Lindsey, there lived a wise woman. Some said she was a witch, but they said it in a whisper, lest she should overhear and do them a mischief, and truly it was not a thing one could be sure of, for she was never known to hurt any one, which, if she were a witch, she would have been sure to do. But she could tell you what your sickness was, and how to cure it with herbs, and she could mix rare possets that would drive the pain out of you in a twinkling; and she could advise you what to do if your cows were ill, or if you'd got into trouble, and tell the maids whether their sweethearts were likely to be faithful.

But she was ill-pleased if folks questioned her too much or too long, and she sore misliked fools. A many came to her asking foolish things, as was their nature, and to them she never gave counsel—at least of a kind that could aid them much.

Well, one day, as she sat at her door paring potatoes, over the stile and up the path came a tall lad with a long nose and goggle eyes and his hands in his pockets.

"That's a fool, if ever was one, and a fool's luck in his face," said the wise woman to herself with a nod of her head, and threw a potato skin over her left shoulder to keep off ill-chance.

"Good-day, missis," said the fool. "I be come to see thee."

"So thou art," said the wise woman; "I see that. How's all in thy folk this year?"

"Oh, fairly," answered he. "But they say I be a fool."

"Ay, so thou art," nodded she, and threw away a bad potato. "I see that too. But what wouldst o' me? I keep no brains for sale."

"Well, see now. Mother says I'll ne'er be wiser all my born days; but folks tell us thou canst do everything. Can't thee teach me a bit, so they'll think me a clever fellow at home?"

"Hout-tout!" said the wise woman; "thou'rt a bigger fool than I thought. Nay, I can't teach thee nought, lad; but I tell thee summat. Thou'lt be a fool all thy days till thou gets a coat o' clay; and then thou'lt know more than me."

"Hi, missis; what sort of a coat's that?" said he.

"That's none o' my business," answered she. "Thou'st got to find out that."

And she took up her potatoes and went into her house.

The fool took off his cap and scratched his head.

"It's a queer kind of coat to look for, sure-*ly*," said he. "I never heard of a coat o' clay. But then I be a fool, that's true."

So he walked on till he came to the drain near by, with just a pickle of water and a foot of mud in it.

"Here's muck," said the fool, much pleased, and he got in and rolled in it spluttering. "Hi, yi!" said he—for he had his mouth full—"I've got a coat o' clay now to be sure. I'll go home and tell my mother I'm a wise man and not a fool any longer." And he went on home.

Presently he came to a cottage with a lass at the door.

"Morning, fool," said she; "hast thou been ducked in the horsepond?"

"Fool yourself," said he, "the wise woman says I'll know more'n she when I get a coat o' clay, and here it is. Shall I marry thee, lass?"

"Ay," said she, for she thought she'd like a fool for a husband, "when shall it be?"

"I'll come and fetch thee when I've told my mother," said the fool, and he gave her his lucky penny and went on.

When he got home his mother was on the doorstep.

"Mother, I've got a coat o' clay," said he.

"Coat o' muck," said she; "and what of that?"

"Wise woman said I'd know more than she when I got a coat o' clay," said he, "so I down in the drain and got one, and I'm not a fool any longer."

"Very good," said his mother, "now thou canst get a wife."

"Ay," said he, "I'm going to marry so-an'-so."

"What!" said his mother, "*that* lass? No, and that thou'lt not. She's nought but a brat, with ne'er a cow or a cabbage o' her own."

"But I gave her my luck penny," said the fool.

"Then thou'rt a bigger fool than ever, for all thy coat o' clay!" said his mother, and banged the door in his face.

"Dang it!" said the fool, and scratched his head, "that's not the right sort o' clay sure-*ly.*"

So back he went to the highroad and sat down on the bank of the river close by, looking at the water, which was cool and clear.

By-and-by he fell asleep, and before he knew what he was about—plump—he rolled off into the river with a splash, and scrambled out, dripping like a drowned rat.

"Dear, dear," said he, "I'd better go and get dry in the sun." So up he went to the highroad, and lay down in the dust, rolling about so that the sun should get at him all over.

Presently, when he sat up and looked down at himself, he found that the dust had caked into a sort of skin over his wet clothes till you could not see an inch of them, they were so well covered. "Hi, yi!" said he, "here's a coat o' clay ready made, and a fine one. See now, I'm a clever fellow this time sure-*ly,* for I've found what I wanted without looking for it! Wow, but it's a fine feeling to be so smart!"

And he sat and scratched his head, and thought about his own cleverness.

But all of a sudden, round the corner came the squire on horseback, full gallop, as if the boggles were after him; but the fool had to jump, even though the squire pulled his horse back on his haunches.

"What the dickens," said the squire, "do you mean by lying in the middle of the road like that?"

"Well, master," said the fool, "I fell into the water and got wet, so I lay down in the road to get dry; and I lay down a fool an' got up a wise man."

"How's that?" said the squire.

So the fool told him about the wise woman and the coat o' clay.

"Ah, ah!" laughed the squire, "whoever heard of a wise man lying in the middle of the highroad to be ridden over? Lad, take my word for it, you are a bigger fool than ever," and he rode on laughing.

"Dang it!" said the fool, as he scratched his head. "I've not got the right sort of coat yet, then." And he choked and spluttered in the dust that the squire's horse had raised.

So on he went in a melancholy mood till he came to an inn, and the landlord at his door smoking.

"Well, fool," said he, "thou'rt fine and dirty."

"Ay," said the fool, "I be dirty outside an' dusty in, but it's not the right thing yet."

And he told the landlord all about the wise woman and the coat o' clay.

"Hout-tout!" said the landlord, with a wink. "I know what's wrong. Thou'st got a skin o' dirt outside and all dry dust inside. Thou must moisten it, lad, with a good drink, and then thou'lt have a real all-over coat o' clay."

"Hi," said the fool, "that's a good word."

So down he sat and began to drink. But it was wonderful how much liquor it took to moisten so much dust; and each time he got to the bottom of the pot he found he was still dry. At last he began to feel very merry and pleased with himself.

"Hi, yi!" said he. "I've got a real coat o' clay now outside and in—what a difference it do make, to be sure. I feel another man now—so smart."

And he told the landlord he was certainly a wise man now, though he couldn't speak over-distinctly after drinking so much. So up he got, and thought he would go home and tell his mother she hadn't a fool for a son any more.

But just as he was trying to get through the inn-door which would scarcely keep still long enough for him to find it, up came the landlord and caught him by the sleeve.

"See here, master," said he, "thou hastn't paid for thy score—where's thy money?"

"Haven't any!" said the fool, and pulled out his pockets to show they were empty.

"What!" said the landlord, and swore; "thou'st drunk all my liquor and haven't got nought to pay for it with!"

"Hi!" said the fool. "You told me to drink so as to get a coat o' clay; but as I'm a wise man now I don't mind helping thee along in the world a bit, for though I'm a smart fellow I'm not too proud to my friends."

"Wise man! smart fellow!" said the landlord, "and help me along, wilt thee? Dang it! thou'rt the biggest fool I ever saw, and it's I'll help *thee* first—out o' this!"

And he kicked him out of the door into the road and swore at him.

"Hum," said the fool, as he lay in the dust, "I'm not so wise as I thought. I guess I'll go back to the wise woman and tell her there's a screw loose somewhere."

So up he got and went along to her house, and found her sitting at the door.

"So thou'rt come back," said she, with a nod. "What dost thou want with me now?"

So he sat down and told her how he'd tried to get a coat o' clay, and he wasn't any wiser for all of it.

"No," said the wise woman, "thou'rt a bigger fool than ever, my lad."

"So they all say," sighed the fool; "but where can I get the right sort of coat o' clay, then, missis?"

"When thou'rt done with this world, and thy folk put thee in the ground," said the wise woman. "That's the only coat o' clay as'll make such as *thee* wise, lad. Born a fool, die a fool, and be a fool thy life long, and that's the truth!"

And she went into the house and shut the door.

"Dang it," said the fool. "I must tell my mother she was right after all, and that she'll never have a wise man for a son!"

And he went off home.

ᘐ *The Three Cows* ᘐ

THERE was a farmer, and he had three cows; fine fat beauties they were. One was called Facey, the other Diamond, and the third Beauty. One morning he went into his cowshed, and there he found Facey so thin that the wind would have blown her away. Her skin hung loose about her, all her flesh was gone, and she stared out of her great eyes as though she'd seen a ghost; and what was more, the fireplace in the kitchen was one great pile of wood-ash. Well, he was bothered with it; he could not see how all this had come about.

Next morning his wife went out to the shed, and see! Diamond was for all the world as wisht a looking creature as Facey—nothing but a bag of bones, all the flesh gone, and half a rick of wood was gone too; but the fireplace was piled up three feet high with white wood-ashes. The farmer determined to watch the third night; so he hid in a closet which opened out of the parlour, and he left the door just ajar, that he might see what passed.

Tick, tick, went the clock, and the farmer was nearly tired of waiting; he had to bite his little finger to keep himself awake, when suddenly the door of his house flew open, and in rushed maybe a thousand pixies, laughing and dancing and dragging at Beauty's halter till they had brought the cow into the middle of the room. The farmer really thought he should have died with fright, and so perhaps he would had not curiosity kept him alive.

Tick, tick, went the clock, but he did not hear it now. He was too intent staring at the pixies and his last beautiful cow. He saw them throw her down, fall on her, and kill her; then with their knives they ripped her open, and flayed her as clean as a whistle. Then out ran some of the little people and brought in firewood and made a roaring blaze on the hearth, and there they cooked the flesh of the cow—they baked and they boiled, they stewed and they fried.

"Take care," cried one, who seemed to be the king, "let no bone be broken."

Well, when they had all eaten, and had devoured every scrap of beef on the cow, they began playing games with the bones, tossing them one to another.

One little leg-bone fell close to the closet-door, and the farmer was so afraid lest the pixies should come there and find him in their search for the bone, that he put out his hand and drew it in to him. Then he saw the king stand on the table and say, "Gather the bones!"

Round and round flew the imps, picking up the bones. "Arrange them," said the king; and they placed them all in their proper positions in the hide of the cow. Then they folded the skin over them, and the king struck the heap of bone and skin with his rod. Whisht! up sprang the cow and lowed dismally. It was alive again; but, alas! as the pixies dragged it back to its stall, it halted in the off forefoot, for a bone was missing.

> "The cock crew,
> Away they flew,"

and the farmer crept trembling to bed.

Ᏸ *The Blinded Giant* Ᏸ

AT Dalton, near Thirsk, in Yorkshire, there is a mill. It has quite recently been rebuilt; but when I was at Dalton, six years ago, the old building stood. In front of the house was a long mound which went by the name of "the giant's grave," and in the mill you can see a long blade of iron something like a scythe-blade, but not curved, which was called "the giant's knife," because of a very curious story which is told of this knife. Would you like to hear it? Well, it isn't very long.

There once lived a giant at this mill who had only one eye in the middle of his forehead, and he ground men's bones to make his bread. One day he captured on Pilmoor a lad named Jack, and instead of grinding him in the mill he kept him grinding as his servant, and never let him get away. Jack served the giant seven years, and never was allowed a holiday the whole time. At last he could bear it no longer. Topcliffe fair was coming on, and Jack begged that he might be allowed to go there.

"No, no," said the giant, "stop at home and mind your grinding."

"I've been grinding and grinding these seven years," said Jack, "and not a holiday have I had. I'll have one now, whatever you say."

"We'll see about that," said the giant.

Well, the day was hot, and after dinner the giant lay down in the mill with his head on a sack and dozed. He had been eating in the mill, and had laid down a great loaf of bone bread by his side, and the knife I told you about was in his hand, but his fingers relaxed their hold of it in sleep. Jack seized the knife, and holding it with both his hands drove the blade into the single eye of the giant, who woke with a howl of agony, and starting up, barred the door. Jack was again in difficulties, for he couldn't get out, but he soon found a way out of them. The giant had a favourite dog, which had also been sleeping when his master was blinded. So Jack killed the dog, skinned it, and threw the hide over his back.

"Bow, wow," says Jack.

"At him, Truncheon," said the giant; "at the little wretch that I've fed these seven years, and now has blinded me."

"Bow, wow," says Jack, and ran between the giant's legs on all-fours, barking till he got to the door. He unlatched it and was off, and never more was seen at Dalton Mill.

〜 Scrapefoot 〜

ONCE upon a time, there were three Bears who lived in a castle in a great wood. One of them was a great big Bear, and one was a middling Bear, and one was a little Bear. And in the same wood there was a Fox who lived all alone, his name was Scrapefoot. Scrapefoot was very much afraid of the Bears, but for all that he wanted very much to know all about them. And one day as he went through the wood he found himself near the Bears' Castle, and he wondered whether he could get into the castle. He looked all about him everywhere, and he could not see any one. So he came up very quietly, till at last he came up to the door of the castle, and he tried whether he could open it. Yes! the door was not locked, and he opened it just a little way, and put his nose in and looked, and he could not see any one. So then he opened it a little way farther, and put one paw in, and then another paw, and another and another, and then he was all in the Bears' Castle. He found he was in a great hall with three chairs in it—one big, one middling, and one little chair; and he thought he would like to sit down and rest and look about him; so he sat down on the big chair. But he found it so hard and uncomfortable that it made his bones ache, and he jumped down at once and got into the middling chair, and he turned round and round in it, but he couldn't make himself comfortable. So then he went to the little chair and sat down in it, and it was so soft and warm and comfortable that Scrapefoot was quite happy; but all at once it broke to pieces under him and he couldn't put it together again! So he got up and began to look about him again, and on one table he saw three saucers, of which one was very big, one was middling, one was quite a little saucer. Scrapefoot was very thirsty, and he began to drink out of the big saucer. But he only just tasted the milk in the big saucer, which was so sour and so nasty that he would not taste another drop of it.

Then he tried the middling saucer, and he drank a little of that. He tried two or three mouthfuls, but it was not nice, and then he left it and went to the little saucer, and the milk in the little saucer was so sweet and so nice that he went on drinking it till it was all gone.

Then Scrapefoot thought he would like to go upstairs; and he listened and he could not hear any one. So upstairs he went, and he found a great room with three beds in it; one was a big bed, and one was a middling bed, and one was a little white bed; and he climbed up into the big bed, but it was so hard and lumpy and uncomfortable that he jumped down again at once, and tried the middling bed. That was rather better, but he could not get comfortably in it, so after turning about a little while he got up and went to the little bed; and that was so soft and so warm and so nice that he fell fast asleep at once.

And after a time the Bears came home, and when they got into the hall the big Bear went to his chair and said, "WHO'S BEEN SITTING IN MY CHAIR?" and the middling Bear said, "WHO'S BEEN SITTING IN MY

CHAIR?" and the little Bear said, "*Who's been sitting in my chair and has broken it all to pieces?*" And then they went to have their milk, and the big Bear said, "WHO'S BEEN DRINKING MY MILK?" and the middling Bear

said, "WHO'S BEEN DRINKING MY MILK?" and the little Bear said, "*Who's been drinking my milk and has drunk it all up?*" Then they went upstairs and into the bedroom, and the big Bear said, "WHO'S BEEN SLEEPING IN MY BED?" and the middling Bear said, "WHO'S BEEN SLEEPING IN MY BED?" and the little Bear said, "*Who's been sleeping in my bed?—and see here he is!*" So then the Bears came and wondered what they should do with him; and the big Bear said, "Let's hang him!" and then the middling Bear said, "Let's drown him!" and then the little Bear said, "Let's throw him out of the window." And then the Bears took him to the window, and the big Bear took two legs on one side and the middling Bear took two legs on the other side, and they swung him backwards and forwards, backwards and forwards, and out of the window. Poor Scrapefoot was so frightened, and he thought every bone in his body must be broken. But he got up and first shook one leg—no, that was not broken; and then another, and that was not broken; and another and another, and then he wagged his tail and found there were no bones broken. So then he galloped off home as fast as he could go, and never went near the Bears' Castle again.

⤳ *The Pedlar of Swaffham* ⤳

IN the old days when London Bridge was lined with shops from one end to the other, and salmon swam under the arches, there lived at Swaffham, in Norfolk, a poor pedlar. He'd much ado to make his living, trudging about with his pack at his back and his dog at his heels, and at the close of the day's labour was but too glad to sit down and sleep. Now it fell out that one night he dreamed a dream, and therein he saw the great bridge of London town, and it sounded in his ears that if he went there he should hear joyful news. He made little count of the dream, but on the following night it come back to him, and again on the third night.

Then he said within himself, "I must needs try the issue of it," and so he trudged up to London town. Long was the way and right glad was he when he stood on the great bridge and saw the tall houses on right hand and left, and had glimpses of the water running and the ships sailing by. All day long he paced to and fro, but he heard nothing that might yield him comfort. And again on the morrow he stood and he gazed—he paced afresh the length of London Bridge, but naught did he see and naught did he hear.

Now the third day being come as he still stood and gazed, a shopkeeper hard by spoke to him.

"Friend," said he, "I wonder much at your fruitless standing. Have you no wares to sell?"

"No, indeed," quoth the pedlar.

"And you do not beg for alms."

"Not so long as I can keep myself."

"Then what, I pray thee, dost thou want here, and what may thy business be?"

"Well, kind sir, to tell the truth, I dreamed that if I came hither, I should hear good news."

Right heartily did the shopkeeper laugh.

"Nay, thou must be a fool to take a journey on such a silly errand. I'll tell thee, poor silly country fellow, that I myself dream too o' nights, and that last night I dreamt myself to be in Swaffham, a place clean unknown to me, but in Norfolk if I mistake not, and methought I was in an orchard behind a pedlar's house, and in that orchard was a great oak tree. Then meseemed that if I digged I should find beneath that tree a great treasure. But think you I'm such a fool as to take on me a long and wearisome journey and all for a silly dream. No, my good fellow, learn wit from a wiser man than thyself. Get thee home, and mind thy business."

When the pedlar heard this he spoke no word, but was exceeding glad in himself, and returning home speedily, digged underneath the great oak-tree, and found a prodigious great treasure. He grew exceeding rich, but he did not forget his duty in the pride of his riches. For he built up again the church at Swaffham, and when he died they put a statue of him therein all in stone with his pack at his back and his dog at his heels. And there it stands to this day to witness if I lie.

❧ *The Old Witch* ❧

ONCE upon a time there were two girls who lived with their mother and father. Their father had no work, and the girls wanted to go away and seek their fortunes. Now one girl wanted to go to service, and her mother said she might if she could find a place. So she started for the town. Well, she went all about the town, but no one wanted a girl like her. So she went on farther into the country, and she came to a place where there was an oven where there was lots of bread baking. And the bread said, "Little girl, little girl, take us out, take us out. We have been baking seven years, and no one has come to take us out." So the girl took out the bread, laid it on the ground, and went on her way. Then she met a cow, and the cow said, "Little girl, little girl, milk me, milk me! Seven years have I been waiting, and no one has come to milk me." The girl milked the cow into the pails that stood by. As she was thirsty she drank some, and left the rest in the pails by the cow. Then she went on a little bit farther, and came to an apple-tree, so loaded with fruit that its branches were breaking down, and the tree said, "Little girl, little girl, help me shake my fruit. My branches are breaking, it is so heavy." And the girl said, "Of course I will, you poor tree." So she shook the fruit all off, propped up the branches, and left the fruit on the ground under the tree. Then she went on again till she came to a house. Now in this house there lived a witch, and this witch took girls into her house as servants. And when she heard that this girl had left her home to seek service, she said that she would try her, and give her good wages. The witch told the girl what work she was to do. "You must keep the house clean and tidy, sweep the floor and the fireplace; but there is one thing you must never do. You must never look up the chimney, or something bad will befall you."

So the girl promised to do as she was told, but one morning as she was cleaning, and the witch was out, she forgot what the witch said, and looked up the chimney. When she did this a great bag of money fell down in her lap. This happened again and again. So the girl started to go off home.

When she had gone some way she heard the witch coming after her. So she ran to the apple-tree and cried:

> "Apple-tree, apple-tree hide me,
> So the old witch can't find me;
> If she does she'll pick my bones,
> And bury me under the marble stones."

So the apple-tree hid her. When the witch came up she said:

> "Tree of mine, tree of mine,
> Have you seen a girl
> With a willy-willy wag, and a long-tailed bag,
> Who's stole my money, all I had?"

And the apple-tree said, "No, mother; not for seven year."

When the witch had gone down another way, the girl went on again, and just as she got to the cow she heard the witch coming after her again, so she ran to the cow and cried:

> "Cow, cow, hide me,
> So the old witch can't find me;
> If she does she'll pick my bones,
> And bury me under the marble stones."

So the cow hid her.

When the old witch came up, she looked about and said to the cow:

> "Cow of mine, cow of mine,
> Have you seen a girl
> With a willy-willy wag, and a long-tailed bag,
> Who's stole my money, all I had?"

And the cow said, "No, mother; not for seven year."

When the witch had gone off another way, the little girl went on again, and when she was near the oven she heard the witch coming after her again, so she ran to the oven and cried:

> "Oven, oven, hide me,
> So the old witch can't find me;
> If she does she'll break my bones,
> And bury me under the marble stones."

And the oven said, "I've no room, ask the baker." And the baker hid her behind the oven.

When the witch came up she looked here and there and everywhere, and then said to the baker:

> "Man of mine, man of mine,
> Have you seen a girl,
> With a willy-willy wag, and a long-tailed bag,
> Who's stole my money, all I had?"

So the baker said, "Look in the oven." The old witch went to look, and the oven said, "Get in and look in the furthest corner." The witch did so, and when she was inside the oven shut her door, and the witch was kept there for a very long time.

The girl then went off again, and reached her home with her money bags, married a rich man, and lived happy ever afterwards.

The other sister then thought she would go and do the same. And she went the same way. But when she reached the oven, and the bread said, "Little girl, little girl, take us out. Seven years have we been baking, and no one has come to take us out." The girl said, "No, I don't want to burn my fingers." So she went on till she met the cow, and the cow said, "Little girl, little girl, milk me, milk me, do. Seven years have I been waiting, and no one has come to milk me." But the girl said, "No, I can't milk you, I'm in a hurry," and went on faster. Then she came to the apple-tree, and the apple-tree asked her to help shake the fruit. But the girl said, "No, I can't; another day p'raps I may," and went on till she came to the witch's house. Well, it happened to her just the same as to the other girl—she forgot what she was told, and one day when the witch was out, looked up the chimney, and down fell a bag of money. Well, she thought she would be off at once. When she reached the apple-tree, she heard the witch coming after her, and she cried:

> "Apple-tree, apple-tree, hide me,
> So the old witch can't find me;
> If she does she'll break my bones,
> And bury me under the marble stones."

But the tree didn't answer, and she ran on further. Presently the witch came up and said:

> "Tree of mine, tree of mine,
> Have you seen a girl,
> With a willy-willy wag, and a long-tailed bag,
> Who's stole my money, all I had?"

The Old Witch

The tree said, "Yes, mother; she's gone down that way."

So the old witch went after her and caught her, she took all the money away from her, beat her, and sent her off home just as she was.

✧ The Three Wishes ✧

ONCE upon a time, and be sure 'twas a long time ago, there lived a poor woodman in a great forest, and every day of his life he went out to fell timber. So one day he started out, and the goodwife filled his wallet and slung his bottle on his back, that he might have meat and drink in the forest. He had marked out a huge old oak, which, thought he, would furnish many and many a good plank. And when he was come to it, he took his axe in his hand and swung it round his head as though he were minded to fell the tree at one stroke. But he hadn't given one blow, when what should he hear but the pitifullest entreating, and there stood before him a fairy who prayed and beseeched him to spare the tree. He was dazed, as you may fancy, with wonderment and affright, and he couldn't open his mouth to utter a word. But he found his tongue at last, and, "Well," said he, "I'll e'en do as thou wishest."

"You've done better for yourself than you know," answered the fairy, "and to show I'm not ungrateful, I'll grant you your next three wishes, be they what they may." And therewith the fairy was no more to be seen, and the woodman slung his wallet over his shoulder and his bottle at his side, and off he started home.

But the way was long, and the poor man was regularly dazed with the wonderful thing that had befallen him, and when he got home there was nothing in his noddle but the wish to sit down and rest. Maybe, too, 'twas a trick of the fairy's. Who can tell? Anyhow down he sat by the blazing fire, and as he sat he waxed hungry, though it was a long way off supper-time yet.

"Hasn't thou naught for supper, dame?" said he to his wife.

"Nay, not for a couple of hours yet," said she.

"Ah!" groaned the woodman, "I wish I'd a good link of black pudding here before me."

No sooner had he said the word, when clatter, clatter, rustle, rustle, what should come down the chimney but a link of the finest black pudding the heart of man could wish for.

If the woodman stared, the goodwife stared three times as much. "What's all this?" says she.

Then all the morning's work came back to the woodman, and he told his tale right out, from beginning to end, and as he told it the goodwife glowered and glowered, and when he had made an end of it she burst out, "Thou bee'st but a fool, Jan, thou bee'st but a fool; and I wish the pudding were at thy nose, I do indeed."

And before you could say Jack Robinson, there the goodman sat and his nose was the longer for a noble link of black pudding.

He gave a pull but it stuck, and she gave a pull but it stuck, and they both pulled till they had nigh pulled the nose off, but it stuck and stuck.

"What's to be done now?" said he.

"'Tisn't so very unsightly," said she, looking hard at him.

Then the woodman saw that if he wished, he must need wish in a hurry; and wish he did, that the black pudding might come off his nose. Well! there it lay in a dish on the table, and if the goodman and goodwife didn't ride in a golden coach, or dress in silk and satin, why they had at least as fine a black pudding for their supper as the heart of man could desire.

ᗡ᚜ *The Buried Moon* ᗡ᚜

LONG ago, in my grandmother's time, the Car-land was all in bogs, great pools of black water, and creeping trickles of green water, and squishy mools which squirted when you stepped on them.

Well, granny used to say how long before her time the Moon herself was once dead and buried in the marshes, and as she used to tell me, I'll tell you all about it.

The Moon up yonder shone and shone, just as she does now, and when she shone she lighted up the bog-pools, so that one could walk about almost as safe as in the day.

But when she didn't shine, out came the Things that dwelt in the darkness and went about seeking to do evil and harm; Bogles and crawling Horrors, all came out when the Moon didn't shine.

Well, the Moon heard of this, and being kind and good—as she surely is, shining for us in the night instead of taking her natural rest—she
was main troubled. "I'll see for myself, I will," said she, "maybe it's not so
bad as folks make out."

Sure enough, at the month's end down she stept, wrapped up in a black
cloak, and a black hood over her yellow shining hair. Straight she went
to the bog edge and looked about her. Water here and water there; waving tussocks and trembling mools, and great black snags all twisted and
bent. Before her all was dark—dark but for the glimmer of the stars in
the pools, and the light that came from her own white feet, stealing out
of her black cloak.

The Moon drew her cloak faster about and trembled, but she wouldn't
go back without seeing all there was to be seen; so on she went, stepping
as light as the wind in the summer from tuft to tuft between the greedy
gurgling water-holes. Just as she came near a big black pool her foot
slipped and she was nigh tumbling in. She grabbed with both hands at a
snag near by to steady herself with, but as she touched it, it twined itself round her wrists, like a pair of handcuffs, and gript her so that she
couldn't move. She pulled and twisted and fought, but it was no good.
She was fast, and must stay fast.

Presently as she stood 'trembling in the dark, wondering if help would
come, she heard something calling in the distance, calling, calling, and
then dying away with a sob, till the marshes were full of this pitiful crying sound; then she heard steps floundering along, squishing in the mud
and slipping on the tufts, and through the darkness she saw a white face
with great feared eyes.

'Twas a man strayed in the bogs. Mazed with fear he struggled on
toward the flickering light that looked like help and safety. And when
the poor Moon saw that he was coming nigher and nigher to the deep
hole, further and further from the path, she was so mad and so sorry that
she struggled and fought and pulled harder than ever. And though she
couldn't get loose, she twisted and turned, till her black hood fell back
off her shining yellow hair, and the beautiful light that came from it
drove away the darkness.

Oh, but the man cried with joy to see the light again. And at once all
evil things fled back into the dark corners, for they cannot abide the light.
So he could see where he was, and where the path was, and how he could
get out of the marsh. And he was in such haste to get away from the
quicks, and bogles and things that dwelt there, that he scarce looked at

the brave light that came from the beautiful shining yellow hair, stream-ing out over the black cloak and falling to the water at his feet. And the Moon herself was so taken up with saving him, and with rejoicing that he was back on the right path, that she clean forgot that she needed help herself, and that she was held fast by the Black Snag.

So off he went; spent and gasping, and stumbling and sobbing with joy, flying for his life out of the terrible bogs. Then it came over the Moon, she would main like to go with him. So she pulled and fought as if she were mad, till she fell on her knees, spent with tugging, at the foot of the snag. And as she lay there, gasping for breath, the black hood fell forward over her head. So out went the blessed light and back came the darkness, with all its evil Things, with a screech and a howl. They came crowding round her, mocking and snatching and beating; shrieking with rage and spite, and swearing and snarling, for they knew her for their old enemy, that drove them back into the corners, and kept them from working their wicked wills.

"Drat thee!" yelled the witch-bodies, "thou'st spoiled our spells this year agone!"

"And us thou sent'st to brood in the corners!" howled the Bogles.

And all the Things joined in with a great "Ho, ho!" till the very tus-socks shook and the water gurgled. And they began again.

"We'll poison her—poison her!" shrieked the witches.

And "Ho, ho!" howled the Things again.

"We'll smother her—smother her!" whispered the crawling Horrors, and twined themselves round her knees.

And "Ho, ho!" mocked the rest of them.

And again they all shouted with spite and ill-will. And the poor Moon crouched down, and wished she was dead and done with.

And they fought and squabbled what they should do with her, till a pale grey light began to come in the sky; and it drew nigh the dawning. And when they saw that, they were feared lest they shouldn't have time to work their will; and they caught hold of her, with horrid bony fingers, and laid her deep in the water at the foot of the snag. And the Bogles fetched a strange big stone and rolled it on top of her, to keep her from rising. And they told two of the will-o'-the-wykes to take turns in watching on the black snag, to see that she lay safe and still, and couldn't get out to spoil their sport.

And there lay the poor Moon, dead and buried in the bog, till some one would set her loose; and who'd know where to look for her.

Well, the days passed, and 'twas the time for the new moon's coming, and the folk put pennies in their pockets and straws in their caps so as to be ready for her, and looked about, for the Moon was a good friend to the marsh folk, and they were main glad when the dark time was gone, and the paths were safe again, and the Evil Things were driven back by the blessed Light into the darkness and the water-holes.

But days and days passed, and the new moon never came, and the nights were aye dark, and the Evil Things were worse than ever. And still the days went on, and the new moon never came. Naturally the poor folk were strangely feared and mazed, and a lot of them went to the Wise Woman who dwelt in the old mill, and asked if so be she could find out where the Moon was gone.

"Well," said she, after looking in the brewpot, and in the mirror, and in the Book, "it be main queer, but I can't rightly tell ye what's happed to her. If ye hear of aught, come and tell me."

So they went their ways; and as days went by, and never a moon come, naturally they talked—my word! I reckon they *did* talk! their tongues wagged at home, and at the inn, and in the garth. But so came one day, as they sat on the great settle in the Inn, a man from the far end of the bog lands was smoking and listening, when all at once he sat up and slapped his knee. "My faicks!" says he, "I'd clean forgot, but I reckon I kens where the Moon be!" and he told them of how he was lost in the bogs, and how, when he was nigh dead with fright, the light shone out, and he found the path and got home safe.

So off they all went to the Wise Woman, and told her about it, and she looked long in the pot and the Book again, and then she nodded her head.

"It's dark still, childer, dark!" says she, "and I can't rightly see, but do as I tell ye, and ye'll find out for yourselves. Go all of ye, just afore the night gathers, put a stone in your mouth, and take a hazel-twig in your hands, and say never a word till you're safe home again. Then walk on and fear not, far into the midst of the marsh, till ye find a coffin, a candle, and a cross. Then ye'll not be far from your Moon; look, and m'appen ye'll find her."

So came the next night in the darklings, out they went all together, every man with a stone in his mouth, and a hazel-twig in his hand, and feeling, thou may'st reckon, main feared and creepy. And they stumbled and stottered along the paths into the midst of the bogs; they saw nought, though they heard sighings and flutterings in their ears, and felt cold wet fingers touching them; but all at once, looking around for the coffin, the candle, and the cross, while they came nigh to the pool beside the great snag, where the Moon lay buried. And all at once they stopped, quaking and mazed and skeery, for there was the great stone, half in, half out of the water, for all the world like a strange big coffin; and at the head was the black snag, stretching out its two arms in a dark gruesome cross, and on it a tiddy light flickered, like a dying candle. And they all knelt down in the mud, and said, "Our Lord," first forward, because of the cross, and then backward, to keep off the Bogles; but without speaking out, for they knew that the Evil Things would catch them, if they didn't do as the Wise Woman told them.

Then they went nigher, and they took hold of the big stone, and shoved it up, and afterwards they said that for one tiddy minute they saw a strange and beautiful face looking up at them glad-like out of the black water; but the light came so quick and so white and shining, that they stept back mazed with it, and the very next minute, when they could see again, there was the full Moon in the sky, bright and beautiful and kind as ever, shining and smiling down at them, and making the bogs and the paths as clear as day, and stealing into the very corners, as though she'd have driven the darkness and the Bogles clean away if she could.

✺ *A Son of Adam* ✺

A MAN was one day working. It was very hot, and he was digging. By-and-by he stopped to rest and wipe his face; and he was very angry to think he had to work so hard only because of Adam's sin. So he complained bitterly, and said some very hard words about Adam.

It happened that his master heard him, and he asked, "Why do you blame Adam? You'd ha' done just like Adam, if you'd a-been in his place."

"No, I shouldn't," said the man; "I should ha' know'd better."

"Well, I'll try you," says his master; "come to me at dinner-time."

So come dinner-time, the man came, and his master took him into a room where the table was a-set with good things of all sorts. And he said: "Now, you can eat as much as ever you like from any of the dishes on the table; but don't touch the covered dish in the middle till I come back." And with that the master went out of the room and left the man there all by himself.

So the man sat down and helped himself, and ate some o' this dish and some o' that, and enjoyed himself finely. But after awhile, as his master didn't come back, he began to look at the covered dish, and to wonder whatever was in it. And he wondered more and more, and he says to himself, "It must be something very nice. Why shouldn't I just look at it? I won't touch it. There can't be any harm in just peeping." So at last he could hold back no longer, and he lifted up the cover a tiny bit; but he couldn't see anything. Then he lifted it up a bit more, and out popped a mouse. The man tried to catch it; but it ran away and jumped off the table and he ran after it. It ran first into one corner, and then, just as he thought he'd got it, into another, and under the table, and all about the room. And the man made such a clatter, jumping and banging and running round after the mouse, a-trying to catch it, that at last his master came in.

"Ah!" he said; "never you blame Adam again, my man!"

✺ *The Children in the Wood* ✺

NOW ponder well, you parents dear,
    These words which I shall write;
A doleful story you shall hear,
    In time brought forth to light.
A gentleman of good account,

In Norfolk dwelt of late,
Who did in honour far surmount
    Most men of his estate.

Sore sick he was and like to die,
    No help his life could save;
His wife by him as sick did lie,
    And both possest one grave.
No love between these two was lost,
    Each was to other kind;
In love they lived, in love they died,
    And left two babes behind.

The one a fine and pretty boy
    Not passing three years old,
The other a girl more young than he,
    And framed in beauty's mould.
The father left his little son,
    As plainly did appear,
When he to perfect age should come,
    Three hundred pounds a year;

And to his little daughter Jane
    Five hundred pounds in gold,
To be paid down on marriage-day,
    Which might not be controlled.
But if the children chanced to die
    Ere they to age should come,
Their uncle should possess their wealth;
    For so the will did run.

"Now, brother," said the dying man,
    "Look to my children dear;
Be good unto my boy and girl,
    No friends else have they here;
To God and you I recommend
    My children dear this day;
But little while be sure we have
    Within this world to stay.

"You must be father and mother both,
　　And uncle, all in one;
God knows what will become of them
　　When I am dead and gone."
With that bespake their mother dear:
　　"O brother kind," quoth she,
"You are the man must bring our babes
　　To wealth or misery.

"And if you keep them carefully,
　　Then God will you reward;
But if you otherwise should deal,
　　God will your deeds regard."
With lips as cold as any stone,
　　They kissed their children small:
"God bless you both, my children dear!"
　　With that the tears did fall.

These speeches then their brother spake
　　To this sick couple there:
"The keeping of your little ones,
　　Sweet sister, do not fear;
God never prosper me nor mine,
　　Nor aught else that I have,
If I do wrong your children dear
　　When you are laid in grave!"

The parents being dead and gone,
　　The children home he takes,
And brings them straight unto his house
　　Where much of them he makes.
He had not kept these pretty babes
　　A twelvemonth and a day,
But, for their wealth, he did devise
　　To make them both away.

He bargained with two ruffians strong,
　　Which were of furious mood,
That they should take these children young,

And slay them in a wood.
He told his wife an artful tale
    He would the children send
To be brought up in London town
    With one that was his friend.

Away then went those pretty babes,
    Rejoicing at that tide,
Rejoicing with a merry mind
    They should on cock-horse ride.
They prate and prattle pleasantly,
    As they ride on the way,
To those that should their butchers be
    And work their lives' decay:

So that the pretty speech they had
    Made Murder's heart relent;
And they that undertook the deed
    Full sore now did repent.

Yet one of them, more hard of heart,
    Did vow to do his charge,
Because the wretch that hirèd him
    Had paid him very large.

The other won't agree thereto,
    So there they fall to strife;
With one another they did fight
    About the children's life;
And he that was of mildest mood
    Did slay the other there,
Within an unfrequented wood;
    The babes did quake for fear!

He took the children by the hand,
    Tears standing in their eye,
And bade them straightway follow him,
    And look they did not cry;
And two long miles he led them on,
    While they for food complain:
"Stay here," quoth he, "I'll bring you bread,
    When I come back again."

These pretty babes, with hand in hand,
    Went wandering up and down;
But never more could see the man
    Approaching from the town.
Their pretty lips with blackberries
    Were all besmeared and dyed;
And when they saw the darksome night,
    They sat them down and cried.

Thus wandered these poor innocents,
    Till death did end their grief;
In one another's arms they died,
    As wanting due relief:
No burial this pretty pair
    From any man receives,

Till Robin Redbreast piously
 Did cover them with leaves.

And now the heavy wrath of God
 Upon their uncle fell;
Yea, fearful fiends did haunt his house,
 His conscience felt an hell:
His barns were fired, his goods consumed,
 His lands were barren made,
His cattle died within the field,
 And nothing with him stayed.

And in a voyage to Portugal
 Two of his sons did die;
And to conclude, himself was brought
 To want and misery:
He pawned and mortgaged all his land
 Ere seven years came about.
And now at last this wicked act
 Did by this means come out,

The fellow that did take in hand
 These children for to kill,
Was for a robbery judged to die,
 Such was God's blessèd will:
Who did confess the very truth,
 As here hath been displayed:
The uncle having died in jail,
 Where he for debt was laid.

You that executors be made,
 And overseers eke,
Of children that be fatherless,
 And infants mild and meek,
Take you example by this thing,
 And yield to each his right,
Lest God with suchlike misery
 Your wicked minds requite.

ᔓ *The Hobyahs* ᔓ

ONCE there was an old man and woman and a little girl, and they all lived in a house made of hempstalks. Now the old man had a little dog named Turpie; and one night the Hobyahs came and said, "Hobyah! Hobyah! Hobyah! Tear down the hempstalks, eat up the old man and woman, and carry off the little girl!" But little dog Turpie barked so, that

the Hobyahs ran off; and the old man said, "Little dog Turpie barks so that I cannot sleep nor slumber, and if I live till morning I will cut off his tail." So in the morning the old man cut off little dog Turpie's tail.

The next night the Hobyahs came again, and said, "Hobyah! Hobyah! Hobyah! Tear down the hempstalks, eat up the old man and woman, and carry off the little girl!" But little dog Turpie barked so that the Hobyahs ran off; and the old man said, "Little dog Turpie barks so

that I cannot sleep nor slumber, and if I live till morning I will cut off one of his legs." So in the morning the old man cut off one of little dog Turpie's legs.

The next night the Hobyahs came again, and said, "Hobyah! Hobyah! Hobyah! Tear down the hempstalks, eat up the old man and woman, and carry off the little girl!" But little dog Turpie barked so, that the Hobyahs ran off; and the old man said, "Little dog Turpie barks so that I cannot sleep nor slumber, and if I live till morning I will cut off another of his legs."

So in the morning the old man cut off another of little dog Turpie's legs.

The next night the Hobyahs came again, and said, "Hobyah! Hobyah! Hobyah! Tear down the hempstalks, eat up the old man and woman, and carry off the little girl." But little dog Turpie barked so that the Hobyahs ran off; and the old man said, "Little dog Turpie barks so that I cannot sleep nor slumber,

and if I live till morning I will cut off another of his legs." So in the morning the old man cut off another of little dog Turpie's legs.

The next night the Hobyahs came again, and said, "Hobyah! Hobyah! Hobyah! Tear down the hempstalks, eat up the old man and woman, and carry off the little girl!" But little dog Turpie barked so that the Hobyahs ran off; and the old man said, "Little dog Turpie barks so that I cannot sleep nor slumber, and if I live till morning I will cut off another of his legs." So in the morning the old man cut off another of little dog Turpie's legs.

The next night the Hobyahs came again, and said, "Hobyah! Hobyah! Hobyah! Tear down the hempstalks, eat up the old man and woman, and carry off the little girl!" But little dog Turpie barked so that the Hobyahs ran off; and the old man said, "Little dog Turpie barks so that I cannot sleep nor slumber, and if I live till morning I will cut off little dog Turpie's head." So in the morning the old man cut off little dog Turpie's head.

The next night the Hobyahs came again, and said, "Hobyah!

Hobyah! Hobyah! Tear down the hempstalks, eat up the old man and woman, and carry off the little girl!" And when the Hobyahs found that little dog Turpie's head was off they tore down the hempstalks, ate up the old man and woman, and carried the little girl off in a bag.

And when the Hobyahs came to their home they hung up the bag with the little girl in it, and every Hobyah knocked on the top of the bag and said, "Look me! look me!" And then they went to sleep until the next night, for the Hobyahs slept in the daytime.

The little girl cried a great deal, and a man with a big dog came that way and heard her crying. When he asked her how she came there and she told him, he put the dog in the bag and took the little girl to his home.

The next night the Hobyahs took down the bag and knocked on the top of it, and said, "Look me! look me!" and when they opened the bag———

the big dog jumped out and ate them all up; so there are no Hobyahs now.

✣ A Pottle o' Brains ✣

ONCE in these parts, and not so long gone neither, there was a fool that wanted to buy a pottle o' brains, for he was ever getting into scrapes through his foolishness, and being laughed at by every one. Folk told him that he could get everything he liked from the wise woman that lived on the top o' the hill, and dealt in potions and herbs and spells and things, and could tell thee all as'd come to thee or thy folk. So he told his mother, and asked her if he could seek the wise woman and buy a pottle o' brains.

"That ye should," says she: "thou'st sore need o' them, my son; and if I should die, who'd take care o' a poor fool such's

273

thou, no more fit to look after thyself than an unborn baby? but mind thy manners, and speak her pretty, my lad; for they wise folk are gey and light mispleased."

So off he went after his tea, and there she was, sitting by the fire, and stirring a big pot.

"Good e'en, missis," says he, "it's a fine night."

"Aye," says she, and went on stirring.

"It'll maybe rain," says he, and fidgeted from one foot to t'other.

"Maybe," says she.

"And m'appen it won't," says he, and looked out o' the window.

"M'appen," says she.

And he scratched his head and twisted his hat.

"Well," says he, "I can't mind nothing else about the weather, but let me see; the crops are getting on fine."

"Fine," says she.

"And—and—the beasts is fattening," says he.

"They are," says she.

"And—and—" says he, and comes to a stop—"I reckon we'll tackle business now, having done the polite like. Have you any brains for to sell?"

"That depends," says she, "if thou wants king's brains, or soldier's brains, or schoolmaster's brains, I dinna keep 'em."

"Hout no," says he, "jist ordinary brains—fit for any fool—same as every one has about here; something clean common-like."

"Aye so," says the wise woman, "I might manage that, if so be thou'lt help thyself."

"How's that for, missis?" says he.

"Jest so," says she, looking in the pot; "bring me the heart of the thing thou likest best of all, and I'll tell thee where to get thy pottle o' brains."

"But," says he, scratching his head, "how can I do that?"

"That's no for me to say," says she, "find out for thyself, my lad! if thou doesn't want to be a fool all thy days. But thou'll have to read me a riddle so as I can see thou'st brought the right thing, and if thy brains is about thee. And I've something else to see to," says she, "so gode'en to thee," and she carried the pot away with her into the back place.

So off went the fool to his mother, and told her what the wise woman said.

"And I reckon I'll have to kill that pig," says he, "for I like fat bacon better than anything."

"Then do it, my lad," said his mother, "for certain 'twill be a strange and good thing fur thee, if thou canst buy a pottle o' brains, and be able to look after thy own self."

So he killed his pig, and next day off he went to the wise woman's cottage, and there she sat, reading in a great book.

"Gode'en, missis," says he, "I've brought thee the heart o' the thing I like best of all; and I put it hapt in paper on the table."

"Aye so?" says she, and looked at him through her spectacles. "Tell me this then, what runs without feet?"

He scratched his head, and thought, and thought, but he couldn't tell.

"Go thy ways," says she, "thou'st not fetched me the right thing yet. I've no brains for thee to-day." And she clapt the book together, and turned her back.

So off the fool went to tell his mother.

But as he got nigh the house, out came folk running to tell him that his mother was dying.

And when he got in, his mother only looked at him and smiled as if to say she could leave him with a quiet mind since he had got brains enough now to look after himself—and then she died.

So down he sat and the more he thought about it the badder he felt. He minded how she'd nursed him when he was a tiddy brat, and helped him with his lessons, and cooked his dinners, and mended his clouts, and bore with his foolishness; and he felt sorrier and sorrier, while he began to sob and greet.

"Oh, mother, mother!" says he, "who'll take care of me now! Thou shouldn't have left me alone, for I liked thee better than everything!"

And as he said that, he thought of the words of the wise woman. "Hi, yi!" says he, "must I take mother's heart to her?"

"No! I can't do that," says he. "What'll I do! what'll I do to get that pottle of brains, now I'm alone in the world?" So he thought and thought and thought, and next day he went and borrowed a sack, and bundled his mother in, and carried it on his shoulder up to the wise woman's cottage.

"Gode'en, missis," says he, "I reckon I've fetched thee the right thing this time, surely," and he plumped the sack down kerflap! in the doorsill.

"Maybe," says the wise woman, "but read me this, now, what's yellow and shining but isn't gold?"

And he scratched his head, and thought and thought but he couldn't tell.

"Thou'st not hit the right thing, my lad," says she. "I doubt thou'rt a bigger fool than I thought!" and shut the door in his face.

"See there!" says he, and set down by the road side and greets.

"I've lost the only two things as I cared for, and what else can I find to buy a pottle of brains with!" and he fair howled, till the tears ran down into his mouth. And up came a lass that lived near at hand, and looked at him.

"What's up with thee, fool?" says she.

"Oo, I've killed my pig, and lost my mother and I'm nobbut a fool myself," says he, sobbing.

"That's bad," says she; "and haven't thee anybody to look after thee?"

"No," says he, "and I canna buy my pottle of brains, for there's nothing I like best left!"

"What art talking about!" says she.

And down she sets by him, and he told her all about the wise woman and the pig, and his mother and the riddles, and that he was alone in the world.

"Well," says she, "I wouldn't mind looking after thee myself."

"Could thee do it?" says he.

"Ou, ay!" says she; "folk says as fools make good husbands, and I reckon I'll have thee, if thou'rt willing."

"Can'st cook?" says he.

"Ay, I can," says she.

"And scrub?" says he.

"Surely," says she.

"And mend my clouts?" says he.

"I can that," says she.

"I reckon thou'lt do then as well as anybody," says he; "but what'll I do about this wise woman?"

"Oh, wait a bit," says she, "something may turn up, and it'll not matter if thou'rt a fool, so long's thou'st got me to look after thee."

"That's true," says he, and off they went and got married. And she kept his house so clean and neat, and cooked his dinner so fine, that one night he says to her: "Lass, I'm thinking I like thee best of everything after all."

"That's good hearing," says she, "and what then?"

"Have I got to kill thee, dost think, and take thy heart up to the wise woman for that pottle o' brains?"

"Law, no!" says she, looking skeered, "I winna have that. But see here; thou didn't cut out thy mother's heart, did thou?"

"No; but if I had, maybe I'd have got my pottle o' brains," says he.

"Not a bit of it," says she; "just thou take me as I be, heart and all, and I'll wager I'll help thee read the riddles."

"Can thee so?" says he, doubtful like; "I reckon they're too hard for women folk."

"Well," says she, "let's see now. Tell me the first."

"What runs without feet?" says he.

"Why, water!" says she.

"It do," says he, and scratched his head.

"And what's yellow and shining but isn't gold?"

"Why, the sun!" says she.

"Faith, it be!" says he. "Come, we'll go up to the wise woman at once," and off they went. And as they came up the pad, she was sitting at the door, twining straws.

"Gode'en, missis," says he.

"Gode'en, fool," says she.

"I reckon I've fetched thee the right thing at last," says he.

The wise woman looked at them both, and wiped her spectacles.

"Canst tell me what that is as has first no legs, and then two legs, and ends with four legs?"

And the fool scratched his head, and thought and thought, but he couldn't tell.

And the lass whispered in his ear:

"It's a tadpole."

"M'appen," says he then, "it may be a tadpole, missis."

The wise woman nodded her head.

"That's right," says she, "and thou'st got thy pottle o' brains already."

"Where be they?" says he, looking about and feeling in his pockets.

"In thy wife's head," says she. "The only cure for a fool is a good wife to look after him, and that thou'st got, so gode'en to thee!" And with that she nodded to them, and up and into the house.

So they went home together, and he never wanted to buy a pottle o' brains again, for his wife had enough for both.

⤳ The King of England and his Three Sons ⤳

ONCE upon a time there was an old king who had three sons; and the old king fell very sick one time and there was nothing at all could make him well but some golden apples from a far country. So the three brothers went on horseback to look for some of these apples. They set off together, and when they came to cross-roads they halted and refreshed themselves a bit; and then they agreed to meet on a certain time, and not one was to go home before the other. So Valentine took the right, and Oliver went straight on, and poor Jack took the left.

To make my long story short I shall follow poor Jack, and let the other two take their chance, for I don't think there was much good in them. Off poor Jack rides over hills, dales, valleys, and mountains, through woolly woods and sheepwalks, where the old chap never sounded his hollow bugle-horn, farther than I can tell you to-night or ever intend to tell you.

At last he came to an old house, near a great forest, and there was an old man sitting out by the door, and his look was enough to frighten you or any one else; and the old man said to him:

"Good morning, my king's son."

"Good morning to you, old gentleman," was the young prince's answer; frightened out of his wits though he was, he didn't like to give in.

The old gentleman told him to dismount and to go in to have some refreshment, and to put his horse in the stable, such as it was. Jack soon felt much better after having something to eat, and began to ask the old gentleman how he knew he was a king's son.

"Oh dear!" said the old man, "I knew that you were a king's son, and I know what is your business better than what you do yourself. So you will have to stay here to-night; and when you are in bed you mustn't be frightened whatever you may hear. There will come all manner of frogs and snakes, and some will try to get into your eyes and your mouth, but mind, don't stir the least bit or you will turn into one of those things yourself."

Poor Jack didn't know what to make of this, but, however, he ventured to go to bed. Just as he thought to have a bit of sleep, round and over and under him they came, but he never stirred an inch all night.

"Well, my young son, how are you this morning?"

"Oh, I am very well, thank you, but I didn't have much rest."

"Well, never mind that; you have got on very well so far, but you have a great deal to go through before you can have the golden apples to go to your father. You'd better come and have some breakfast before you start on your way to my other brother's house. You will have to leave your own horse here with me until you come back again, and tell me everything about how you get on."

After that out came a fresh horse for the young prince, and the old man gave him a ball of yarn, and he flung it between the horse's two ears.

Off he went as fast as the wind, which the wind behind could not catch the wind before, until he came to the second oldest brother's house. When he rode up to the door he had the same salute as from the first old man, but this one was even uglier than the first one. He had long grey hair, and his teeth were curling out of his mouth, and his finger- and toe-nails had not been cut for many thousand years. He put the horse into a much better stable, and called Jack in, and gave him plenty to eat and drink, and they had a bit of a chat before they went to bed.

"Well, my young son," said the old man, "I suppose you are one of the king's children come to look for the golden apples to bring him back to health."

"Yes, I am the youngest of the three brothers, and I should like to get them to go back with."

"Well, don't mind, my young son. Before you go to bed to-night I will send to my eldest brother, and will tell him what you want, and he won't have much trouble in sending you on to the place where you must get the apples. But mind not to stir to-night no matter how you get bitten and stung, or else you will work great mischief to yourself."

The young man went to bed and bore all, as he did the first night, and got up the next morning well and hearty. After a good breakfast out comes a fresh horse, and a ball of yarn to throw between his ears. The old man told him to jump up quick, and said that he had made it all right with his eldest brother, not to delay for anything whatever, "For," said he, "you have a good deal to go through in a very short and quick time."

He flung the ball, and off he goes as quick as lightning, and comes to the eldest brother's house. The old man receives him very kindly and told him he long wished to see him, and that he would go through his work like a man and come back safe and sound. "To-night," said he, "I will give you rest; there shall nothing come to disturb you, so that you may not feel sleepy for to-morrow. And you must mind to get up middling early, for you've got to go and come all in the same day; there will be no place for you to rest within thousands of miles of that place; and if there was, you would stand in great danger never to come from there in your own form. Now, my young prince, mind what I tell you. To-morrow, when you come in sight of a very large castle, which will be surrounded with black water, the first thing you will do you will tie your horse to a tree, and you will see three beautiful swans in sight, and you will say, 'Swan, swan, carry me over in the name of the Griffin of the Greenwood,' and the swans will swim you over to the earth. There will be three great entrances, the first guarded by four great giants and drawn swords in their hands, the second by lions, the other by fiery serpents and dragons. You will have to be there exactly at one o'clock; and mind and leave there precisely at two, and not a moment later. When the swans carry you over to the castle, you will pass all these things, all fast asleep, but you must not notice any of them.

"When you go in, you will turn up to the right; you will see some grand rooms, then you will go downstairs and through the cooking kitchen, and through a door on your left you go into a garden, where you will find the apples you want for your father to get well. After you fill your wallet, you make all speed you possibly can, and call out for the swans to carry you over the same as before. After you get on your horse, should you hear anything shouting or making any noise after you, be sure not to look back, as they will follow you for thousands of miles; but when the time is up and you get near my place, it will be all over. Well now, my young man, I have told you all you have to do to-morrow; and mind, whatever you do, don't look about you when you see all those frightful things asleep. Keep a good heart, and make haste from there, and come back to me with all the speed you can. I should like to know how my two brothers were when you left them, and what they said to you about me."

The Castle of Melvales

"Well, to tell the truth, before I left London my father was sick, and said I was to come here to look for the golden apples, for they were the only things that would do him good; and when I came to your youngest brother, he told me many things I had to do before I came here. And I thought once that your youngest brother put me in the wrong bed, when he put all those snakes to bite me all night long, until your second brother told me 'So it was to be,' and said, 'It is the same here,' but said you had none in your beds."

"Well, let's go to bed. You need not fear. There are no snakes here."

The young man went to bed, and had a good night's rest, and got up the next morning as fresh as newly caught trout. Breakfast being over, out comes the other horse, and, while saddling and fettling, the old man began to laugh, and told the young gentleman that if he saw a pretty young lady, not to stay with her too long, because she might waken, and then he would have to stay with her or to be turned into one of those unearthly monsters, like those he would have to pass by going into the castle.

"Ha! ha! ha! you make me laugh so that I can scarcely buckle the saddle-straps. I think I shall make it all right, my uncle, if I see a young lady there, you may depend."

"Well, my boy, I shall see how you will get on."

So he mounts his Arab steed, and off he goes like a shot out of a gun. At last he comes in sight of the castle. He ties his horse safe to a tree, and pulls out his watch. It was then a quarter to one, when he called out, "Swan, swan, carry me over, for the name of the old Griffin of the Greenwood." No sooner said than done. A swan under each side, and one in front, took him over in a crack. He got on his legs, and walked quietly by all those giants, lions, fiery serpents, and all manner of other frightful things too numerous to mention, while they were fast asleep, and that only for the space of one hour, when into the castle he goes neck or nothing. Turning to the right, upstairs he runs, and enters into a very grand bedroom, and sees a beautiful Princess lying full stretch on a gold bedstead, fast asleep. He gazed on her beautiful form with admiration, and he takes her garter off, and buckles it on his own leg, and he buckles his on hers; he also takes her gold watch and pocket-handkerchief, and exchanges his for hers; after that he ventures to give her a kiss, when she very nearly opened her eyes. Seeing the time short, off he runs downstairs, and passing through the kitchen to go into the garden for the apples, he could see the cook all-fours on her back on the middle of the floor, with the knife in one hand and the fork in the other. He found the apples, and filled the wallet; and on passing through the kitchen the cook near wakened, but he was obliged to make all the speed he possibly could, as the time was nearly up. He called out for the swans, and they managed to take him over; but they found that he was a little heavier than before. No sooner than he had mounted his horse he could hear a tremendous noise, the enchantment was broke, and they tried to follow him, but all to no purpose. He was not long before he came to the oldest brother's house; and glad enough he was to see it, for the sight and the noise of all those things that were after him nearly frightened him to death.

"Welcome, my boy; I am proud to see you. Dismount and put the horse in the stable, and come in and have some refreshments; I know you are hungry after all you have gone through in that castle. And tell me all you did, and all you saw there. Other kings' sons went by here to go to that castle, but they never came back alive, and you are the only one that ever broke the spell. And now you must come with me, with a sword in your hand, and must cut my head off, and must throw it in that well."

The young Prince dismounts, and puts his horse in the stable, and they go in to have some refreshments, for I can assure you he wanted some; and after telling everything that passed, which the old gentleman was very pleased to hear, they both went for a walk together, the young Prince looking around and seeing the place looking dreadful, as did the old man. He could scarcely walk from his toe-nails curling up like ram's horns that had not been cut for many hundred years, and big long hair. They come to a well, and the old man gives the Prince a sword, and tells him to cut his head off, and throw it in that well. The young man has to do it against his wish, but has to do it.

No sooner has he flung the head in the well, than up springs one of the finest young gentlemen you would wish to see; and instead of the old house and the frightful-looking place, it was changed into a beautiful hall and grounds. And they went back and enjoyed themselves well, and had a good laugh about the castle.

The young Prince leaves this young gentleman in all his glory, and he tells the young Prince before leaving that he will see him again before long. They have a jolly shake-hands, and off he goes to the next oldest brother; and, to make my long story short, he has to serve the other two brothers the same as the first.

Now the youngest brother began to ask him how things went on. "Did you see my two brothers?"

"Yes."

"How did they look?"

"Oh! they looked very well. I liked them much. They told me many things what to do."

"Well, did you go to the castle?"

"Yes, my uncle."

"And will you tell me what you see in there? Did you see the young lady?"

"Yes, I saw her, and plenty of other frightful things."

"Did you hear any snake biting you in my oldest brother's bed?"

"No, there were none there; I slept well."

"You won't have to sleep in the same bed to-night. You will have to cut my head off in the morning."

The young Prince had a good night's rest, and changed all the appearance of the place by cutting his friend's head off before he started in the morning. A jolly shake-hands, and the uncle tells him it's very probable he shall see him again soon when he is not aware of it. This one's mansion was very pretty, and the country around it beautiful, after his head was cut off. Off Jack goes, over hills, dales, valleys, and mountains, and very near losing his apples again.

At last he arrives at the cross-roads, where he has to meet his brothers on the very day appointed. Coming up to the place, he sees no tracks of horses, and, being very tired, he lays himself down to sleep, by tying the horse to his leg, and putting the apples under his head. Presently up come the other brothers the same time to the minute, and found him fast asleep; and they would not waken him, but said one to another, "Let us see what sort of apples he has got under his head." So they took and tasted them, and found they were different to theirs. They took and changed his apples for theirs, and off to London as fast as they could, and left the poor fellow sleeping.

After a while he awoke, and, seeing the tracks of other horses, he mounted and off with him, not thinking anything about the apples being changed. He had still a long way to go, and by the time he got near London he could hear all the bells in the town ringing, but did not know what was the matter until he rode up to the palace, when he came to know that his father was recovered by his brother's apples. When he got there, his two brothers were off to some sports for a while; and the King was glad to see his youngest son, and very anxious to taste his apples. But when he found out that they were not good, and thought that they were more for poisoning him, he sent immediately for the headsman to behead his youngest son, who was taken away there and then in a carriage. But instead of the headsman taking his head off, he took him to a forest not far from the town, because he had pity on him, and there left him to take his chance, when presently up comes a big hairy bear, limping upon three legs. The Prince, poor fellow, climbed up a tree, frightened of him, but the bear told him to come down, that it was no use of him to stop there. With hard persuasion poor Jack comes down, and the bear speaks to him and bids him "Come here to me; I will not do you any harm. It's better for you to come with me and have some refreshments; I know that you are hungry all this time."

The poor young Prince says, "No, I am not hungry; but I was very frightened when I saw you coming to me first, as I had no place to run away from you."

The bear said, "I was also afraid of you when I saw that gentleman setting you down from the carriage. I thought you would have guns with you, and that you would not mind killing me if you saw me; but when I saw the gentleman going away with the carriage, and leaving you behind by yourself, I made bold to come to you, to see who you were, and now I know who you are very well. Are you not the King's youngest son? I have seen you and your brothers and lots of other gentlemen in this wood many times. Now before we go from here, I must tell you that I am in disguise; and I shall take you where we are stopping."

The young Prince tells him everything from first to last, how he started in search of the apples, and about the three old men, and about the castle, and how he was served at last by his father after he came home; and instead of the headsman taking his head off, he was kind enough to leave him his life, "and here I am now, under your protection."

The bear tells him, "Come on, my brother; there shall no harm come to you as long as you are with me."

So he takes him up to the tents; and when they see 'em coming, the girls begin to laugh, and say, "Here is our Jubal coming with a young gentleman." When he advanced nearer the tents, they all knew that he was the young Prince that had passed by that way many times before; and when Jubal went to change himself, he called most of them together into one tent, and told them all about him, and to be kind to him. And so they were, for there was nothing that he desired but what he had, the same as if he was in the palace with his father and mother. Jubal, after he pulled off his hairy coat, was one of the finest young men amongst them, and he was the young Prince's closest companion. The young Prince was always very sociable and merry, only when he thought of the gold watch he had from the young Princess in the castle, and which he had lost he knew not where.

He passed off many happy days in the forest; but one day he and poor Jubal were strolling through the trees, when they came to the very spot where they first met, and, accidentally looking up, he could see his watch hanging in the tree which he had to climb when he first saw poor Jubal coming to him in the form of a bear; and he cries out, "Jubal, Jubal, I can see my watch up in that tree."

"Well, I am sure, how lucky!" exclaimed poor Jubal; "shall I go and get it down?"

"No, I'd rather go myself," said the young Prince.

Now whilst all this was going on, the young Princess in that castle, seeing that one of the King of England's sons had been there by the changing of the watch and other things, got herself ready with a large army, and sailed off for England. She left her army a little out of the town, and she went with her guards straight up to the palace to see the King, and also demanded to see his sons. They had a long conversation together about different things. At last she demands one of the sons to come before her; and the oldest comes, when she asks him, "Have you ever been at the Castle of Melvales?" and he answers, "Yes." She throws down a pocket-handkerchief and bids him to walk over it without stumbling. He goes to walk over it, and no sooner did he put his foot on it, than he fell down and broke his leg. He was taken off immediately and made a prisoner of by her own guards. The other was called upon, and was asked the same questions, and had to go through the same performance, and he also was made a prisoner of. Now she says, "Have you not another son?" when the King began to shiver and shake and knock his two knees together that he could scarcely stand upon his legs, and did not know what to say to her, he was so much frightened. At last a thought came to him to send for his headsman, and inquire of him particularly, Did he behead his son, or was he alive?

"He is saved, O King."

"Then bring him here immediately, or else I shall be done for."

Two of the fastest horses they had were put in the carriage, to go and look for the poor Prince; and when they got to the very spot where they left him, it was the time when the Prince was up the tree, getting his watch down, and poor Jubal standing a distance off. They cried out to him, Had he seen another young man in this wood? Jubal, seeing such a nice carriage, thought something, and did not like to say No, and said Yes, and pointed up the tree; and they told him to come down immediately, as there was a young lady in search of him with a young child.

"Ha! ha! ha! Jubal, did you ever hear such a thing in all your life, my brother?"

"Do you call him your brother?"

"Well, he has been better to me than my brothers."

"Well, for his kindness he shall accompany you to the palace, and see how things turn out."

After they go to the palace, the Prince has a good wash, and appears before the Princess, when she asks him, Had he ever been at the Castle of Melvales? With a smile upon his face, he gives a graceful bow. And says my Lady, "Walk over that handkerchief without stumbling." He walks over it many times, and dances upon it, and nothing happened to him. She said, with a proud and smiling air, "That is the young man"; and out come the objects exchanged by both of them. Presently she orders a very large box to be brought in and to be opened, and out come some of the most costly uniforms that were ever worn on an emperor's back; and when he dressed himself up, the King could scarcely look upon him from the dazzling of the gold and diamonds on his coat. He orders his two brothers to be in confinement for a period of time; and before the Princess asks him to go with her to her own country, she pays a visit to the bear's camp, and she makes some very handsome presents for their kindness to the young Prince. And she gives Jubal an invitation to go with them, which he accepts; wishes them a hearty farewell for a while, promising to see them all again in some little time.

They go back to the King and bid farewell, and tell him not to be so hasty another time to order people to be beheaded before having a proper cause for it. Off they go with all their army with them; but while the soldiers were striking their tents, the Prince bethought himself of his Welsh harp, and had it sent for immediately to take with him in a beautiful wooden case. They called to see each of those three brothers whom the Prince had to stay with when he was on his way to the Castle of Melvales; and I can assure you, when they all got together, they had a very merry time of it. And there we will leave them.

᧡ King John and the Abbot of Canterbury ᧡

IN the reign of King John there lived an Abbot of Canterbury who kept up grand state in his Abbey. A hundred of the Abbot's men dined each day with him in his refectory, and fifty knights in velvet coats and gold chains waited upon him daily. Well, King John, as you know, was a very bad king, and he couldn't brook the idea of any one in his kingdom, however holy he might be, being honoured more than he. So he summoned the Abbot of Canterbury to his presence.

The Abbot came with a goodly retinue, with his fifty knights-at-arms in velvet cloaks and gold chains. The King went to meet him, and said to him, "How now, father Abbot? I hear it of thee, thou keepest far greater state than I. This becomes not our royal dignity, and savours of treason in thee."

"My liege," quoth the Abbot, bending low, "I beg to say that all I spend has been freely given to the Abbey out of the piety of the folk. I trust your Grace will not take it ill that I spend for the Abbey's sake what is the Abbey's."

"Nay, proud prelate," answered the King, "all that is in this fair realm of England is our own, and thou hast no right to put me to shame by holding such state. However, of my clemency I will spare thee thy life and thy property if you can answer me but three questions."

"I will do so, my liege," said the Abbot, "so far as my poor wit can extend."

"Well, then," said the King, "tell me where is the centre of all the world round; then let me know how soon can I ride the whole world about; and, lastly, tell me what I think."

"Your Majesty jesteth," stammered the Abbot.

"Thou wilt find it no jest," said the King. "Unless thou canst answer me these questions three before a week is out, thy head will leave thy body"; and he turned away.

Well, the Abbot rode off in fear and trembling, and first he went to Oxford to see if any learned doctor could tell him the answer to those questions three; but none could help him, and he took his way to Canterbury, sad and sorrowful, to take leave of his monks. But on his way he met his shepherd as he was going to the fold.

"Welcome home, Lord Abbot," quoth the shepherd; "what news from good King John?"

"Sad news, sad news, my shepherd," said the Abbot, and told him all that had happened.

"Now, cheer up, Sir Abbot," said the shepherd. "A fool may perhaps answer what a wise man knows not. I will go to London in your stead; grant me only your apparel and your retinue of knights. At the least I can die in your place."

"Nay, shepherd, not so," said the Abbot; "I must meet the danger in my own person. And to that, thou canst not pass for me."

"But I can and I will, Sir Abbot. In a cowl, who will know me for what I am?"

So at last the Abbot consented, and sent him to London in his most splendid array, and he approached King John with all his retinue as before, but dressed in his simple monk's dress and his cowl over his face.

"Now welcome, Sir Abbot," said King John; "thou art prepared for thy doom, I see."

"I am ready to answer your Majesty," said he.

"Well, then, question first—where is the centre of the round earth?" said the King.

"Here," said the shepherd Abbot, planting his crozier in the ground; "an' your Majesty believe me not, go measure it and see."

"By St. Botolph," said the King, "a merry answer and a shrewd; so to question the second. How soon may I ride this round world about?"

"If your Majesty will graciously rise with the sun, and ride along with him until the next morning he rise, your Grace will surely have ridden it round."

"By St. John," laughed King John, "I did not think it could be done so soon. But let that pass, and tell me question third and last, and that is—What do I think?"

"That is easy, your Grace," said he. "Your Majesty thinks I am my lord the Abbot of Canterbury; but as you may see," and here he raised his cowl, "I am but his poor shepherd, that am come to ask your pardon for him and for me."

Loud laughed the King. "Well caught. Thou hast more wit than thy lord, and thou shalt be Abbot in his place."

"Nay, that cannot be," quoth the shepherd; "I know not to write nor to read."

"Well, then, four nobles a week thou shalt have for thy ready wit. And tell the Abbot from me that he has my pardon." And with that King John sent away the shepherd with a right royal present, besides his pension.

❧ Rushen Coatie ❧

THERE was once a king and a queen, as many a one has been; few have we seen, and as few may we see. But the queen died, leaving only one bonny girl, and she told her on her death-bed: "My dear, after I am gone, there will come to you a little red calf, and whenever you want anything, speak to it, and it will give it you."

Now, after a while, the king married again an ill-natured wife, with three ugly daughters of her own. And they hated the king's daughter because she was so bonny. So they took all her fine clothes away from her, and gave her only a coat made of rushes. So they called her Rushen Coatie, and made her sit in the kitchen nook, amid the ashes. And when dinner-time came, the nasty stepmother sent her out a thimbleful of broth, a grain of barley, a thread of meat, and a crumb of bread. But when she had eaten all this, she was just as hungry as before, so she said to herself: "Oh! how I wish I had something to eat." Just then, who should come in but a little red calf, and said to her: "Put your finger into my left ear." She did so, and found some nice bread. Then the calf told her to put her finger into its right ear, and she found there some cheese, and made a right good meal off the bread and cheese. And so it went on from day to day.

Now the king's wife thought Rushen Coatie would soon die from the scanty food she got, and she was surprised to see her as lively and healthy as ever. So she set one of her ugly daughters on the watch at meal times to find out how Rushen Coatie got enough to live on. The daughter soon found out that the red calf gave food to Rushen Coatie, and told her mother. So her mother went to the king and told him she was longing to have a sweetbread from a red calf. Then the king sent for his butcher, and had the little red calf killed. And when Rushen Coatie heard of it, she sate down and wept by its side, but the dead calf said:

> "Take me up, bone by bone,
> And put me beneath yon grey stone;
> When there is aught you want
> Tell it me, and that I'll grant."

So she did so, but could not find the shank-bone of the calf.

Now the very next Sunday was Yuletide, and all the folk were going to church in their best clothes, so Rushen Coatie said: "Oh! I should like to go to church too"; but the three ugly sisters said: "What would you do at the church, you nasty thing? You must bide at home and make the dinner." And the king's wife said: "And this is what you must make the soup of, a thimbleful of water, a grain of barley, and a crumb of bread."

When they all went to church, Rushen Coatie sat down and wept, but looking up, who should she see coming in limping, lamping, with a shank wanting, but the dear red calf? And the red calf said to her: "Do not sit there weeping, but go, put on these clothes, and above all, put on this pair of glass slippers, and go your way to church."

"But what will become of the dinner?" said Rushen Coatie.

"Oh, do not fash about that," said the red calf, "all you have to do is to say to the fire:

> "Every peat make t'other burn,
> Every spit make t'other turn,
> Every pot make t'other play,
> Till I come from church this good Yuleday,"

and be off to church with you. But mind you come home first."

So Rushen Coatie said this, and went off to church, and she was the grandest and finest lady there. There happened to be a young prince there, and he fell at once in love with her. But she came away before service was over, and was home before the rest, and had off her fine clothes and on with her rushen coatie, and she found the calf had covered the table, and the dinner was ready, and everything was in good order when the rest came home. The three sisters said to Rushen Coatie: "Eh, lassie, if you had seen the bonny fine lady in church today, that the young prince fell in love with!" Then she said: "Oh! I wish you would let me go with you to the church to-morrow," for they used to go three days together to church at Yuletide.

But they said: "What should the like of you do at church, nasty thing? The kitchen nook is good enough for you."

So the next day they all went to church, and Rushen Coatie was left behind, to make dinner out of a thimbleful of water, a grain of barley, a crumb of bread, and a thread of meat. But the red calf came to her help again, gave her finer clothes than before, and she went to church, where all the world was looking at her, and wondering where such a grand lady came from, and the prince fell more in love with her than ever, and tried to find out where she went to. But she was too quick for him, and got home long before the rest, and the red calf had the dinner all ready.

The next day the calf dressed her in even grander clothes than before, and she went to the church. And the young prince was there again, and this time he put a guard at the door to keep her, but she took a hop and a run and jumped over their heads, and as she did so, down fell one of her glass slippers. She didn't wait to pick it up, you may be sure, but off she ran home, as fast as she could go, on with the rushen coatie, and the calf had all things ready.

Then the young prince put out a proclamation that whoever could put on the glass slipper should be his bride. All the ladies of his court went and tried to put on the slipper. And they tried and tried and tried, but it was too small for them all. Then he ordered one of his ambassadors to mount a fleet horse and ride through the kingdom and find an owner for the glass shoe. He rode and he rode to town and castle, and made all the ladies try to put on the shoe. Many a one tried to get it on that she might be the prince's bride. But no, it wouldn't do, and many a one wept, I warrant, because she couldn't get on the bonny glass shoe. The ambassador rode on and on till he came at the very last to the house where there were the three ugly sisters. The first two tried it and it wouldn't do, and the queen, mad with spite, hacked off the toes and heels of the third sister, and she could then put the slipper on, and the prince was brought to marry her, for he had to keep his promise. The ugly sister was dressed all in her best and was put up behind the prince on horseback, and off they rode in great gallantry. But ye all know, pride must have a fall, for as they rode along a raven sang out of a bush—

"Hackèd Heels and Pinchèd Toes
Behind the young prince rides,
But Pretty Feet and Little Feet
Behind the cauldron bides."

"What's that the birdie sings?" said the young prince.

"Nasty lying thing," said the step-sister, "never mind what it says."

But the prince looked down and saw the slipper dripping with blood, so he rode back and put her down. Then he said: "There must be some one that the slipper has not been tried on."

"Oh, no," said they, "there's none but a dirty thing that sits in the kitchen nook and wears a rushen coatie."

But the prince was determined to try it on Rushen Coatie, but she ran away to the grey stone, where the red calf dressed her in her bravest dress, and she went to the prince and the slipper jumped out of his pocket on to her foot, fitting her without any chipping or paring. So the prince married her that very day, and they lived happy ever after.

❧ The King o' the Cats ❧

ONE winter's evening the sexton's wife was sitting by the fireside with her big black cat, Old Tom, on the other side, both half-asleep and waiting for the master to come home. They waited and they waited, but still he didn't come, till at last he came rushing in, calling out, "Who's Tommy Tildrum?" in such a wild way that both his wife and his cat stared at him to know what was the matter.

"Why, what's the matter?" said his wife, "and why do you want to know who Tommy Tildrum is?"

"Oh, I've had such an adventure. I was digging away at old Mr. Fordyce's grave when I suppose I must have dropped asleep, and only woke up by hearing a cat's *Miaou*."

"*Miaou!*" said Old Tom in answer.

"Yes, just like that! So I looked over the edge of the grave, and what do you think I saw?"

"Now, how can I tell?" said the sexton's wife.

"Why, nine black cats all like our friend Tom here, all with a white spot on their chestesses. And what do you think they were carrying? Why, a small coffin covered with a black velvet pall, and on the pall was a small coronet all of gold, and at every third step they took they cried all together, *Miaou——*"

"*Miaou!*" said Old Tom again.

"Yes, just like that!" said the Sexton; "and as they came nearer and nearer to me I could see them more distinctly, because their eyes shone out with a sort of green light. Well, they all came towards me, eight of them carrying the coffin, and the biggest cat of all walking in front for all the world like—but look at our Tom, how he's looking at me. You'd think he knew all I was saying."

"Go on, go on," said his wife; "never mind Old Tom."

"Well, as I was a-saying, they came towards me slowly and solemnly, and at every third step crying all together, *Miaou——*"

"*Miaou!*" said Old Tom again.

"Yes, just like that, till they came and stood right opposite Mr. Fordyce's grave, where I was, when they all stood still and looked straight at me. I did feel queer, that I did! But look at Old Tom; he's looking at me just like they did."

"Go on, go on," said his wife; "never mind Old Tom."

"Where was I? Oh, they all stood still looking at me, when the one that wasn't carrying the coffin came forward and, staring straight at me, said to me—yes, I tell 'ee, *said* to me—with a squeaky voice, 'Tell Tom Tildrum that Tim Toldrum's dead,' and that's why I asked you if you knew who Tom Tildrum was, for how can I tell Tom Tildrum Tim Toldrum's dead if I don't know who Tom Tildrum is?"

"Look at Old Tom, look at Old Tom!" screamed his wife.

And well he might look, for Tom was swelling and Tom was staring, and at last Tom shrieked out, "What—old Tim dead! then I'm the King o' the Cats!" and rushed up the chimney and was never more seen.

❧ *Tamlane* ❧

YOUNG TAMLANE was son of Earl Murray, and Burd Janet was daughter of Dunbar, Earl of March. And when they were young they loved one another and plighted their troth. But when the time came near for their marrying, Tamlane disappeared, and none knew what had become of him.

Many, many days after he had disappeared, Burd Janet was wandering in Carterhaugh Wood, though she had been warned not to go there. And as she wandered she plucked the flowers from the bushes. She came at last to a bush of broom and began plucking it. She had not taken more than three flowerets when by her side up started young Tamlane.

"Where come ye from, Tamlane, Tamlane?" Burd Janet said; "and why have you been away so long?"

"From Elfland I come," said young Tamlane. "The Queen of Elfland has made me her knight."

"But how did you get there, Tamlane?" said Burd Janet.

"I was a-hunting one day, and as I rode widershins round yon hill, a deep drowsiness fell upon me, and when I awoke, behold! I was in Elfland. Fair is that land and gay, and fain would I stop but for thee and one other thing. Every seven years the Elves pay their tithe to the Nether world, and for all the Queen makes much of me, I fear it is myself that will be the tithe."

"Oh can you not be saved? Tell me if aught I can do will save you, Tamlane?"

"One only thing is there for my safety. To-morrow night is Hallowe'en, and the fairy court will then ride through England and Scotland, and if you would borrow me from Elfland you must take your stand by Miles Cross between twelve and one o' the night, and with holy water in your hand you must cast a compass all around you."

"But how shall I know you, Tamlane," quoth Burd Janet, "amid so many knights I've ne'er seen before?"

"The first court of Elves that come by let pass, let pass. The next court you shall pay reverence to, but do naught nor say aught. But the third court that comes by is the chief court of them, and at the head rides the Queen of all Elfland. And by her side I shall ride upon a milk white steed with a star in my crown; they give me this honour as being a christened knight. Watch my hands, Janet, the right one will be gloved but the left one will be bare, and by that token you will know me."

"But how to save you, Tamlane?" quoth Burd Janet.

"You must spring upon me suddenly, and I will fall to the ground. Then seize me quick, and whatever change befall me, for they will exercise all their magic on me, cling hold to me till they turn me into red-hot iron. Then cast me into this pool and I will be turned back into a mother-naked man. Cast then your green mantle over me, and I shall be yours, and be of the world again."

So Burd Janet promised to do all for Tamlane, and next night at midnight she took her stand by Miles Cross and cast a compass round her with holy water.

Soon there came riding by the Elfin court, first over the mound went a troop on black steeds, and then another troop on brown. But in the third court, all on milk white steeds, she saw the Queen of Elfland and by her side a knight with a star in his crown with right hand gloved and the left bare. Then she knew this was her own Tamlane, and springing forward she seized the bridle of the milk-white steed and pulled its rider down. And as soon as he had touched the ground she let go the bridle and seized him in her arms.

"He's won, he's won amongst us all," shrieked out the eldritch crew, and all came around her and tried their spells on young Tamlane.

First they turned him in Janet's arms like frozen ice, then into a huge flame of roaring fire. Then, again, the fire vanished and an adder was skipping through her arms, but still she held on; and then they turned him into a snake that reared up as if to bite her, and yet she held on. Then suddenly a dove was struggling in her arms, and almost flew away. Then they turned him into a swan, but all was in vain, till at last he was changed into a red-hot glaive, and this she cast into a well of water and then he turned back into a mother-naked man. She quickly cast her green mantle over him, and young Tamlane was Burd Janet's for ever.

Then sang the Queen of Elfland as the court turned away and began to resume its march.

> "She that has borrowed young Tamlane
>   Has gotten a stately groom,
> She's taken away my bonniest knight,
>   Left nothing in his room.
>
> "But had I known, Tamlane, Tamlane,
>   A lady would borrow thee,
> I'd hae ta'en out thy two grey eyne,
>   Put in two eyne of tree.
>
> "Had I but known, Tamlane, Tamlane,
>   Before we came from home,
> I'd hae ta'en out thy heart o' flesh,
>   Put in a heart of stone.
>
> "Had I but had the wit yestreen
>   That I have got to-day,
> I'd paid the Fiend seven times his teind
>   Ere you'd been won away."

And then the Elfin court rode away, and Burd Janet and young Tamlane went their way homewards and were soon after married after young Tamlane had again been sained by the holy water and made Christian once more.

ᴄᴦ *The Stars in the Sky* ᴦᴄ

ONCE on a time and twice on a time, and all times together as ever I heard tell of, there was a tiny lassie who would weep all day to have the stars in the sky to play with; she wouldn't have this, and she wouldn't have that, but it was always the stars she would have. So one fine day off she went to find them. And she walked and she walked and she walked, till by-and-by she came to a mill-dam.

"Gooden to ye," says she; "I'm seeking the stars in the sky to play with. Have you seen any?"

"Oh, yes, my bonny lassie," said the mill-dam. "They shine in my own face o' nights till I can't sleep for them. Jump in and perhaps you'll find one."

So she jumped in, and swam about and swam about and swam about, but ne'er a one could she see. So she went on till she came to a brooklet.

"Gooden to ye, Brooklet, Brooklet," says she; "I'm seeking the stars in the sky to play with. Have you seen any?"

"Yes, indeed, my bonny lassie," said the Brooklet. "They glint on my banks at night. Paddle about, and maybe you'll find one."

So she paddled and she paddled and she paddled, but ne'er a one did she find. So on she went till she came to the Good Folk.

"Gooden to ye, Good Folk," says she; "I'm looking for the stars in the sky to play with. Have ye seen e'er a one?"

"Why, yes, my bonny lassie," said the Good Folk. "They shine on the grass here o' night. Dance with us, and maybe you'll find one."

And she danced and she danced and she danced, but ne'er a one did she see. So down she sate; I suppose she wept.

"Oh dearie me, oh dearie me," says she, "I've swam and I've paddled and I've danced, and if ye'll not help me I shall never find the stars in the sky to play with."

But the Good Folk whispered together, and one of them came up to her and took her by the hand and said, "If you won't go home to your mother, go forward, go forward; mind you take the right road. Ask Four Feet to carry you to No Feet at all, and tell No Feet at all to carry you to the stairs without steps, and if you can climb that——"

"Oh, shall I be among the stars in the sky then?" cried the lassie.

"If you'll not be, then you'll be elsewhere," said the Good Folk, and set to dancing again.

So on she went again with a light heart, and by-and-by she came to a saddled horse, tied to a tree.

"Gooden to ye, Beast," said she; "I'm seeking the stars in the sky to play with. Will you give me a lift, for all my poor bones are a-aching."

"Nay," said the horse, "I know nought of the stars in the sky, and I'm here to do the bidding of the Good Folk, and not my own will."

"Well," said she, "it's from the Good Folk I come, and they bade me tell Four Feet to carry me to No Feet at all."

"That's another story," said he; "jump up and ride with me."

So they rode and they rode and they rode, till they got out of the forest and found themselves at the edge of the sea. And on the water in front of them was a wide glistening path running straight out towards a beautiful thing that rose out of the water and went up into the sky, and was all the colours in the world, blue and red and green, and wonderful to look at.

"Now get you down," said the horse; "I've brought ye to the end of the land, and that's as much as Four Feet can do. I must away home to my own folk."

"But," said the lassie, "where's No Feet at all, and where's the stair without steps?"

"I know not," said the horse, "it's none of my business neither. So gooden to ye, bonny lassie"; and off he went.

So the lassie stood still and looked at the water, till a strange kind of fish came swimming up to her feet.

"Gooden to ye, big Fish," says she; "I'm looking for the stars in the sky, and for the stairs that climb up to them. Will ye show me the way?"

"Nay," said the Fish, "I can't, unless you bring me word from the Good Folk."

"Yes, indeed," said she. "They said Four Feet would bring me to No Feet at all, and No Feet at all would carry me to the stairs without steps."

"Ah, well," said the Fish; "that's all right, then. Get on my back and hold fast."

And off he went—Kerplash!—into the water, along the silver path, towards the bright arch. And the nearer they came the brighter the sheen of it, till she had to shade her eyes from the light of it.

And as they came to the foot of it, she saw it was a broad bright road, sloping up and away into the sky, and at the far, far end of it she could see wee shining things dancing about.

"Now," said the Fish, "here ye are, and yon's the stair: climb up, if you can, but hold on fast. I'll warrant you'll find the stair easier at home than

by such a way: 'twas ne'er meant for lassies' feet to travel"; and off he splashed through the water.

So she clomb and she clomb and she clomb, but ne'er a step higher did she get: the light was before her and around her, and the water behind her, and the more she struggled the more she was forced down into the dark and the cold, and the more she clomb the deeper she fell.

But she clomb and she clomb, till she got dizzy in the light and shivered with the cold, and dazed with the fear; but still she clomb, till at last, quite dazed and silly-like, she let clean go, and sank down—down—down.

And bang she came on to the hard boards, and found herself sitting, weeping and wailing, by the bedside at home all alone.

⤳ *News!* ⤳

MR. G. Ha! Steward, how are you, my old boy? How do things go on at home?

STEWARD. Bad enough, your honour; the magpie's dead!

MR. G. Poor Mag! so he's gone. How came he to die?

STEWARD. Over-ate himself, Sir.

MR. G. Did he indeed? a greedy dog. Why, what did he get that he liked so well?

STEWARD. Horseflesh; he died of eating horseflesh.

MR. G. How came he to get so much horseflesh?

STEWARD. All your father's horses, Sir.

MR. G. What! are they dead too?

STEWARD. Ay, Sir; they died of over-work.

MR. G. And why were they over-worked?

STEWARD. To carry water, Sir.

MR. G. To carry water, and what were they carrying water for?

STEWARD. Sure, Sir, to put out the fire.

MR. G. Fire! what fire?

STEWARD. Your father's house is burned down to the ground.

MR. G. My father's house burnt down! and how came it to be on fire?

STEWARD. I think, Sir, it must have been the torches.

MR. G. Torches! what torches?

STEWARD. At your mother's funeral.

MR. G. My mother dead?

STEWARD. Ay, poor lady, she never looked up after it.

MR. G. After what?

STEWARD. The loss of your father.

MR. G. My father gone too?

STEWARD. Yes, poor gentleman, he took to his bed as soon as he heard of it.

MR. G. Heard of what?

STEWARD. The bad news, an' it please your honour.

MR. G. What? more miseries, more bad news!

STEWARD. Yes, Sir, your bank has failed, your credit is lost and you're not worth a shilling in the world. I made bold, Sir, to come and wait on you about it; for I thought you would like to hear the news.

ᔭ *Puddock, Mousie, and Ratton* ᔭ

THERE lived a Puddock in a well,
And a merry Mousie in a mill.

Puddock he would a-wooing ride,
Sword and pistol by his side.

Puddock came to the Mousie's inn,
"Mistress Mousie, are you within?"

MOUSIE.
"Yes, kind Sir, I am within,
Softly do I sit and spin."

PUDDOCK.
"Madam, I am come to woo,
Marriage I must have of you."

MOUSIE.
"Marriage I will grant you none
Till Uncle Ratton he comes home."

PUDDOCK.
"See, Uncle Ratton's now come in
Then go and bask the bride within."

Who is it that sits next the wall
But Lady Mousie both slim and small?

Who is it that sits next the bride
But Lord Puddock with yellow side?

But soon came Duckie and with her Sir Drake;
Duckie takes Puddock and makes him squeak.

Then came in the old carl cat
With a fiddle on his back:
"Do ye any music lack?"

Puddock he swam down the brook,
Sir Drake he catched him in his fluke.

The cat he pulled Lord Ratton down,
The kittens they did claw his crown.

But Lady Mousie, so slim and small,
Crept into a hole beneath the wall;
"Squeak," quoth she, "I'm out of it all."

The Little Bull-Calf

CENTURIES of years ago, when almost all this part of the country was wilderness, there was a little boy, who lived in a poor bit of property and his father gave him a little bull-calf, and with it he gave him everything he wanted for it.

But soon after his father died, and his mother got married again to a man that turned out to be a very vicious stepfather, who couldn't abide the little boy. So at last the stepfather said: "If you bring that bull-calf into this house, I'll kill it." What a villain he was, wasn't he?

Now this little boy used to go out and feed his bull-calf every day with barley bread, and when he did so this time, an old man came up to him—we can guess who that was, eh?—and said to him: "You and your bull-calf had better go away and seek your fortune."

So he went on and he went on and he went on, as far as I could tell you till to-morrow night, and he went up to a farmhouse and begged a crust of bread, and when he got back he broke it in two and gave half of it to the bull-calf. And he went to another house and begs a bit of cheese crud, and when he went back he wanted to give half of it to the bull-calf. "No," says the bull-calf, "I'm going across the field, into the wild-wood wilderness country, where there'll be tigers, leopards, wolves, monkeys, and a fiery dragon, and I'll kill them all except the fiery dragon, and he'll kill me."

The little boy did cry, and said! "Oh, no, my little bull-calf; I hope he won't kill you."

The Little Bull–Calf

"Yes, he will," said the little bull-calf, "so you climb up that tree, so that no one can come nigh you but the monkeys, and if they come the cheese crud will save you. And when I'm killed, the dragon will go away for a bit, then you must come down the tree and skin me, and take out my bladder and blow it out, and it will kill everything you hit with it. So when the fiery dragon comes back, you hit it with my bladder and cut its tongue out."

(We know there were fiery dragons in those days, like George and his dragon in the Bible; but, there! it's not the same world nowadays. The world is turned topsy-turvy since then, like as if you'd turned it over with a spade!)

Of course, he did all the little bull-calf told him. He climbed up the tree, and the monkeys climbed up the tree after him. But he held the cheese crud in his hand, and said: "I'll squeeze your heart like the flint-stone." So the monkey cocked his eye as much as to say: "If you can squeeze a flint-stone to make the juice come out of it, you can squeeze me." But he didn't say anything, for a monkey's cunning, but down he went. And all the while the little bull-calf was fighting all the wild beasts on the ground, and the little lad was clapping his hands up the tree, and calling out: "Go in, my little bull-calf! Well fought, little bull-calf!" And he mastered everything except the fiery dragon, but the fiery dragon killed the little bull-calf.

But the lad waited and waited till he saw the dragon go away, then he came down and skinned the little bull-calf, and took out its bladder and went after the dragon. And as he went on, what should he see but a king's daughter, staked down by the hair of her head, for she had been put there for the dragon to destroy her.

So he went up and untied her hair, but she said: "My time has come, for the dragon to destroy me; go away, you can do no good." But he said: "No! I can master it, and I won't go"; and for all her begging and praying he would stop.

And soon he heard it coming, roaring and raging from afar off, and at last it came near, spitting fire and with a tongue like a great spear, and you could hear it roaring for miles, and it was making for the place where the king's daughter was staked down. But when it came up to them, the lad just hit it on the head with the bladder and the dragon fell down dead, but before it died, it bit off the little boy's forefinger.

Then the lad cut out the dragon's tongue and said to the king's daughter: "I've done all I can, I must leave you." And sorry she was he had to go, and before he went she tied a diamond ring in his hair, and said goodbye to him.

By-and-by, who should come along but the old king, lamenting and weeping, and expecting to see nothing of his daughter but the prints of the place where she had been. But he was surprised to find her there alive and safe, and he said: "How came you to be saved?" So she told him how she had been saved, and he took her home to his castle again.

Well, he put it into all the papers to find out who saved his daughter, and who had the dragon's tongue and the princess's diamond ring, and was without his forefinger. Whoever could show these signs should marry his daughter and have his kingdom after his death. Well, any number of gentlemen came from all parts of England, with forefingers cut off, and with diamond rings and all kinds of tongues, wild beasts' tongues and foreign tongues. But they couldn't show any dragons' tongues, so they were turned away.

At last the little boy turned up, looking very ragged and desolated like, and the king's daughter cast her eye on him, till her father grew very angry and ordered them to turn the little beggar boy away. "Father," says she; "I know something of that boy."

Well, still the fine gentlemen came, bringing up their dragons' tongues that weren't dragons' tongues, and at last the little boy came up, dressed a little better. So the old king says: "I see you've got an eye on that boy. If it has to be him it must be him." But all the others were fit to kill him, and cried out: "Pooh, pooh, turn that boy out, it can't be him." But the king said: "Now, my boy, let's see what you have to show." Well, he showed the diamond ring with her name on it, and the fiery dragon's tongue. How the others were thunderstruck when he showed his proofs! But the king told him: "You shall have my daughter and my estate."

So he married the princess, and afterwards got the king's estate. Then his step-father came and wanted to own him, but the young king didn't know such a man.

᧖ *The Wee, Wee Mannie* ᧖

ONCE upon a time, when all big folks were wee ones and all lies were true, there was a wee, wee Mannie that had a big, big Coo. And out he went to milk her of a morning, and said—

> "Hold still, my Coo, my hinny,
>   Hold still, my hinny, my Coo,
> And ye shall have for your dinner
>   What but a milk white doo."

But the big, big Coo wouldn't hold still. "Hout!" said the wee, wee Mannie—

> "Hold still, my Coo, my dearie,
>   And fill my bucket wi' milk,
> And if ye'll be no contrairy
>   I'll gi'e ye a gown o' silk."

But the big, big Coo wouldn't hold still. "Look at that, now!" said the wee, wee Mannie—

> "What's a wee, wee mannie to do,
>   Wi' such a big contrairy Coo?"

So off he went to his mother at the house. "Mother," said he, "Coo won't stand still, and wee, wee Mannie can't milk big, big Coo."
   "Hout!" says his mother, "take stick and beat Coo."
   So off he went to get a stick from the tree, and said—

> "Break, stick, break,
> And I'll gi'e ye a cake."

But the stick wouldn't break, so back he went to the house. "Mother," says he, "Coo won't hold still, stick won't break, wee, wee Mannie can't beat big, big Coo."

"Hout!" says his mother, "go to the Butcher and bid him kill Coo."

So off he went to the Butcher, and said—

> "Butcher, kill the big, big Coo,
> She'll gi'e us no more milk noo."

But the Butcher wouldn't kill the Coo without a silver penny, so back the Mannie went to the house. "Mother," says he, "Coo won't hold still, stick won't break, Butcher won't kill without a silver penny, and wee, wee Mannie can't milk big, big Coo."

"Well," said his mother, "go to the Coo and tell her there's a weary, weary lady with long yellow hair weeping for a cup o' milk."

So off he went and told the Coo, but she wouldn't hold still, so back he went and told his mother.

"Well," said she, "tell the Coo there's a fine, fine laddie from the wars sitting by the weary, weary lady with golden hair, and she weeping for a sup o' milk."

So off he went and told the Coo, but she wouldn't hold still, so back he went and told his mother.

"Well," said his mother, "tell the big, big Coo there's a sharp, sharp sword at the belt of the fine, fine laddie from the wars who sits beside the weary, weary lady with the golden hair, and she weeping for a sup o' milk."

And he told the big, big Coo, but she wouldn't hold still.

Then said his mother, "Run quick and tell her that her head's going to be cut off by the sharp, sharp sword in the hands of the fine, fine laddie, if she doesn't give the sup o' milk the weary, weary lady weeps for."

And wee, wee Mannie went off and told the big, big Coo.

And when Coo saw the glint of the sharp, sharp sword in the hand of the fine, fine laddie come from the wars, and the weary, weary lady weeping for a sup o' milk, she reckoned she'd better hold still; so wee, wee Mannie milked big, big Coo, and the weary, weary lady with the golden hair hushed her weeping and got her sup o' milk, and the fine, fine laddie new come from the wars put by his sharp, sharp sword, and all went well that didn't go ill.

ᔑ Habetrot and Scantlie Mab ᔐ

A WOMAN had one fair daughter, who loved play better than work, wandering in the meadows and lanes better than the spinning-wheel and distaff. The mother was heartily vexed at this, for in those days no lassie had any chance of a good husband unless she was an industrious spinster. So she coaxed, threatened, even beat her daughter, but all to no purpose; the girl remained what her mother called her, "an idle cuttie."

At last, one spring morning, the gudewife gave her seven heads of lint, saying she would take no excuse; they must be returned in three days spun into yarn. The girl saw her mother was in earnest, so she plied her distaff as well as she could; but her hands were all untaught, and by the evening of the second day only a very small part of her task was done. She cried herself to sleep that night, and in the morning, throwing aside her work in despair, she strolled out into the fields, all sparkling with dew. At last she reached a knoll, at whose feet ran a little burn, shaded with woodbine and wild roses; and there she sat down, burying her face in her hands. When she looked up, she was surprised to see by the margin of the stream an old woman, quite unknown to her, drawing out the thread as she basked in the sun. There was nothing very remarkable in her appearance, except the length and thickness of her lips, only she was seated on a self-bored stone. The girl rose, went to the good dame, and gave her a friendly greeting, but could not help inquiring "What makes you so long lipped?"

"Spinning thread, my hinnie," said the old woman pleased with her. "I wet my fingers with my lips, as I draw the thread from the distaff."

"Ah!" said the girl, "I should be spinning too, but it's all to no purpose. I shall ne'er do my task": on which the old woman proposed to do it for her. Overjoyed, the maiden ran to fetch her lint, and placed it in her new friend's hand, asking where she should call for the yarn in the evening; but she received no reply; the old woman passed away from her among the trees and bushes. The girl, much bewildered, wandered about a little, sat down to rest, and finally fell asleep by the little knoll.

When she awoke she was surprised to find that it was evening. Causleen, the evening star, was beaming with silvery light, soon to be lost in the moon's splendour. While watching these changes, the maiden was startled by the sound of an uncouth voice, which seemed to issue from below the self-bored stone, close beside her. She laid her ear to the stone and heard the words: "Hurry up, Scantlie Mab, for I've promised the yarn and Habetrot always keeps her promise." Then looking down the hole saw her friend, the old dame, walking backwards and forwards in a deep cavern among a group of spinsters all seated on colludie stones, and busy with distaff and spindle. An ugly company they were, with lips more or less disfigured, like old Habetrot's. Another of the sisterhood, who sat in a distant corner reeling the yarn, was marked, in addition, by grey eyes, which seemed starting from her head, and a long hooked nose.

While the girl was still watching, she heard Habetrot address this dame by the name of Scantlie Mab, and say, "Bundle up the yarn, it is time the young lassie should give it to her mother." Delighted to hear this, the girl got up and returned homewards. Habetrot soon overtook her, and placed the yarn in her hands. "Oh, what can I do for ye in return?" exclaimed she, in delight. "Nothing—nothing," replied the dame; "but dinna tell your mother who spun the yarn."

Scarcely believing her eyes, the girl went home, where she found her mother had been busy making sausters, and hanging them up in the chimney to dry, and then, tired out, had retired to rest. Finding herself very hungry after her long day on the knoll, the girl took down pudding after pudding, fried and ate them, and at last went to bed too. The mother was up first the next morning, and when she came into the kitchen and found her sausters all gone, and the seven hanks of yarn lying beautifully smooth and bright upon the table, she ran out of the house wildly, crying out—

"My daughter's spun seven, seven, seven,
My daughter's eaten seven, seven, seven,
And all before daylight."

A laird who chanced to be riding by, heard the exclamation, but could not understand it; so he rode up and asked the gudewife what was the matter, on which she broke out again—

"My daughter's spun seven, seven, seven,
My daughter's eaten seven, seven, seven

before daylight; and if ye dinna believe me, why come in and see it." The laird, he alighted and went into the cottage, where he saw the yarn, and admired it so much he begged to see the spinner.

The mother dragged in her girl. He vowed he was lonely without a wife, and had long been in search of one who was a good spinner. So their troth was plighted, and the wedding took place soon afterwards, though the bride was in great fear that she should not prove so clever at her spinning-wheel as he expected. But old Dame Habetrot came to her aid. "Bring your bonnie bridegroom to my cell," said she to the young bride soon after her marriage; "he shall see what comes o' spinning, and never will he tie you to the spinning-wheel."

Accordingly the bride led her husband the next day to the flowery knoll, and bade him look through the self-bored stone. Great was his surprise to behold Habetrot dancing and jumping over her rock, singing all the time this ditty to her sisterhood, while they kept time with their spindles:—

> "We who live in dreary den,
>   Are both rank and foul to see;
> Hidden from the glorious sun,
>   That teems the fair earth's canopie:
> Ever must our evenings lone
>   Be spent on the colludie stone.
>
> "Cheerless is the evening grey.
>   When Causleen hath died away,
> But ever bright and ever fair,
>   Are they who breathe this evening air;
> And lean upon the self-bored stone
>   Unseen by all but me alone."

The song ended, Scantlie Mab asked Habetrot what she meant by her last line, "Unseen by all but me alone."

"There is one," replied Habetrot, "whom I bid to come here at this hour, and he has heard my song through the self-bored stone." So saying she rose, opened another door, which was concealed by the roots of an old tree, and invited the pair to come in and see her family.

The laird was astonished at the weird-looking company, as he well might be, and enquired of one after another the cause of their strange lips. In a different tone of voice, and with a different twist of the mouth, each answered that it was occasioned by spinning. At least they tried to say so, but one grunted out "Nakasind," and another "Owkasaänd," while a third murmured "O-a-a-send." All, however, made the bridegroom understand what was the cause of their ugliness; while Habetrot slily hinted that if his wife were allowed to spin, her pretty lips would grow out of shape too, and her pretty face get an ugsome look. So before he left the cave he vowed that his little wife should never touch a spinning-wheel, and he kept his word. She used to wander in the meadows by his side, or ride behind him over the hills, but all the flax grown on his land was sent to old Habetrot to be converted into yarn.

❧ Old Mother Wiggle-Waggle ❧

THE fox and his wife they had a great strife,
They never ate mustard in all their whole life;
They ate their meat without fork or knife,
    And loved to be picking a bone, e-ho!

The fox went out, one still, clear night,
And he prayed the moon to give him light,
For he'd a long way to travel that night,
    Before he got back to his den-o!

The fox when he came to yonder stile,
He lifted his lugs and he listened a while!
"Oh, ho! " said the fox, "it's but a short mile
    From this unto yonder wee town, e-ho!"

And first he arrived at a farmer's yard,
Where the ducks and the geese declared it was hard,
That their nerves should be shaken and their rest
    should be marred

By the visits of Mister Fox-o!

The fox when he came to the farmer's gate,
Who should he see but the farmer's drake;
"I love you well for your master's sake,
    And long to be picking your bones, e-ho!"

The grey goose she ran round the hay-stack,
"Oh, ho!" said the fox, "you are very fat;
You'll grease my beard and ride on my back
    From this into yonder wee town, e-ho!"

Then he took the grey goose by her sleeve,
And said: "Madam Grey Goose, by your leave
I'll take you away without reprieve,
    And carry you back to my den-o!"

And he seized the black duck by the neck,
And slung him all across his back,
The black duck cried out "quack, quack, quack,"
    With his legs all dangling down-o!

Old Mother Wiggle-Waggle hopped out of bed,
Out of the window she popped her old head;
"Oh! husband, oh! husband, the grey goose is gone,
    And the fox is off to his den, oh!"

Then the old man got up in his red cap,
And swore he would catch the fox in a trap;
But the fox was too cunning, and gave him the slip,
    And ran through the town, the town, oh!

When he got to the top of the hill,
He blew his trumpet both loud and shrill,
For joy that he was safe and sound
    Through the town, oh!

But at last he arrived at his home again,
To his dear little foxes, eight, nine, ten,

Says he "You're in luck, here's a fine fat duck,
With his legs all dangling down-o"!

So he sat down together with his hungry wife,
And they did very well without fork or knife,
They never ate a better duck in all their life,
And the little ones picked the bones-o!

⤞ Catskin ⤝

WELL, there was once a gentleman who had fine lands and houses, and he very much wanted to have a son to be heir to them. So when his wife brought him a daughter, bonny as bonny could be, he cared naught for her, and said, "Let me never see her face."

So she grew up a bonny girl, though her father never set eyes on her till she was fifteen years old and was ready to be married. But her father said, "Let her marry the first that comes for her." And when this was known, who should be first but a nasty rough old man. So she didn't know what to do, and went to the henwife and asked her advice. The henwife said, "Say you will not take him unless they give you a coat of silver cloth." Well, they gave her a coat of silver cloth, but she wouldn't take him for all that, but went again to the henwife, who said, "Say you will not take him unless they give you a coat of beaten gold." Well, they gave her a coat of beaten gold, but still she would not take him, but went to the henwife, who said, "Say you will not take him unless they give you a coat made of the feathers of all the birds of the air." So they sent a man with a great heap of pease; and the man cried to all the birds of the air, "Each bird take a pea, and put down a feather." So each bird took a pea and put down one of its feathers: and they took all the feathers and made a coat of them and gave it to her; but still she would not, but asked the henwife once again, who said, "Say they must first make you a coat of catskin." So they made her a coat of catskin; and she put it on, and tied up her other coats, and ran away into the woods.

So she went along and went along and went along, till she came to the end of the wood, and saw a fine castle. So there she hid her fine dresses, and went up to the castle gates, and asked for work. The lady of the castle saw her, and told her, "I'm sorry I have no better place, but if you like you may be our scullion." So down she went into the kitchen, and they called her Catskin, because of her dress. But the cook was very cruel to her and led her a sad life.

Well, it happened soon after that the young lord of the castle was coming home, and there was to be a grand ball in honour of the occasion. And when they were speaking about it among the servants, "Dear me, Mrs. Cook," said Catskin, "how much I should like to go."

"What! you dirty impudent slut," said the cook, "you go among all the fine lords and ladies with your filthy catskin? a fine figure you'd cut!" and with that she took a basin of water and dashed it into Catskin's face. But she only briskly shook her ears, and said nothing.

When the day of the ball arrived, Catskin slipped out of the house and went to the edge of the forest where she had hidden her dresses. So she bathed herself in a crystal waterfall, and then put on her coat of silver cloth, and hastened away to the ball. As soon as she entered all were overcome by her beauty and grace, while the young lord at once lost his heart to her. He asked her to be his partner for the first dance, and he would dance with none other the livelong night.

When it came to parting time, the young lord said, "Pray tell me, fair maid, where you live." But Catskin curtsied and said:

> "Kind sir, if the truth I must tell,
> At the sign of the 'Basin of Water' I dwell."

Then she flew from the castle and donned her catskin robe again, and slipped into the scullery again, unbeknown to the cook.

The young lord went the very next day to his mother, the lady of the castle, and declared he would wed none other but the lady of the silver dress, and would never rest till he had found her. So another ball was soon arranged for in hope that the beautiful maid would appear again.

So Catskin said to the cook, "Oh, how I should like to go!" Whereupon the cook screamed out in a rage, "What, you, you dirty impudent slut! you would cut a fine figure among all the fine lords and ladies." And with that she up with a ladle and broke it across Catskin's back. But she only shook her ears, and ran off to the forest, where she first of all bathed, and then put on her coat of beaten gold, and off she went to the ball-room.

As soon as she entered all eyes were upon her; and the young lord soon recognised her as the lady of the "Basin of Water," and claimed her hand for the first dance, and did not leave her till the last. When that came, he again asked her where she lived. But all that she would say was:

> "Kind sir, if the truth I must tell,
> At the sign of the 'Broken Ladle' I dwell";

and with that she curtsies, and flew from the ball, off with her golden robe, on with her catskin, and into the scullery without the cook's knowing.

Next day when the young lord could not find where was the sign of the "Basin of Water," or of the "Broken Ladle," he begged his mother to have another grand ball, so that he might meet the beautiful maid once more.

All happened as before. Catskin told the cook how much she would like to go to the ball, the cook called her "a dirty slut," and broke the skimmer across her head. But she only shook her ears, and went off to the forest, where she first bathed in the crystal spring, and then donned her coat of feathers, and so off to the ball-room.

When she entered every one was surprised at so beautiful a face and form dressed in so rich and rare a dress; but the young lord soon recognised his beautiful sweetheart, and would dance with none but her the whole evening. When the ball came to an end, he pressed her to tell him where she lived, but all she would answer was:

> "Kind sir, if the truth I must tell,
> At the sign of the 'Broken Skimmer' I dwell";

and with that she curtsied, and was off to the forest. But this time the young lord followed her, and watched her change her fine dress of feathers for her catskin dress, and then he knew her for his own scullery-maid.

Next day he went to his mother, the lady of the castle, and told her that he wished to marry the scullery-maid, Catskin. "Never," said the lady, and rushed from the room. Well, the young lord was so grieved at that, that he took to his bed and was very ill. The doctor tried to cure him, but he would not take any medicine unless from the hands of Catskin. So the doctor went to the lady of the castle, and told her her son would die if she did not consent to his marriage with Catskin. So she had to give way, and summoned Catskin to her. But she put on her coat of beaten gold, and went to the lady, who soon was glad to wed her son to so beautiful a maid.

Well, so they were married, and after a time a dear little son came to them, and grew up a bonny lad; and one day, when he was four years old, a beggar woman came to the door, so Lady Catskin gave some money to the little lord and told him to go and give it to the beggar woman. So he went and gave it, but put it into the hand of the woman's child, who leant forward and kissed the little lord. Now the wicked old cook—why hadn't she been sent away?—was looking on, so she said, "Only see how beggars' brats take to one another." This insult went to Catskin's heart, so she went to her husband, the young lord, and told him all about her father, and begged he would go and find out what had become of her parents. So they set out in the lord's grand coach, and travelled through the forest till they came to Catskin's father's house, and put up at an inn near, where Catskin stopped, while her husband went to see if her father would own her.

Now her father had never had any other child, and his wife had died; so he was all alone in the world and sate moping and miserable. When the young lord came in he hardly looked up, till he saw a chair close up to him, and asked him, "Pray, sir, had you not once a young daughter whom you would never see or own?"

The old gentleman said, "It is true; I am a hardened sinner. But I would give all my worldly goods if I could but see her once before I die." Then the young lord told him what had happened to Catskin, and took him to the inn, and brought his father-in-law to his own castle, where they lived happy ever afterwards.

֍ Stupid's Cries ֍

THERE was once a little boy, and his mother sent him to buy a sheep's head and pluck; afraid he should forget it, the lad kept saying all the way along:

> "Sheep's head and pluck!
> Sheep's head and pluck!"

Trudging along, he came to a stile; but in getting over he fell and hurt himself, and beginning to blubber, forgot what he was sent for. So he stood a little while to consider: at last he thought he recollected it, and began to repeat:

> "Liver and lights and gall and all!
> Liver and lights and gall and all!"

Away he went again, and came to where a man had a pain in his liver, bawling out:

> "Liver and lights and gall and all!
> Liver and lights and gall and all!"

Whereon the man laid hold of him and beat him, bidding him say:

> "Pray God send no more!
> Pray God send no more!"

The youngster strode along, uttering these words, till he reached a field where a hind was sowing wheat:

"Pray God send no more!
Pray God send no more!"

This was all his cry. So the sower began to thrash him, and charged him to repeat:

"Pray God send plenty more!
Pray God send plenty more!"

Off the child scampered with these words in his mouth till he reached a churchyard and met a funeral, but he went on with his:

"Pray God send plenty more!
Pray God send plenty more!"

The chief mourner seized and punished him, and bade him repeat:

"Pray God send the soul to heaven!
Pray God send the soul to heaven!"

Away went the boy, and met a dog and a cat going to be hung, but his cry rang out!

"Pray God send the soul to heaven!
Pray God send the soul to heaven!"

The good folk nearly were furious, seized and struck him, charging him to say:
"A dog and a cat agoing to be hung!
A dog and a cat agoing to be hung!"

This the poor fellow did, till he overtook a man and a woman going to be married. "Oh! oh!" he shouted:

"A dog and a cat agoing to be hung!
A dog and a cat agoing to be hung!"

The man was enraged, as we may well think, gave him many a thump, and ordered him to repeat:

"I wish you much joy!
I wish you much joy!"

This he did, jogging along, till he came to two labourers who had fallen into a ditch. The lad kept bawling out:

"I wish you much joy!
I wish you much joy!"

This vexed one of the folk so sorely that he used all his strength, scrambled out, beat the crier, and told him to say:

"The one is out, I wish the other was!
The one is out, I wish the other was!"

On went young 'un till he found a fellow with only one eye; but he kept up his song:

"The one is out, I wish the other was!
The one is out, I wish the other was!"

This was too much for Master One-eye, who grabbed him and chastised him, bidding him call:

"The one side gives good light,
    I wish the other did!
The one side gives good light,
    I wish the other did!"

So he did, to be sure, till he came to a house, one side of which was on fire. The people here thought it was he who had set the place a-blazing, and straightway put him in prison. The end was, the judge put on his black cap, and condemned him to die.

↝ *The Lambton Worm* ↝

A WILD young fellow was the heir of Lambton, the fine estate and hall by the side of the swift-flowing Wear. Not a Mass would he hear in

Brugeford Chapel of a Sunday, but a-fishing he would go. And if he did not haul in anything, his curses could be heard by the folk as they went by to Brugeford.

Well, one Sunday morning he was fishing as usual, and not a salmon had risen to him, his basket was bare of roach or dace. And the worse his luck, the worse grew his language, till the passers-by were horrified at his words as they went to listen to the Mass-priest.

At last young Lambton felt a mighty tug at his line. "At last," quoth he, "a bite worth having!" and he pulled and he pulled, till what should appear above the water but a head like an eft's, with nine holes on each side of its mouth. But still he pulled till he had got the thing to land, when it turned out to be a Worm of hideous shape. If he had cursed before, his curses were enough to raise the hair on your head.

"What ails thee, my son?" said a voice by his side, "and what hast thou caught, that thou shouldst stain the Lord's Day with such foul language?"

Looking round, young Lambton saw a strange old man standing by him.

"Why, truly," he said, "I think I have caught the devil himself. Look you and see if you know him."

But the stranger shook his head, and said, "It bodes no good to thee or thine to bring such a monster to shore. Yet cast him not back into the Wear; thou hast caught him, and thou must keep him," and with that away he turned, and was seen no more.

The young heir of Lambton took up the gruesome thing, and, taking it off his hook, cast it into a well close by, and ever since that day that well has gone by the name of the Worm Well.

For some time nothing more was seen or heard of the Worm, till one day it had outgrown the size of the well, and came forth full-grown. So it came forth from the well and betook itself to the Wear. And all day long it would lie coiled round a rock in the middle of the stream, while at night it came forth from the river and harried the country side. It sucked the cow's milk, devoured the lambs, worried the cattle, and frightened all the women and girls of the district, and then it would retire for the rest of the night to the hill, still called the Worm Hill, on the north side of the Wear, about a mile and a half from Lambton Hall.

This terrible visitation brought young Lambton, of Lambton Hall, to his senses. He took upon himself the vows of the Cross, and departed for the Holy Land, in the hope that the scourge he had brought upon his district would disappear. But the grisly Worm took no heed, except that it crossed the river and came right up to Lambton Hall itself where the old lord lived on all alone, his only son having gone to the Holy Land. What to do? The Worm was coming closer and closer to the Hall; women were shrieking, men were gathering weapons, dogs were barking and horses neighing with terror. At last the steward called out to the dairy maids, "Bring all your milk hither," and when they did so, and had brought all the milk that the nine kye of the byre had yielded, he poured it all into the long stone trough in front of the Hall.

The Worm drew nearer and nearer, till at last it came up to the trough. But when it sniffed the milk, it turned aside to the trough and swallowed all the milk up, and then slowly turned round and crossed the river Wear, and coiled its bulk three times round the Worm Hill for the night.

Henceforth the Worm would cross the river every day, and woe betide the Hall if the trough contained the milk of less than nine kye. The Worm would hiss, and would rave, and lash its tail round the trees of the park, and in its fury it would uproot the stoutest oaks and the loftiest firs. So it went on for seven years. Many tried to destroy the Worm, but all had failed, and many a knight had lost his life in fighting with the monster, which slowly crushed the life out of all that came near it.

At last the Childe of Lambton came home to his father's Hall, after seven long years spent in meditation and repentance on holy soil. Sad and desolate he found his folk: the lands untilled, the farms deserted, half the trees of the park uprooted, for none would stay to tend the nine kye that the monster needed for his food each day.

The Childe sought his father, and begged his forgiveness for the curse he had brought on the Hall.

"Thy sin is pardoned," said his father; "but go thou to the Wise Woman of Brugeford, and find if aught can free us from this monster."

To the Wise Woman went the Childe, and asked her advice.

"'Tis thy fault, O Childe, for which we suffer," she said; "be it thine to release us."

"I would give my life," said the Childe.

"Mayhap thou wilt do so," said she. "But hear me, and mark me well. Thou, and thou alone, canst kill the Worm. But, to this end, thou go to the smithy and have thy armour studded with spear-heads. Then go to the Worm's Rock in the Wear, and station thyself there. Then, when the Worm comes to the Rock at dawn of day, try thy prowess on him, and God gi'e thee a good deliverance."

The Lambton Worm

"And this I will do," said Childe Lambton.

"But one thing more," said the Wise Woman, going back to her cell. "If thou slay the Worm, swear that thou wilt put to death the first thing that meets thee as thou crossest again the threshold of Lambton Hall. Do this, and all will be well with thee and thine. Fulfil not thy vow, and none of the Lambtons, for generations three times three, shall die in his bed. Swear, and fail not."

The Childe swore as the Wise Woman bid, and went his way to the stithy. There he had his armour studded with spear-heads all over. Then he passed his vigils in Brugeford Chapel, and at dawn of day took his post on the Worm's Rock in the River Wear.

As dawn broke, the Worm uncoiled its snaky twine from around the hill, and came to its rock in the river. When it perceived the Childe waiting for it, it lashed the waters in its fury and wound its coils round the Childe, and then attempted to crush him to death. But the more it pressed, the deeper dug the spear-heads into its sides. Still it pressed and pressed, till all the water around was crimsoned with its blood. Then the Worm unwound itself, and left the Childe free to use his sword. He raised it, brought it down, and cut the Worm in two. One half fell into the river, and was carried swiftly away. Once more the head and the remainder of the body encircled the Childe, but with less force, and the spear-heads did their work. At last the Worm uncoiled itself, snorted its last foam of blood and fire, and rolled dying into the river, and was never seen more.

The Childe of Lambton swam ashore, and, raising his bugle to his lips, sounded its note thrice. This was the signal to the Hall, where the servants and the old lord had shut themselves in to pray for the Childe's success. When the third sound of the bugle was heard, they were to release Boris, the Childe's favourite hound. But such was their joy at learning of the Childe's safety and the Worm's defeat, that they forgot orders, and when the Childe reached the threshold of the Hall his old father rushed out to meet him, and would have clasped him to his breast.

"The vow! the vow!" called out the Childe of Lambton, and blew still another blast upon his horn. This time the servants remembered, and released Boris, who came bounding to his young master. The Childe raised his shining sword, and severed the head of his faithful hound.

But the vow was broken, and for nine generations of men none of the Lambtons died in his bed. The last of the Lambtons died in his carriage as he was crossing Brugeford Bridge, one hundred and thirty years ago.

ꙅ The Wise Men of Gotham ꙅ

Of Buying of Sheep.

THERE were two men of Gotham, and one of them was going to market to Nottingham to buy sheep, and the other came from the market, and they both met together upon Nottingham bridge.

"Where are you going?" said the one who came from Nottingham.

"Marry," said he that was going to Nottingham, "I am going to buy sheep."

"Buy sheep?" said the other, "and which way will you bring them home?"

"Marry," said the other, "I will bring them over this bridge."

"By Robin Hood," said he that came from Nottingham, "but thou shalt not."

"By Maid Marion," said he that was going thither, "but I will."

"You will not," said the one.

"I will," said the other.

Then they beat their staves against the ground one against the other, as if there had been a hundred sheep between them.

"Hold in," said one; "beware lest my sheep leap over the bridge."

"I care not," said the other; "they shall not come this way."

"But they shall," said the other.

Then the other said: "If that thou make much to do, I will put my fingers in thy mouth."

"Will you?" said the other.

Now, as they were at their contention, another man of Gotham came from the market with a sack of meal upon a horse, and seeing and hearing his neighbours at strife about sheep, though there were none between them, said:

"Ah, fools! will you ever learn wisdom? Help me, and lay my sack upon my shoulders."

They did so, and he went to the side of the bridge, unloosened the mouth of the sack, and shook all his meal out into the river.

"Now, neighbours," he said, "how much meal is there in my sack?"

"Marry," said they, "there is none at all."

"Now, by my faith," said he, "even as much wit as is in your two heads to stir up strife about a thing you have not."

Which was the wisest of these three persons, judge yourself.

Of Hedging a Cuckoo.

Once upon a time the men of Gotham would have kept the Cuckoo so that she might sing all the year, and in the midst of their town they made a hedge round in compass and they got a Cuckoo, and put her into it, and said, "Sing there all through the year, or thou shalt have neither meat nor

water." The Cuckoo, as soon as she perceived herself within the hedge, flew away. "A vengeance on her!" said they. "We did not make our hedge high enough."

Of Sending Cheeses.

There was a man of Gotham who went to the market at Nottingham to sell cheese, and as he was going down the hill to Nottingham bridge, one of his cheeses fell out of his wallet and rolled down the hill. "Ah, gaffer," said the fellow, "can you run to market alone? I will send one after another after you." Then he laid down his wallet and took out the cheeses, and rolled them down the hill. Some went into one bush, and some went into another.

"I charge you all to meet me near the market-place"; and when the fellow came to the market to meet his cheeses, he stayed there till the market was nearly done. Then he went about to inquire of his friends and neighbours, and other men, if they did see his cheeses come to the market.

"Who should bring them?" said one of the market men.

"Marry, themselves," said the fellow; "they know the way well enough."

He said, "A vengeance on them all. I did fear, to see them run so fast, that they would run beyond the market. I am now fully persuaded that they must be now almost at York." Whereupon he forthwith hired a horse to ride to York, to seek his cheeses where they were not, but to this day no man can tell him of his cheeses.

Of Drowning Eels.

When Good Friday came, the men of Gotham cast their heads together what to do with their white herrings, their red herrings, their sprats, and other salt fish. One consulted with the other, and agreed that such fish should be cast into their pond (which was in the middle of the town), that they might breed against the next year, and every man that had salt fish left cast them into the pool.

"I have many white herrings," said one.

"I have many sprats," said another.

"I have many red herrings," said the other.

"I have much salt fish. Let all go into the pond or pool, and we shall fare like lords next year."

At the beginning of next year following the men drew near the pond to have their fish, and there was nothing but a great eel. "Ah," said they all, "a mischief on this eel, for he has eaten up all our fish."

"What shall we do to him?" said one to the other.

"Kill him," said one.

"Chop him into pieces," said another. "Not so," said another; "let us drown him."

"Be it so," said all. And they went to another pond, and cast the eel into the pond. "Lie there and shift for yourself, for no help thou shalt have from us"; and they left the eel to drown.

Of Sending Rent.

Once on a time the men of Gotham had forgotten to pay their land-lord. One said to the other, "To-morrow is our pay-day, and what shall we find to send our money to our landlord?"

The one said, "This day I have caught a hare, and he shall carry it, for he is light of foot."

"Be it so," said all; "he shall have a letter and a purse to put our money in, and we shall direct him the right way." So when the letters were written and the money put in a purse, they tied it round the hare's neck, saying, "First you go to Lancaster, then thou must go to Loughborough, and Newarke is our landlord, and commend us to him, and there is his dues."

The hare, as soon as he was out of their hands, ran on along the country way. Some cried, "Thou must go to Lancaster first."

"Let the hare alone," said another; "he can tell a nearer way than the best of us all. Let him go."

Another said, "It is a subtle hare, let her alone; she will not keep the highway for fear of dogs."

Of Counting.

On a certain time there were twelve men of Gotham who went fish-ing, and some went into the water and some on dry ground; and, as they were coming back, one of them said, "We have ventured much this day wading; I pray God that none of us that did come from home be drowned."

"Marry," said one, "let us see about that. Twelve of us came out," and every man did count eleven, and the twelfth man did never count him-self.

"Alas!" said one to another, "one of us is drowned." They went back to the brook where they had been fishing, and looked up and down for him that was drowned, and made great lamentation. A courtier came riding by, and he did ask what they were seeking, and why they were so sorrow-ful. "Oh," said they, "this day we came to fish in this brook, and there were twelve of us, and one is drowned."

"Why," said the courtier, "count me how many of you there be," and one counted eleven and did not count himself. "Well," said the courtier, "what will you give me if I find the twelfth man?"

"Sir," said they, "all the money we have."

"Give me the money," said the courtier; and he began with the first, and gave him a whack over the shoulders that he groaned, and said, "There is one," and he served all of them that they groaned; but when he came to the last he gave him a good blow, saying, "Here is the twelfth man."

"God bless you on your heart," said all the company; "you have found our neighbour."

᧬ Princess of Canterbury ᧬

THERE lived formerly in the County of Cumberland a nobleman who had three sons, two of whom were comely and clever youths, but the other a natural fool, named Jack, who was generally engaged with the sheep: he was dressed in a parti-coloured coat, and a steepled-crowned hat with a tassel, as became his condition. Now the King of Canterbury had a beautiful daughter, who was distinguished by her great ingenuity and wit, and he issued a decree that whoever should answer three questions put to him by the princess should have her in marriage, and be heir to the crown at his decease. Shortly after this decree was published, news of it reached the ears of the nobleman's sons, and the two clever ones determined to have a trial, but they were sadly at a loss to prevent their idiot brother from going with them. They could not, by any means, get rid of him, and were compelled at length to let Jack accompany them. They had not gone far, before Jack shrieked with laughter, saying, "I've found an egg." "Put it in your pocket," said the brothers. A little while afterwards, he burst out into another fit of laughter on finding a crooked hazel stick, which he also put in his pocket: and a third time he again laughed extravagantly because he found a nut. That also was put with his other treasures.

When they arrived at the palace, they were immediately admitted on mentioning the nature of their business, and were ushered into a room where the princess and her suite were sitting. Jack, who never stood on ceremony, bawled out, "What a troop of fair ladies we've got here!"

"Yes," said the princess, "we are fair ladies, for we carry fire in our bosoms."

"Do you?" said Jack, "then roast me an egg," pulling out the egg from his pocket.

"How will you get it out again?" said the princess.

"With a crooked stick," replied Jack, producing the hazel.

"Where did that come from?" said the princess.

"From a nut," answered Jack, pulling out the nut from his pocket. "I've answered the three questions, and now I'll have the lady." "No, no," said the king, "not so fast. You have still an ordeal to go through. You must come here in a week's time and watch for one whole night with the princess, my daughter. If you can manage to keep awake the whole night long you shall marry her next day."

"But if I can't?" said Jack.

"Then off goes your head," said the king. "But you need not try unless you like."

Well, Jack went back home for a week, and thought over whether he should try and win the princess. At last he made up his mind. "Well," said Jack, "I'll try my vorton; zo now vor the king's daughter, or a headless shepherd!"

And taking his bottle and bag, he trudged to the court. In his way thither, he was obliged to cross a river, and pulling off his shoes and stockings, while he was passing over he observed several pretty fish bobbing against his feet; so he caught some and put them into his pocket. When he reached the palace he knocked at the gate loudly with his crook, and having mentioned the object of his visit, he was immediately conducted to the hall where the king's daughter sat ready prepared to see her lovers. He was placed in a luxurious chair, and rich wines and spices were set before him, and all sorts of delicate meats. Jack, unused to such fare, ate and drank plentifully, so that he was nearly dozing before midnight.

"Oh, shepherd," said the lady, "I have caught you napping!"

"Noa, sweet ally, I was busy a-feeshing."

"A fishing," said the princess in the utmost astonishment: "Nay, shepherd, there is no fish-pond in the hall."

"No matter vor that, I have been fishing in my pocket, and have just caught one."

"Oh me!" said she, "let me see it."

The shepherd slyly drew the fish out of his pocket and pretending to have caught it, showed it her, and she declared it was the finest she ever saw.

About half an hour afterwards, she said, "Shepherd, do you think you could get me one more?"

He replied, "Mayhap I may, when I have baited my hook"; and after a little while he brought out another, which was finer than the first, and the princess was so delighted that she gave him leave to go to sleep, and promised to excuse him to her father.

In the morning the princess told the king, to his great astonishment, that Jack must not be beheaded, for he had been fishing in the hall all night; but when he heard how Jack had caught such beautiful fish out of his pocket, he asked him to catch one in his own.

Jack readily undertook the task, and bidding the king lie down, he pretended to fish in his pocket, having another fish concealed ready in his hand, and giving him a sly prick with a needle, he held up the fish, and showed it to the king.

His majesty did not much relish the operation, but he assented to the marvel of it, and the princess and Jack were united the same day, and lived for many years in happiness and prosperity.

OYEZ·OYEZ·OYEZ
THE·ENGLISH·FAIRY·TALES
ARE·NOW·CLOSED
LITTLE·BOYS·AND·GIRLS
MUST·NOT·READ·ANY·FURTHER·

Warning to Children

~⁊~

Notes and References

FOR some general remarks on the English Folk-Tale and previous collectors, I must refer to the introductory observations added to the Notes and References of *English Fairy Tales,* in the second edition. With the present instalment the tale of English Fairy Stories that are likely to obtain currency among the young folk is complete. I do not know of more than half-a-dozen "outsiders" that deserve to rank with those included in my two volumes which, for the present, at any rate, must serve as the best substitute that can be offered for an English Grimm. I do not despair of the future. After what Miss Fison (who, as I have recently learned, was the collector of *Tom Tit Tot* and *Cap o' Rushes*), Mrs. Balfour, and Mrs. Gomme have done in the way of collecting among the folk, we may still hope for substantial additions to our stock to be garnered by ladies from the less frequented portions of English soil. And from the United States we have every reason to expect a rich harvest to be gathered by Mr. W. W. Newell, who is collecting the English folk-tales that still remain current in New England. If his forthcoming book equals in charm, scholarship, and thoroughness his delightful *Games and Songs of American Children,* the Anglo-American folk-tale will be enriched indeed. A further examination of English nursery rhymes may result in some additions to our stock. I reserve these for separate treatment in which I am especially interested, owing to the relations which I surmise between the folk-tale and the *cante-fable.*

Meanwhile the eighty-seven tales (representing some hundred and twenty variants) in my two volumes must represent the English folk-tale as far as my diligence has been able to preserve it at this end of the nineteenth century. There is every indication that they form but a scanty survival of the whole *corpus* of such tales which must have existed in this country. Of the seventy European story-radicles which I have enumerated in the Folk-Lore Society's *Handbook,* pp. 117–35, only forty are represented in our collection: I have little doubt that the majority of the remaining thirty or so also existed in these isles, and especially in England. If I had reckoned in the tales current in the English pale of Ireland, as well as those in Lowland Scots, there would have been even less missing. The result of my investigations confirms me in my impression that the scope of the English folk-tale should include all those current among the folk in English, no matter where spoken, in Ireland, the Lowlands, New England, or Australia. Wherever there is community of language, tales can spread, and it is more likely that tales should be preserved in those parts where English is spoken with most of dialect. Just as the Anglo-Irish Pale preserves more of the

pronunciation of Shakespeare's time, so it is probable that Anglo-Irish stories preserve best those current in Shakespeare's time in English. On the other hand, it is
possible that some, nay, many of the Anglo-Irish stories have been imported from the
Celtic districts, and are positively folk-translations from the Gaelic. Further research
is required to determine which is English and which Celtic among Anglo-Irish folk-
tales. Meanwhile my collection must stand for the nucleus of the English folk-tale,
and we can at any rate judge of its general spirit and tendencies from the eighty-seven
tales now before the reader.

Of these, thirty-eight are *märchen* proper, *i.e.*, tales with definite plot and evolution;
ten are sagas or legends locating romantic stories in definite localities; no less than
nineteen are drolls or comic anecdotes; four are cumulative stories; six beast tales; while
ten are merely ingenious nonsense tales put together in such a form as to amuse children. The preponderance of the comic element is marked, and it is clear that humour
is a characteristic of the English *folk*. The legends are not of a very romantic kind, and
the *märchen* are often humorous in character. So that a certain air of un-romance is
given by such a collection as that we are here considering. The English folk-muse
wears homespun and plods afoot, albeit with a cheerful smile and a steady gaze.

Some of this effect is produced by the manner in which the tales are told. The
colloquial manner rarely rises to the dignified, and the essence of the folk-tale manner in English is colloquial. The opening formulæ are varied enough, but none of
them has much play of fancy. "Once upon a time and a very good time it was, though
it wasn't in my time nor in your time nor in any one else's time," is effective enough
for a fairy epoch, and is common, according to Mayhew (*London Labour*, iii.), among
tramps. We have the rhyming formula:

> Once upon a time when pigs spoke rhyme,
> And monkeys chewed tobacco,
> And hens took snuff to make them tough,
> And ducks went quack, quack, quack Oh!

on which I have variants not so refined. Some stories start off without any preliminary formula, or with a simple "Well, there was once a———" A Scotch formula
reported by Mrs. Balfour runs, "Once on a time when a' muckle folk were wee and
a' lees were true," while Mr. Lang gives us "There was a king and a queen as mony
ane's been, few have we seen and as few may we see." Endings of stories are even
less varied. "So they married and lived happy ever afterwards," comes from folk-
tales, not from novels. "All went well that didn't go ill," is a somewhat cynical formula given by Mrs. Balfour, while the Scotch have "they lived happy and died
happy, and never drank out of a dry cappie."

In the course of the tale the chief thing to be noticed is the occurrence of rhymes
in the prose narrative, tending to give the appearance of a *cante-fable*. I have enumerated those occurring in *English Fairy Tales* in the Notes to *Childe Rowland* (No.
xxi.). In the present volume rhyme occurs in Nos. xlvi., xlviii., xlix., lviii., lx., lxiii.
(see Note), lxiv., lxxiv., lxxxi., lxxxv., while lv., lxix., lxxiii., lxxvi., lxxxiii., lxxxiv., are
either in verse themselves or derived from verse versions. Altogether one-third of
our collection gives evidence in favour of the *cante-fable* theory which I adduced in

my notes to *Childe Rowland.* Another point of interest in English folk-narrative is the repetition of verbs of motion, "So he went along and went along and went along." Still more curious is a frequent change of tense from the English present to the past. "So he gets up and went along." All this helps to give the colloquial and familiar air to the English fairy-tale, not to mention the dialectal and archaic words and phrases which occur in them.

But their very familiarity and colloquialism make them remarkably effective with English-speaking little ones. The rhythmical phrases stick in their memories; they can remember the exact phraseology of the English tales much better, I find, than that of the Grimms' tales, or even of the Celtic stories. They certainly have the quality of coming home to English children. Perhaps this may be partly due to the fact that a larger proportion of the tales are of native manufacture. If the researches contained in my Notes are to be trusted only i.-ix., xi., xvii., xxii., xxv., xxvi., xxvii., xliv., l., liv., lv., lviii., lxi., lxii., lxv., lxvii., lxxviii., lxxxiv., lxxxvii. were imported; nearly all the remaining sixty are home produce, and have their roots in the hearts of the English people which naturally respond to them.

In the following Notes I have continued my practice of giving (1) *Source* where I obtained the various tales. (2) *Parallels,* so far as possible, in full for the British Isles, with bibliographical references when they can be found; for occurrences abroad I generally refer to the lists of incidents contained in my paper read before the International Folk-Lore Congress of 1891 and republished in the *Transactions* 1892, pp. 87–98. (3) *Remarks* where the tale seems' to need them. I have mainly been on the search for signs of diffusion rather than of "survivals" of antiquarian interest, though I trust it will be found I have not neglected these.

XLIV. THE PIED PIPER

Source.—Abraham Elder, *Tales and Legends of the Isle of Wight,* (London, 1839), pp. 157–164. Mr. Nutt, who has abridged and partly rewritten the story from a copy of Elder's book in his possession, has introduced a couple of touches from Browning.

Parallels.—The well-known story of the Pied Piper of Hameln (Hamelin), immortalised by Browning, will at once recur to every reader's mind. Before Browning, it had been told in English in books as well known as Verstegan's *Restitution of Decayed Intelligence,* 1605; Howell's *Familiar Letters* (see my edition, p. 357, *n.*); and Wanley's *Wonders of the Little World.* Browning is said to have taken it from the last source (Furnivall, *Browning Bibliography,* 158), though there are touches which seem to me to come from Howell (see my note *ad loc.*), while it is not impossible he may have come across Elder's book, which was illustrated by Cruikshank. The Grimms give the legend in their *Deutsche Sagen* (ed. 1816, 330–33), and in its native land it has given rise to an elaborate poem *à la* Scheffel by Julius Wolff, which has in its turn been the occasion of an opera by Victor Nessler. Mrs. Gutch, in an interesting study of the myth in *Folk-Lore,* iii. pp. 227–52, quotes a poem, *The Sea Piece,* published by Dr. Kirkpatrick in 1750, as showing that a similar legend was told of the Cave Hill, near Belfast.

> Here, as Tradition's hoary legend tells,
> A blinking Piper once with magic Spells

And strains beyond a vulgar Bagpipe's sound,
Gathered the dancing Country wide around.
When hither as he drew the tripping Rear
(Dreadful to think and difficult to swear!)
The gaping Mountain yawned from side to side,
A hideous Cavern, darksome, deep, and wide;
In skipt th' exulting Demon, piping loud,
With passive joy succeeded by the Crowd.

*　　*　　*　　*

There firm and instant closed the greedy Womb,
Where wide-born Thousands met a common Tomb.

Remarks.—Mr. Baring-Gould, in his *Curious Myths of the Middle Ages,* has explained the Pied Piper as a wind myth; Mrs. Gutch is inclined to think there may be a substratum of fact at the root of the legend, basing her conclusions on a pamphlet of Dr. Meinardus, *Der historische Kern,* which I have not seen. She does not, however, give any well-authenticated historical event at Hameln in the thirteenth century which could have plausibly given rise to the legend, nor can I find any in the *Urkundenbuch* of Hameln (Luneberg, 1883). The chief question of interest attaching to the English form of the legend as given in 1839 by Elder, is whether it is independent of the German myth. It does not occur in any of the local histories of the Isle of Wight which I have been able to consult of a date previous to Elder's book—*e.g.,* J. Hassel, *Tour of the Isle of Wight,* 1790. Mr. Shore, in his *History of Hampshire,* 1891, p. 185, refers to the legend, but evidently bases his reference on Elder, and so with all the modern references I have seen. Now Elder himself quotes Verstegan in his comments on the legend, pp. 168–9 and note, and it is impossible to avoid conjecturing that he adapted Verstegan to the locality. Newtown, when Hassel visited it in 1790, had only six or seven houses (*l.c.* i. 137–8), though it had the privilege of returning two members to Parliament; it had been a populous town by the name of Franchville before the French invasion of the island of *temp.* Ric. II. It is just possible that there may have been a local legend to account for the depopulation by an exodus of the children. But the expression "pied piper" which Elder used clearly came from Verstegan, and until evidence is shown to the contrary the whole of the legend was adapted from him. It is not without significance that Elder was writing in the days of the *Ingoldsby Legends,* and had possibly no more foundation for the localisation of his stories than Barham.

There still remains the curious parallel from Belfast to which Mrs. Gutch has drawn attention. Magic pipers are not unknown to English folk-lore, as in the Percy ballad of *The Frere and the Boy,* or in the nursery rhyme of Tom Piperson in its more extended form. But beguiling into a mountain is not known elsewhere except at Hameln, which was made widely known in England by Verstegan's and Howell's accounts, so that the Belfast variant is also probably to be traced to the *Rattenfänger.* Here again, as in the case of Beddgellert (*Celtic Fairy Tales,* No. xxi.), the Blinded Giant and the Pedlar of Swaffham (*infra,* Nos. lxi., lxiii.), we have an imported legend adapted to local conditions.

XLV. Hereafterthis

Source.—Sent me anonymously soon after the appearance of *English Fairy Tales*. From a gloss in the MS. "vitty" = Devonian for "decent," I conclude the tale is current in Devon. I should be obliged if the sender would communicate with me.

Parallels.—The latter part has a certain similarity with "Jack Hannaford" (No. viii.). Halliwell's story of the miser who kept his money "for luck" (p. 153) is of the same type. Halliwell remarks that the tale throws light on a passage in Ben Jonson:

> Say we are robbed,
> If any come to borrow a spoon or so
> I will not have Good Fortune or God's Blessing
> Let in, while I am busy.

The earlier part of the tale has resemblance with "Lazy Jack" (No. xxvii.), the European variants of which are given by M. Cosquin, *Contes de Lorraine*, i. 241. Jan's satisfaction with his wife's blunders is also European (Cosquin, *l.c.* i. 157). On minding the door and dispersing robbers by its aid see "Mr. Vinegar" (No. vi.).

Remarks.—"Hereafterthis" is thus a *mélange* of droll incidents, yet has characteristic folkish touches ("can you milk-y, bake-y," "when I lived home") which give it much vivacity.

XLVI. The Golden Ball

Source.—Contributed to the first edition of Henderson's *Folk-Lore of the Northern Counties*, pp. 333–5, by Rev. S. Baring-Gould.

Parallels.—Mr. Nutt gave a version in *Folk-Lore Journal,* vi. 144. The man in instalments occurs in "The Strange Visitor" (No. xxxii.). The latter part of the tale has been turned into a game for English children, "Mary Brown," given in Miss Plunket's *Merry Games,* but not included in Newell, *Games and Songs of American Children.*

Remarks.—This story is especially interesting as having given rise to a game. Capture and imprisonment are frequently the gruesome *motif* of children's games, as in "Prisoner's base." Here it has been used with romantic effect.

XLVII. My Own Self

Source.—Told to Mrs. Balfour by Mrs. W., a native of North Sunderland, who had seen the cottage and heard the tale from persons who had known the widow and her boy, and had got the story direct from them. The title was "Me A'an Sel'," which I have altered to "My Own Self."

Parallels.—Notwithstanding Mrs. Balfour's informant, the same tale is widely spread in the North Country. Hugh Miller relates it, in his *Scenes from my Childhood,* as "Ainsel"; it is given in Mr. Hartland's *English Folk and Fairy Tales;* Mr. F. B. Jevons has heard it in the neighbourhood of Durham; while a further version appeared in *Monthly Chronicle of North Country Folk Lore.* Further parallels abroad are enumerated by Mr. Clouston in his *Book of Noodles,* pp. 194–5, and by the late Prof. Köhler in *Orient und Occident,* ii. 331. The expedient by which Ulysses outwits Polyphemus in the Odyssey by calling himself οὐτισ is clearly of the same order.

Remarks.—The parallel with the Odyssey suggests the possibility that this is the ultimate source of the legend, as other parts of the epic have been adapted to local requirements in Great Britain, as in the "Blinded Giant" (No. lxi.), or "Conall Yellow-claw" (*Celtic Fairy Tales,* No. v.). The fact of Continental parallels disposes of the possibility of its being a merely local legend. The fairies might appear to be in a some-what novel guise here as something to be afraid of. But this is the usual attitude of the folk towards the "Good People," as indeed their euphemistic name really implies.

XLVIII. THE BLACK BULL OF NORROWAY

Source.—Chambers's *Popular Rhymes of Scotland,* much Anglicised in language, but otherwise unaltered.

Parallels.—Chambers, *l.c.,* gave a variant with the title "The Red Bull o' Nor-roway." Kennedy, *Legendary Fictions,* p. 87, gives a variant with the title "The Brown Bear of Norway." Mr. Stewart gave a Leitrim version, in which "Norroway" becomes "Orange," in *Folk Lore* for June 1893, which Miss Peacock follows up with a Lin-colnshire parallel (showing the same corruption of name) in the September number. A reference to the "Black Bull o' Norroway" occurs in Sidney's *Arcadia,* as also in the *Complaynt of Scotland,* 1548. The "sale of bed" incident at the end has been bibli-ographised by Miss Cox in her volume of variants of *Cinderella,* p. 481. It probably existed in one of the versions of Nix Nought Nothing (No. vii.).

Remarks.—The Black Bull is clearly a Beast who ultimately wins a Beauty. But the tale as is told is clearly not sufficiently motivated. Miss Peacock's version renders it likely that a fuller account may yet be recovered in England.

XLIX. YALLERY BROWN

Source.—Mrs. Balfour's "Legends of the Lincolnshire Fens," in *Folk Lore,* ii. It was told to Mrs. Balfour by a labourer, who professed to be the hero of the story, and related it in the first person. I have given him a name, and changed the narration into the oblique narration, and toned down the dialect.

Parallels.—"Tiddy Mun," the hero of another of Mrs. Balfour's legends (*l.c.,* p. 151) was "none bigger 'n a three years old bairn," and had no proper name.

Remarks.—One might almost suspect Mrs. Balfour of being the victim of a piece of invention on the part of her autobiographical informant. But the scrap of verse, especially in its original dialect, has such a folkish ring that it is probable he was only adapting a local legend to his own circumstances.

L. THE THREE FEATHERS

Source.—Collected by Mrs. Gomme from some hop-pickers near Deptford.

Parallels.—The beginning is *à la* Cupid and Psyche, on which Mr. Lang's mono-graph in the Carabas series is the classic authority. The remainder is an Eastern tale, the peregrinations of which have been studied by Mr. Clouston in his *Pop. Tales and Fictions,* ii. 289, *seq. The Wright's Chaste Wife,* is the English *fabliau* on the subject. M. Bédier, in his recent work on *Les Fabliaux,* pp. 411–13, denies the Eastern origin of the fabliau, but in his Indiaphobia M. Bédier is "capable de tout." In the Indian version the various messengers are sent by the king to test the chastity of a peerless wife of whom he has heard. The incident occurs in some versions of the *Battle of the Birds* story (*Celtic Fairy Tales,* No. xxiv.), and considering the wide spread of this in the British Isles, it was possibly from this source that it came to Deptford.

LI. Sir Gammer Vans

Source.—Halliwell's *Nursery Rhymes and Tales.*

Parallels.—There is a Yorkshire Lying Tale in Henderson's *Folk Lore,* first edition, p. 337, a Suffolk one, "Happy Borz'l," in *Suffolk Notes and Queries,* while a similar jingle of inconsequent absurdities, commencing "So he died, and she unluckily married the barber, and a great bear coming up the street popped his head into the window, saying, 'Do you sell any soap?'" is said to have been invented by Charles James Fox to test Sheridan's memory, who repeated it after one hearing. (Others attribute it to Foote.) Similar *Lugenmärchen* are given by the Grimms, and discussed by them in their Notes, Mrs. Hunt's translation, ii. pp. 424, 435, 442, 450, 452, *cf.* Crane, *Ital. Pop. Tales,* p. 263.

Remarks.—The reference to venison warrants, and bows and arrows, seem to argue considerable antiquity for this piece of nonsense. The honorific prefix "Sir" may in that case refer to clerkly qualities rather than to knighthood.

LII. Tom Hickathrift

Source.—From the Chapbook, *c.* 1660, in the Pepysian Library, edited for the Villon Society by Mr. G. L. Gomme. Mr. Nutt, who kindly abridged it for me, writes, "Nothing in the shape of incident has been omitted, and there has been no re-writing beyond a phrase here and there rendered necessary by the process of abridgment. But I have in one case altered the sequence of events, putting the fight with the giant last."

Parallels.—There are similar adventures of giants in Hunt's Cornish *Drolls.* Sir Francis Palgrave (*Quart. Rev.,* vol. xxi.), and, after him, Mr. Gomme, have drawn attention to certain similarities with the Grettir Saga, but they do not extend beyond general resemblances of great strength. Mr. Gomme, however, adds that the cart-wheel "plays a not unimportant part in English folk-lore as a representative of old runic faith" (Villon Soc. edition, p. xv.).

Remarks.—Mr. Gomme, in his interesting Introduction, points out several indications of considerable antiquity for the legend, various expressions in the Pepysian chapbook ("in the marsh of the Isle of Ely," "good ground"), indicating that it could trace back to the sixteenth century. On the other hand, there is evidence of local tradition persisting from that time onward till the present day (Weaver, *Funerall Monuments,* 1631, pp. 866–7; Spelman, *Icenia,* 1640, p. 138; Dugdale, *Imbanking,* 1662 (ed. 1772, p. 244); Blomefield, *Norfolk,* 1808, ix. pp. 79, 80). These refer to a sepulchral monument in Tylney churchyard which had figured on a stone coffin an axle-tree and cart-wheel. The name in these versions of the legend is given as Hickifric, and he is there represented as a village Hampden who withstood the tyranny of the local lord of the manor. Mr. Gomme is inclined to believe, I understand him, that there is a certain amount of evidence for Tom Hickathrift being a historic personality round whom some of the Scandinavian mythical exploits have gathered. I must refer to his admirable Introduction for the ingenious line of reasoning on which he bases these conclusions. Under any circumstances no English child's library of folk-tales can be considered complete that does not present a version of Mr. Hickathrift's exploits.

LIII. The Hedley Kow

Source.—Told to Mrs. Balfour by Mrs. M. of S. Northumberland. Mrs. M.'s mother told the tale as having happened to a person she had known when young: she had herself seen the Hedley Kow twice, once as a donkey and once as a wisp of straw. "Kow" must not be confounded with the more prosaic animal with a C.

Parallels.—There is a short reference to the Hedley Kow in Henderson, *l.c.,* first edition, pp. 234–5. Our story is shortly referred to thus: "He would present himself to some old dame gathering sticks, in the form of a truss of straw, which she would be sure to take up and carry away. Then it would become so heavy that she would have to lay her burden down, on which the straw would become 'quick,' rise upright and shuffle away before her, till at last it vanished from her sight with a laugh and shout." Some of Robin Goodfellow's pranks are similar to those of the Hedley Kow. The old woman's content with the changes is similar to that of "Mr. Vinegar." An ascending scale of changes has been studied by Prof. Crane, *Italian Popular Tales,* p. 373.

LIV. Gobborn Seer

Source.—Collected by Mrs. Gomme from an old woman at Deptford. It is to be remarked that "Gobborn Seer" is Irish (Goban Saor = free carpenter), and is the Irish equivalent of Wayland Smith, and occurs in several place names in Ireland.

Parallels.—The essence of the tale occurs in Kennedy, *l.c.,* p. 67 *seq.* Gobborn Seer's daughter was clearly the clever lass who is found in all parts of the Indo-European world. An instance in my *Indian Fairy Tales,* "Why the Fish laughed" (No. xxiv.). She has been made a special study of by Prof. Child, *English and Scotch Ballads,* i. 485, while an elaborate monograph by Prof. Benfey under the title "Die Kluge Dirne" (reprinted in his *Kleine Schriften,* ii. 156 *seq.*), formed the occasion for his first presentation of his now well-known hypothesis of the derivation of all folk-tales from India.

Remarks.—But for the accident of the title being preserved there would have been nothing to show that this tale had been imported into England from Ireland, whither it had probably been carried all the way from India.

LV. Lawkamercyme

Source.—Halliwell, *Nursery Rhymes.*

Parallels.—It is possible that this is an Eastern "sell": it occurs at any rate as the first episode in Fitzgerald's translation of Jami's *Salámán and Absál.* Jami, *ob.* 1492, introduces the story to illustrate the perplexities of the problem of individuality in a pantheistic system.

> Lest, like the simple Arab in the tale,
> I grow perplext, O God! 'twixt ME and THEE,

> If I—this Spirit that inspires me whence?
> If Thou—then what this sensual impotence?

In other words, M. Bourget's *Cruelle Enigme*. The Arab yokel corning to Bagdad is fearful of losing his identity, and ties a pumpkin to his leg before going to sleep. His companion transfers it to his own leg. The yokel awaking is perplexed like the pantheist.

> If I—the pumpkin why on you?
> If you—then where am I, and who?

LVI. Tattercoats

Source.—Told to Mrs. Balfour by a little girl named Sally Brown, when she lived in the Cars in Lincolnshire. Sally had got it from her mother, who worked for Mrs. Balfour. It was originally told in dialect, which Mrs. Balfour has omitted.

Parallels.—Miss Cox has included "Tattercoats" in her exhaustive collection of parallels of *Cinderella* (Folk-Lore Society Publications, 1892), No. 274 from the MS. which I had lent her. Miss Cox rightly classes it as "Indeterminate," and it has only the *Menial Heroine* and *Happy Marriage* episodes in common with stories of the Cinderella type.

Remarks.—"Tattercoats" is of interest chiefly as being without any "fairy" or supernatural elements, unless the magic pipe can be so considered; it certainly gives the tale a fairy-like element. It is practically a prose variant of "King Cophetua and the Beggar Maid," and is thus an instance of the folk-novel pure and simple, without any admixture of those unnatural incidents which transform the folk-novel into the serious folk-tale as we are accustomed to have it. Which is the prior, folk-novel or tale, it would be hard to say.

LVII. The Wee Bannock

Source.—Chambers's *Popular Rhymes of Scotland*. I have attempted an impossibility, I fear, in trying to anglicise, but the fun of the original tempted me. There still remain several technical trade terms requiring elucidation. I owe the following to the kindness of the Rev. Mr. Todd Martin, of Belfast. *Lawtrod* = lap board on which the tailor irons; *tow cards*, the comb with which tow is carded; the *clove*, a heavy wooden knife for breaking up the flax. *Heckling* is combing it with a *heckle* or wooden comb; *binnings* are halters for cattle made of *sprit* or rushes. *Spurtle* = spoon; *whins* = gorse.

Parallels.—This is clearly a variant of "Johnnycake" = journey cake, No. xxviii., where see Notes.

Remarks.—But here the interest is with the pursuers rather than with the pursued. The subtle characterisation of the various occupations reaches a high level of artistic merit. Mr. Barrie himself could scarcely have succeeded better in a very difficult task.

LVIII. Johnny Gloke

Source.—Contributed by Mr. W. Gregor to *Folk-Lore Journal*, vii. I have rechristened "Johnny Glaik" for the sake of the rhyme, and anglicised the few Scotticisms.

Parallels.—This is clearly "The Valiant Tailor" of the Grimms: "*x* at a blow" has been bibliographised. (See my list of Incidents in Trans. Folk-Lore Congress, 1892, *sub voce.*)

Remarks.—How "The Valiant Tailor" got to Aberdeen one cannot tell, though the resemblance is close enough to suggest a direct "lifting" from some English version of "Grimm's Goblins." At the same time it must be remembered that "Jack the Giant Killer" (see Notes on No. xix.) contains some of the incidents of the Valiant Tailor.

LIX. Coat o' Clay

Source.—Contributed by Mrs. Balfour originally to *Longman's Magazine,* and thence to *Folk-Lore,* Sept. 1890.

Remarks.—A rustic apologue, which is scarcely more than a prolonged pun on "Coat o' Clay." Mrs. Balfour's telling redeems it from the usual dulness of folk-tales with a moral or a double meaning.

LX. The Three Cows

Source.—Contributed to Henderson, *l.c.,* pp. 321–2, by the Rev. S. Baring-Gould.

Parallels.—The incident "Bones together" occurs in "Rushen Coatie" *(infra,* No. lxx.), and has been discussed by the Grimms, i. 399, and by Prof. Köhler, *Or. und Occ.* ii. 680.

LXI. The Blinded Giant

Source.—Henderson's *Folk-Lore of Northern Counties.* See also *Folk-Lore.*

Parallels.—Polyphemus in the Odyssey and the Celtic parallels in *Celtic Fairy Tales,* No. v., "Conall Yellowclaw." The same incident occurs in one of Sindbad's voyages.

Remarks.—Here we have another instance of the localisation of a well-known myth. There can be little doubt that the version is ultimately to be traced back to the Odyssey. The one-eyed giant, the barred door, the escape through the blinded giant's legs in the skin of a slaughtered animal, are a series of incidents that could not have arisen independently and casually. Yet till lately the mill stood to prove if the narrator lied, and every circumstance of local particularity seemed to vouch for the autochthonous character of the myth. The incident is an instructive one, and I have therefore included it in this volume, though it is little more than an anecdote in its present shape.

LXII. Scrapefoot

Source.—Collected by Mr. Batten from Mrs. H., who heard it from her mother over forty years ago.

Parallels.—It is clearly a variant of Southey's "Three Bears" (No. xviii.).

Remarks.—This remarkable variant raises the question whether Southey did anything more than transform Scrapefoot into his naughty old woman, who in her turn has been transformed by popular tradition into the naughty girl Silverhair. Mr. Nutt ingeniously suggests that Southey heard the story told of an old vixen, and mistook the rustic name of a female fox for the metaphorical application to women of fox-like temper. Mrs. H.'s version to my mind has all the marks of priority. It is throughout an animal tale, the touch at the end of the shaking the paws and the name Scrapefoot are too *volkstümlich* to have been conscious variations on Southey's tale. In introducing the story in his *Doctor,* the poet laureate did not claim to do more than repeat a popular tale. I think that there can be little doubt that in Mrs. H.'s version we have now recovered this in its original form. If this is so, we may here have one more incident of the great northern beast epic of bear and fox, on which Prof. Krohn has written an instructive monograph. *Bär (Wolf.) und Fuchs* (Helsingfors, 1889).

LXIII. The Pedlar of Swaffham

Source.—*Diary of Abraham de la Pryme* (Surtees Soc.) under date 10th Nov., 1699, but re-written by Mr. Nutt, who has retained the few characteristic seventeenth century touches of Pryme's dull and colourless narration. There is a somewhat fuller account in Blomfield's *History of Norfolk,* vi. 211–13, from Twysden's *Reminiscences,* ed. Hearne, p. 299. In this there is a double treasure; the first in an iron pot with a Latin inscription, which the pedlar, whose name is John Chapman, does not understand. Inquiring its meaning from a learned friend, he is told—

> Under me doth lie
> Another much richer than I.

He accordingly digs deeper and finds another pot of gold.

Parallels.—Bloomfield refers to Fungerus, *Etymologicum Latino-Græcum,* pp. 1110–11, where the same story is told of a peasant of Dort, in Holland, who was similarly directed to go to Kempen Bridge. Prof. E. B. Cowell, who gives the passage from Fungerus in a special paper on the subject in the *Journal of Philology,* vi. 189–95, points out that the same story occurs in the *Masnávi* of the Persian port Jalaluddin, whose *floruit* is 1260 A.D. Here a young spendthrift of Bagdad is warned in a dream to repair to Cairo, with the usual result of being referred back.

Remarks.—The artificial character of the incident is sufficient to prevent its having occurred in reality or to more than one inventive imagination. It must therefore have been brought to Europe from the East and adapted to local conditions at Dort and Swaffham. Prof. Cowell suggests that it was possibly adapted at the later place to account for the effigy of the pedlar and his dog.

LXIV. The Old Witch

Source.—Collected by Mrs. Gomme at Deptford.

Parallels.—I have a dim memory of hearing a similar tale in Australia in 1860. It is clearly parallel with the Grimms' "Frau Holle," where the good girl is rewarded and the bad punished in a similar way. Perrault's "Toads and Diamonds" is of the same *genus.*

LXV. The Three Wishes

Source.—Sternbergs *Folk-Lore of Northamptonshire,* 1851, but entirely re-written by Mr. Nutt, who has introduced from other variants one touch at the close—viz., the readiness of the wife to allow her husband to remain disfigured.

Parallels.—Perrault's "Trois Souhaits" is the same tale, and Mr. Lang has shown in his edition of Perrault (pp. xlii.-li.) how widely spread is the theme throughout the climes and the ages. I do not, however, understand him to grant that they are all derived from one source—that represented in the Indian *Pantschatantra*. In my *Æsop*, i. 140–1, I have pointed out an earlier version in Phædrus where it occurs (as in the prose versions) as the fable of *Mercury and the two Women*, one of whom wishes to see her babe when it has a beard; the other, that everything she touches may follow her, which she would find useful in her profession. The babe becomes bearded, and the other woman raising her hand to wipe her eyes finds her nose following her hand—*dénouement* on which the scene closes. M. Bédier, as usual, denies the Indian origin, *Les Fabliaux*, pp. 177 *seq.*

Remarks.—I have endeavoured to show, *l.c.*, that the Phædrine form is ultimately to be derived from India, and there can be little doubt that all the other variants, which are only variations on one idea, and that an absurdly incongruous one, were derived from India in the last resort. The case is strongest for drolls of this kind.

LXVI. The Buried Moon

Source.—Mrs. Balfour's "Legends of the Lincolnshire Cars" in *Folk-Lore*, ii., somewhat abridged and the dialect removed. The story was derived from a little girl named Bratton, who declared she had heard it from her "grannie." Mrs. Balfour thinks the girl's own weird imagination had much to do with framing the details.

Remarks.—The tale is noteworthy as being distinctly mythical in character, and yet collected within the last ten years from one of the English peasantry. The conception of the moon as a beneficent being, the natural enemy of the bogles and other dwellers of the dark, is natural enough, but scarcely occurs, so far as I recollect, in other mythological systems. There is, at any rate, nothing analogous in the Grimms' treatment of the moon in their *Teutonic Mythology*, tr. Stallybrass, pp. 701–21.

LXVII. A Son of Adam

Source.—From memory, by Mr. E. Sidney Hartland, as heard by him from his nurse in childhood.

Parallels.—Jacques de Vitry, *Exempla*, ed. Prof. Crane, No. xiii., and references given in notes, p. 139. It occurs in Swift and in modern Italian folk-lore.

Remarks.—The *Exempla* were anecdotes, witty and otherwise, used by the monks in their sermons to season their discourse. Often they must have been derived from the folk of the period, and at first sight it might seem that we had found still extant among the folk the story that had been the original of Jacques de Vitry's *Exemplum*. But the theological basis of the story shows clearly that it was originally a monkish invention and came thence among the folk.

LXVIII. The Children in the Wood

Source.—Percy, *Reliques*. The ballad form of the story has become such a nursery classic that I had not the heart to "prose" it. As Mr. Allingham remarks, it is the best of the ballads of the pedestrian order.

Parallels.—The second of R. Yarrington's *Two Lamentable Tragedies*, 1601, has the same plot as the ballad. Several chapbooks have been made out of it, some of them enumerated by Halliwell's *Popular Histories* (Percy Soc.) No. 18. From one of these I am in the fortunate position of giving the names of the *dramatis personæ* of this domestic tragedy. Androgus was the wicked uncle, Pisaurus his brother who married Eugenia, and their children in the wood were Cassander and little Kate. The ruffians were appropriately named Rawbones and Woudkil. According to a writer in 3 *Notes and Queries*, ix. 144, the traditional burial-place of the children is pointed out in Norfolk. The ballad was known before Percy, as it is mentioned in the *Spectator*, Nos. 80 and 179.

Remarks.—The only "fairy" touch—but what a touch!—is the pall of leaves collected by the robins.

LXIX. The Hobyahs

Source.—*American Folk-Lore Journal*, iii. 173, contributed by Mr. S. V. Proudfit as current in a family deriving from Perth.

Remarks.—But for the assurance of the tale itself that Hobyahs are no more, Mr. Batten's portraits of them would have convinced me that they were the bogles or spirits of the comma bacillus. Mr. Proudfit remarks that the cry "Look me" was very impressive.

LXX. A Pottle o' Brains

Source.—Contributed by Mrs. Balfour to *Folk-Lore*, II.

Parallels.—The fool's wife is clearly related to the Clever Lass of "Gobborn Seer," where see notes.

Remarks.—The fool is obviously of the same family as he of the "Coat o' Clay" (No. lix.), if he is not actually identical with him. His adventures might be regarded as a sequel to the former ones. The Noodle family is strongly represented in English folk-tales, which would seem to confirm Carlyle's celebrated statistical remark.

LXXI. The King of England

Source.—Mr. F. Hindes Groome, "In Gypsy Tents," told him by John Roberts, a Welsh gypsy, with a few slight changes and omission of passages insisting upon the gypsy origin of the three helpful brothers.

Parallels.—The king and his three sons are familiar figures in European *märchen*. Slavonic parallels are enumerated by Leskien Brugman in their *Lithauische Märchen*, notes on No. 11, p. 542. The Sleeping Beauty is of course found in Perrault.

Remarks.—The tale is scarcely a good example for Mr. Hindes Groome's contention (in *Transactions Folk-Lore Congress)* for the diffusion of all folk-tales by means of gypsies as *colporteurs*. This is merely a matter of evidence, and of evidence there is singularly little, though it is indeed curious that one of Campbell's best equipped informants should turn out to be a gypsy. Even this fact, however, is not too well substantiated.

LXXII. King John and the Abbot

Source.—"Prosed" from the well-known ballad in Percy. I have changed the first query: What am I worth? Answer: Twenty-nine pence—one less, I ween, than the Lord. This would have sounded somewhat bold in prose.

Parallels.—Vincent of Beauvais has the story, but the English version comes from the German Joe Miller, Pauli's *Schimpf und Ernst,* No. lv., p. 46, ed. Oesterley, where see his notes. The question I have omitted exists there, and cannot have "independently arisen." Pauli was a fifteenth century worthy or unworthy.

Remarks.—Riddles were once on a time serious things to meddle with, as witness Samson and the Sphynx, and other instances duly noted with his customary erudition by Prof. Child in his comments on the ballad, *English and Scotch Ballads,* i. 403–14.

LXXIII. Rushen Coatie

Source.—I have concocted this English, or rather Scotch, Cinderella from the various versions given in Miss Cox's remarkable collection of 345 variants of *Cinderella* (Folk-Lore Society, 1892); see *Parallels* for an enumeration of those occurring in the British Isles. I have used Nos. 1–3, 8–10. I give my composite the title "*Rushen Coatie,*" to differentiate it from any of the Scotch variants, and for the purposes of a folk-lore experiment. If this book becomes generally used among English-speaking peoples, it may possibly re-introduce this and other tales among the folk. We should be able to trace this re-introduction by the variation in titles. I have done the same with "Nix Nought Nothing," "Molly Whuppie," and "Johnny Gloke."

Parallels.—Miss Cox's volume gives no less that 113 variants of the pure type of Cinderella—her type A. "Cinderella, or the Fortunate Marriage of a despised Scullery-maid by aid of an *Animal* Godmother through the Test of a Slipper"—such might be the explanatory title of a chapbook dealing with the pure type of Cinderella. This is represented in Miss Cox's book, so far as the British Isles are concerned, by no less than seven variants, as follows:—(1) Dr. Blind, in *Archæological Review,* iii. 24–7, "Ashpitell" (from neighbourhood of Glasgow). (2) A. Lang, in *Revue Celtique,* t. iii., reprinted in "Folk-Lore," September, 1890, "Rashin Coatie" (from Morayshire). (3) Mr. Gregor, in *Folk-Lore Journal,* ii. 72–4 (from Aberdeenshire), "The Red Calf"—all these in Lowland Scots. (4) Campbell, *Popular Tales,* No. xliii. ii. 286 *seq.,* "The Sharp Grey Sheep." (5) Mr. Sinclair, in *Celtic Mag.,* xiii. 454–65, "Snow-white Maiden." (6) Mr. Macleod's variant communicated through Mr. Nutt to Miss Cox's volume, p. 533; and (7) Curtin, *Myths of Ireland,* pp. 78–92, "Fair, Brown, and Trembling"—these four in Gaelic, the last in Erse. To these I would add (8, 9) Chambers's two versions in *Pop. Rhymes of Scotland,* pp. 66–8, "Rashie Coat," though Miss Cox assimilates them to Type B. Catskin; and (10) a variant of Dr. Blind's version, unknown to Miss Cox, but given in 7 *Notes and Queries,* x. 463 (Dumbartonshire). Mr. Clouston has remarks on the raven as omen-bird in his notes to Mrs. Saxby's *Birds of Omen in Shetland* (privately printed, 1893).

Remarks.—In going over these various versions, the first and perhaps most striking thing that comes out is the substantial agreement of the variants in each *language.* The English—*i.e.,* Scotch, variants go together; the Gaelic ones agree to differ from the English. I can best display this important agreement and difference by the accompanying two tables, which give, in parallel columns, Miss Cox's abstracts of her tabulations, in which each incident is shortly given in technical phraseology. It is practically impossible to use the long tabulations for comparative purposes without some such shorthand.

Now, in the "English" versions there is practical unanimity in the concluding portions of the tale. *Magic dresses—Meeting-place (Church)—Flight—Lost Shoe—Shoe Marriage-test—Mutilated foot—False Bride—Bird witness—Happy Marriage,* follow one another with exemplary regularity in all four (six) versions.* The introductory incidents vary somewhat. Chambers has evidently a maimed version of the introduction of Catskin (see No. lxxxiii.). The remaining three enable us, however, to restore with some confidence the *Ur*-Cinderella in English somewhat as follows: *Helpful animal given by dying mother—Ill-treated heroine—Menial heroine—Ear cornucopia—Spy on heroine—Slaying by helpful animal—Tasks—Revivified bones.* I have

ENGLISH VARIANTS OF CINDERELLA

GREGOR.	LANG.	CHAMBERS, I. AND II.	BLIND.
Ill-treated heroine (by parents).	Calf given by dying mother.	*Heroine dislikes husband.*	Ill-treated heroine (by stepmother).
Helpful animal (red calf).	Ill-treated heroine (by stepmother) and sisters).	*Henwife aid.*	Menial heroine.
Spy on heroine.	Heroine disguise (rashin coatie).	*Countertasks.*	Helpful animal (black sheep).
Slaying of helpful animal threatened.	Hearth abode.	*Heroine disguise.*	Ear cornucopia.
Heroine flight.	Helpful animal.	*Heroine flight.*	Spy on heroine.
Heroine disguise (rashin coatie).	Slaying of helpful animal.	Menial heroine.	Slaying of helpful animal.
Menial heroine.	Revivified bones.	(Fairy) aid.	Old woman advice.
	Help at grave.		Revivified bones.
	Dinner cooked (by helpful animal).		Task-performing animal.
Magic dresses (given by calf).	Magic dresses.	Magic dresses.	Meeting-place (church).
Meeting-place (church).	Meeting-place (church).	Meeting-place (church).	Dresses (not magic).
Flight.	Flight threefold.	Flight threefold.	Flight twofold.
Lost shoe.	Lost shoe.	Lost shoe.	Lost shoe.
Shoe marriage test.	Shoe marriage test.	Shoe marriage test.	Shoe marriage test.
Mutilated foot (housewife's daugh.)	Mutilated foot.	Mutilated foot.	Mutilated foot.
Bird witness.	False bride.	False bride.	False bride.
Happy marriage.	Bird witness.	Bird witness.	Bird witness (raven).
House for red calf.	Happy marriage.	Happy marriage.	Happy marriage.

*Chambers, II., consists entirely and solely of these incidents

attempted in my version to reconstruct the "English" Cinderella according to these formulæ. It will be observed that the helpful animal is helpful in two ways—*(a)* in helping the heroine to perform tasks; *(b)* in providing her with magic dresses. It is the same with the Grimms' Aschenputtel and other Continental variants.

Turning to the Celtic variants, these divide into two sets. Campbell's and Macleod's versions are practically at one with the English formula, the latter with an important variation which will concern us later. But the other two, Curtin's and Sinclair's, one collected in Ireland and the other in Scotland, both continue the formula with the conclusion of the Sea Maiden tale (on which see the notes of my *Celtic Fairy Tales,* No. xvii.). This is a specifically Celtic formula, and would seem therefore to claim Cinderella for the Celts. But the welding of the Sea Maiden ending on to the Cinderella formula is clearly a later and inartistic junction, and implies rather imperfect assimilation of the Cinderella formula. To determine the question of origin we must turn to the purer type given by the other two Celtic versions.

Campbell's tale can clearly lay no claim to represent the original type of Cinderella. The golden shoes are a gift of the hero to the heroine which destroys the

CELTIC VARIANTS OF CINDERELLA

MACLEOD.	CAMPBELL.	SINCLAIR.	CURTIN.
Heroine, daughter of sheep, king's wife.	Ill-treated heroine (by stepmother).	Ill-treated heroine (by stepmother and sisters).	Ill-treated heroine (by elder sisters).
	Menial heroine.	Menial heroine.	Menial heroine.
	Helpful animal.	Helpful cantrips.	Henwife aid.
Spy on heroine.	Spy on heroine.	Magic dresses (+starlings on shoulders).	Magic dresses (honey-bird, finger and stud).
Eye sleep threefold.	Eye sleep.	Meeting-place (church).	Meeting-place (church).
Slaying of helpful animal mother.	Slaying of helpful animal.	Flight twofold.	Flight threefold.
Revivified bones.	Revivified bones.	Lost shoe.	Lost shoe.
Magic dresses.	Stepsister substitute.	Shoe marriage test.	Shoe marriage test.
	Golden shoe gift (from hero).	Heroine under washtub.	Mutilated foot.
Meeting-place (feast).	Meeting-place (sermon).	Happy marriage.	Happy marriage.
Flight threefold.	Flight threefold.	Substituted bride.	Substituted bride (eldest sister).
Lost shoe (golden).	Lost shoe.	Jonah heroine.	Jonah heroine.
Shoe marriage test.	Shoe marriage test.	Three reappearances.	Three reappearances.
Mutilated foot.	Mutilated foot.	Reunion.	Reunion.
	False bride.		Villain Nemesis.
Bird witness.	Bird witness.		
Happy marriage.	Happy marriage.		

whole point of the *Shoe marriage-test*, and cannot have been in the original, wherever it originated. Mr. Macleod's version, however, contains an incident which seems to bring us nearer to the original form than any version contained in Miss Cox's book. Throughout the variants it will be observed what an important function is played by the helpful animal. This in some of the versions is left as a legacy by the heroine's dying mother. But in Mr. MacLeod's version the helpful animal, a sheep, is the heroine's mother herself! This is indeed an archaic touch, which seems to hark back to primitive times and totemistic beliefs. And more important still, it is a touch which vitalises the other variants in which the helpful animal is rather dragged in by the horns. Mr. Nutt's lucky find at the last moment seems to throw more light on the origin of the tale than almost the whole of the remaining collection.

But does this find necessarily prove an original Celtic origin for Cinderella? Scarcely. It remains to be proved that this introductory part of the story with helpful animal was necessarily part of the original. Having regard to the feudal character underlying the whole conception, it remains possible that the earlier part was ingeniously dovetailed on to the latter from some pre-existing and more archaic tale, perhaps that represented by the Grimms' "One Eyed, Two Eyes, and Three Eyes." The possibility of the introduction of an archaic formula which had become a convention of folk-telling cannot be left out of account.

The "Youngest-best" formula which occurs in Cinderella, and on which Mr. Lang laid much stress in his treatment of the subject in his *Perrault* as a survival of the old tenure of "junior right," does not throw much light on the subject. Mr. Ralston, in the *Nineteenth Century*, 1879, was equally unenlightening with his sun-myths.

LXXIV. KING O' CATS

Source.—I have taken a point here and a point there from the various English versions mentioned in the next section. I have expanded the names, so as to make a jingle from the Dildrom and Doldrum of Harland.

Parallels.—Five variants of this quaint legend have been collected in England: (1) Halliwell, *Pop. Rhymes*, 167, "Molly Dixon"; (2) *Choice Notes—Folk-Lore*, p. 73, "Colman Grey"; (3) *Folk-Lore Journal*, ii. 22, "King o' the Cats"; (4) *Folk-Lore—England* (Gibbings), "Johnny Reed's Cat"; (5) Harland and Wilkinson, *Lancashire Legends*, p. 13, "Dildrum Doldrum." Sir F. Palgrave gives a Danish parallel; *cp.* Halliwell, *l.c.*

Remarks.—An interesting example of the spread and development of a simple anecdote throughout England. Here again we can scarcely imagine more than a single origin for the tale which is, in its way, as weird and fantastic as E. A. Poe.

LXXV. TAMLANE

Source.—From Scott's *Minstrelsy*, with touches from the other variants given by Prof. Child in his *Eng. and Scotch Ballads*, i. 335–58.

Parallels.—Prof. Child gives no less than nine versions in his masterly edition, *l.c.*, besides another fragment "Burd Ellen and Young Tamlane," i. 258. He parallels the marriage of Peleus and Thetis in Apollodorus III., xiii. 5, 6, which still persists in modern Greece as a Cretan ballad.

Remarks.—Prof. Child remarks that dipping into water or milk is necessary before transformation can take place, and gives examples, *l.c.* 338, to which may be added that of Catskin (see Notes *infra*). He gives as the reason why the Elf-queen would have "ta'en out Tamlane's two grey eyne," so that henceforth he should not be able to see the fairies. Was it not rather that he should not henceforth see Burd Janet?—a subtle touch of jealousy. On dwelling in fairyland Mr. Hartland has a monograph in his *Science of Fairy Tales,* pp. 161–254.

LXXVI. The Stars in the Sky

Source.—Mrs. Balfour's old nurse, now in New Zealand. The original is in broad Scots, which I have anglicised.

Parallels.—The tradition is widespread that at the foot of the rainbow treasure is to be found; *cf.* Mr. John Payne's *Sir Edward's Questing* in his "Songs of Life and Death."

Remarks.—The "sell" at the end is scarcely after the manner of the folk, and various touches throughout indicate a transmission through minds tainted with culture and introspection.

LXXVII. News!

Source.—Bell's *Speaker.*

Parallels.—Jacques de Vitry, *Exempla,* ed. Crane, No. ccv., a servant being asked the news by his master returned from a pilgrimage to Compostella, says the dog is lame, and goes on to explain: "While the dog was running near the mule, the mule kicked him and broke his own halter and ran through the house, scattering the fire with his hoofs, and burning down your house with your wife." It occurs even earlier in Alfonsi's *Disciplina Clericalis,* No. xxx., at beginning of the twelfth century, among the *Fabliaux,* and in Bebel, *Werke,* iii., 71, whence probably it was reintroduced into England. See Prof. Crane's note *ad loc.*

Remarks.—Almost all Alfonsi's *exempla* are from the East. It is characteristic that the German version finishes up with a loss of honour, the English climax being loss of fortune.

LXXVIII. Puddock, Mousie and Ratton

Source.—Kirkpatrick Sharpe's *Ballad Book,* 1824, slightly anglicised.

Parallels.—Mr. Bullen, in his *Lyrics from Elizabethan Song Books,* p. 202, gives a version "The Marriage of the Frog and the Mouse" from T. Ravenscroft's *Melismata,* 1611. The nursery rhyme of the frog who would a-wooing go is clearly a variant of this, and has thus a sure pedigree of three hundred years; *cf.* "Frog husband" in my List of Incidents, or notes to "The Well of the World's End" (No. xli.).

LXXIX. Little Bull-Calf

Source.—*Gypsy Lore Journal,* iii., one of a number of tales told "In a Tent" to Mr. John Sampson. I have re-spelt and euphemised the bladder.

Parallels.—The Perseus and Andromeda incident is frequent in folk tales; see my List of Incidents *sub voce* "Fight with Dragon." "Cheese squeezing," as a test of prowess, is also common, as in "Jack the Giant Killer" and elsewhere (Köhler, *Jahrbuch*, vii. 252).

LXXX. The Wee Wee Mannie

Source.—From Mrs. Balfour's old nurse. I have again anglicised.

Parallels.—This is one of the class of accumulative stories like the *Old Woman who led her Pig to Market* (No. v.). The class is well represented in these isles.

LXXXI. Habetrot and Scantlie Mab

Source.—Henderson's *Folk-Lore of Northern Counties*, pp. 258–62 of Folk-Lore Society's edition. I have abridged and to some extent re-written.

Parallels.—This in its early part is a parallel to the "Tom Tit Tot," which see. The latter part is more novel, and is best compared with the Grimms' *Spinners*.

Remarks.—Henderson makes out of Habetrot a goddess of the spinning-wheel, but with very little authority as it seems to me.

LXXXII. Old Mother Wiggle Waggle

Source.—I have inserted into Halliwell's version one current in Mr. Batten's family, except that I have substituted "Wiggle-Waggle" for "Slipper-Slopper." The two versions supplement one another.

Remarks.—This is a pure bit of animal satire, which might have come from a rural Jefferies with somewhat more of wit than the native writer.

LXXXIII. Catskin

Source.—From the chapbook reprinted in Halliwell. I have introduced the demand for magic dresses from Chambers's "Rashie Coat," into which it had clearly been interpolated from some version of Catskin.

Parallels.—Miss Cox's admirable volume of variants of *Cinderella* also contains seventy-three variants of Catskin, besides thirteen "indeterminate" ones which approximate to that type. Of these eighty-six, five exist in the British Isles, two chap-books given in Halliwell and in Dixon's *Songs of English Peasantry*, two by Campbell, Nos. xiv. and xiv*a*., "The King who wished to marry his Daughter," and one by Kennedy's *Fireside Stories*, "The Princess in the Catskins." Goldsmith knew the story by the name of "Catskin," as he refers to it in the *Vicar*. There is a fragment from Cornwall in *Folk-Lore*, i. App. p. 149.

Remarks.—"Catskin, or the Wandering Gentlewomen," now exists in English only in two chapbook ballads. But Chambers's first variant of "Rashie Coat" begins with the Catskin formula in a euphemised form. The full formula may be said to run in abbreviated form—*Death-bed promise—Deceased wife's resemblance marriage test—Unnatural father* (desiring to marry his own daughter)—*Helpful animal—Counter Tasks—Magic dresses—Heroine flight—Heroine disguise—Menial* *heroine—Meeting-place—Token objects named—Threefold flight—Lovesick prince—Recognition ring—Happy marriage.* Of these the chapbook versions contain scarcely anything of the opening *motifs.* Yet they existed in England, for Miss Isabella Barclay, in a variant which Miss Cox has overlooked (*Folk-Lore;* i. *l.c.),* remembers having heard the Unnatural Father incident from a Cornish servant-girl. Campbell's two versions also contain the incident, from which one of them receives its name. One wonders in what form Mr. Burchell knew Catskin, for "he gave the [Primrose] children the Buck of Beverland,* with the history of Patient Grissel, the adventures of Catskin and the Fair Rosamond's Bower" (*Vicar of Wakefield,* 1766, c. vi.). Pity that "Goldy" did not tell the story himself, as he had probably heard it in Ireland, where Kennedy gives a poor version in his *Fireside Stories.*

Yet, imperfect as the chap-book versions are, they yet retain not a few archaic touches. It is clear from them, at any rate, that the Heroine was at one time transformed into a Cat. For when the basin of water is thrown in her face she "shakes her ears" just as a cat would. Again, before putting on her magic dresses she bathes in a pellucid pool. Now, Professor Child has pointed out in his notes on Tamlane and elsewhere (*English and Scotch Ballads,* i. 338; ii. 505; iii. 505) that dipping into water or milk is necessary before transformation can take place. It is clear, therefore, that Catskin was originally transformed into an animal by the spirit of her mother, also transformed into an animal.

If I understand Mr. Nutt rightly (*Folk-Lore,* iv. 135 *seq.*), he is inclined to think, from the evidence of the hero-tales which have the unsavoury *motif* of the Unnatural Father, that the original home of the story was England, where most of the hero-tales locate the incident. I would merely remark on this that there are only very slight traces of the story in these islands nowadays, while it abounds in Italy, which possesses one almost perfect version of the formula (Miss Cox No. 142, from Sardinia).

Mr. Newell, on the other hand (*American Folk-Lore Journal,* ii.160), considers Catskin the earliest of the three types contained in Miss Cox's book, and considers that Cinderella was derived from this as a softening of the original. His chief reason appears to be the earlier appearance of Catskin in Straparola,† 1550, a hundred years earlier than Cinderella in Basile, 1636. This appears to be a somewhat insufficient basis for such a conclusion. Nor is there, after all, so close a relation between the two types in their full development as to necessitate the derivation of one from the other.

LXXXIV. STUPID'S CRIES

Source.—*Folk-Lore Record.* iii. 152–5, by the veteran Prof. Stephens. I have changed "dog and bitch" of original to "dog and cat," and euphemised the liver and lights.

Parallels.—Prof. Stephens gives parallels from Denmark, Germany, (the Grimms' *Up Riesensohn*) and Ireland (Kennedy, *Fireside Stories,* p. 30).

* Who knows the Buck of Beverland nowadays?
† It is practically in Des Perier's *Récréations,* 1544

LXXXV. THE LAMBTON WORM

Source.—Henderson's *Folk-Lore of Northern Counties,* pp. 287–9, I have re-written, as the original was rather high falutin'.

Parallels.—Worms or dragons form the subject of the whole of the eighth chapter of Henderson. "The Laidly Worm of Spindleston Heugh" (No. xxxiii.) also requires the milk of nine kye for its daily rations, and cow's milk is the ordinary provender of such kittle cattle (Grimm's *Teut. Myth,* 687), the mythological explanation being that cows = the clouds and the dragon = the storm. Jephtha vows are also frequent in folk-tales: Miss Cox gives many examples in her *Cinderella,* p. 511.

Remarks.—Nine generations back from the last of the Lambtons, Henry Lambton, M.P., ob. 1761, reaches Sir John Lambton, Knight of Rhodes, and several instances of violent death occur in the interim. Dragons are possibly survivals into historic times of antedeluvian monsters, or reminiscences of classical legend (Perseus, etc.). Who shall say which is which, as Mr. Lang would observe.

LXXXVI. WISE MEN OF GOTHAM

Source.—The chap-book contained in Mr. Hazlitt's *Shakesperian Jest Book,* vol. iii. I have selected the incidents and modernised the spelling; otherwise the droll remains as it was told in Elizabethan times.

Parallels.—Mr. Clouston's *Book of Noodles* is little else than a series of parallels to our droll. See my list of incidents under the titles, "One cheese after another," "Hare postman," "Not counting self," "Drowning eels." In most cases Mr. Clouston quotes Eastern analogies.

Remarks.—All countries have their special crop of fools, Bœotians among the Greeks, the people of Hums among the Persians (how appropriate!), the Schildburgers in Germany, and so on. Gotham is the English representative, and as witticisms call to mind well-known wits, so Gotham has had heaped on its head all the stupidities of the Indo-European world. For there can be little doubt that these drolls have spread from East to West. This "Not counting self" is in the *Gooroo Paramastan,* the cheeses "one after another" in M. Rivière's collection of Kabyle tales, and so on. It is indeed curious how little originality there is among mankind in the matter of stupidity. Even such an inventive genius as the late Mr. Sothern had considerable difficulty in inventing a new "sell."

LXXXVII. PRINCESS OF CANTERBURY

Source.—I have inserted into the old chap-book version of the *Four Kings of Colchester, Canterbury,* &c., an incident entitled by Halliwell "The Three Questions."

Parallels.—The "riddle bride wager" is a frequent incident of folk tales (see my List of Incidents); the sleeping tabu of the latter part is not so common, though it occurs, *e.g.,* in the Grimms' "Twelve Princesses," who wear out their shoes with dancing.

Index

Aarne, Annti, xxvi
"Abbot of Canterbury, King John
    and the," 288–290
"Adam, A Son of," 264
"All Fur," xxvi
America, 12
Animal courting rhyme, 301–303
Animals, help Jack frighten some
    robbers, 32–34
Anthrophagic creatures, "The
    Hobyahs," 270–273
Anti-Semitism, xii, xxiii
Apple tree, two girls and a witch
    and, 254–258
Apples, golden, quest for, 278–287
Arm of gold, 102–103
Arthur, King, 77, 83, 87, 103
    Tom Thumb and, 105–106
"The Ass, the Table, and the Stick,"
    145–148
"Aucassin et Nicolette," 12
Australia, xi–xii, xxx, 12

Bagpipes, 35
Balfour, M. C., xxviii
Ballads, 12
Ballygan, 98
Basile, Giambattista, ix
Batten, J. D., xxv, 13
Beans, magical, 53–54
Bears
    disguise, 285

fox "Scrapefoot" and the three
    bears, 250–252
"The Story of the Three Bears,"
    74–77
Beelzebub, 62–63
Beheading, 28, 154, 283
"Binnorie," xxv, 44–45
Birds
    enchanted husband and the
        "Three Feathers," 218–221
    enchanted prince, 117–120
    "Henny-Penny" and other
        foolish fowl, 87–89
    King of, 71
    magpie's nest-building lessons,
        140–141
    revenge on a wicked stepmother,
        28–30
"Black Bull of Norroway," 208–213
Bladder, 305–306
"The Blinded Giant," 249–250
Bloody clothes, cleaned pure and
    clean by a damosel, 211
Blunderbore, a giant, 79
Bogles, 144
    adventure of the Golden Ball,
        204–205
    and "The Buried Moon,"
        259–263
    See also Fairies; Imps; Pixies
Bone, "Teeny-Tiny," 51–52
Bow Church, Bells of, 125

357

About the Editor

Donald Haase is chair of the Department of German and Slavic Studies at Wayne State University. A specialist in comparative literature, he has published on English, French, and German writers, as well as on fairy tales and children's literature in European, Anglo-American, and intercultural contexts. He edited *The Reception of Grimms' Fairy Tales: Responses, Reactions, Revisions* (1993) and is the editor of *Marvels & Tales: Journal of Fairy-Tale Studies*.